Rome Reborn on Western Shores

★ ★ ★ ★ ★ ★ ★ ★ ★ ★ ★ ★ ★

ROME REBORN
ON WESTERN SHORES

Historical Imagination and the Creation
of the American Republic

Eran Shalev

University of Virginia Press *Charlottesville and London*

First published 2009

1 3 5 7 9 8 6 4 2

LIBRARY OF CONGRESS CATALOGING-IN-PUBLICATION DATA
Shalev, Eran, 1970–
   Rome reborn on western shores : historical imagination and the creation of the
American republic / Eran Shalev.
      p. cm. — (Jeffersonian America)
   Includes bibliographical references and index.
   ISBN 978-0-8139-2833-3 (cloth : alk. paper) — ISBN 978-0-8139-2839-5 (e-book)
   1. Political science—United States—History—18th century. 2. Political culture—
United States—History—18th century. 3. United States—History—Revolution,
1775–1783—Literature and the revolution. 4. Civilization, Classical—Study and
teaching—United States—History—18th century. 5. Classical literature—Study and
teaching—United States—History—18th century. 6. United States—Civilization— '
Classical influences. I. Title.
   JA84.U5S48 2009
   973.3′1—dc22   2009007720

To the memory of my father, Shaul Shalev (1940–73),
deprived by war of becoming a great historian

The world has been empty since the Romans.

—LOUIS SAINT-JUST

CONTENTS

ACKNOWLEDGMENTS

W HEN I TOOK THE FIRST steps toward writing the manuscript on which this book is based, a friend warned me of the intellectual sharks swimming in the Hobbesian waters of academia. They will, my good-intentioned adviser cautioned, take a snap whenever they get a chance. That friend could not have been more wrong. In terms of mentors, I was lucky twice. Jack Greene has inspired and encouraged my work since I arrived at Johns Hopkins University as a graduate student and served ever since as an unsurpassed model of how to conduct diligent and critical scholarship. As all of Jack's numerous students have learned, the quest for (intellectual) power is intrinsic to the pursuits of happiness, academic and otherwise. I cannot thank Jack enough for all this, as well as for braving, for the second time in his long and distinguished career, to accept an Israeli student. His first was Avihu Zakai, whom I thank not only for being the most dedicated and generous M.A. mentor, but also, especially, for teaching me invaluable lessons outside the strict academic curriculum, including the worth and beauty of humanistic erudition and true friendship.

Peter Onuf was (understandably) skeptical when I could not recite the exact (and obviously too long) working title of my manuscript. However, ever since I imposed on him one of my chapters, he has proved a wonderful friend and caring mentor in the Greenesque style. Laura Kalman has provided help, academically and otherwise, in her signature ways (including answering e-mails before they were sent) every step of the way. Words cannot convey my gratitude for her friendship. To Dorothy Ross I owe my broad view of American intellectual history, and I thank her for generously commenting on my work. Her perceptive insights improved this study greatly. I thank Michael Johnson for many uplifting and edifying discussions on topics that include, but are not restricted to, American history and for setting an admirable model for intellectual curiosity and stimulating teaching. I am grateful to Phil Morgan for his helpful advice and assistance and for reading portions of this work and offering criticism in private and public forums.

Friends have enriched the years I spent in Baltimore in ideal as well as in corporal ways. David Nirenberg made me think and rethink ideas with his paradigm-shifting observations between sets in the gym and runs in Roland Park. David Bell, a great historian of a European republic, insisted and verified that I made clear—to myself and to him—"what is at stake." He has ever since made sure I do not forget. Ken Moss read and astutely commented on my work and endured discussions on history in environments that were not always accommodating for intellectual discourse. Jane Dailey provided me with perceptive observations that could come only from a post-eighteenth-century historian.

Chris Brown provided me with many insights on the nature of the American Revolution, while Matt Roller expanded exponentially my knowledge of the classics, and Dan Richter provided timely and much needed help and encouragement. I was lucky to benefit from the friendship and criticism of Michael Zakim, Amit Yahav, Dror Wahrman, Maurizio Valsania, and Zur Shalev (for the protocol: other than curiously parallel careers and a shared name, no relation). I am especially thankful to John Pocock, whose epoch-making studies have shaped my view of history. Professor Pocock has also provided me with invaluable advice. Perhaps the timeliest came after I presented to him a half-baked prospectus: "But someone has already written the Machiavellian Moment." I wish to thank the anonymous readers at the University of Virginia Press for their comments, which made me think harder about my work and improved this study significantly.

I benefited from comments on chapters I presented to the members of the Early American Seminar at Johns Hopkins. I especially thank Molly Warsh, Jessica Spivey, Justin Roberts, and Catherine Molineux for their cherished friendship and valuable comments. Mary Ashburn Miller has provided excellent criticism and editorial advice. I thank Dimtri Shevchenko for his editorial assistance and the University of Pennsylvania

Press for permitting the re-publication of early versions of chapters 2 and 5 in *Early American Studies* 4, no. 1 (2006), and the *Journal of the Early Republic* 23, no. 2 (2003), respectively.

I especially thank my family for enduring many transatlantic flights while this study was being written. They would not have come so far so often if not for my beloved Yonatan and Yuli, who were born together with this study. They, and Michal, made, and still make, the long ride gratifying and meaningful. Without them, this Rome would have never been reborn.

Rome Reborn on Western Shores

INTRODUCTION

REFLECTING ON THE AMERICAN REVOLUTION from his retirement in 1805, the second president of the United States "read the history of all ages and nations in every page" of a Roman history he was studying at the time. Indeed, it was "especially the history of our country for forty years past" that John Adams could recognize and discover in the Roman annals. If one would only "change the names," then "every anecdote [would] be applicable to us."[1] Adams had already manifested his inclination to identify repetitions and reoccurrences in history exactly half a century before he read the history of the young United States in Roman narratives. Indeed, even "immortal Rome," he wrote at the age of twenty in a letter to a friend, "was at first but an insignificant village . . . but by degrees it rose to a stupendous Height." When Rome sank into debauchery, the young Adams concluded, it became "easy prey to Barbarians." Similarly, when England, "the greatest Nation upon the globe," declined, he wrote, "the great seat of Empire" might transfer "into America."[2] Years later, as a representative to the First Continental Congress, Adams was willing to bring his and the Roman worlds even closer yet. He believed that the reaction of that body's delegates to the horrid, and false, news of the bombardment of Boston in September 1774—they vigorously chanted "War! War! War!"—would "have done honour to the oratory of a Briton or a Roman."[3] Defending the proposed Federal Constitution in the late 1780s, more than a decade later, Adams elaborated on how classical antiquity should serve as "what is called in many families of the continent a boudoir; an octagonal apartment in a house, with a full-length mirror on every side, and another in the ceiling" where Americans could "see their own faces and figures multiplied without end," shaped in the forms and structures of antiquity "in whatever direction they turn their eyes."[4] Americans, Adams thought, should imagine themselves dressed in togas.

Adams's lifelong thinking of, through, and with the classics about revolutionary American reality may seem extraordinary today, but it was anything but unique for his generation of revolutionaries and nation builders. *Rome Reborn on Western Shores* seeks to trace and analyze the remarkable duality that John Adams articulated and that many patriots experienced—namely, the ambivalence of being Americans participating in a modern revolution while fashioning themselves and acting as if they were ancient republicans. Students of late-eighteenth-century America have long been aware that throughout the Revolution, Americans appealed to classical antiquity to provide historical meaning for their political endeavors. This study aims to demonstrate, however, that this classical discourse has had an overlooked but very significant role in the intellectual history of the Revolution. That is, we have not yet appreciated how American patriots made use of the classical discourse to articulate and express their attitudes toward history and time. *Rome Reborn on Western Shores* thus reveals the ways in which the classical discourse of the American Revolution functioned as a distinct mode of historical thought.[5]

The contention of this book is that we cannot properly understand the political choices and claims made by the American revolutionaries unless we realize that to them, in many ways, the world of the ancient Mediterranean was as vivid and recognizable as the world in which they were living; that classical heroes such as Cincinnatus and Cicero and villains such as Catiline and Jugurtha were meaningful and familiar figures. Indeed, in a world in which numerous Americans thought in terms of classical narratives, styled themselves as ancients, and acted out classical roles, it is possible to see how patriots habitually reflected on and represented their experiences through the classics. So powerful was this mode of thought that many patriots wished they would get a chance to re-experience that revered history, while others feared that classical history, especially the decline and dissolution of the ancient polities, would repeat itself in America. Occasionally, when stakes were especially high, they thought they were, as Edmund Pendleton, president of the Virginia Convention, put it in 1776, "treading upon the Republican ground of Greece and Rome."[6] Without a full grasp of this peculiar and compelling historical consciousness, so different from our contemporary sensibilities, we cannot fully appreciate how revolutionaries decided to make the break with Britain, how they justified that rupture, and how they constructed their new, independent states.[7] This classical idiom, or "language," like its parallel natural languages, limited what might be said. Like natural languages, however, it enriched American patriots' ability to discourse and imagine by providing them with a spectacular cosmos of classical images and meanings through which to comprehend their own situations. Hence, the Greek and Roman example gave Americans the courage to rebel; at the same time, however, it proscribed them from certain courses of action and swayed them toward others. Classical antiquity, then, played a crucial role in articulating the revolutionaries' quarrel and their coming to terms with history and time.[8]

Decades of fruitful scholarly studies of the classics in early America have given us a good idea of the extent and contours of their use in the formative years of the United States.[9] However, if we know when and why Americans chose to discourse on the classics, we still lack an understanding of the processes through which revolutionaries made the world of ancient Greece and Rome meaningful to their political endeavors. In particular, we still need to assess the relationship between the classics and revolutionary Americans' modes of thought and action. By stressing the ideological aspects of civic humanism, scholars may have overlooked a significant feature of that powerful tradition—namely, the ways in which the revolutionary classical discourse, a language of and about history, articulated and reflected peculiar understandings of, and attitudes toward, historical time.[10] If scholars have already shown the impressive degree to which American patriots plundered the classics for models and *exempla*, *Rome Reborn on Western Shores* will demonstrate the extent to which the incessant appeal to the classics entailed specific comprehension of, and ways of thinking about, time.[11] This study will thus be the first attempt to understand American patriots' uses of the world of classical antiquity as a distinct way in which they thought of and through history.

The unprecedented levels of engagement in late-eighteenth-century America with the "culture of classicism" (perhaps most obviously seen through the explosion in the use of classical pseudonyms during the 1770s) provided the foundations for revolutionaries to express, and audiences to make sense of, classically tainted attitudes toward time and history, which stand at the center of this study. The classics were becoming meaningful after 1750 to ever growing numbers of North Americans (a people "steeped in the classics," according to the historian Paul Rahe), which made Greece and especially Rome such a fruitful and meaningful discursive sphere throughout the Revolution.[12] The complex cultural and economic processes that late colonial American societies experienced, from a consumer revolution to the expansion of erudition and a culture of print, enabled the reception and permeation of the classics to a degree that, while never matching the universality of the Bible, was still unthinkable only decades earlier.[13] While the prevalence of the classics in revolutionary culture reflected the neoclassical resurgence experienced in contemporary Europe, the context of that cultural surge in America was different from its European counterpart.[14] Indeed, the following chapters demonstrate the various ways in which the severe ideological strains they were experiencing after 1765 encouraged American leaders and patriots to use the classical world to promote revolutionary ends, while the classics became a medium for legitimizing and constructing reality in terms of a venerated republican past.

The American Revolution, which witnessed the unyoking of the British Crown and subsequently the construction of republican governments and federal institutions, enticed American patriots to free the reins of their classical imagination. Patriots constructed their revolutionary present through the histories of Greece and Rome in remarkable ways, in a variety of contexts, and to diverse ends. Revolutionaries referred to the venerated ancients in their private moments and in their public performances. They appealed to the classics for consolation, justification, and validation as they experienced an intense intellectual and emotional relationship with the narratives and heroes of antiquity. Invoking the inspiring examples of ancient republics was a vital tool in the hands of American orators and writers, who provided the *exempla* of the virtuous ancients and emphasized their relevance to the American situation. The classics encouraged and roused the Americans collectively before crossing the Rubicon of independence and consoled them in private at times when war tried their souls.

When they created a federal system, the ancients were there to inspire them even as American state makers seemed to break every rule of classical wisdom. In short, the classics had an immense influence on the ways in which individuals interpreted and made sense of the Revolution. Charles Lee, Washington's future attorney-general, attesting to his own experience, asserted that it was "natural to a young person whose chief companions are the Greek and Roman historians and Orators to be dazzled with the splendid picture" of antiquity.[15] Indeed, another Charles Lee, the revolutionary general, an Englishman who rallied to the American cause, asserted that Plutarch had converted him into an "enthusiastick for liberty . . . and for liberty in a republican garb."[16] Adorning reality "in a republican garb" was common practice in revolutionary America.

American Whigs found the classics so appealing because they perceived the ancient republics as the origin and embodiment of some of the most powerful ideals they cherished—namely, the ideological bundle modern scholarship understands under the common framework of "the republican synthesis."[17] Indeed, many revolutionaries envisioned a society and government based on virtue and disinterested citizenship, the main sources of classical republicanism.[18] Unsurprisingly, a powerful ideal of many of the Revolution's leaders and their followers was not a democracy (a government still associated with the rule of the mob) but, rather, an organic hierarchy led by patricians who would embody the classical virtues.[19] It is thus republican Rome more than any other classical polity that dominates this study, as its title attests. Rome enticed, for reasons that will be elaborated in chapter 1, revolutionaries' political imagination and historical inquisitiveness more than any other historical society. Yet it is the fact that this book is designed not as an overview of the classical tradition in America or as a review of late-eighteenth-century American intellectual history (studies that should allocate a proper share to the role of the Greek and Hellenic worlds) but, rather, as an examination of the ways in which American revolutionaries put the classical world to use in articulating their attitudes toward history and time, that dictates that Rome shall be its focus.

Understanding the classical discourse as a unique mode of historical thought, as a way of thinking about the nature of time and of America's place in history, may present unexpected results. Revolutionary Americans,

it becomes apparent, frequently stretched and blurred conventional understandings of historical time. When patriots looked at Britain, they saw an
amazing "picture" drawn from its "original," the malevolent Roman Empire of the corrupt Caesars.[20] When they turned to look at themselves,
revolutionaries recognized a different Rome, one that was still pristine,
republican, and virtuous. They predicted that "Columbian *Livies* ... [a] *Cicero* ... some future *Virgil*" would rise in America and were confident when
they endured crises that America's Brutus "will not be wanting."[21] Numerous Americans, most notably George Washington, seemed to have fulfilled
such roles, as their compatriots repeatedly described them as American
Fabii, Cati, or Cincinnati. There were moments particularly ominous.
During the years leading to independence, many Americans acted according to scripts they associated with the heroes of the classical pantheon.
It is thus no wonder that spectators of Patrick Henry delivering a celebrated speech in which he challenged his foes to "give me liberty or give
me death," an immortal line derived from Addison's popular neo-Roman
play *Cato,* imagined they were watching not a Virginian urging the House
of Burgesses but, rather, Cato of Utica preaching to the Roman Senate.
Such a classical ecology could culminate in remarkable performances, such
as the revolutionary leader Joseph Warren delivering a Boston Massacre
oration in front of a crowd of thousands donned in a "Ciceronian Toga."
Numerous patriots throughout the Revolution acted out classical roles as
they covered themselves with pseudonymous masks, reviving ancient history on American prints by discoursing with other Americans who also
masqueraded as classical heroes. Once the Revolution was over, American
historians recounting the events of the past decades were heavily disposed
to describe their recent history as a reoccurrence of classical events.

The chapters in *Rome Reborn on Western Shores* follow a chronological as
well as a thematic logic and point to the changing genres and contexts in
which revolutionaries perceived their eighteenth-century present and classical antiquity as deeply related to, and drawing meaning from, each other.
Following the revolutionaries from the early days of the imperial quarrel
to their tortured decision to declare independence and subsequently to
construct a federal republic and beyond, *Rome Reborn on Western Shores*
will demonstrate the various ways in which patriots represented America
in terms of classical, usually Roman, history. We will see how during moments of crisis in the American Revolution, when the level of anxiety and

concern was high enough, the conventional habits of speech, arguably also of thought, seemed to have collapsed to a certain degree, and people began to represent themselves as if they really were, or were like, or were the immediate followers of—revolutionaries demonstrated a variety of attitudes toward their historical role—the heroes of antiquity. This book's chapters examine the revolutionaries during critical moments of tension when they described the British Empire as a corrupt Roman Empire; when during the months leading to independence they elaborated on their assumed relation to the ancients and performed publicly as ancient heroes; when they assumed classical identities to engage in the debate on the Constitution; and when they looked back once the Revolution was over and chose to write their recent history as an epic tale of classical proportions. During these critical moments, we will see, classical sensibilities arose, and language and action—or, rather, history and revolution—converged and transformed the ways in which patriots represented and assimilated their experiences and endowed their feats with significance and meaning.

This study concentrates on the remarkable and intriguing revolutionary sensibilities that enabled American patriots to imagine themselves as part of a historical process that originated in classical antiquity. It would be hard to overestimate the classics' role in shaping revolutionary discourse and language and, consequently, in leading American patriots through classically tainted modes of action. Indeed, without appreciating the immense influence of history on late-eighteenth-century Americans we are in danger of misrepresenting the revolutionaries' Revolution, the ways in which patriots represented, made sense of, and acted out their political endeavors. Finally, *Rome Reborn on Western Shores* sheds light on the recent and surprising surge in comparisons between America and Rome. Indeed, to fully understand the meaning of the intense identifications of America as the overextended, declining "Roman Empire" of the twenty-first century, we need to trace back and identify the origins of this classical discourse—namely, the way in which American revolutionaries constructed the new nation as a Roman republic reborn on western shores. This investigation will reveal the curious trajectory of representations of America as a Roman republic turned empire during the past two hundred and thirty years. It will also demonstrate how anxious assessments of the nature of the dangers the American republic has faced, as well as the gloomy predictions regarding its fate, were embedded in the vocabulary of, and have thus characterized, the classical discourse from the early days of the Revolution until the dawning of the third millennium.

Through analyzing the long-gone world of the American Revolution, we will come to see how many of its participants thought and acted, as John Adams suggested in 1775, in ways they believed would not only honor them as Britons (and consequently as Americans), but would also represent them as virtuous, stern Romans. The following chapters demonstrate how the American Revolution was repeatedly contemplated and performed by patriots who acted according to classical roles. Hence, they saw their Revolution at times, and we should interpret it accordingly, as a Roman revolution. *Rome Reborn on Western Shores* attempts to come to terms with this remarkable ambivalence.

I

A REVOLUTIONARY LANGUAGE

History and the Classics in the Age of Revolution

AMERICAN PATRIOTS FOUND classical history, its narratives and patterns, instrumental from the early days of the constitutional disputes with Britain in the mid-1760s. Indeed, revolutionaries articulated grievances and gained the imperial contest's rhetorical and moral high ground over and again through appeals to the classics. Along the way, they developed a unique, classicized approach to interpreting history and to linking it to their present. This book is designed as a study not of the uses that were made of the classical world in political argument, but of the ways in which such uses reflect on American revolutionaries' attitudes toward history and time. However, the former question is inevitably inseparable from the latter. The chapters that follow will examine the role of the classics in constructing a distinct revolutionary historical consciousness. Yet to come to terms with the patriots' attitudes toward history and time, one needs to understand how the classics functioned in late-eighteenth-century American discourse. Therefore, this chapter will examine the broad common modes and structures, shared throughout the colonies-turned-states, through which American patriots employed the classics.

The assumptions that Americans shared regarding how, why, and when the classical civilizations were relevant for their cause demonstrate the ways in which they intellectualized their Revolution and how they evaluated their role in history. Accordingly, this chapter will initially portray the breadth and depth of "the culture of classicism" in late-eighteenth-century America and explain Rome's dominant role in that discourse. Then it will examine the configurations into which references to the classics usually fell and will show that, once their pervasiveness is put aside, the revolutionary discourse of the classics still left some white men, most women, and virtually all blacks out of its discursive boundaries. Following the examination of the common forms and patterns in the revolutionary classical discourse, I will proceed to identify the meta-historical assumptions underlying that discourse. Scholars have long been aware of the prevalence in America of what has been lately formulated as the "civic-humanist view of history," an outlook that understood history to consist of a set of universal moralistic and exemplary narratives.[1] This chapter, however, identifies widespread revolutionary beliefs beyond the assumptions of humanist history regarding the historical process and the nature and meaning of time. By recognizing the ways in which American revolutionaries made use of the classics, as well as the assumptions regarding the nature of history that underlay the revolutionary classical discourse, this chapter lays the groundwork for analyzing the revolutionary attitudes toward time and history that will be at the center of this study.

Interest in the history, culture, and languages of classical antiquity today is considered a high-culture endeavor (regardless of Hollywood mega-movies inspired by Greek and Roman themes and other expressions of pop-culture derived from the classics). This, however, should not mislead us into thinking that such has always been the case. To the contrary, many indicators suggest that the world of classical antiquity was becoming meaningful after 1750 to growing numbers of North Americans. Contemporaries certainly felt so. Thomas Jefferson, for instance, thought that the entirety of the white male yeomanry, which he considered the backbone of American society, consisted of potential classical discoursers. In a letter of January 15, 1787, to J. Hector St. John de Crevecoeur, Jefferson stated, "Ours are the only farmers who can read Homer."[2] From the other side of the political divide, the arch-Tory Jonathan Boucher also had an expansionary view of the prevalence of classical antiquity in America. Boucher, as opposed to Jefferson, deplored the inflammatory influence of antiquity on "an abundance of men" who read "only classics."[3]

The foundations of what would become, in the words of the historian Caroline Winterer, a "culture of classicism" during the eighteenth and nineteenth centuries were as old as settlement in North America. American elites have always been preoccupied with the classics; their formal education was based on a strict and uniform curriculum that stressed Latin, Greek, and Hebrew (in this order of importance) derived from the admission requirements of contemporary colleges, of which there were nine in 1776 and twenty-five by 1800. Students graduating from grammar school would be expected to read Cicero and Virgil in Latin and the New Testament in Greek if they wished to be admitted to college. The years spent in college deepened the familiarity of generations of Americans with antiquity and its languages.[4] The holdings of public and private libraries reflected these cultural interests: Classical materials, both original and translations, consistently made up 10 to 12 percent of their catalogues.[5] Yet even Americans who were not privileged enough to enjoy the benefit of years of rigid classical studies could still develop formidable knowledge and a sense of familiarity with the world of antiquity. Men such as George Washington and Patrick Henry never learned Latin or Greek. Nonetheless, they and many like them were able to make the classics meaningful to their private and public lives to a remarkable degree.

The permeation of the classics during the second half of the eighteenth century, however, went beyond the few thousand college graduates and traditional elites. The increasing popularity, accessibility, and penetration of the classics occurred in a context of rising prosperity, commercialism, and aspirations toward gentility among a broad swathe of Americans, processes closely linked to what the historian Jack Greene has described as cultural convergence, reinforced by Timothy Breen's documentation of a new consumer culture.[6] Indeed, new cultural aspirations supported by the proliferation of print and the expansion of the public sphere exposed numerous middling Americans across the colonies to mores and spheres of knowledge that were traditionally out of their cultural reach. Among those areas was the world of antiquity.

The steep rise in the importation of books and multiplication of bookstores, as well as the bustling colonial scene of printers producing a growing number of local newspapers and imprints by the 1770s, provided eager Americans with "a new abundance of printed matter," as prints of all kinds became cheaper and more widely available.[7] As their output grew, the importance of newspapers increased, and by the mid-eighteenth century, they came to occupy "an essential niche in the social ecology."[8] By and large, newspapers portrayed the worldview of the middle and upper classes: cultivated, ethnocentric, Protestant, English, predominantly male. Indeed, most subscribers naturally came from these categories and were concentrated in the cities.[9] However, because of their low cost and frequent appearance, newspapers were readily available in homes and in public spaces to many thousands who were not white, genteel, or male. Scholars have thus concluded that newspapers "almost certainly reached well beyond the audience most publishers had in mind."[10] Thus, it does thus not seem a long jump "to assume that the information and the knowledge that colonists acquired through the press . . . did indeed influence them."[11] The newspapers, as anyone who has examined a random sample of contemporary papers even superficially can tell, abounded with classical quotations, tags, pseudonyms, histories, parallels, and parables. The staggering expansion of print culture was not confined to books and newspapers, however. More printed material in the form of pamphlets and broadsides, two main venues for manifesting classical wisdom, came into the view of growing numbers of readers.[12] The "cult of antiquity" in America could thus be transformed and expanded into a widespread "culture of classicism."[13]

Late-eighteenth-century Americans developed a "vernacular classical" canon of modern histories of antiquity and translations from the Latin and Greek; that category "was rapidly encroaching on the cultural reverence for ancient texts in Greek and Latin." Obviously, such "vernacular classicism" vastly extended the potential number of participators in the classical discourse to Americans who could read English but were not proficient in Latin or Greek.[14] The backdrop to this sea of literary and literacy-related change was the substantial increase in private and public schooling after about 1750, as schools of all kinds were being opened across the American provinces.[15] Even elite white women, who in the mid-eighteenth century still found it hard to benefit from institutional classical education, "began in growing numbers to immerse themselves in the wondrous literary and material vestiges of classical antiquity" during the revolutionary decades. The wives, siblings and daughters of patriots became more noticeable discoursers of the classics as the Revolution progressed, as they became more proficient classicists with their numbers steadily growing.[16]

Americans, however, did not even need to participate in the expanding text-based print culture to relate to the classical world. A classical visual culture emerged during those decades through which they were introduced to classical pictorial representations and symbolisms by way of paintings, broadsides, coins, paper currency, seals, almanacs, magazines, bowls, banners, wallpaper, furniture, and fashion.[17] The venues in which they were bombarded with classical themes expanded, as well, including by the late eighteenth century salons, coffeehouses, literary societies and clubs, theaters, and public orations.[18] The rise of such discursive institutions converged with the permeation of antique forms into the sphere of art, architecture, and nomenclature. Indeed, historians of the classical tradition in America seem to agree that the novel oral, visual, and printed modes of communication in early America "broadly diffused" the classical tradition in late-eighteenth-century America, a tradition that by the last quarter of the eighteenth century had a "palpable presence."[19]

Even if the reach of the classical world has never attained the universality of the Bible, and the elite and educated would always feel more comfortable within its borders than their social inferiors, as the eighteenth century reached its final decades more Americans found themselves participating, both as cultural producers and as consumers, in a wide-ranging, continuous conversation of and through the classics. Instances such as a quotation from Addison's neo-Roman drama *Cato* inscribed on a hanged effigy during a Stamp Act riot or a pamphlet by "a Black" that used many classical allusions and examples demonstrates the extent (and perhaps the limits) of the exposure to, as well as the accessibility and potential influence of, the classics among Americans who could never have been formally trained in them.[20] Indeed, when imperial tensions began escalating after the mid-1760s, this widespread and ever growing familiarity with classical antiquity could be quickly transformed into an overtly political and most effective revolutionary language.

While examining the various ways in which the classical language functioned during the Revolution, we should keep in mind that revolutionary Americans participating in that discourse were not classical scholars. Indeed, they would commonly conflate and collapse the histories of the Hellenic and Roman worlds into each other, ignoring basic historiographical conventions and divisions of space and time. Suffering from what Winterer has recently diagnosed as "an acute temporal flabbiness," Americans tended to think of "the classics" as a monolithic historical unit and were frequently unable to differentiate clearly between "Greece and Rome," two civilizations that they repeatedly paired.[21] This intellectual conflation and the fact that the Greek legacy is itself the product of borrowing from a variety of later cultures makes the task of distinguishing "within the classical tradition [in America] between the legacies of Greece and Rome" formidable.[22] Nevertheless, historians have identified significant strands of Greek Stoicism and Epicureanism that are imperative in understanding Revolutionary-age Americans' "assumptions about God, the universe, and human nature from the basis of human thought and Action."[23] Furthermore, the historian Eric Nelson has recently stressed the impact of a vibrant "Greek tradition in republican thought" on the American Founding.[24] It is thus indisputable that late-eighteenth-century Americans were attracted to the culture, philosophy, morality, and historiography of Greece. Nevertheless, historians of the classical tradition in America concur that, while they adulated Greece, revolutionary Americans demonstrated an "overwhelming preference for Rome."[25] If many contemporaries, in the words of John Warren in a July 4 oration in 1783, saw Greece as "the seat of arts and sciences," Rome was to them the "mistress of the world."[26] While they admired Greece, to Rome they were "addicted."[27]

There were deep-rooted reasons for such a preference. The Western curriculum had always put more emphasis on Latin, the Catholic Church's language and Medieval Europe's lingua franca, than on Greek. This preference was further cultivated in the New World. "Greek," Meyer Reinhold, a pioneering historian of the classical tradition in America, concluded, "had only a token role in the traditional humanistic curriculum of the colonial period."[28] Even more important was republican Rome's perceived relevance—and Greece's, especially democratic Athens's, irrelevance—to the American political predicament: While a republic governed by a mixed constitution and led by a "natural aristocracy" on the Roman model seemed ideal to many Americans, an Athenian-styled democracy seemed as good as the rule of the mob.[29] Such sensibilities would change only during the nineteenth century with the advent of Jacksonian Democracy.[30] Americans could not stop contemplating Rome's greatness, culminating in the possession of unparallel imperial domains. And while Rome provided a coherent narrative of a minute republic's rise to world domination, its subsequent transformation into an empire, and its eventual decline, revolutionary-age Americans could not find in the Greek past a "chronological specificity, a clear beginning or end, or even a clear geographical boundary of what was Greek and non-Greek."[31] The cumulative effect of these factors translated in late-eighteenth-century America into a much more frequent use of and a profound inclination toward everything that was Roman. It is no wonder then that when classical learning was politicized in the revolutionary era, Greek and Hellenism "receded into the shadows."[32] It was thus Rome that revolutionaries "saw as the noblest achievement of free men aspiring to govern themselves."[33] It was republican Rome, not a Greek polis, that patriots envisioned while erecting their own republic on western shores.[34] This is not to say that Greece did not hold a strong grip on revolutionary classical imagination. It certainly did. But Rome more than any other polity dominated revolutionary Americans' historical reflection and, thus, the attempts to articulate their attitudes toward history and time.

With the connection to the mother country gradually but surely eroding during the decade following the Stamp Act of 1765, American patriots put their classical imagination to constant use. The world of classical civilizations rendered itself meaningful to revolutionary Americans by providing paradigmatic examples of republican ideals and standards of conduct. Patriots turned repeatedly to the classical republican societies, first and foremost to Rome, to define their own republicanism and to situate their ideologies in a historical context. However, revolutionaries did not perceive republicanism merely as an ideology or as a model of structure of government or political system. Rather, they understood it as a particular attitude toward political life. Such an attitude was based on public civic virtue, an attitude that historically originated in classical antiquity. The foundation of such virtue, which lay at the core of a republican society, was the ancients' love of liberty and hatred of tyranny. Accordingly, many of the revolutionary references to the classics involved examples of those noble sentiments that underlay the glorious commonwealths of the past. Henry Steele Commager has pointed out that "the scorn of luxury and effeminacy and the acceptance of austerity; the preference for the rural life . . . the eloquence . . . the devotion to the law; the dedication to public service; the sense of honor and dignity and virtue—all of this was American as it was Roman."[35] This Roman–American double consciousness played out in the wake of the Revolution through classical *exempla* intended to educate and inspire the American public.

Patriot writers attempted to inculcate civic virtue through allusions to classical history, frequently Greek but even more often Roman, and ancient glory. A revolutionary writer in the *Virginia Gazette*, wishing to "secure this valuable blessing [of classical virtue], and learn the greatness of its worth," wished to recommend to his "countrymen, especially the younger part of it, a thorough acquaintance with these records of illustrious liberty, the histories of Greece and Rome." The writer intended this recommendation not as a theoretical or academic exercise, but rather as a spur to urge Americans to "a glorious emulation of those virtues, which have immortalized their names." Classical examples would surely instill Americans with "a just hatred of tyranny and zeal for freedom," and induce them to follow "the godlike actions of those heroes and patriots, whose lives are delivered down to us by Plutarch."[36] Similarly, in Hugh Henry Brackenridge's drama *The Death of General Montgomery* (1777), the protagonist Montgomery reminded Americans just before expiring in the battlefield that "it is in a commonwealth only that you can expect to find every man a patriot . . . a hero. Aristedes, Epaminondas, Pericles, Scipio, Camillus, and a thousand other illustrious Grecian and Roman heroes, would never have astonished the world with their name, had they lived under a royal government."[37] Patriots deemed a government that enabled and promoted freedom as a necessary condition to liberate man's spirit and facilitate manly glory.[38] Unsurprisingly, in the classical formulation that so many revolutionaries adopted, great men, recognized by their ability to "astonish the world," were military leaders and heroes.

New Englanders too often conceived liberty in classical terms and performed as a classical act. "Cato of Utica," a Bostonian styling his literary persona as the ideal type of classical republicans, Cato the Younger, told his audience that "the heroic ages were the most free, and in proportion to the progress of tyranny, pusillanimity and barbarism have prevailed . . . liberty invigorates the spirit and refines the understanding, while slavery debilitates the one, and rapines the other."[39] Another writer from New Hampshire, endeavoring to make clear how well Bostonians, suffering of the economic consequences of the Intolerable Acts, were situated on the spectrum of freedom and tyranny, deemed them "in general [to] have that fortitude which did honor to the ancient Romans."[40]

When the war eventually began, yet another American "Cato" explained to the readers of the *South Carolina Gazette* what role the classics should play in the American psyche. "The history of the Grecian colonies affects an animating example," this Cato argued, balancing a Roman pseudonym and Greek content, for "how far the laws of freedom were deemed sacred, even in the savage ages of the world."[41] The ancient societies indeed provided an "animating example," and patriot writers kept returning to the narratives and patterns supplied by the liberty-loving ancients for deductive moral lessons. Patriots shared a classical dislike of the symbols of tyranny. "A Commonwealth's man" from New Hampshire characteristically praised the "simple language" of the Romans and their self-effacement to attack titles and aristocratic appellations, "the offsprings of monarchical or arbitrary governments." "The Roman Senate," the writer pointed out, "in the height of its glory and happiness, had no other title than *senatus populus que romanus,* that is, the senate and people of Rome. Scipio was addressed by the name of Scipio at the head of his army. . . . Let us leave the titles of excellency [to the] servants of the king of Britain."[42]

The American Revolution's leaders were, as we will see throughout this study, repeatedly valorized as classical ancients. Nevertheless, even "the common sort" were occasionally commended as such. A nameless "mechanic" who asserted in 1774 that he would prefer eating acorns in the forest to submitting to British tyranny, extracted from William Tudor a classicized praise: "What a Roman! By Heavens, I glory in being this Man's fellow citizen. When I meet with such Sentiments from such a person, I easily anticipate the Period when Bostonian shall equal Spartan Virtue, and the American colonies rival in Patriotism the most celebrated Grecian Republic."[43] It was quite typical for Tudor to perceive the nameless "mechanic" as a Roman while envisioning America's future as Greek. American revolutionaries were not trained or critical readers of history, and they repeatedly lumped together the Greek and Roman annals. Indeed, Howard Mumford Jones was correct in asserting that, "except among specialists . . . , the chronology of the ancient world was as blurred in the eighteenth century . . . as it is to us."[44] Thus, while repeatedly attracted to the Roman example, patriots nonetheless often appealed to the Greeks, as well. Motivated politically, revolutionaries habitually de-historicized antiquity as they scavenged the classical narrative for useful morals and parables. In that process, the temporal and semantic borders between Greece and Rome were often blurred.

In an apparent attempt to buttress Americans' attachment to and knowledge of classical history, Dixon and Hunter's *Virginia Gazette* made an extraordinary editorial decision: The newspaper published during the whole of February and March 1776, in weekly installments, the Earl of Chesterfield's *Letters* as the leading piece, often occupying most of the front page. There was obviously no lack of other items to publish in the tumultuous months immediately preceding independence, and the enormous space the *Letters* occupied points to their perceived importance and their predicted popularity.[45] From February 3 to March 30, 1776, nine issues of the *Virginia Gazette* printed selections of the *Letters,* the vast majority dealing with classical history (as well as mythology), which is not the case of the *Letters* as a whole. The editorial selection of the *Letters* of the fourth Earl of Chesterfield, Philip Stanhope, especially those concerned with Roman history—which, according to Chesterfield, was "of all ancient histories . . . the most instructive and furnishes most examples of virtue, wisdom, and courage"—was a conscious attempt to tutor Virginians in the facts and merits of classical history in the critical months preceding independence.[46]

By providing ideals and standards for revolutionary Americans, the classics helped forge communal ties in the emerging imagined pan-American community, demonstrated by motions taken in both Continental Congresses. On October 22, 1774, during the final days of the session of the First Continental Congress, "an Address from C. Tully [Cicero] was read and ordered to be [laid] on the table." Some six months later, in a session of the succeeding Congress, an unidentified delegate asked his peers to "consult history: did not the Grecian republic prosper amid continual warfare? Their prosperity, their power, their splendor, grew from the all-animating spirit of war. Did not the cottagers and shepherds rise into imperial Rome, the mistress of the world, the nurse of heroes, the delight of gods!"[47] A Ciceronian oration read aloud and "consultations" with classical history were among the few ways to unite the motley crew gathered in Philadelphia from the various British North American colonies to conduct America's business. Apparently, the classical world provided patriots with what the anthropologist Roy D'Andrade has called a "cultural model," a cognitive schema inter-subjectively shared by a social group, in which everybody knows the schema, and everybody knows that everyone else knows the schema and everybody knows that everyone knows that everyone knows the schema.[48]

Nomenclature and imagery were among the most salient intellectual manifestations that patriots tied between themselves and the classics. Names of political institutions such as "Congress" and "Senate," state and federal seals and emblems, paper money, and coins all involved classical imagery "on an unprecedented scale" during the separation from the British Empire.[49] As Winterer points out, late-eighteenth-century American neoclassical prints of images, such as the goddesses Liberty and Minerva, stand out as strikingly new and strikingly political.[50] Although this study cannot cover the vast field of classical visual texts and the variety of its manifestations, we should note that these representations further suggest the vigor and meaning of the imagined links between patriots and the long-gone world of the ancients and underscore the public roles of such ties. Indeed, the revolutionary classical images may be understood as additional ways to reinforce republican behavior and inculcate classical standards.

Military examples were another major arena of comparison, contrast, and appraisal between American and classical endeavors. The great classical polities were militaristic social organizations, embattled throughout most of their existence, a characteristic that spurred them to conquer and overcome numerous peoples and annex vast territories. Americans, then, had good reasons to look into the classical martial example, as well as a strong incentive to depict themselves as classical warriors. Not only would such representations situate their war within an intelligible and well-known historical-military context, but it would also portray them as equals to the world's most famed warrior states and could uplift their fragile Revolution and bleak prospects beyond its seeming tenuousness.[51]

As one of the first major maneuvers of the War of Independence, the Quebec campaign provided Americans with an opportunity to elaborate on similarities between classical and American men of war and ways of war. Lacking a substantial national martial heritage, American orators, poets, and politicians capitalized on what they constructed as a classicized and heroic—if ultimately vain—effort and sacrifice to route the British out of Canada. The author of *Remarks on a Late Pamphlet Entitled Plain*

Truth, for example, attributed the Continental Army's "painful and tedious marches over frozen lakes . . . [and the crossing] of snow and icy mountains, in the most inclement season of the year" to true "Spartan or Roman enthusiasm."[52] *An Impartial History of the War in America between Great Britain and the United States* ascribed the behavior of American soldiers in the same campaign to their "Roman" virtue. The "Roman soldiers in the time of the commonwealth," Americans knew, "without force of constraint, served their country, and maintained good discipline from mutual choice." Like in America, "the soldiers . . . were free Romans, and had an interest in the happiness of their country." Like the Americans, the Roman soldiers "endured hardships and encountered dangers, not from force, but because they considered themselves members of the commonwealth, and mutual sharers of the honours and privileges which they were fighting for, with the greatest senators of Rome." Similarly, American troops were nobly motivated. They "did not follow Montgomery to Canada for the sake of plunder or from any wanton desire of laying waste the country," but in a manifestation of disinterested patriotism.[53] Americans, who found significant similarities in the motivation and execution between the American soldiers of the Canadian campaign and the Romans of old, continued to elaborate on similar patterns throughout the long years of the war.[54]

None other than the commander of the Continental Army himself acknowledged those relationships and provided a remarkable demonstration of the perceived ties between American and Roman soldiers. Responding to a British peace offer in 1777, George Washington wrote to his opponent, General John Burgoyne: "The associated armies in America act from the noblest motives, liberty. The same principles actuated the arms of Rome in the days of her glory; and the same object was the reward of Roman valour."[55] Washington, pointing at a meaningful correlation between the American and Roman armies, emphasized to his imperial opponent the perceived connection between the army he commanded and those who conquered the greatest of empires. Washington underscored the republican nature of both armies, implying the stark difference between what he perceived as a British mercenary army and his subordinates, who, like the Romans, were citizen-soldiers fighting out of their own will for their country's cause. Lower-ranking soldiers also suggested similarities to the ancients. The anonymous "Field-Officer in the Northern Army" who described how American "troops rushed on the enemy with more than

Roman bravery" implied, as Washington had, that such bravery stemmed not from brute rage or greed but was, rather, the corollary of patriotism—or, in Washington's words, the outcome of "the noblest of motives, liberty."[56]

An epic clash that stirred revolutionaries was the Battle of Thermopylae, remembered as the ultimate stance of a few virtuous against a corrupt multitude, of westerners—Spartans, against their eastern—Persian—enemies. Hence "Cato of Utica" valorized the few "who defended the pass of Thermopilae against millions of armed slaves, commanded by their emperor."[57] Patriots, however, tended to tie historical battles such as Thermopylae to specific American engagements which they perceived as analogous. Accordingly, Henry Hugh Brackenridge, in his play *The Battle of Bunker Hill*, had one of his protagonists pledge that "should Faithless Gage, pour forth his lean, half starv'd myrmidons," referring to the members of the warlike Thessalian people who were ruled by Achilles and followed him—unquestionably—on the fateful expedition against Troy, "we'll make them taste our cartridges." If, however, Gage would dare discharge his "myrmidons" against the American line, they, in turn, even "if o'er charged, with numbers, [would] bravely fall, Like those three hundred at Thermopylae, And give our country credit in our deaths."[58] For Brackenridge the Americans entrenched on Bunker Hill reincarnated the three hundred Spartans led by Leonidas and situated in the pass of Thermopylae, fighting until their glorious death by an overwhelming Persian foe. Americans remembered that the Persians may have won the day in Thermopylae, but were eventually hurled back, defeated, to their eastern empire.

The classics also provided constitutional reasoning and argumentation for rebelling Americans, as they read their current legal situation and grievances back to antiquity. Patriots provided numerous comparisons between ancient and modern colonization and the nature of the relation in antiquity between the imperial center and its colonial peripheries. Colonists repeatedly looked back to the classical centuries to understand better the nature of colonialism, to contextualize their own situation historically, and to make use of that history for propagandistic ends. The most common interpretation of ancient colonization idealized the imperial relationship in ancient Greece, understanding that connection as consisting mostly of honor and reverence from the colony toward the mother *polis*. The Romans, by contrast, were usually thought to have conducted a brutal imperial policy, keeping their colonies in a servile state. James Otis summed up this view: "'Tis well known the Grecians were kind, humane, just and generous towards theirs [colonies]. 'Tis as notorious that the Romans were severe, cruel, brutal and barbarous towards theirs. I have ever pleased myself in thinking that Great-Britain, since the [Glorious] revolution, might be justly compared to Greece, in its care and protection of its colonies. I also imagined that the French and Spaniards followed the Roman example."[59] Otis's use of the past tense throughout the passage was indicative: After 1765, he and many of his fellow Americans perceived Britain not as a humane Greece but as a malicious Rome reincarnate.

This particular reading of ancient constitutional history, of the Greeks as humanitarian and the Romans as tyrannical, although widely accepted among American patriots, was not the only available interpretation of the classical colonial experience. American writers occasionally put forward a nuanced version of the familiar narrative in which both Greece and Rome were seen as worthy models of center–periphery relations. Addressing "the inhabitants of the colony of Massachusetts Bay," a writer in the *Boston Gazette* pointed out in March 1775 that "the practice of nations has been different" from that of Britain in treating their colonies. "The Greeks," for instance, "planted colonies, and neither demanded nor pretended any authority over them, but they became independent commonwealths." However, the Romans, the *Gazette* (now less traditional) stated, "continued their colonies under the jurisdiction of the mother commonwealth, but, nevertheless, she allowed them the privileges of cities . . . but these Italian cities . . . were always allow'd all the rights of Roman citizens and were govern'd by senates of their own. It was the policy of Rome to conciliate her colonies by allowing them equal liberty with her citizens."[60]

Advancing their constitutional argument from history, patriots did not restrict themselves to understanding the Roman treatment of colonies as heavy-handed and unjust. They could also, as just shown, interpret the Romans' conduct as proper and equitable. A comparison of that interpretation of Rome as an empire of justice to the perceived British mishandling of colonial policy justified rebellion and contextualized such radical action in a genealogy of historical struggles between liberty and tyranny, which has come to be known as the Whig interpretation of History. These instances further demonstrate how Americans, in their constitutional and propagandistic front against their mother country, were thinking through the classics by reading and molding history to fit their specific needs and current situations.

Another popular mode in which many of the classical allusions functioned was that of a prestigious metaphor, usually intended to praise a specific American within the context of the most esteemed and honored of secular discourses. Many of the instances we have examined so far were also intended to bestow classical auras on people and events. However, there were contexts within which the primary aim of the allusion was to adorn Americans with a classical "halo," with minimal intent to furnish a specific republican *exemplum*. Thus, when the Committee of Correspondence of the town of Chelsea, Massachusetts, wrote in a letter published by the *Boston Gazette* to "the worthy Committee of Correspondence in the Town of Boston," it praised the "noble patriots" that its town had "cheerfully contributed [to] . . . the Grand Congress." The Chelseans found it important to note that their representatives "supported the dignity of ancient Roman Senators."[61] Southerners, too, imagined their representatives as Roman senators whose "resolution and conduct" bore "all the character of ancient magnanimity."[62] Similarly, a pseudonymous writer under the Greek name "Coloni" described the great pleasure he had reading "General Lee's letter to General Burgoyne." The American general, Coloni added, "writes like a Roman senator."[63] Americans found the highest measure of honor in representations as Roman statesmen of old: dignified and firm, resolute and disinterested, and above all dedicated to the common good, those ancients embodied republican virtues.

Prestigious metaphors were not reserved for statesmen, however, as writers honored soldiers, too, often the fallen, with classical appellations. Hence, in *An Elegy to the Memory of Charles Lewis*, published in the *Virginia Gazette* on May 25, 1775, the eulogist described the Lewis's conduct in his mortal moments in Roman terms: "Where death his leaden vollies round him shot . . . [l]ike Caesar, nobly brave, [he] maintained his ground, and calm as Cato bore the fatal wound."[64] Distorting the historical picture by attributing to the fallen American patriot the distinctions of the two nemeses of antiquity—Julius Caesar and Cato Uticensis—the eulogist bestowed on Lewis what he certainly believed were the highest commendations. However, American revolutionaries employed classical history not only to bestow prestigious metaphors but also to confer derogative ones. Christopher Gadsden of South Carolina wrote in 1779 in a diary entry that "Catiline's Gang was not more atrocious than such as are daily deluded over to the enemy from our back [western] parts."[65] American Tories were easily understood in terms of Rome's rogues. Such seemingly trivial allusions were no mere "intellectual window dressing," for these classical references functioned beyond their obvious purpose of ornamenting mundane experiences.[66] Indeed, the discourse of antiquity was central to an attempt to situate the American endeavor in the historical context of classical republicanism. Within this frame of reference, specific allusions received significant meaning when understood not as discrete speech acts but, rather, as elements in an ongoing, extensive, and profound historical discourse.

The effect of the classics on patriots' perceptions is demonstrated in the ways revolutionaries evaluated and set their expectations for how their fellow Americans behaved. Indeed, the severe criteria of the ancients were applied to critique revolutionary America. Josiah Quincy, for example, called on his compatriots to act "Brutus-like" by dedicating themselves "to the service of your country."[67] Quincy was asking and expecting revolutionaries to give up their personal interests en masse in favor of the communal good. People who called for such deeds did so in a way that provided historical meaning to such radical, "Brutus-like" action. Quincy may have been referring either to Lucius Junius Brutus, the Roman republic's founder who executed his sons for the sake of the commonwealth, or to Marcus Junius Brutus, Julius Caesar's assassin. In any event, Quincy derived the meaning of his anticipations from classical narratives of republican citizens devoting themselves to the common good. Such high expectations nurtured by the classical standards often turned into admonitions and sour disappointments. John Adams also revealed classically driven expectations and dissatisfactions. In 1774, he contrasted the first Continental Congress's economic responses to the Coercive Acts with the bolder policies of Demosthenes and Cicero. Adams posed a counter-factual question: If those revered ancients had been delegates to the American Congress, "is it easy to believe they would propose non Importation? Non exportation? Non consumption? ...If I mistake not, Something a little more sublime and mettlesome would come from such kind of spirits."[68] Adams expected his peers to identify with his own classical sensibilities and act accordingly; subsequently, he was bewildered by what he considered to be timid American action. Only a year later, Adams was once again puzzled by the discrepancy between his classical expectations and his compatriots' behavior. Commenting on the American retreat from Canada, he remarked: "Flight was unknown to the Romans . . . I wish it was [so] to Americans."[69] Such hopes and anticipations, nurtured through a worldview committed to understanding history as a field of action in which America's fate was deeply implicated with classical history, revealed the tightness of the ancients' hold on the reins of contemporary interpretations of the Revolution.

Adams was by no means alone in comparing Americans to Romans and in the balance choosing the Romans as worthier. William Smith's critique, in *An Oration, in Memory of General Montgomery,* demonstrates the problematic appeal of an ascetic republican virtue to a modern society busy pursuing its happiness. Americans have "minds so little," Smith lamented, "that they can conceive nothing great, which does not court the eye in all the trappings of dress, titles and external splendor. . . . A General from the plough! [a term] of ridicule and reproach among many [in America]. Yet such was Cincinnatus, in the best days of Roman virtue."[70] Hence, as opposed to the dominant strand of comparing America to classical antiquity and Americans to ancients, some used classical examples to demonstrate the shortcomings of American virtue. The idiom of antiquity could be further used to mock Americans' pretensions to "play ancient." The *Pennsylvania Gazette* reported that, at the siege of Louisburg, a company of American soldiers "talked of the wondrous feats they would perform, and compared themselves to Romans; but finding the place likely to make resistance, these Romans very courageously ran away. And thus they would do on every occasion if real danger approached, when at a distance they would bluster, resolve, write, protest, and look big."[71] At least some contemporaries thought that there was a significant discrepancy between the Roman rhetoric and American reality.

The Humble Confession, Declaration, Recantation, and Apology of Benjamin Towne, a satirical tract said to have been written by John Witherspoon, provides an exception that proves the rule. Towne was an English-born publisher who changed sides from patriot to loyalist after the British occupation of Philadelphia in 1777. When the British evacuated the city in the following year, patriots forced Towne to publish his "humble confession" in an attempt to return to the patriot fold. "I remember to have read in the Roman history that when Cato of Utica had put himself to death, being unable to survive the dissolution of the republic, and the extinction of liberty; another senator of inferior note, whose name I cannot recollect, did the same thing," wrote Towne (or whoever wrote the pamphlet in his name). Yet Towne had no intention of becoming a republican martyr. To the contrary, he believed that "to pass the same judgment on the conduct of an obscure printer" such as himself "is miserable reasoning indeed." Towne was evoking classical history to demonstrate how inapplicable that history's teachings were, at least in the case of a humbled ex-loyalist. Indeed, "had a Hancock, or an Adams changed sides, I grant you they would have deserved no quarter, and I believe would have received none."[72] However, how many Hancocks and Adamses did America have? And how many Catos did Rome have? Towne—or, rather, the witty Witherspoon—elaborated, perhaps unwittingly, the problem of the attempt to impose an extremely demanding elitist culture such as classical republicanism on a heterogeneous, permissive, and market-oriented society. However, a white Anglo-American and prosperous artisan such as Towne was automatically a member of the community of the classical-idiom discoursers. For many North Americans, that was not the case.

As mentioned earlier, by the late colonial period elite white women already spoke "classic." Upper-class women were interested in political affairs (in later years they could astonish male observers, as Mrs. Robert Carter did, with their "perfect acquaintance with the American constitution"), and indeed they were able to acquire impressive, if limited, knowledge of classical culture.[73] Mercy Otis Warren offers a remarkable example of an American woman who was fluent in discoursing the classics, as her revolutionary neo-Roman plays *The Adulateur* and *The Defeat*, which were unmatched in their ability to merge Roman and American narratives, attest.[74] Warren was, however, the exception that proves the rule. Contemporary perceptions of women's condition in classical societies in which "the fair sex were . . . neglected and despised" did not leave much room for American women to perform in a classicized public sphere.[75] The servile state of women in antiquity echoed the conspicuous lack of sexual equality in American society and was not especially appealing to female writers as a possible source for textual expression. Hypothetically, American women could have identified with and embodied classical virtues with the aid of protagonists such as Portia, Cato's daughter and Brutus's wife who committed suicide when her republic—and husband—were destroyed. Indeed,

Winterer and the historian Philip Hicks have demonstrated convincingly how elite white women such as Mercy Otis Warren and Abigail Adams viewed "political events through a classical lens," especially that of Rome.[76] It was through the ancient model of the Roman matron that some American women were able to participate in, and contribute to, the revolutionary classical discourse. Much more effective in the political sphere than their Greek counterparts, Roman matrons did not, however, provide very useful models for public action. Always in the background, either supporting or plotting, they did not occupy the front stage of public life.[77] Women were not supposed to engage actively in the civic spheres of the res publica—neither in ancient Rome nor in early America. Early American political discourse was male-centered, a "grammar of virility" steeped in a "culture of manhood" that ignored women as potential public figures.[78]

Nevertheless, women's voices occasionally conversed publicly in the classical discourse. "Aurelia," a Roman pseudonym chosen by a woman for an essay published in the *Boston Gazette,* admitted that "ladies have no benefits in politics" and that it was only after her husband had "gone forth in defence of his country" that she felt free to indulge "in the privilege of reading the newspapers."[79] Male writers occasionally appealed to women in a classical idiom. A piece entitled "To the Female Inhabitants of the Colony of Rhode Island" appealed to the women of the colony, "like the Roman and our ancestorial matrons, [to] animate us in the defense of our liberties."[80] Nevertheless, such appeals were rare and demonstrate the extent to which women were regularly excluded from the classical sphere, as they were from many other areas of revolutionary American life.

Blacks, unsurprisingly, fared even worse than women in the classical sphere. An obvious characteristic America shared with the ancient civilizations was that both were slaveholding societies. Unlike in antiquity, however, black slaves in the New World had little access to the intellectual fundamentals of that society and hence held little, if any, knowledge of the classics. Although we find some instances of freed slaves who were acquainted with the classics—notably, Phillis Wheatley, who knew Latin and displayed sophisticated classicism in her poems—those cases were rare and are in no way indicative of widespread black (or, in Wheatley's case, black *and* female) participation in the most Western of discourses. That said, Wheatley was not the only African American who discoursed in the classical idiom. A sermon written by "A Black Whig" in 1782 and addressed to "the Americans in general, but to the citizens of South Carolina in particular," revealed a remarkable use of the classics. The black "son of freedom" chose a classicized fashion to glorify American valor. The British, he pointed out, "have been fought with bravery equal to that of Romans, by the raw and undisciplined Americas." When he came to praise "the virtuous daughters of Carolina," he glorified their "courage, perseverance and fortitude [that] are equal to the daughters of ancient Rome and Sparta."[81] Was the member of the lowest social and racial caste aware of the irony of praising women, who were also deprived of meaningful participation in the classical discourse, in a language that must have been foreign to many of them, as it was to vast majority of African Americans? To make even more glaring the marginality of non-privileged groups in the classical sphere, masters mockingly gave classical names to black slaves, who were mostly dispossessed of any chance to obtain and relate to classical knowledge. Ironically, most of the Catos, Caesars, and Brutuses of America were not white Americans signing newspaper articles with classical pseudonyms or taking pleasure in the classical names and metaphors that their peers bestowed on them. Rather, they were enslaved human beings deprived of liberty, classical or otherwise.

We have thus far examined different patterns and modes through which revolutionary Americans appealed to the classics. As we have seen, those rhetorical forms were in common use throughout the colonies-turned-states. A mere few symbolic spheres other than the classics could produce meaningful connotations for such a wide swath of the diverse lot of participators in the American revolutionary discourse. However, Americans shared more than rhetorical classical structures. The classical discourse also implied certain meta-historical assumptions that underlay the discoursers of antiquity. The first of those assumptions was the *translatio imperii*, which cultivated the widespread belief in America's ultimate rise to Roman heights.

American revolutionaries' depictions of themselves in terms of, and as, Roman incarnations throughout the Revolution rested on a long-held belief in the transfer of political dominion westward, toward America, the *translatio imperii*. This meta-historical concept, "whose existence entailed historical events but was not to be critically evaluated within the context that events provided," underlay patriots' perception that their destiny was correlated with Roman annals.[82] Visions of "western shores" as the locus of a new empire were in no way an American invention, however; they had a long pedigree by the last quarter of the eighteenth century. The belief in *translatio imperii*, the constant travel of the "transfer of rule" westward, was ingrained in the European faith in the perpetual movement of political and cultural legitimacy from one civilization to another, passed down from classical antiquity to the dominant forces of Western Europe. It was, as J. G. A. Pocock points out, "a key concept in the structure of medieval Latin thinking."[83] Such a belief was indebted, but not restricted, to cyclical understandings of historical time: As one civilization declined, another would soon arise to replace it as the seat of *imperium*, or political dominion. Originating in Roman historiography and introduced into Christian thought by St. Jerome in the fourth century, the *translatio* by the twelfth century had acquired its characteristic form, described by Otto Bishop of Freising as "the process of world history," which "became a movement of power from East to the West."[84] The discovery of the New World and the Reformation drove Europeans increasingly to incorporate the Americas into the framework of the *translatio imperii*.[85] By the eighteenth century both England and France wished to prove their superior claims to cultural and political hegemony to the "glory that was Rome." The logic of *translatio imperii* presumed, however, not only that supreme political power moves constantly westward, but also that there could ever be only one dominant imperial power at any single moment. Eighteenth-century oppositional Whig understandings conditioned contemporaries to perceive European powers as irredeemably corrupt, setting the stage for a new force in the west to assume imperial power.

As early as 1725, some analysts believed *imperium* to be crossing the Atlantic. George Berkeley's *Verses on the Prospect of the Arts and Learning in America* predicted that "there shall be sung another golden age, The rise of empire and arts . . . Westward the course of empire takes its way."[86] In his old age John Adams recalled in a letter to Benjamin Rush a vivid memory from his childhood during the 1740s: "There is nothing . . . more ancient in my memory than the observation that arts, sciences and empire had traveled westward; and in conversation it was always added since I was a child, that their next leap would be over the Atlantic into America."[87] An English traveler was impressed at midcentury that the concept of *translatio* carried a new "idea, strange as it was visionary," which presumed that at some approaching "destined moment . . . America is to give law to the rest of the world."[88] Nathaniel Ames observed during the 1750s that "the progress of Human literature (like the sun) is from East to the West; thus it has traveled thro' Asia and Europe, and now is arrived at the Eastern Shore of *America*."[89] When William Hooper, a North Carolinian, asserted in 1774 that the colonies "ere long will build an empire upon the ruins of Great Britain," he was expressing what had become a common notion about the rising empire of liberty in the west. A South Carolinian under the pseudonym "Non Quis Sed Quid (Not Measures, Men)" elaborated the notion of *translatio* in the context of the gathering Continental Congress. Encouraging his compatriots to choose "deputies for a general congress; solemnly enter into a non importation agreement, and religiously adhere to it," the author promised that "great things" awaited America. He could be confident in America's future greatness, since "learning, liberty, and every thing that ennobles the human mind, have constantly been traveling westward."[90] Understandings of *translatio imperii* had conditioned Americans by Independence to imagine effortlessly the transfer of the seat of empire across the ocean from its former locus in corrupt Britain to its new American habitat. It indeed seems to have been common for patriots to expect by 1776 that America would become "the theatre where human nature will soon receive its greatest military, civil, and literary honours."[91]

Once metropolitan decision makers abandoned the policy known as "salutary neglect" and chose to carry out stricter control over the colonies, including the repeated attempts to extract revenue, they disturbed the imperial equilibrium politically, constitutionally, and intellectually. During the following years, residents of the separate colonies began to realize that they shared an identity of interests, an idea that had been conspicuously underdeveloped during most of the colonial era. If still a long way from full blown "nationalism," such notions might indeed be seen as the first step toward the construction of a pan-American imagined community.[92] As the political coherence among the colonies intensified and the prospects of war with Britain materialized, understandings of the *translatio imperii* to America took a significant turn. Rome became crucial to making sense of America's historical role as the next locus of civilization, power, and glory. The 1770s indeed played a pivotal role in reshaping notions of *translatio* in America and witnessed a remarkable change in colonists' rhetoric: When conveying visions of transfer of empire thereafter, Americans did not simply imagine the imperial relocation as a transfer of political supremacy. Rather, a revolutionary context accompanied by an ardent belief in the degraded state of Britain became the pretext for asserting repeatedly that America would either re-create Rome on western shores or would enjoy grandeur defined in Roman and classical terms.

Jacob Duché elaborated in October 1772 in his "Letters of Caspipina" an American *translatio* with a Roman edge. "Caspipina" described "new kingdoms and empires rushing forth from the embryo state, eager to disclose their latent powers," while "the setting rays of the sun of Righteousness shinning forth with seven fold luster to the utmost bourn of this western continent." Caspipina's millennial picture positioned America as a place deserving pilgrimage and respect even more than the consecrated Old World spaces. Indeed, he went on to remark how he treaded "the hallowed soil [of America] with far higher pleasures from anticipation than your classic enthusiasts feel from reflection, whilst they kiss the floor of Tusculum," the Latin city in which Pliny and Cicero resided.[93] That year witnessed other visions of a *translatio* defined in antique terms. "No more of Memphis, Athens, Rome, Britain," exclaimed Philip Freneau (1752–1832) in the 1772 edition of his "Rising Glory of America." The poet's thoughts "on this auspicious day" were set on "a theme more new, tho' not less noble . . . The rising glory of this western world."[94] In the 1775 edition of that poem, Freneau further rhapsodized that "the sun towards the west retreats" and kindles a "blest region" in which "Greece and Rome [are] no more."[95] America, Freneau believed, was about to occupy the role of the revered ancient republics of old. Josiah Quincy's pamphlet *Observations on the Act of Parliament Commonly Called the Boston Port-Bill,* published in the watershed year of 1774, was even more straightforward in its conception of America as a new Rome. Quincy mused that the republican, self-sacrificing spirit that "rose in Rome" would "one day make glorious this more Western world." America, Quincy felt, was on the verge of unfolding its imperial, Roman-like potential; she "hath in her store her Bruti and Cassii—her Hampdens and Sydneys."[96] Quincy understood history as a succession of empires in which Rome and Britain assumed the role of America's predecessors. Quincy's use of the plural tense in referring to "Bruti" and "Cassii," alluding to the Roman senators Brutus (Junius Marcus Brutus, 85–42 BC) and Cassius (Cassius Longinus Gaius, d. 42 BC), who led the conspiracy to murder Julius Caesar when he overthrew the republic, suggested at this early point of the conflict what would become obvious in years to come: the belief that America would not only repeat Roman grandeur, but would indeed surpass the empires of the past with its native "Romans." Rome, we recall, could boast only one of each virtuous specimen. *An Elegy on the Times,* also published in 1774, invited its readers to "meet the Fathers of this western clime; Nor names more noble graced the rolls of fame, When Spartan firmness brav'd the wrecks of time, or Rome's bold virtues fann'd th' heroic flame."[97] Once again, the poet envisioned America in a succession of ancient and glorious polities. Owing its greatness to its "fathers," the American–Romans who equaled the virtue of the patriots of old, America would rise, and eventually it, too, would ennoble the wrecks of time.

Authors elaborating on the *translatio imperii* were often critical of the classical inheritance in light of America's prospects. Envisioning classical armies drenched in "fields of blood and mighty battles lost," a writer in the *Boston Gazette* pointed out that in America there were "no Caesars, Sylla, or old Phillip's son [Alexander], who sigh'd and wept when he'd one world undone." The Bostonian would rather "sing of nations, Empires, yet unborn." The American empire, "yet unborn," would realize "justice . . . o'er the land," and rescue "freedom from the tyrant's hand." Utopian prospects awaited America, a patriot state adorned "in laurel crowns": "commerce revives, and arts and science rise. Whole empires lofty spreading sails unfurl'd / Roll swiftly toward the Western world." It was quite common for New Englanders, as we shall see in following chapters, to merge such classical visions with millennial apparitions.[98] Two weeks later the *Boston Gazette* published yet another prediction of the transfer of empire westward, which, if not outright critical toward its imperial predecessors, did not pay them the usual reverence. Calling on his peers to examine "Greece and Athens! And . . . proud mistress Rome" who were wiped off the historical map, the writer turned confrontationally to the British. The author called on his "lordly tyrants," pointing out how "beneath this Western sky, We've form'd a new dominion, and Land of liberty."[99] Such belief in American superiority was not a mere expression of insecurity and anxiety, as one could assume from the apparent fragility of the colonies vis-à-vis Britain.[100] Such self-confidence demonstrated a structural element characteristic of the use of the classical idiom. That aspect of the classical discourse consisted of the belief that America was both fulfilling and surpassing its ancient historical parallels.[101]

"A Dialogue from the Year of Independence," which introduced two characters—an American and a Frenchman—who discussed America's place in the imperial succession, expressed similar ideas. Narvon, the American, conveyed to the Frenchman Massilon an outline of the east-to-west trajectory of world history: "See empires first in eastern regions rise; arts, science, freedom and religion there, first spread and flourish—see them bend their way, and flow advance to these far western climes." This dynamic progress of power, science, and arts culminated in America, where "from ev'ry province, by the gen'ral voice / Of all the land, a senate [shall] constitute, As wise, as great, as prudent as august, As Rome, when mistress of the universe, Or Athens, when her pride was in it's bloom, Or Britain, e'er she fell, could ever boast."[102] Narvon emphasized that America was *as* (a word used five times in these few lines quoted) magnanimous as her imperial predecessors, Athens, Rome, and Britain. As such, the senates that the now united states would erect would compare favorably to, if not outshine, the senates of old. Narvon further asserted that in America, "each one's a Cato; each a Socrates."[103] This generous attribution of classical virtues placed America as a more perfect incarnation of the ancient mold. In independent America, Narvon foresaw "a grand republic rise and rule; extend her limits to the ambient seas . . . see arts increase; see science rear her head; behold her flourish thro' this wide domain, and Egypt, Rome and Athens, far excel." Such a republic would "give law to Europe" and "rise on western shores, [and] for ages far surpass all former empires."[104] Nonetheless, even while patriots repeatedly alleged that America exceeded the ancient civilizations, they affirmed a special relation between Rome and America. America was not merely Rome's successor, it was commonly held, but was connected metaphysically to that revered polity: "What now gleams with dawning ray, at home, Once blaz'd . . . at Rome."[105] The belief in historical, as well as meta-historical, ties that bonded America to the ancient republics was a mainstay of this classical idiom.

Americans continued to work out notions of reconstituting a classical empire in America after independence during wartime. David Ramsay, the South Carolinian historian who delivered the *Oration on the Advantages of American Independence* in 1778, was impressed by America's obvious potential, alluding to the continent's territorial extent, which indeed dwarfed the territories of European monarchies: "What a substratum for empire! Compared with which the foundation of the Macedonian, the Roman, and the British, sink into insignificance," he marveled.[106] Ramsay's oration also introduced a concept that reinforced the notion of the transfer of political dominion, the *translatio imperii:* The transfer of knowledge, *translatio studii,* described a westward movement not only of *imperium* but also of learning and the arts, or the whole gamut of "civilization." Here, Ramsay hoped, "the free governments of America will produce poets, orators, criticks, and historians, equal to the most celebrated of the ancient commonwealths of Greece and Italy."[107] Hence, the American *imperium* would be accompanied by cultural and intellectual dominance, measuring up to the empires of old. The poem "Anticipation of the Literary Fame of America" articulated the notion of *translatio studii* to its fullest extent, predicting, "Columbian *Livies* . . . another *Plato* . . . *Cicero* . . . some new *Euripides* . . . some future *Virgil* . . . some modern *Ovid*," who would all "throng the historick field" in America. When all these incarnations of the classical masters were recast, "Tully's Tusculum [would] again be seen . . . in our western clime."[108] Patriots predicted that America would rise as a cultural crucible that would witness the resurrection of an Augustan Rome on western shores.

Reverend Samuel Cooper's sermon in Boston on the day of the commencement of the Massachusetts Constitution of 1780 demonstrated similar reasoning. Cooper explained to his adherents: "Rome rose to empire because she early thought herself destined for it," and Romans "did great things because they believed themselves capable, and born to do them." Americans, however, have "an object more truly great and honourable. We seem called by heaven to make a large portion of this globe a seat of knowledge and liberty, of agriculture, commerce, and arts, and what is more important than all, of Christian piety and virtue."[109] The American empire, at least in this cleric's vision, would become a Protestant Rome (not to be confused, of course, with the popish Rome), fulfilling providential notions of *translatio religionis,* the incorporation of America within the confines of an ecclesiastical history.[110] Here again, America was described as better than its original, pagan predecessor. Nevertheless, it would always be understood in and compared to its predecessor's terms.

In claiming inheritance of Europe's religious, cultural, and political dominance, and in asserting the possibility of a more perfect *imperium,*

Americans justified their break with declining Britain. In *America Invincible,* a poem by an officer with the Continental Army dedicated to General Horatio Gates in 1779, America replaced Britain as the seat of empire: "Britain's in awe, and totters from her base, while blooming freedom seems to claim the place, where free born sons . . . [r]ous'd to support its justice with delight."[111] Yet if America had proclaimed its independence from Britain, it had not severed its ties to antiquity by any means. America's citizens, the poet foretold, were bound to establish "young Senates with their tender laws" and to call "new Catos to their Country's cause."[112] America was once more represented as a new Rome, establishing Roman institutions and nurturing Roman citizens. Yet America's mission was not emulative but one that would transform it into a new and better Rome. When after the conclusion of the War of Independence Phillis Wheatley's poem *Liberty and Peace* portrayed America as a "New-born Rome" who "shall give Britannia Law," such imagery was already a common trope.[113] America, in the minds of its inhabitants, had replaced Britain in the role of a new Rome; *imperium* had been transferred to American soil.

The *translatio imperii* was not the only paradigm that pervaded the classico-historical discourse. An additional meta-historical position revolutionary-era Americans shared was a discomfort with secular, scientific concepts of time. Understanding time as a linear, enlightened, Newtonian concept indifferent to human existence and experience became an option for contemporaries for the first time through eighteenth-century scientific discourse.[114] The classical discourse, however, reveals that the burden of a history perceived as occurring within a void, meaningless continuum, having neither an apparent beginning nor an end, seemed unbearable to many Americans (if it was indeed a stance seriously taken by any contemporary). These patriots revealed their apprehensions through the distinct ways in which they repeatedly evaluated and understood their own epoch in relation to classical antiquity.

Patriots commonly looked backward to antiquity to evaluate their present achievements and prospects. Philip Freneau asked, after prophesizing that America would become a new Greece or Rome, "How could I weep that we were born so soon,/In the beginning of more happy times!"[115] The "more happy times" to which Freneau referred were those when Americans

35

would equal the Romans. John Adams referred to such an epoch in a letter dated 1776 to George Wythe (described by Thomas Jefferson as a "Cato without the avarice of the Roman").[116] "You and I, my dear friend," Adams wrote, "have been sent into life at a time when the greatest lawgivers of antiquity would have wished to have lived."[117] Within a historicized understanding of time, in which every occurrence stood independently and would be considered as singular and distinct, Adams's temporal conjunction of the American present and classical antiquity would make little sense. So would Charles Lee's reflection, again during the year of independence: "I us'd to regret not being thrown into the world in the glamorous third or fourth century [BC] of the Romans; but now I am thoroughly reconcil'd to my lot."[118] Similarly, the South Carolinian "Vox Populi" asserted late in 1774 that, although "some extol Roman Greatness . . . , the heart of every son of these provinces may distend with joy when he reflects that he is born an American."[119] These remarks demonstrate how revolutionaries compared their deeds to those of the revered ancients to evaluate, and eventually present, their lives and times as significant in historical perspective. These revolutionaries' reconciliation and eventual delight with being born in eighteenth-century America instead of during classical antiquity's greatest hour reveals the extent to which the appraisal of the revolutionary present depended on the classical past for self-realization, as they insisted on assessing and contextualizing their experiences vis-à-vis republican Rome's past. The classical discourse thus provided the revolutionaries' deeds with meanings that were gained and revealed through history.

Patriots did not stop articulating their achievements through the lens of classical history even after independence, when they could plausibly feel that American annals had matured and acquired a respectability of their own. For Americans obsessed with their future fame, the narratives of classical history offered intellectual means and contexts to evaluate and interpret their own endeavors. The historical alignments American revolutionaries made between modern and ancient history prescribed, however, that time could not be viewed as contingent and arbitrary. Rather, history had to entail an extra-historical logic: The present would repeatedly refer to a glorified, or at times a vilified, past to attain meaning and significance. By the late eighteenth century, such historical attitudes may have been falling out of fashion in Europe, but they were still holding their ground in revolutionary America.[120]

The modes we have thus far discussed, patriots' frequent statements regarding the western movement of empire and the historical meanings embedded in time, were accompanied by an additional presumption regarding the nature of history—namely, that they were operating in a historical dimension that had precedence. Present events were not unique but, rather, grounded in past occurrences. Indeed, many revolutionaries perceived their actions as *not* exceptional (in the historiographical sense of the word). Hence, they often provided accounts suggesting that they witnessed, participated in, or anticipated paradigmatic repetitions of classical episodes. Thus, William Henry Drayton genuinely expected that when America needed a savior, an American "Brutus [would] not be wanting."[121] Such representations of repetition, imitation, and imagined relations to classical history were, as we shall see, staples of the revolutionary classical discourse.[122] Instructively, Edmund Pendleton recalled that, at the Virginia Convention of 1776, "The young boasted that they were treading upon the Republican ground of Greece and Rome."[123] Pendleton expressed the notion that the "ground" Virginians were stomping—or, rather, the history in which they were participating—had its origins, and found its meaning, in the events of a classical past. Indeed, it appeared as if the events that the ancients had experienced ages ago were not only similar but also inherently connected to those that Americans were currently going through.

William Hooper's letter of 1774 to James Iredell is revealing in the context of understanding the ways in which the present could derive meaning from such alleged relations to the classics, while history was seen as a dimension of time that was subject to reoccurrences. At the end of a remarkable epistle describing the Roman decadence that led to the rise of the Caesars, Hooper asked: "Reverse the catastrophe [of Roman corruption and decline], and might not Great Britain be the original from which this picture is taken?" Hooper's imagery reveals how history was perceived as a canvas that potentially represented more than one reality, or "original." In Hooper's view, the British Empire did not merely resemble decadent Rome of the first century BC; Britain was an imprint of a Roman mold. Josiah Quincy also described history as playing out reoccurrences of well-known patterns and events when he suggestively asked in 1774: "Is not Britain to America, what Caesar was to Rome?" A decade later, Alexander Hamilton asked under the Roman pseudonym "Catullus" whether "Caesar, who overturned the republic, was the Whig, [and] Cato, who died for it, the Tory of Rome?"[124] Such a debate assigning the contemporary labels "patriot" and "loyalist" to ancient Romans reveals the extent to which American revolutionaries viewed history as a medium that manifested repetitions and reoccurrences. Searching for the contemporary incarnation of the relationship between Caesar and Rome and finding it in the liaison between Britain and America, as Quincy did, was a common practice, a contemporary mode of unlocking and revealing history's logic. As late as 1805, John Adams could still assert that he seemed "to read the history of all ages and nations in every page, and especially the history of our country for forty years past. Change the names and every anecdote will be applicable to us."[125] Such modes of constructing history as a medium that bore witness to the repetition of narratives, a stance that was arguably even more robust during the Revolution—thirty years before Adams's remarkable observation—indicate the potential of the possible connections Americans could make between classical and their own history. Indeed, Americans repeatedly suggested that they were witnessing and re-experiencing "circumstances similar to those which produced the greatest orators of ancient days."[126] Time's alleged repetitive qualities were not necessarily benign, however: If the Continental Congress's rule was compared to that of the benevolent Augustus, Americans should expect the historical narrative to repeat and witness the malicious "twelve Caesars [to] succeed it."[127] In light of such an outlook, revolutionaries persistently searched for and provided evidence of the assumed correspondences and parallels between their own experiences and the classical narratives. Put otherwise, they became proficient figurative readers of history.

Such understandings went beyond the standard Enlightenment view of history—namely, that history was "philosophy teaching by example."[128] The revolutionary classical discourse suggests that history did not merely provide instructive models from earlier periods. Rather, that discourse gave expression to views suggesting that history consisted of processes that brought about reoccurrences of events and episodes from the past. These reoccurrences consisted both of large historical trajectories, such as the rise and fall of empires, and much more specific occasions, such as the rise of an "American Brutus" who would supposedly solve America's Roman-like tribulations. It was due to the very nature of history's unfolding, not because of the common Enlightenment-age truism that similar causes produced similar effects, that America and antiquity were bonded.[129]

The coming chapters will demonstrate how prescribing classical meaning to American history, and interpreting the one in light of the other, could culminate in various understandings of, and attitudes toward, time and history. For the time being, however, it is important to underscore the strong similarities in the modes in which revolutionary Americans employed the classics as well as in the assumptions they shared about history and its meaning. The common structures and shared clusters of meanings examined in this chapter emerged during the Revolution and harnessed the language of antiquity to projecting classical history on American endeavors—indeed, to styling an image of America as a newborn republican Rome. Such commonalities in trans-American attitudes toward antiquity that prevailed throughout the different regions, colonies, and states of revolutionary America were anything but inevitable. In fact, as we shall see, revolutionary Americans manifested through their uses of the classics striking differences in their historical sensibilities and attitudes toward time.

2

BRITANNIA CORRUPT

The British Empire in the Revolutionary
Classical Imagination

THE DISTINGUISHED SOUTH CAROLINIAN planter and merchant Henry Laurens, imprisoned in the Tower of London during the last years of the War for American Independence on charges of high treason against the British Crown, had plenty of time to contemplate the origins and meaning of the enduring imperial contest. Caught on a boat sailing to Holland to negotiate a loan for his struggling republic, Laurens, while awaiting judgment in the tower, kept a prison journal and spent "many days . . . penciling [in] large extracts from Gibbon's Decline and Fall of the Roman Empire." Throughout the journal, Laurens, the former president of the South Carolina Provincial Congress, compared the British and Roman empires and drew "parallels and reflexions from the conduct of Great Britain in the commencement and prosecution of the war against the American Colonies." As he viewed it, the example of the demise of the Roman Empire paralleled "the impolicy and folly" of Britain's conduct, as well as Britain's "injustice and cruelty of proceeding in the War."[1] In understanding and representing Britain in terms of the corrupt Roman Empire, Laurens was by no means expressing an outlandish position. He was, rather, drawing on a historical paradigm that Americans had been circulating and articulating for more than two decades. This chapter traces an intellectual revolution that took place in North America in the years following the French and Indian War. Whereas colonists represented Britain as a conquering, glorious, world-dominating Rome in the early 1760s, over the course of the next twenty years they proceeded to characterize the metropole by employing the image of a different Rome—the Rome of the corrupt tyranny of the most hated Caesars. Identifying this rapid deterioration in the representations of Britain from heights of glory to depths of tyranny and madness provides a richer understanding of the ways in which the political and psychological separation from Britain became possible, acceptable, and finally inevitable.

Furthermore, by illuminating the ways in which Americans shed their British identity through transforming their classical imagination, this chapter will provide the necessary background to understand the classicized identity they would eventually adopt. Moreover, the trajectory presented in this chapter questions notions advocated by the so-called republican synthesizers of undisrupted domination of Whig ideas in the colonies throughout the eighteenth century. Finally, this chapter will contribute to our understanding of a largely overlooked framework through which civic humanistic ideology could be expressed and articulated. Focusing on the revolutionary use of antiquity, or on classical form rather than on republican content, reveals a remarkable historical hermeneutics, a classical exegesis employed throughout the Revolution. If this chapter elaborates on a specific aspect of that exegesis, of interpretations of Britain as a degenerate Roman Empire, the following chapters will focus on the ways in which Americans perceived themselves as virtuous ancients. Hence, the remainder of this study will underscore the centrality of the peculiar historical consciousness suggested by the revolutionary classical discourse to our understanding of the American Revolution and its unlikely creation, the United States of America.

During the Seven Years' War, the global fighting conducted by France and Britain was not confined to the fields of Mars. As a contemporary French journal concluded, "The future will scarcely believe it, but the war between the English and the French has been as lively on paper as on the high seas."[2] One of the issues of the intellectual melees between France and Britain was the dispute over *translatio imperii,* or who was to be anointed the new Rome. Early on in the war, after the French victory in Minorca, the Abbe Seran de la Tour published *Comparison of the Conduct of the Carthagians with Respect to the Romans in the Second Punic War.* The subtitle of that work revealed the author's intention: "With the Conduct of England with Regard to France in the Declared War between These Two Powers in 1756." Seran's dissertation, among several other works published in those years, viewed the rivalry between Britain and France as a reenactment of one of the great rivalries of antiquity: the fierce competition between republican Rome and commercial Carthage.[3] That epic battle was preserved in European collective memory as a struggle in which a reluctant, virtuous Rome was forced to engage in three "Punic" wars before finally annihilating the avaricious, commercial Carthage on its way to world domination.[4] Thus, as one scholar has commented, "The Punic wars became a dramatic if not always revealing way for the rivals to think about their respective strengths and the designs each had upon the other."[5] The French were tempted to view themselves as Romans and the commercial, seagoing England as Carthage. The British, however, were potentially more ambivalent in regard to their ancient identity, because they could not ignore the fact that they were indeed a seafaring, commercial nation, just like Carthage of old.

However, when William Pitt's war strategy finally bore fruit, leading to a string of crushing British victories, identifying the heirs of the Romans seemed an easy task, at least in the minds of the inhabitants of the Anglophone world. The successive conquests that gave India and North America to the little island kingdom had made Englishmen, in Horace Walpole's phrase, "heirs apparent of the Romans."[6] After the successes of the year 1759, crowned by the capture of Quebec, English national self-esteem and self-assertion grew, as did that already deep-rooted sense that Britain was especially favored by providence.[7] By the end of the war, as Britain gained territory and power unequaled by any of its contemporaries, Britons began frequently and seamlessly to identify their imperial achievements with those of the empires of antiquity. During the 1760s and 1770s, they proclaimed time and again the affinity of their imperial project to that of classical Rome's and understood their achievements in light of the Romans'. They made such claims despite the profound historical differences between Rome and Britain: "Unlike Rome—Britain had become a guarantor of a balance of power in Europe ... unlike Rome again—it stood at the head of an empire of commerce rather than [of] conquest."[8]

This chapter examines the changing representations of Britain as Rome by American colonists-turned-rebels and the function and significance of those representations. Before turning to American depictions of Britain, however, I will briefly review the reflexive classical discourse within Britain of its Romanized identity. This review intends not only to contextualize the American discourse in a broad Atlantic setting but also to demonstrate the extent to which Americans abruptly deviated from the contemporaneous British discourse after 1765.

After the Treaty of Paris of 1763, British historians were busy producing narratives and histories of the late war in which they depicted Britons, like Romans, as possessing the *civitas* that enabled them to extend dominion over cultural and national outsiders.[9] One such history in which Britain and Rome were repeatedly compared was Oliver Goldsmith's *A History of England*, published in 1764. Goldsmith asserted that the British Empire could "now boast more power than even the Great Roman empire," especially because the huge expanse of Canada now "fell totally under the power of his Britannic majesty."[10] Goldsmith understood the British achievement by means of comparison to that of the Romans and derived its significance from surpassing Rome in power and territorial extent. Numerous British and Anglo-American writers would repeat this pattern during the early 1760s.[11]

Geographical surveys perpetuated the same line of reasoning, relying further on the Roman example and metaphor to assess and invest meaning in British imperial accomplishments. Accordingly, while the anonymously written *The Present State of the British Empire in Europe, America, Africa and Asia*, published in 1768, closed by stating that the British Empire was "more extensive and perhaps more powerful than any that had hitherto existed; even the great Roman Empire not excepted,"[12] Abercromby's *De Jure*, written in 1774, chose to pursue contemporary problems through a historical examination of ancient colonization. "There is great affinity, between this [Roman] form of Government and ours,"[13] Abercromby asserted, following a line of reasoning prevalent since the early days of the English imperial project in Ireland and the New World that appealed to the colonization project in terms of the Roman model in "the neo-Roman language of empire (*imperium*) and colony (*colonia*)."[14] Such notions gained particular significance thanks to the extraordinary territorial expansion of the British Empire in the years immediately preceding 1763. Abercromby went on to present the common motivations for colonizing that the two empires shared: subduing natives to gain dominion; expansion to prevent enemy attacks and increase the number of subjects; and emigration to purge deviant citizens from the metropolis, therefore diminishing urban tumults, and reward war veterans. Romans therefore could serve as models "from whom modern nations (ours in particular) have borrowed Maxims of State."[15] Such observations were useful also in understanding the imperial situation in the political arena. Hence, in 1766 Philip Yorke, a member of the "American Committee" of the House of Commons, could declare, "Our own colonies are more like those of Rome [as opposed to Greek colonies]. They went out upon charter, carrying with them the laws and enjoying the protection of the mother country."[16] John Entick's *The Present State of the British Empire,* published a mere two years before the American colonists' Declaration of Independence, pointed out that "the British Empire is arrived at that height of power and glory, to which none of the states and monarchies upon earth could ever lay the like claim. Rome, in all her grandeur, did not equal Great Britain, either in constitution, dominion, commerce, riches or strength . . . [Britain's empire] in its present state excels the ancient and modern states."[17] Entick, however, did not praise the British achievement merely for surpassing Rome in sheer power and extent, as has already been noted in other writings. Romans could not "boast of the liberty, rights and privileges, and of that security of property and person" enjoyed by an English subject. In contradistinction to the Roman Empire, one "founded in blood, plunder and rapine and upon an ambition that could not bear an equal," the countries that formed the British Empire across the globe were brought under the crown of Great Britain "by sound policy."[18] Hence, British pride in its empire was not restricted to visions of power and territory. It stemmed also from founding an unprecedented empire of liberty. Such a perception combined Whig notions of liberty and commerce and Tory notions of territorial expansion.

Rome therefore filled an important intellectual space within which Britons reflected on their extensive empire—its virtues and historical significance—during the 1760s and 1770s. Their recent achievements were validated, assessed, recognized, and imagined in relation to the antique and awesome Mediterranean empire. Most writers seemed to have agreed not only that the comparison was valid, but also that Britain had actually surpassed Rome. As we shall now see, Americans were participating in this imperial discourse, showing by the late 1750s an unbounded pride in taking part in the British venture, the greatest "since the days of Julius Caesar."[19]

When Benjamin Prime Young published his lyric poem *The Unfortu-nate Hero* in 1758, the war in America was still far from being determined. Nonetheless, Young chose to write an ode following the Greek poet Pindar's style to classicize the memory of the fallen British General George Howe.[20] In this eulogium, Young compared Howe, "the unfortunate hero," to the greatest warriors of the Roman republic in a manner that would repeat itself numerous times in different occasions and contexts during the coming decades: "Such were the warriors of days of old / such Cincinnatus, such Camillus bold, and the great Scipio's rose."[21] In Young's description, Howe was as virtuous as Rome's famed soldiers; he envisioned Howe in a classical context and imagined him as inflicting defeats on Rome's enemies: "Heroes like these [Howe] extensive vengeance hurl'd / on Rome's perfidious foes.... By thunderbolts like these she once subdu'd the world."[22] Young, after establishing the Roman quality of Howe and his soldiers, promised his readers that "Thro' every Age, Th' historic page, Their deeds with honor shall rehearse."[23] The British soldiers would go down in memory like their Roman predecessors, Young reassured his readers, and would share infinite glory with the empire that nurtured Cincinnatus, Camillus, and Scipio, the venerated soldier-republicans.

While the outcome of the Seven Years' War was still uncertain and Britons could only dream of an outcome as favorable as they would embrace in a mere few months, Young extensively employed allusions from the symbolic world of republican Rome. *The Conquest of Louisburg,* by John Maylem, which classicized William Pitt's first major victory in the war, chose a different path in the classicization of Britain. Maylem did not depict the warriors in the fields as classical heroes the way Young did. Rather, he glorified the imperial throne of George II, which he portrayed as surpassing "Olimpus's craggy height."[24] Maylem went on to claim that the British monarch, "Like Jove," the supreme Roman god, "who while on Olympus shone, so shone he," was the supreme British leader. The monarch was not alone on the "Olympus" but "throng'd by sages in the Dome, Like the fam'd senate of Imperial Rome."[25] In this imagined, heavenly Roman Senate, the king used "his sacred tongue" to deliver heroic, Roman-like speeches.

Maylem equated Britain and the Roman Empire not solely through its martial boldness or virtue but also by representing the king's advisers as the Roman Senate. Where else than in a classical empire could Jupiter command Roman legislatures? Maylem chose to depict Britain as the Roman Empire, not as its preceding republic. Once the contest between Britain and its American colonies started a mere few years after the publication of Maylem's poem, representations of Britain as the Roman Empire would become the norm. Those portrayals, however, would depict Britain as a corrupt, tyrannical Rome.

The victory on the Plains of Abraham and the capture of Quebec in 1759 triggered a jubilee in America, as the French menace subsided significantly. After that battle, a string of victories ensured the Anglo-American triumph, and Americans deemed the cooperation of British Redcoats and American soldiers to have been crucial in the successful conclusion of the war. Numerous published tracts glorified the epic extent of the victory. The re-publication in 1760 of *The Recruiting Officer*, a marching hymn originally published in Massachusetts in 1748 during the War of the Austrian Succession (named King George's War in the colonies), further entrenched correlations between republican Rome and Great Britain.[26] The last stanza of this jingoistic marching song reminded Americans, "For at Carthage there's Money store, Besides great Quantities of Ore, We'll have a Share as well as they, When over the Hills and far away, King George commands and we'll obey."[27] This poem blended with the discourse discussed earlier in which Britain and France competed for their Roman–Carthaginian identities throughout the eighteenth century. That this poem was picked for re-publication twelve years after it was originally published was no coincidence. It was indeed convenient that George II remained on the throne and that the Carthaginian French foe was as relevant as ever.

Two sermons given during 1760 in Boston, a city greatly relieved when the Carthaginian French danger to the north abated, illustrated a similar trend. The Reverend Jonathan Mayhew admonished his colonial brethren about the dangers that befell ancient Rome after it defeated Carthage. "When her citizens had no longer any foreign enemy to fear," Mayhew asserted, the Romans lost their moral cohesiveness and fell into "violent factions, contentions, and civil wars. They lost their liberty in the end; became wretched by means of their own prosperity and greatness; and so the Roman power was destroyed."[28] In case such similarities were not clear enough, Mayhew drove the point home: "Something not wholly un-like to this, may possibly befall us in time, the American Carthage being subdued."[29] The "American Carthage" stood for the vanquished French Canada, defeated by implication by a new Rome. Total victory heightened Mayhew's anxiety that peace would lead to moral decline depicted in Ro-man terms, "unless God should give us the wisdom to avoid those rocks and shelves."[30]

Thomas Foxcroft was sanguine in his sermon for "what is now so hap-pily accomplished," the complete conquest of Canada without which "we could hope for no lasting Quiet in these Parts."[31] Foxcroft added: "Long had it been the common Opinion (CARTHAGO *est delenda*) The American Carthage must be reduced, Canada must be conquer'd."[32] Here, even more explicitly than in Mayhew's sermon, Foxcroft depicted the victory over the French in terms of the Punic Wars, implying that "the American Carthage" had been reduced by a new Rome. Furthermore, by reiterating "Carthage must be utterly destroyed"—the phrase with which Cato the Elder ended every speech he gave in the Roman Senate to urge the Roman people to destroy Carthage—Foxcroft wove together seamlessly the histories of Rome and Carthage, Britain and France. Those histories intertwined as he applied Cato the Elder's famous maxim to French Canada, transforming Canada's defeat into an event of epic, classical dimensions. In this drama, Americans positioned themselves as Roman provincials acting under the auspices of a mighty empire.

Once the amazement over and celebration of the defeat of the the "American Carthage" faded, colonists began to look forward to the future of the British Empire. The perception of the British Empire as a new Rome could proceed virtually uninterrupted and, in effect, undisputed. *The Mili-tary Glory of Great-Britain* endowed British achievements with classical splendor and drew meaningful parallels between the vast Roman expan-sion during the last two centuries BC and the enormous territorial growth of British America. In fact, this ode defined British territorial gains by the fact that British regiments had surpassed the Roman legions by conquer-ing territory in "in those golden Climes, Where the first Sun beskirts the Eastern Clouds. And where the Roman Eagle never flew."[33] Astonishingly, the British Empire had exceeded its Roman predecessor in conquering the whole of North America. Obviously, however, British subjects still needed such comparisons and juxtapositions with Rome to derive their empire's meaning and historical significance.[34] Another lyric poem from the same year, Nathaniel Evans's *Ode on the Late Glorious Successes of His Majesty's Arms,* further articulated the comparisons of Britain and Rome. Evans, a Philadelphian bard, actually implied in the poem that Britain *was* a new Rome. The mode, tone, and language of the ode (itself a Horatian, classical genre) were thoroughly classicized: As in a classical epic, Evans called on the "sacred Muse" to "stamp her Honours on the Page of Time," a time destined to see Britannia's rule.[35] He went on to evoke "the harmonious sounding lyre" for "sweet Clio," the Roman goddess of history, to "pour the rich Tide of Melody along."[36] Classically narrating "the late glorious successes" of His Majesty's armies, Evans advised Britain how to rule its newly conquered territories: "Well doth Britannia take the noble ways / Which ancient Rome victoriously pursu'd, / At home her People's peerless Worth to raise, / While by her Arms abroad the Foe's subdu'd."[37] Evans was encouraging Britain to adopt expansionist, Roman-like imperial policies in which metropolitans and provincials enjoyed equal rights, as in Rome. As colonists, Evans and his American brethren would naturally qualify for equal rights. The poet then turned to recount the British victory by using the well-known *figura* of the Punic Wars: "Dauntless Hannibal withstood; Till Latian [British] Ardor" subdued "Punic [French] rage" and "drenched the field with Carthaginian [again, French] blood." Evans's work represents an elaboration of the Roman–Carthaginian British–French scheme to its fullest extent by an American voice, which left no doubt about his verdict in the decades-old debate of who was to qualify as the Romans' heir. In a piece he wrote in the following year, Evans compared the British king to one of the early and benevolent Roman kings before the foundation of the republic: "Rome's glorious Numa shall be seen in thee," he promised George III.[38] The poet thus expressed the ambivalence inherent in comparing Roman history, a monarchy-turned-republic-turned-empire, with the British monarchy, an ambivalence that did not seem to bother his peers and apparently occurred to him only fleetingly, if at all.[39]

A symbolic verse by George Cockings published in New Hampshire in 1762, entitled *War: An Heroic Poem,* again described military British leaders in terms of ancient warriors. Hence, Robert Clive, who in India "made Nabobs, [and thus] Nabobs could depose," had achieved "what conqu'ring Rome has," although Rome's conquests surely had not reached as far as the Indian subcontinent.[40] Cockings's militaristic poem described British victories over the French as those of Ajax, the Homeric Trojan hero who "turn'[d] and frown'd at Illium's tower; when Grecians fled, from conquering pow'rs." In another scene, Cockings said that one Captain Macdonald, "a Scotch gentleman," acted "like Scipio," who "took his father on his shoulders, when in danger and carried him thro' the enemy's battle." Similarly, "'Midst volleys, flame, & deaths, & Gallie fire," Macdonald lifted "his fallen friend" and "bore him from the field of battle dead." In one of the poem's climaxes, Cockings juxtaposed General Wolfe's heroic death in battle with the epic death of Sparta's King Leonidas in Thermopylae. Like "the gallant king of Lacadeamon . . . faint with loss of blood, at pain, his body throng'd with wounds . . . he [Wolfe] fell, a notable instance of that magnanimity, with which the spirit of freedom animates a patriot's soul." If Wolfe's death equaled the Spartan king's, it surpassed that of Cato the Younger, who committed suicide in besieged Utica when the Roman Republic was doomed: "Cato, self wounded dy'd and scorn'd to yield: / But, Wolfe was slain, amid the glorious field." Wolfe's destruction, Cockings concluded, "may be equall'd! never be outdone! . . . Like great Leonidas, and Titus dy'd!" "Titus," Cockings explained in a footnote, "was a young Roman warrior . . . with that magnanimity, and spirit of freedom, and valour, for which the ancient Romans were so much famed . . . [who died] not until they had formed an heap of carnage round them."[41] Wolfe's Roman-like death took part in Cockings's tapestry of comparisons between British and Roman soldiers. The significance of such tropes were not their literary and rhetoric value but, rather, their articulation of a deep correlation between the ancient and modern empires, a correspondence that would shortly come back to haunt British imperialists.

The Conquest of Canada, a "Historical Tragedy" written by Cockings after the war was over, did not contain many classical references, but its introduction, written by the author and addressed "To the Public," described Britain once more as a new, conquering Rome.[42] The late war, "gloriously successful to great Britain, beyond all parallel," was so remarkable, "and so much worth, and bravery, was there displayed" that Cockings, "as a historian," asserted that it was "amply worthy of being registered in the annals of fame, as rival actions of those patriotic deeds, of the so much admired ancient Greeks and Romans!"[43] Complying with the imperial sensibilities we have been examining, Cockings portrayed British history as equal in glory and significance to the annals of ancient empires.[44] Oxenbridge

Thatcher took a similar stance in the same year, in *The Sentiments of a British American.* "Great Britain at this day,"Thatcher asserted, "is arrived to a height of glory and wealth which no European nations hath ever reached since the decline of the Roman Empire."[45] These Americans left no doubt regarding the intellectual and historical prisms through which they believed British American achievements ought to be interpreted. Linking the British Empire to Rome provided these colonists with historical meaning and significance. To Americans who viewed themselves as Britons occupying peripheral imperial outposts, such imaginative liaisons were crucial for evaluating their place in history as participants, albeit marginal ones, in the imperial framework.

We have seen how Americans repeatedly understood and presented the British Empire, its leaders and its victories, during the short Pax Britannica as equaling and even as surpassing Rome at its height. Like their contemporary oppositional Whigs in England, these writers, glorifying the British imperial achievement, looked back to Rome for inspiration and precedent. However, if Whig language was preoccupied with liberty and encroachments on it, the imperial discourse that we have been tracing here, which Herbert Butterfield has called "the real Tory alternative" to the Whig interpretation of history, was based on colonization and overseas expansion.[46] This imperial discourse did not have much time to develop uninterrupted in North America, however. Soon after the Treaty of Paris of 1763 had ended the Seven Years' War, British policymakers felt the need to deal with the fiscal crisis and the predicament governing North America, which became more pronounced after the conclusion of the war. As we shall soon see, Americans' angry reactions to the Proclamation of 1763, the Sugar Act of 1764, and especially the Stamp Act of 1765 led them to reformulate radically their understanding of Britain as Rome. Once an idiom of Tory veneration, antiquity rapidly became a venue for expressions of anger and frustration, aligning with the classical vernacular of radical Whiggism. As this language escalated, it expressed and articulated the centrifugal forces that would eventually tear apart the first British Empire.

A close examination of the short years of the Pax Britannica may cast doubt on certain hypotheses forwarded by the "republican synthesis" school.[47]

Bernard Bailyn, a leader of that historiographical paradigm, argued for a continuing American suspicion of British civic morality throughout the eighteenth century. Bailyn claimed that the defiant voices of the Whig opposition, marginal in British politics, became dominant in colonial debates leading up to independence.[48] As evidence, he pointed to colonists who described British lavishness and decadence, occasionally depicting Britain in terms of a corrupt Rome. As an example, Bailyn quoted young John Dickinson, who summed up his impression of England in 1754 in a letter from London, where he was studying law: "I think the character of Rome will suit this nation: 'easy to be bought, if there was but a purchaser,'" referring to Sallust's depiction of Rome in the years of the decline of the republic.[49] Descriptions such as Dickinson's, conveying England as a corrupt Rome, have apparently persuaded many scholars that, by the eve of the revolution, the inhabitants of the colonies were intellectually conditioned for rebellion and eventual separation from a corrupt England. However, an examination of the texts reviewed earlier shows clearly that Americans residing in the colonies (as opposed to Dickinson writing from London) repeatedly referred to the might and glory of the British Empire—not to its corruption—in Roman terms. The classical idiom has thus employed Rome for Tory expansionist ends, not for corruption-obsessed radical Whig ends. In fact, it is hard to find examples of Americans describing British decadence in terms of a corrupt Rome during the 1750s and early 1760s while residing in the colonies.[50] Examining how Americans employed images of Rome in relation to Britain reveals an abrupt discontinuity in the use of the classical language before and after the Stamp Act. Such language certainly does not support the continuity of the commonwealth idiom that Bailyn suggested. This transformation from prominently Tory to radical Whig classical representations of Britain implies that the time may have come to revisit other assumptions made by the republican synthesizers.

Once the Pax Britannica disintegrated, Tory conceptualizations of Britain as a glorious and conquering Rome were transformed, giving way to interpretations aligned with the radical Whig view of Britain as a malevolent Rome of the emperors. One realizes then that the radicalizing influence of oppositional Whig thought should not be given full credit for harnessing antiquity to the patriot cause. As we have seen, imperial Tory imagination might have played an important role in this transformation.

Once Britain donned the garb of a Roman victor, it was only too easy for Americans a decade later to imagine the metropolis as wearing the blood-stained toga of a tyrant.

In the years that elapsed between the Stamp Act and the beginning of the War of Independence, the relationship between the metropole and the North American colonies deteriorated rapidly. With each new round of taxation, opposition, violence, and repeal, the imperial connection, described repeatedly by both sides in filial terms, fractured and weakened.[51] In the rest of this chapter, I will consider a certain strand of the American Whig discourse, which will shed new light on the way Americans understood their deteriorating relations with Britain after the Stamp Act. By concentrating on the creative uses made of the image of the Roman Empire to explain the British Empire after 1765, I intend to demonstrate how Americans attempted to historicize their desertion by a once benevolent "mother" country and how such perceptions substantiated claims to political as well as historical independence. The imaginative use of a classical rhetoric that, as we shall see, time and again depicted Britain as a tyrannical Rome was a significant factor in expressing and elaborating the colonists' increasing animosity toward Britain and hence their own nascent patriotism.

The depictions of Britain as a tyrannical Rome were part of a civic-humanistic discourse in which corruption, virtue, luxury, and self-sacrifice framed an intellectual paradigm that understood the present in terms of antiquity.[52] However, by examining the classical discourse on its own terms as an autonomous language, not as a subsidiary dialect of civic humanism, we may gain new perspectives on American historical consciousness and its debt and relation to classical antiquity. Because of the relative lack of focused attention paid to the classical idiom in scholarship, historians have failed to notice the role Rome played in the imperial disintegration. By paying as much attention to form as to content, and to imagery and metaphor as well as to ideology, I intend to demonstrate how revolutionary Americans used the classics creatively to express and understand their separation from Britain and the dissolution of imperial ties.

The discourse this book traces brings to the fore an important facet of revolutionary logic: The colonists' historical language suggest that the way they represented and made sense of the present was deeply indebted to their classical-historical imagination. Americans perceived Britain as a corrupt Rome and its leaders and colonial representatives as depraved Romans of the time of the Caesars. The cognitive aspects of the republican-civic humanistic language cannot be fully understood without recognizing the major role played by the historico-imaginative components of that discourse. The form in which the republican message was delivered—namely, the classical *topoi*— was a crucial component of American understanding and adaptation of the civic-humanistic language.

The shifting representations of Britain as an imperial Rome took place on two levels. On a national level, colonials depicted Britain as a corrupt, tyrannical Rome; on an ad hominem level, they portrayed colonial magistrates and English officers as malevolent, debauched Romans. Equations and juxtapositions of Britain as a corrupt Rome were the first to emerge, before the stakes were raised and the trans-Atlantic rift became apparently unbridgeable. At first, then, comparisons on the national level tended to be general and impersonal. Such attacks on Britain's corporate body could indeed wound the pride of Englishmen and Loyalists, but were usually less damaging and generally less effective than ad hominem diatribes. When Americans extended their imagery into the realm of the personal, comparing Loyalists and crown magistrates, native and Britons, to the Julio-Claudian emperors from Caesar to Nero, they crossed a Rubicon. Those Caesars who epitomized the perverse and tyrannical image of imperial Rome became models in service of the patriot imagination in a gradual and escalating process. The increasing anger and desperation on behalf of colonial resistance was the motivating factor behind the outraged depictions of British magistrates as Roman emperors. After all, describing royal colonial agents, ministers, and finally the monarch himself as the most despised rulers in Western collective memory required deep rage that gradually increased over time. As the stakes became higher, then, writers interpreted occurrences and developments within a radicalized cognitive framework. Thus, if at the beginning of the trans-Atlantic contest the references to Britain as a tyrannical Roman Empire were withheld and abstract, as the years went by the discourse became not only more aggressive but suggestively ad hominem. As this chapter demonstrates, this discourse ultimately culminated in the desecration of the monarch's persona in the "Nerofication" of George III.[53]

Even before an overt quarrel between Britain and the colonies erupted in 1765, colonists began to rankle at the first signs of what they would soon interpret as a dramatic change in imperial policy or, worse, as a conspiracy to rob them of their liberties. They saw the renewal of the Writs of Assistance, the Proclamation of 1763, and the Sugar Act of 1764, among other measures, as unprecedented and as violations of the British constitution as interpreted from the western shores of the Atlantic. The novel fashion in which James Otis employed the imagery of antiquity reflects the initial discomfort American colonists felt during the years between the end of the war and the Stamp Act. *The Rights of the British Colonies Asserted and Proved*, a passionate rebuttal of Parliament's right to tax the colonies that was published after the passage of the Sugar Act and the spread of rumors about impending revenue legislation, signaled a new mode of employing antiquity. Comparing the Roman and British constitutions, the author of the pamphlet, the lawyer James Otis, asserted that Britain had the greatest opportunity for "honest wealth and grandeur" since the days of Julius Caesar.[54] His message, however, was rather pessimistic. Addressing the question of standing armies in North America, he asked, "Are all ambitious generals dead? Will no more rise hereafter? . . . [T]he experience of past times will show that an army of 20 or 30 thousand veterans half [of them] 3000 miles from Rome, were apt to proclaim Caesars."[55] Not withstanding that Britain was still a potentially prosperous Rome, one can already sense the ambivalence that Americans were feeling toward their Roman "mother." By linking standing armies, alluding to the Redcoats stationed in North America, to the rise of the Caesars in Rome, Otis prefigured the discourse of the next twenty years. Still, he had to wait until Parliament passed a genuine revenue act such as the Stamp Act for many others to follow his lead not only in resisting Parliament's authority to tax, but also in embracing a depiction of Britain as a potentially tyrannical Roman Empire.

The Stamp Act was a watershed in the way Americans imagined their mother country. After that act passed, references to Britain as a glorious Rome became the mainstay of Englishmen and loyalists. As mobs burned effigies and tore down houses belonging to stamp collectors, it soon became evident that the loudest voices in the colonies were no longer willing to portray the mother country as a magnanimous Rome. Soon those voices began to make use of a less glorious stage in Roman history to describe the actions and historical significance of their mother country.[56] One of the earliest examples of the conflation of British and Roman imperial histories is found in Patrick Henry's renowned "treason speech," delivered in the Virginia House of Burgesses. Reacting to the Stamp Act, Henry introduced a set of radical resolutions denouncing the British Parliament's usurpation of powers vested in the colonial legislature, which alone, according to Henry, had the power to tax. He praised his resolves in a heated speech and ended by warning: "Caesar had his Brutus—Charles the First his Cromwell—and George III—may he profit from their example." According to another account, Henry supposedly cried, "Tarquin and Caesar had each his Brutus, Charles the First his Cromwell, and George the Third—"; upon which cries of "Treason" prevented him from continuing. In this speech, Henry evoked notorious autocratic rulers whose own people murdered and dethroned them. Roman citizens belonging to the Brutus *gen* dethroned both Tarquin, the last king of pre-republican Rome, and Julius Caesar, the republic's destroyer. But while they drove Tarquin out, a group of senators in the Forum led by Marcus Junius Brutus stabbed Caesar to death. Charles I was, of course, the last monarch to suffer regicide in recent British memory. This early and inflamed use of the Roman analogy, however, seems to be the exception that proves the rule within the relatively mild Roman discourse of the mid-1760s.[57] The Rome-inspired depictions of Britain and its leadership during the Stamp Act crisis and throughout the 1760s were usually mild, avoiding personal attacks. The colonists had not yet crossed the Rubicon.

Less than two months after Parliament passed the Stamp Act in Westminster, the *Providence Gazette* published "A Letter from a Plain Yeoman" in which "Yeoman" asserted: "Pharaoh, Caligula, and but a few more, have been instances of such abusers of power."[58] The writer hurried to add, though, that he did "not mention those monsters with any design of making an odious parallel between them and any person now in authority."[59] Whether "Yeoman" wished to make odious parallels or not, his analogies were ominous. References to the raving, cruel, and perverse Caligula (AD 12–41), one of the most notorious Caesars of the Julio-Claudian dynasty, and Pharaoh, the enslaver of the Hebrews during their Egyptian captivity, were potentially explosive. If the mention of Caligula in 1765 still required a disclaimer, which "Yeoman" was quick to provide, that infamous Caesar would appear often in coming years in attacks on British magistrates without any such disclaimers.

Stephen Hopkins, the governor of Rhode Island, claimed in a pamphlet published that same year that sending Americans to the courts of the vice-admiralty to be tried without peers "must call to everyone's remembrance Tacitus's account of the miserable condition of the Romans, in the reign of Tiberius their emperor, who let loose and encouraged the informers of that age."[60] Pointing out the resemblance between the situation of the Romans under one of the cruelest emperors, remembered for his reign of terror and draconic legislation in Rome, and the American colonists under Grenville's administration, Hopkins conveyed deep distress at the colonists' condition and suggested the despotism inherent in an apparent subversion of the British constitution. Nevertheless, his unflattering reference to Tiberius's Rome was quite detached and abstract. Hopkins deliberately chose his words, and his juxtaposition, although conveying similarities between the situation of British colonists and Roman citizens, was still cautious in linking Britain and imperial Rome.

In the ensuing debate over the Stamp Act, American Tories attempted to justify the British position by claiming that "the Roman *coloniae* did not enjoy all the rights of Roman citizens; on the contrary, they only used the Roman laws and religion, and served in the legions, but had not the right of suffrage or of bearing honours. In these respects, our English colonies exactly resemble them".[61] James Otis replied to this argument soon after in *A Vindication of the British Colonies Asserted and Proved*, in which he denied the validity of comparing the American situation to the severe Roman model and endorsed instead a comparison to the more humane Greek example.[62] Hence, while Loyalists compared the British colonial project to Rome's, Whigs answered by pointing out the severity and inappropriateness of the Roman *exemplum*.[63] In the years to come, Whigs would repeatedly denounce Britain for reviving and reenacting the Roman Empire's ways.

From the early stages of the contest, colonial Whigs deemed colonial officials, especially governors, the main culprits for what they saw as a dangerous metropolitan policy. Believing such people to have been offenders against the American interest, they often compared those magistrates to corrupt Roman provincial governors. However, perhaps because the public sphere was not yet ready for full-blown representations of Britain as a tyrannical Rome during the Stamp Act crisis, American publishers had recourse to reprinting earlier works that dwelled on similar themes. Such was Jeremiah Dummer's *A Defense of the New-England Charters*, some fifty years old by 1765. That tract, while comparing British to Roman governors, described corruption and luxury as emasculating and degrading civic virtue to such a degree that even virtuous Romans could not stand up to "their proconsuls, consuls or governors [who] were very guilty . . . their corruption was so notorious."[64] Contemporaries would soon blame the whole spectrum of British magistracy in indulging in Roman-like corruption in a language steadily becoming more inflamed.

Nevertheless, during this early imperial crisis, the majority of the colonists still maintained a courteous and deferential position toward their sovereign, however contemptuous they may have been toward colonial agents, Parliament, and ministers. The Connecticut Resolves demonstrated how, while denouncing the Stamp Act, Americans could still "most expressly declare, recognize and acknowledge his majesty king George the third, to be lawful and rightful king of Great Britain, and all other the Dominions and Countries thereto belonging, and that it is the indispensable duty of the people of this colony . . . always to bear faithful and true allegiance to his majesty."[65] Most other colonies used a similarly reverential and respectful language toward the monarch. However, in just a few years, repeated attacks coming from the patriot camp would severely damage and eventually dissolve this deference, together with British authority. The intellectual process of transforming Britain's image from the embodiment of Roman glory and virtue to the incarnation of its worst vices and most infamous rulers not only expressed the crumbling of the practical and psychological authority of Great Britain and its monarch, but has also induced the breakdown of metropolitan authority. By the end of that process, that "rightful king of Great Britain" would be portrayed as the vilest of Caesars: as Nero.

The repeal of the Stamp Act early in 1766 defused tensions and removed momentarily the immediate reason for further agitation and comparisons between Rome and the mother country. However, in a letter to the Committee of London Merchants, George Mason pointed out that George

Grenville, who had planned and attempted to execute the Stamp Act, would lead Britain to disaster and used the idiom of antiquity to drive his point home. Grenville, Mason argued, "dared to act the part that Pericles did, when he engaged his country in the Peloponnesian War which ... ended in the ruin of all of Greece, and fitted it to the Macedonian yoke."[66] Comparing a British minister to the revered, if flawed, Athenian was nonetheless qualitatively different from comparing one to a Roman Caesar. Although Pericles could be deemed wrong-headed in his statesmanship, his personal virtues were beyond reproach. By comparing Grenville to Pericles, Mason was careful not to use insulting imagery, even if his words were harsh. When "An Ode Occasioned by the Repeal of the Stamp Act" appeared in the *Virginia Gazette* and called for Grenville's name to be "Mentioned with Tyrants in historic page, Descend with Infamy thro' every Age, Our Nature's Scorn and Shame," the author instructively mentioned no specific tyrant with relation to Grenville's person.[67] After the repeal of the Stamp Act, this cautious posture was widespread. When, for a brief moment, the rift between the colonies and Britain seemed to have been healed, it was no longer necessary to cast Britain's behavior in an unfavorable Roman light.

The Stamp Act, however, was but the first in a series of contests that ended in the dissolution of the North American British Empire. As such, it demonstrated an early manifestation of an aggressive discourse that eventually depicted Britain and its leaders in Caesarian terms. Nevertheless, if by the end of the Stamp Act crisis the colonists had laid down the line where they believed that Parliament should stop interfering with their legislative business, that line, as Edmund Morgan points out, was "far short of independence."[68] Their continued, if attenuated, allegiance to the king meant that they could not yet use the harsh language that they would in the following years. Consequently, even when comparisons between Britain and imperial Rome were evoked during 1765–66, they still portrayed the mother country in terms of a glorious, if flawed, Rome.

With each new crisis, the atmosphere of anger and distrust toward Britain grew stronger. However, even as the quarrel lengthened and became more and more bitter and the images of Britain became harsher, as long as the colonists saw the situation as redeemable, the process of Nerofication would not begin in earnest. A decade passed before a critical mass of the colonists became convinced that they were suffering under a government ruled by a latter-day Roman tyranny—or, in their words, by "the worst passions of the human heart and the most subtle projects of the human mind."[69] When that judgmental moment occurred, it was accompanied by an epistemological transformation that had far-reaching consequences to the revolutionary psyche. Subsequently, it greatly influenced the classical language of American patriots. As far as we are concerned with depictions of Britain as Rome, this moment (which will reveal itself in following chapters as Catonian), which occurred during the tumultuous years 1774 and 1775, witnessed the remarkable intensification of the depictions of Britain as Rome and especially of individual Britons as Romans. I shall first describe therefore the earlier Romanification of the British Empire in the years following the Stamp Act crisis and then turn to the later and more severe process of Nerofication of its leading men, which began in the mid-1770s.

Arthur Lee used the vocabulary of antiquity extensively in a series of influential essays entitled *The Monitor's Letters* that appeared throughout 1768 in the *Virginia Gazette* in response to the introduction of the Townshend Acts (1767). Lee's rhetoric was still similar in many ways to the language circulating during the Stamp Act crisis two years earlier. While regarding the monarch as "our most Gracious Sovereign,"[70] Lee identified an evil nexus based in Parliament: "The most tremendous tyranny that ever existed would be the House of Commons in England if it were independent of the people."[71] When Lee approximated the extent of potential parliamentary tyranny, he did so vis-à-vis the notoriety of the despotic assemblies of Greece and Rome; an independent Parliament, Lee asserted, would exceed the tyranny both of the Roman *decemviri,* the commission of ten men in early Rome that collapsed into violent and corrupt rule, and that of the Athenian Thirty, the board of the thirty despots that ruled Athens after its capitulation in the Peloponnesian War in the close of the fifth century BC. Instructively, Lee lamented America's current situation, which he understood to be similar to that of "the wretched Romans, in the times of their slavery, when grievously taxed by their emperors."[72] Lee's polemic, as well as that of the majority of writers during the late 1760s, placed America in the perspective of historical tyranny but was reminiscent of the earlier and mild language used during the Stamp Act. Such language still lacked the hyperbole and personal focus that characterized the classical discourse of years to come.

Hence, even the second round of taxation, known as the Townshend Acts, and their repeal in 1769 did not bring about substantive change in classical representation. However, the revival of the dispute after the Period of Quiet, which lasted from 1770 to 1773, saw a dramatic escalation in the articulation and extremity of the depictions of Britain as a corrupt and tyrannical Rome. The epistemological transformation described earlier in this chapter that took place in the mid-1770s performed a significant role in the intensified comparisons between Britain and Rome. In a letter to James Iredell dated April 26, 1774, William Hooper elaborated to its fullest extent the comparison between Britain and imperial Rome. Written just as the Intolerable Acts were passed, Hooper, a North Carolinian, enumerated the causes of decay that the two empires shared: "The extent of the British dominion [like the Roman] is become too unwieldy for her to sustain. Commerce hath generated a profusion of wealth, and luxury and corruption. . . . Venality is at the standard it was when Jugurtha left Rome. . . . [W]hat strikes them [the British] as the glow of health, is but the flushing of fever. . . . Rome in its greatest luster was upon the verge of dissolution."[73] Significantly, as he described the descent from greatness to corruption in standard civic-humanistic form, Hooper alternated the references between the two empires to an extent that at times makes it hard to determine the empire to which he was alluding. Rome, he continued, "from being the nursery of heroes, became the residence of musicians, pimps, panders, and calamities. . . . The Empire . . . fell a sacrifice to a herd of savage miscreants, and the most polished state in the world sunk at once into absolute barbarism. She had been some time ripe for this fate. Some one of enterprise was wanting to make the attempt."[74] Hooper's elaboration, much longer than the portion I have reproduced here, was not composed for antiquarians' sake or to show off the author's classical language. Hooper foresaw and made sense of the fate of England through Roman history, a fact revealed in his remarkable conclusion: "Reverse the catastrophe, and might not Great Britain be the original from which this picture [of Roman decline] is taken?"[75] Hooper's image provides a key with which to unlock the operation of the American classical imagination and the complex role it played in shaping the relationship between American and classical history, "the original" and "the picture." We now see how approximately a decade after the conflict between Britain and its colonies erupted, Americans began expressing notions that conflated their experiences with those of the ancients in ways that surpassed mere analogy and metaphor. In this instance, Hooper articulated a hermeneutics of history that related classical and American histories through the relationship of a classical antetype and an American type, a Roman promise and American fulfillment. I will show in a later chapter how this typological relationship was one of several available ways in which patriot Americans related themselves to classical antiquity.

Similarly, Josiah Quincy of Massachusetts elaborated a vivid image of Britain as a despotic Rome in his *Observations on the Act of Parliament Commonly Called the Boston Port-Bill,* a pamphlet full of classical allusions. The principal villain in Quincy's essay was Julius Caesar, whose benign smile "deceived the Roman Common-wealth, till the increase of his power bid defiance to opposition. . . . [T]he complaisant courtier made his way into the hearts of his countrymen. They would not believe . . . that the smiling Caesar would filch away their liberties, that a native born—born and bred a Roman—would enslave his country."[76] Quincy was reproaching Loyalist native-born Americans who, in his view, were condemning their brethren to servility, just as Caesar had done to his fellow Romans. The real danger that Caesar posed, however, was that in his actions he "prepared the way for a succeeding Nero to spoil and slaughter" Rome.[77] If the danger at that moment seemed containable, it was only because the real peril was lurking unseen and would emerge when Americans put their guard down. As proof, Quincy demonstrated how Caesar left the Roman institutions only in name, devoid of any meaning, as invested in himself all government powers; he "soon became Senate, magistracy and laws."[78] The imminence of a similar process occurring in America was clear. "Is not Britain to America, what Caesar was to Rome?" Quincy asked.[79] What Caesar has done to Rome, according to Quincy, illuminated the British–American relationship. Quincy was constructing a meaningful correspondence between American and Roman history that used the classics as a key to understanding the present. Similarly, Samuel Chase, the Maryland delegate to the Continental Congress, described the Westminster Parliament as the dissolute Roman Senate: "The Roman Senate in the reigns of Claudius Caesar, Domitian or Nero, were not more servilely wicked, than the present House of Commons."[80] Such hermeneutics represented a unique worldview and theory of history that will be explored throughout this study. For the time being, we should note how by 1775 the example of Rome, so recently and often cited for its glory, had been transformed into a paradigm of debauchery. To use Hooper's terminology, the British "picture" was intelligible through the corrupt Roman "original."

Remarkably, after celebrating the removal of the danger of the "French Carthage" after the French and Indian War had been won, Bostonians, after the Coercive Acts were enforced, depicted their city as if it were a Carthage damaged by a cruel British Rome. Adhering to a formerly unconventional view that singled out Carthage as a trading republic and lamented its conquest by a warlike Rome, the *Boston Gazette* admonished: "The town of Boston has been resembled to Carthage, and threatened with the same fate by a member of [the British] parliament: The Execution of the Sentence is already begun."[81] The consequences of the Punic Wars, lengthily described in the *Gazette,* were the "miserable Death of several hundred thousand of people, and of their city [Carthage]!" In short, the *Gazette* concluded, nothing would satisfy the British Rome "but destroying" the Carthaginian Boston. The committee of correspondence of the town of Westerly, Rhode Island, pointed out, too—again in response to the Coercive Acts—how "Rome designing to destroy the city of Carthage, barbarously required the Carthaginians that they should forsake their city." However, "the cruel and unnatural treatment which the town of Boston has received from Great-Britain, will admit of no kind of palliation."[82] Britain, praised in the early 1760s for playing the role of a victorious Rome in the Punic Wars, was reprimanded a decade later by means of the same historical metaphor.

After hostilities commenced, patriots continued to search for similarities in the historical patterns working in both the Roman and the British empires. A South Carolinian addressing General John Burgoyne had pointed out that "the Romans were enslaved by men, who under the specious pretext of names and offices, which had been the safeguard of the liberties of the people, introduced unlimited power." Similarly, the British Empire, which "extended thousands of leagues, and contained millions of subjects," still insisted "on the unlimited supremacy of the representatives of one part over every other part," subverting the constitution, "which is the only safeguard of liberty." "Arbitrary power," it was clear, has "been introduced under the sanction of respectable words" both in Rome and in Britain.[83]

Judge William Henry Drayton of South Carolina believed that "the ruins of *Charlestown, Falmouth,* and *Norfolk,*" American towns that were ravaged by British forces early in the war, paralleled "the ruins of *Carthage, Corinth,* and *Numantium,*" ravaged by the Roman legions.[84] Drayton made further use of the Britain-as-Rome idiom in *A Charge on the Rise of the American Empire,* published in the year of American independence. The tract contains another detailed description of Britain as a fallen Rome, in which Britain's trajectory from glorious empire to complete tyranny is traced along the lines discussed earlier. Addressing his South Carolinian compatriots, Drayton recalled: "Three and thirty years numbered the illustrious Days of the Roman Greatness—Eight Years measure the Duration of the British Grandeur."[85] Indeed, British greatness was achieved in "the Year 1758, when they victoriously pursued their enemy into every quarter of the Globe." Their days of glory were numbered, however, and their cause of decline different than that of the Romans. While Rome had been corrupted by the introduction of "Asiatic Luxury," Britain's decline was due to the "injustice displayed by the Stamp Act."[86] From Drayton's *Charge* one can clearly infer that the intellectual transformation traced in this chapter is not a latter-day construction but one that was obvious to contemporaries: Britain had indeed been a glorious Rome during the years 1758–65, as Drayton pointed out. Unfortunately, by taxing America for revenue, it had been transformed into a despotic, corrupt Rome.[87]

John Leacock's *The Fall of British Tyranny* represents a curious juncture in the road to the Romanification of Britain. In the third act of this tragicomedy, "Lord Boston," General Thomas Gage, the governor of Massachusetts since 1774, states: "I should have been able to have subdued the rebels, and gain'd immortal laurels to myself—have returned to Old England like a Roman Consul."[88] If "Lord Boston" was preoccupied with being perceived as a Roman, "Elbow Room," a character representing General William Howe, commander of the British military in America, disillusioned him: "You must not look for laurels (unless wild ones) nor expect triumphs (unless sham ones)."[89] With this mocking depiction of British generals imagining themselves as victorious Roman officers subduing the colonies, the transformation of Britain from a benevolent Roman-like empire into a corrupt and paralyzed giant, trying unsuccessfully to defeat America, was complete. Leacock's drama suggests that by 1776, Americans were scorning Britons for trying to attain the standards they were believed to embody a mere decade before. In 1778, George Mason asserted that Americans "have been forced into it [revolution], as the only means of self preservation, to guard our country and posterity from the greatest of all evils, such another infernal government (if it deserves the name of government) as the provinces groaned under, in the latter ages of the Roman commonwealth."[90] American patriots had completed the intellectual transformation of Britain as a Rome, from a magnanimous mother country in the early 1760s to a tyrannical empire in the late 1770s.

By the mid-1770s, the depth and complexity of the presumed correspondence between the corrupt Roman Empire and Great Britain was remarkable. Additional, and potentially even more meaningful, expressions of this discourse were the ad hominem comparisons between British officers and magistrates and Roman emperors that emerged during the epistemological transformation of 1774–76. The significance of such comparisons stemmed from the fact that the analogizing between individuals—between specified Britons and Romans—demanded an even deeper merging of British and Roman narratives. As the relationship between the colonies and Britain deteriorated, colonials increasingly demonized the British and consequently imagined and portrayed them as Roman villains. Such attacks escalated both in ferocity and in the rank of targets chosen for defilation.

During December 1766, a mere month after he denounced the royal administration in Boston for inducing treachery "as was never encouraged under any Administration but such as those [of] Nero or Caligula,"[91] Samuel Adams invoked the cruelest of Caesars once again. "The Stamp Act was like the sword that Nero wished for, to have decollated the Roman people at a stroke," Adams wrote in a letter to the South Carolinian Christopher Gadsden.[92] This comparison was communicated in a private letter, and its reference was to an impersonal piece of parliamentary legislation. However, the fact that the Caesarian imagery prevailed in the master agitator's rhetoric *after* the Stamp Act's repeal was foretelling. Adams was referring to Caligula Gaius Caesar, the paranoid, brutal, and presumably mad emperor of the years AD 37–41 and to the murderous, incest-ridden Nero Claudius Caesar, last emperor of the Julio-Claudian dynasty, who reigned during AD 54–68. The two villains conveyed to the patriot sensibility irredeemable debauchery; those Caesars were among the "few men . . .

unalterably excluded from every degree of fame."[93] Early in 1767, John Adams, following the example of his older cousin, remarked, "Nero shall wish the People had but one Neck that he might strike off at one blow, Caligula shall swear to tear up all remaining Virtue among the People."[94] Adams was referring to his belief in the existence of a general conspiracy against liberty in the colonies when he invoked the notorious Caesars, and probably he had in mind Massachusetts's governing elite in general and, specifically, Governor Francis Bernard. Although still hesitant to establish a direct link between Roman Caesars and representatives of the crown, Adams's choice of words was foretelling.

In the following year, John Dickinson published his renowned *Letters from a Farmer in Pennsylvania*. In his second letter, Dickinson warned against civil complacency, which created the situation in which "the Caesars ruined the Roman liberty, under the titles of tribunical and dictatorial authorities." In his mild manner, Dickinson compared British rule to Roman Caesarism, contrasting the harmful historical patterns at work in both polities. He went on to indicate in his next letter that "this mode of taxation [such as practiced by the British] therefore is the mode suited to arbitrary and oppressive governments," and adding that "this policy did not escape the cruel and rapacious NERO."[95] In 1768, it still had been statutes of taxation, not personalities, that colonials were juxtaposing with the policies of Nero Caesar. Accordingly, Arthur Lee, like Dickinson, set side by side what he understood as the slavish condition of the British people and American liberty in his second *Monitor* letter. To dramatize the stakes that he understood as at hand, he described the pitiful Roman people, who "were already wicked . . . [and] were soon to be weak and miserable; they were soon to groan under the most execrable monsters that ever blackened human nature: *Tiberius, Nero, Caligula, Commodus,* and *Domitian*," all notorious Roman emperors.[96] Despite the fact that he evoked this formidable succession of tyrants, Lee left his readers to guess at the modern-day incarnations of the historical villains: Was he referring to a colonial magistrate, a crown adviser, or, perhaps, a minister? Lee, however, went on to pose a rhetorical question: "Shall we not then, my countrymen, combine to oppose this fiend, whenever he shall invade us? Shall we not use every caution, work every nerve, to repeal his open, or elude his concealed attacks?" Roman tyranny was assaulting America, and Lee admonished his brethren for their complacence and encouraged them to confront the impending danger.

The rhetorical groundwork laid in the late 1760s came to fruition during the 1770s as comparisons to the Caesars became increasingly overt. The early 1770s saw an escalation in the depiction of crown magistrates as Roman emperors simultaneous with the construction of the image of Britain as a tyrannical Rome. Even during the Period of Quiet, Samuel Adams employed Roman emperors to vilify the foes of the patriot cause. Now he compared Julius Caesar and Thomas Hutchinson, Massachusetts Bay's governor. Adams warned that Hutchinson's ambition and lust for power might very well transform him into the Caesar of Massachusetts. "Had not Caesar seen that Rome was ready to stoop," Adams reminded the readers of the *Boston Gazette*, "he would not have dared to make himself the Master of that once brave people. . . . [He] led them gently into slavery."[97] "What difference is there between the present state of this province, which in course will be the deplorable state of all America, and that of Rome?" This comparison, however, "would not in all parts hold good," Adams admitted sarcastically. "The Tyrant of Rome, to do him justice, had learning, courage, and great abilities," he wrote, mocking Hutchinson.[98] Adams thus consciously, and polemically, established a direct link between a Roman Caesar and a royal governor.

During 1773, the figure of Nero seems to have emerged as a leading *figura*, captivating Americans' fears, abhorrence, and growing hatred of Britain. Nero epitomized the despised imperial Rome and served as a metonym for the worst type of tyranny, the extreme opposite of everything for which the republican worldview stood. His notoriety was passed down through the ages mainly by Tacitus, who attributed to him cruel rapacity and sadistic debauchery, and by Suetonius, who in a biographical sketch portrayed him as the quintessence of corruption: vain, wanton, greedy, lecherous, brutal, and degraded.[99] Such was the government that a writer using the pseudonym "British Bostonian" envisioned when he described the administration of the American colonies. There has not been "such tyranny since the days of Nero" he cried.[100] Mercy Otis Warren's play *The Adulateur*, a classicized allegory discussed at length in chapter 4, repeatedly evoked Nero, as well as other Caesars. Throughout the play, which takes place in the imaginary Upper Servia—an obvious metaphor for Massachusetts—Warren compares the main villain, Rapatio, representing Thomas Hutchinson, to a Roman tyrant. Early in act four, after describing "Servia" as a corrupt state in which each post is filled with

Rapatio's creatures, Rapatio–Hutchinson promises to "show my pow'r, and trample on my country."[101] Rapatio's crony Gripall assures his master, in what he considers a compliment, "'Twas nobly spoke, there breath'd the soul of Caesar." Soon after, Rapatio imagines the sufferings he will bestow on the people of Servia, a thought that gives him "throbs of joy" as he exclaims: "Nero, I tow'r above thee." During the fifth act, Rapatio envisions once again the miseries of the people he governs and promises to break their resistance and to "execute what Nero durst not." By the end of the play, Servia's governor dreams of becoming "like Nero, at one dread blow to massacre his millions."[102] Seven years after John Adams linked the Stamp Act to the worst of Caesars, American patriots were comparing their crown-appointed governor to that historical villain. This idiom, however, was not confined to New Englanders. Remarkably, Southerners, too, portrayed the Massachusetts governor as the last link in a chain of "Catalines, Caligulas and Neros."[103] Mercy Warren again evoked Nero in 1775 in her satiric play *The Group,* this time comparing a British commander to the hated emperor. In that short play, the character Brigadier Hateall, a pugilistic military leader, claims, "I Nero like, the capital in flames, Could laugh to see her glutted sons expire, Tho' much too rough my soul to touch a lyre." Warren alluded to the heinous image of Nero playing his musical instrument over a roof top as he watched Rome burn, a symbol of the most egotistical and psychopathic of reigns. Such a persistently Nerofied picture of crown representatives demonstrated not only the intensity of what the historian Kenneth Silverman has called "Whig sentimentalism" and tendency for hyperbole, but also the accelerated pace at which colonists were coming to understand their imperial superiors as irredeemable, murderous creatures through the example of antiquity.[104]

Vincent Carretta has demonstrated how British satirists mocked their monarch to the point of depicting him as an ironic Nero, as shown in an engraving from the title page of the 1773 edition of *The New Foundling Hospital for Wit,* which depicted Nero as the blackened figure of George III in an equestrian posture, crowned with laurels and draped in a toga-like cape. The engraving's caption reads, "One of the Headmen of Gotham caused a Statue of himself to be erected in the Character of Marcus Aurelius; but the Statuary, knowing nothing of that Prince, took his likeness from NERO." However, for these satirists, as Carretta points out, George was a Nero not out of strength but out of weakness.[105] If the Island dwellers took their cue for depicting George III as a Roman Caesar from their colonial brethren on the American mainland, their western kin represented the monarch in different Nerofied terms: Americans understood George III as a vicious and powerful Nero tyrant.

Indeed, in 1773 the colonists took a major step toward independence when they began to treat not merely colonial appointees, the Parliament, or cabinet ministers but, significantly, the king's person as a Roman tyrant. John Allan was among the first to assert that, if the rights of Americans were indeed intentionally subverted, "then that man, that King, that minister of state, be who he will [that masterminded the alleged conspiracy], is worse than a Nero TYRANT."[106] While this was not yet a full-fledged identification of the monarch as a Nero—the expression was provisional, and "Nero" was used as an adjective to describe a type of tyranny—Allan was indeed walking a thin line. This harsh idiom nevertheless cut colonial boundaries by 1775 as Southerners, too, were engaged in transforming the way they perceived and depicted their British leaders. "Virginius" had revealed to his readers that what they were viewing "with horror and detestation" as "a Grenville and a North, a Bute and a Mansfield" were reincarnations of "a Catiline, a Clodius, and even the polished Caesar." By 1775, the king's ministers were not deemed the only culprits. "Virginius" went on to admonish the monarch that, "had [Julius] Caesar thought . . . that the laurels of posterity would, instead of honour and estimation, pay him the full tribute of their sovereign execration, while they load the memory of his assassins with the most unbounded honors, he never would have acted the patricide of his country." Similarly, George III should be careful not "to sanctify the most corrupt measures of the most corrupt servants." Otherwise, "History hereafter will do him all the justice he shall be found to deserve," just as it had done to Caesar's memory.[107] The Nerofication of George III was imminent.

As the war broke out, American writers drew parallels more freely and explicitly between Roman tyrants and British leaders. Just before hostilities commenced, John Adams ruminated vaguely that "the present reign may be that of Augustus, but upon my honour I expect twelve Caesars will succeed it."[108] "Philoleutheros Americanus," a Connecticut poet, accused the military governor Thomas Gage ("Tory Tom") of committing atrocious behavior after skirmishes began: "Nero like [Gage murdered] the aged. . . . The blooming virgin and the beardless boy . . . snatch the infant from the streaming breast, Whose spouting veins should maculate his vest."[109] Such was indeed behavior well suited to Nero Caesar. "Cosmopolitan" accused Thomas Hutchinson of acting "Caligula like . . . determined to sever its head from all its members with one stroke," recanting the rhetoric of the Adamses in an earlier and different context.[110] "Orthodoxus," writing in the *New Hampshire Gazette*, accused the "unfit men"—namely, the British legislators—of acting whimsically and mischievously for the sake of "ambition, lust, avarice," just as Caligula had when he carried "coccle shells from the sea shore, in triumph over Neptune."[111] "Orthodoxus" was referring to Caligula's absurd (and most likely apocryphal) behavior in the campaign of AD 39, when he amassed a large army in preparation for an invasion of Britain. At the last minute, Caligula allegedly panicked, changed his mind, and ordered the troops to gather cockle shells from the beach instead, claiming to have won a great triumph over Neptune, the god of the oceans. Like the worst of tyrants, British legislatures were depicted as unworthy and unfit to rule an empire.

Interestingly, even Tories could adopt and adapt the imagery of Roman tyrants to their own ends. While the patriot Governor William Livingston was identified in a Tory publication as "the Nero of New-Jersey,"[112] Samuel Seabury pointed out that "even to Nero and Caligula . . . the Apostles commanded honor and Respect" (the reference is to St. Paul's submission to these tyrants).[113] By presenting such an argument, Seabury in practice admitted that Tories could no longer deny the vigor of the Nerofied images evoked by Whigs. Whigs quoted English members of Parliament as claiming that Americans should "be governed as the Romans used to govern their provinces, by a standing army."[114] Adopting the American idiom, British imperialists accused Americans of inviting the kind of punishment the Romans enforced on their subordinates.

Independence drove yet another escalation in the American sentiment toward Britain and its supreme leader. Historians seem to agree that "Americans of all classes on the patriot side sustained their loyalty to the king throughout the period from 1760 to 1776."[115] Colonists have narrated the repeal of the Stamp Act, for example, as the work of the king intervening as protector of the rights of Englishmen.[116] By declaring the colonies in a state of rebellion, however, George III convinced many that he was the chief architect of the conspiracy to rob the colonies of their rights. Following soon after, the Declaration of Independence signaled how "all grievances [were thrust] onto the person of the king."[117] After independence, George III was reconstituted as *the* enemy, his equestrian statue hacked to pieces in New York and his effigy burned and buried many times over throughout the colonies. The monarch's rapid fall from grace indeed seems "striking" to some.[118] The overt post-1776 discourse of Nerofication articulated and expressed this swift change in esteem for the monarch in America. The mock killings of George III during the year of independence did not merely constitute ritual murder and funeral, as the historian David Waldstreicher instructively points out.[119] They also symbolized George III's resurrection as a Nerofied Caesar.

With the war in its second year and the psychological and legal affiliations between the colonies-turned-states and Britain torn since July 1776, Jonathan Mitchell Sewall produced a notably classicized literary piece, writing a new *Epilogue to Cato* as the concluding section to Addison's tragedy, the most popular play in the colonies throughout the eighteenth century.[120] "Did CAESAR, drunk with pow'r and madly brave, Insatiate burn, his Country to enslave? Did he for this, lead forth a servile host, And spill the choicest blood that Rome cou'd boast?"[121] Sewall asked, and immediately answered: "Our BRITISH CAESAR too, has done the same, and damn'd this Age to everlasting fame!" Referring to the monarch as a "British Caesar" ("Caesar" denoting not a Roman emperor in general but Julius Caesar specifically, the first of Rome's dictators for life and the villain of Addison's *Cato*), Sewall blamed George III for the destruction of the flower of America, as "COLUMBIA's crimson'd fields still smoke with gore! Her bravest heroes cover all the shore!" The *Epilogue* went on to depict General William Howe as a crony in a Caesarian Georgian court: "W've had our DECIUS too, and Howe can say / Health, pardon, peace G——e [Gage] sends America; yet brings destruction, for the olive wreath." The depiction of the British monarch as the tyrant who has destroyed the Roman republic is unmistakable: George III is a British Julius Caesar, and his generals play the part of Caesar's servile cronies. After describing the monarch as Caesar, the last logical step in the escalating discursive ladder of defiling the king would be to equate him with the diabolical tyranny of Nero Claudius Caesar. Americans indeed took this final step and represented their former monarch as the most hated of the emperors of the Julio-Claudian dynasty.

Philip Freneau was among the first to conflate the king's figure with that of Nero. In "America Independent," published in 1778, Freneau, the "poet of the revolution," compared George III to "the dregs of human kind," among them Nero, Herod, and Domitian. By the end of the poem, he asserted that the British king was "the Nero of our times."[122] The image of the worst of Caesars had apparently appealed to Freneau's poetico-historical imagination. In 1782 he charged the king in the pages of the *Freeman's Journal:* "O Nero! The blood of thousands calls aloud for vengeance on your guilty head."[123] *A Dialogue, between the Devil and George III, Tyrant of Britain,* perhaps the most elaborate comparison of George III and Nero, was one of the last instances of Nerofication before the discourse lost its meaning and significance as the war with Britain ended. The *Dialogue* epitomized the Nerofication of King George using hyperbole matched by few other texts, conflating the biblical and classical readings of the Revolution.[124] Written anonymously and paraphrasing a Scottish tract from 1746 entitled *Dialogue between the Devil and George II,* this dialogue satirically depicted the British monarch as a slavish co-conspirer with the Devil. At the very beginning of this outrageous, satanic dialogue between Lucifer and the monarch, the Devil reassured George of his trust: "I doubt not you will equal my antient servants Nero, [and] Caligula."[125] George himself, however, made sure that the point was driven home. "I have a heart of a tyrant," he declared, "and I hope to prove that my head is equal to my heart. . . . Should I succeed, I'll surpass in barbarity any tyrant that ever lived."[126] Willingly, George told the Devil exactly which tyrants he planned to surpass and how. "I will have a saw-mill," he said, divulging his diabolical plan, "carried by a stream of virgin blood to saw off rebels' heads! . . . Did ever Nero, or Caligula, perform any thing equal to this?" "Tyranny," George finally admitted, "has been the plan and pursuit of my life."[127] The British king, sovereign of the American colonies only six years before the publication of the *Dialogue,* surely outdoes the psychotic machinations of the Roman tyrants. In 1783, with the war officially over and the British marginalized as enemies both on the battlefield and in the war of words, the process of Nerofication of the British monarch was complete.

Throughout the chain of events that led to the political and psychological undoing of the imperial connection, the Romanization and Nerofication of Britain and its leadership played a key role in expressing resentment and eroding the sentiments that tied the colonists to the mother country. If American patriots indeed made sense of their separation from Britain in classical terms, as this chapter attempts to demonstrate, such separation did not involve illustrious Romans such as Brutus and Cato or heroic ones such as Cincinnatus or Cassius. As the remainder of this study will reveal, the daring heroes of republican Rome entered the stage only in the mid-1770s and played a different role in the intellectualization of the Revolution. The disintegration of the imperial connection was, instead, imagined through the narratives of imperial Rome of the Caesars. Understanding Britain and its chiefs through such historical types, however, did not serve merely as an allegorical or metaphorical backdrop. It also constituted a cognitive framework for analyzing, justifying, and comprehending contemporary reality. American patriots transformed Britain into a reincarnation of corrupt imperial Rome as their contemporary experiences acquired a historical quality, intertwining contemporary narratives with Roman annals. Such hermeneutics, which repeatedly conflated the present and the past, opened the prospect of infusing classical meaning into present occurrences.

American rebels employed multiple discursive strategies when detaching themselves from Britain. A parallel—and, in several respects, quite similar—intellectual transformation in which "British Israel" devolved into tyrannical and blasphemous, Devil-serving "Assyria" and "Egypt" has been described as the "commanding metaphor" of revolutionary America.[128] Sacvan Bercovitch has noted, however, that in spite of its ubiquity, biblical symbolism during the late eighteenth century may have provided little constructive content—perhaps enough to present the grounds for separation but not to furnish an alternative identity to the British one that was being cast off.[129] While Bercovitch's argument is highly debatable, the following chapters demonstrate the different ways in which the classics participated in and contributed to a discourse of antiquity that provided meanings to their revolutionary endeavors. The narratives and anti-heroes of antiquity were, however, not only handy in justifying war. Rome's history was crucial to making sense of separation and the Empire's disintegration.

3

"JUDGE THE FUTURE BY THE PAST"

The Varieties of Historical Consciousness in Revolutionary America

AT THE FOUNDATION of the classical discourse of the American Revolution lay a set of assumptions about history and its meaning. So effective was that language that by elaborating on their relation to, and the relevance of, the classics to revolutionary America, American patriots rendered the classical discourse as a distinct mode of historical thought. To better understand this innovative language, this chapter examines various ways through which patriots made use of the classical world and thus reflected and gave expression to revolutionary historical consciousness. Competing sets of assumptions about the nature of history and America's place within it emerged through the classical discourse during the crucible of Revolution, especially in 1774–76, years of decision in which notions of America as a discrete political entity began to cohere. Within this discourse, two competing paradigms reflected radically different understandings of the past, its relation to the present as well as disparate expectations from America's national future—that is, they consisted of two distinct historical consciousnesses. Remarkably, those two attitudes toward time and history follow a geographic division: While southerners, mostly elite planters, contemplating ancient history expressed common civic-humanistic notions of time as cyclical and corrupting, northerners discoursing the classics habitually held to a view of history derived from reformed Christian exegesis, which indicated a tendency toward millennial optimism.[1] The middle colonies-turned-states demonstrated in accordance to their trademark religious and ethnic diversity an intellectual middle ground that accommodated and manifested both schools of thought.

Southerners and, occasionally, Americans from the middle colonies-turned-states related to the ancients by believing that they shared a common fate with the republics of antiquity; they understood their revolution, for better or worse, as the latest link in a succession of republics that had unfolded through time and followed similar historical patterns. As such, they were obliged to face the question of decline of political entities. While this view of time originating in the south conformed to contemporary continental republican thinking about the cyclicality of history, northerners, mostly New Englanders, displayed a novel attitude toward time by applying reformed Protestant modes of historical interpretation to classical narratives. Within this forward-looking framework, northern patriots expected to surpass their ancient predecessors and succeed where their republican ancestors had failed. Ultimately, these two distinct visions inspired a revolution in which southerners could not deny that America was working within a historical framework and northerners believed that America was destined to escape time and history. Examined together, they seem to have shaped not a single "revolutionary consciousness" but two distinct conceptions of time, of history, and perhaps even of "revolution." Recognizing this double historical consciousness may modify our understanding of the timing of the development of an American national culture, of distinct northern and southern worldviews. Indeed, the dichotomy of the distinct American cultural regions that we know as the North and the South may have yet unexplored origins in the revolutionary experience, long before the crucible of the antebellum decades and the Civil War, as scholars have commonly assumed. Finally, recognizing the startling differences in revolutionary attitudes toward time will provide a deeper understanding of the variety of historical dispositions that animated revolutionaries in their drive to create an America republic.

The belief in recurring cycles in cosmic and human affairs has far-reaching trajectories in Western thought and can be traced from pre-Socratic thinkers to influential twentieth-century writers.[2] Cyclical paradigms, in which time moved through a repetitive cycle of successive periods, often implied an imperative decline of social conditions as well as a decrease in human physical, intellectual, and spiritual qualities.[3] Typically the cycle would start in a harmonious golden age, followed by decline and destruction, only to be completed at the point of renewal at the gates of another blissful age. This cyclical view of history is commonly associated with the classical world's attitude toward, and understanding of, time, in contrast to a predominantly linear and successive experience driving toward the *eschaton*, prescribed by Judeo-Christian temporal sensibilities.[4]

Cultured southern patriots repeatedly articulated notions of Roman decline as they were contemplating the question of national independence during 1774–76.[5] Historical patterns of rise and decline were entrenched in republican thought from the days of Polybius, and J. G. A. Pocock has recently demonstrated how the cyclical pattern and its ties to the problem of Roman liberty had plagued historians and philosophers for millennia: While Rome achieved empire, it was obvious that it could not retain its republican integrity in the process.[6] Patriots who chose to discourse the Roman experience and its relation to America in the revolutionary south repeatedly placed Roman decline at the center of their discussions. Still, those southerners discussing Rome's demise were not particularly pessimistic. As Stow Persons correctly pointed out more than half a century ago, many of those who employed the cyclical idea in the late eighteenth century generally agreed that contemporary America belonged in the youthful stage of growth, approaching its stage of maturity.[7] Nevertheless, educated southern revolutionaries did not find a way to avoid the necessity of the historical movement toward decline; nor could they deny that that was the direction in which America must be striding, however remote its day of fall might be. If the harsh implications of cyclical thought and the Roman fall for the republican experiment in America were usually submerged in this discourse, they were also inescapable.

In the early months of 1774, the colonies were anxiously waiting to learn of the British response to the Tea Party that destroyed the valuable cargo belonging to the East India Company in Boston Harbor. Speculation ran high, and contemporaries realized that the Period of Quiet might well be over; they were most likely about to face another round of imperial scuffling. On March 17, under the heading "The Reading of History Pleasing and Advantageous," an anonymous writer in the *Virginia Gazette* presented a horrific, if common, historical observation about extensive political entities: "We become acquainted with their Rise and Decline, their grandeur and their fall. One page of history presents us with a powerful Empire stretching her scepter over various kingdoms, and sitting as queen among the nations; in the next, we behold her stripped of her power, and humbled in the dust." The author went on to explain the fall of Rome, the most obvious and infamous instance of such historical disintegration. "When the Romans had subdued all the adjacent nations," the readers of the *Gazette* were told what they must already have known, "their empire, stretched to such a vast extent, [that it] soon lost its spring and force." It was not due to its oversized territory that the empire crumbled, nor to "the violent irruption of the Goths and Vandals"; the barbarian invasions were not the cause but only a symptom of Rome's weakness, which merely "hastened its destruction." The empire "contained, within itself, the seeds of dissolution"—namely, "conveniences and luxuries" that weakened Rome and led it to a magnificent ruin. Luxury, exerting its nefarious influence, was omnipresent, manifested through "the vices of Roman emperors, and the universal corruption of mankind that prevailed among the people." Such were "the causes of that dreadful revolution in the Roman state."[8]

The anonymous author presented the *Gazette*'s readers with a revealing, if quite common, historical analysis. Roman histories ever since Sallust's accounts of the Catiline conspiracy and the Jugurthan war had denounced luxury as the main cause of self-corruption of republican virtue; they saw luxury as the cause of the demise of the empire, which had won it in the first place.[9] In two years' time, across the Atlantic, Edward Gibbon, a member of the British Parliament and historian of the Roman Empire, would also raise the question of Roman liberty, expansion, and demise, and use similar language to explain the same problem. He would describe the "slow and secret poison" that had been introduced "into the vitals of the [Roman] empire."[10] Roman decline sustained an Atlantic discourse.

The writer had a reason for confronting the problem of Roman decline other than denouncing the British Empire.[11] "The large strides it [luxury] has lately made in this kingdom should rouse us from the lethargy of a careless inattention," he warned his compatriots. The fate of the Roman Empire, and the state of the British, should "induce us, before it is too late, to prevent the same destruction from overwhelming our country." Did America, which was beginning to be thought of in terms other than a series of British colonies, contain within itself the seeds of dissolution, too? The acknowledgment of the fragility of America, and the implicit recognition that it might eventually decline, even if it was momentarily on the rise, was, as we are about to see, a mainstay of a southern classical discourse. Significantly, such a historical analysis was virtually absent from the patriot classical discourse in New England during the early years of the Revolution. Revealingly, following the analysis of the Roman decline, the *Gazette*'s editors—were they aware of the irony?—chose to print a detailed "Description of the Manners and Fashion of London," an account of the very things republicans denounced as "luxury" and "corruption."

In the following year, the *Gazettes* of Virginia and Pennsylvania reprinted an oration delivered by William Moore Smith to the Continental Congress on May 23, 1775. Preaching to the assembled congressmen a month after the commencement of hostilities, Smith lengthily retold the well-known story of imperial Rome, which "rose to the summit of human glory, and fell again, low as the dust of the earth . . . trampled under the feet of barbarian swarms." He reiterated the symptoms of Rome's degeneration: "Virtue and honor . . . ceased to distinguished her; that superior genius, and enthusiastic love of liberty which raised her to eminence . . . changed their complexion to rapine and oppression . . . that independent spirit which could derive all the substantial comforts of life from a few acres of ground, degenerated into a capaciousness which whole provinces could not satisfy; generals and commanders were not called from a handy education in the camp or at the plough but from brothels, and all the effeminate senses of voluptuousness and vice." Smith blamed "luxury and her twin daughters, venality and vice," for "this mighty downfall" of the empire. Even the magnificent Rome could not stand long the damage of those poisonous habits; it faltered "on its foundation and the mighty fabric sunk beneath its own weight." Smith's concluded pessimistically: "Such is the flux of human affairs! As the body natural carries from the cradle the seeds of its own dissolution"—that is, luxury—"which ripen faster or slower, as fed by the hand of corruption and sloth, so it is in the body politic."[12]

Here one sees the common tendency among eighteenth-century thinkers to employ an analogy between living bodies and political artifacts. Dating back to the ancient Greeks, such analogies "likened political societies to organisms that were born, matured, decayed and died." According to this view, societies, like men, proceeded from "youth" through "manhood" to maturity and "old age." This metaphor suggested a cyclical view of historical development in which change, the process of time, was eventually and inevitably associated with decay. If social maturity had its advantages, such as power and glory, it also presaged an imperative and imminent decay and collapse.[13] These organic metaphors were in no way exclusively used by Americans during the imperial crisis. Henry Temple Luttrell, an English gentleman supportive of the American cause who found in Americans "the Spartan temperance . . . the urbanity of Athens," believed the Americans would "evince the Roman magnanimity, ere Rome fell under usurpation." "Through melancholy observation, drawn from the fate of the Assyrian, Persian, and Roman empires," Luttrell also found, "national societies, as well as the individual mortals of whom those societies are composed, have their non-age, their adult vigour, and their decline."[14] Smith and other southern writers, however, unlike their northern counterparts, coped not only with the prospects of an aging British society, but with one that was—at least for the time being—situated at its non-age, the rising American (soon to be) republics.

The biological analogy perpetuated the logic of polities that hold their own poison; Aristotle had long before discussed the potential and limits contained in a seed. Consequently, William Smith argued that "empires," which, recall, follow natural laws of birth, growth, and death, "carry in them their own bane, and proceed on fatal ground, from virtuous industry and valour to wealth and conquest; next to luxury then to soul corruption and bloated morals; and last of all, to sloth, anarchy, slavery and political death." This terrible, stadial tale conveyed a moral to the American congressmen in Smith's audience, who by May 1775 were busy executing a war. These ruminations on the fall of empires, Smith judged, "might be to us a beacon set upon a perilous place." America, in other words, was in no way immune to aging and corruption. It would be only in the hand of God, Smith concluded, that "amidst the wide waste of empires, this one corner of the globe may at least remain the last asylum of truth, righteousness, and freedom!"[15] This rhetorical plea to providence contained as much desperation as it did hope. We will soon see that other non-northern intellects similarly perceived America as the last bastion of *libertas*. Those voices, too, however, were conscious of their polity's bleak prospects to sustain its promise for long.

In "Remarks on Annual Elections for the Fairfax Independent Company," written at about the same time as Smith's oration, George Mason wished to preserve the election of militia leaders in Virginia according to the Roman fashion. "While the Roman Commonwealth preserved its vigour new consuls were annually elected, new levies made, and new officers appointed; a general was often recalled from the head of a victorious army, in the midst of a dangerous and important war, and a successor sent to finish the expedition which he had begun." This system seemed to Mason enormously fortunate, for "a long and almost constant series of successes proved the wisdom and utility of measures which carried victory through the world, and at the same time secure the public safety and liberty at home." However, "when by degrees these essential maxims of the state were undermined, and pretences were found to continue commanders beyond the stated times, their army no longer considered themselves the soldiers of the Republic, but as the troops of Marius or of Sylla, of Pompey or of Caesar, of Marc Antony or of Octavius."[16]

Mason was perpetuating a Tacitean explanation of the decline of the empire, which described the Roman polity's failure to deal with the consequences of its suppression of the republic until it became prone to tyranny and crises of succession.[17] This narrative, formulated by Tacitus after the fall of the republic under the rule of the Caesars, portrayed the Roman Empire as imperfect and unstable, exposed to interventions by armies led by warlords outside of Rome that shifted power away from the control of governing senatorial elites. Mason restated the thesis of the Tacitean narrative in which Romans revealed the *arcanum imperii,* the mystery of governance, by recognizing the Roman armies' ability to enthrone their warlords as Caesars away from the city. "The dissolution of that once glorious and happy commonwealth," Mason warned, "was the natural consequence, and has afforded a useful lesson to succeeding generations." Just as Rome had been at the time of its glory, "North America is the only great nursery of freemen now left upon the face of the earth." Mason, recognizing in horror that the rising American commonwealths might share Rome's fate, urged his fellow Virginians to "cherish the sacred deposit" of their liberty and elect their officers for a limited time and scope. Hence, Mason was advocating the Roman fashion of electing the military, as it was practiced before Sulla was nominated to become dictator for life.[18] The "useful lesson" the Tacitean narrative taught Mason was an unsettling one: America was prone to suffer Rome's fate and decline into a state run by military dictators; it could be well on the way toward becoming a principate. There was no millennial confidence in America's future to be found in Mason's words or rhetoric.

"Non Quis Sed Quid" (Not Measures, Men) was the pseudonym chosen by a writer in the *South Carolina Gazette* during July 1774. This pseudonymous writer was buoyant and confident in America's future during July 1774: "When I review the annals of the world, I am constrained to believe that great things await America. . . . When liberty was well nigh banished from every quarter of the globe, we found an asylum in this savage land." "Non Quis Sed Quid" recognized that the *translatio imperii* was working in America's favor: "Learning, liberty, and every thing that ennobles the human mind, have constantly been traveling westward." The South Carolinian went on to assert that he could never believe that, "in this sacred land, slavery shall be so soon permitted to erect her throne on the ruins of freedom." He had a good reason for such overt confidence: The young age and vigor of the American settlements would not allow for a rapid deterioration of morals. If America were to breed despotism when its communities were so recently planted, it would be "contrary to the analogy of things, which gradually have their rise, progress, and declension." To stay on course with the cycle of moral development, Americans should "abandon luxury and indolence" and "encourage industry and frugality."[19] We should note that "Non Quis Sed Quid" did not believe that slavery—he was, of course, referring not to African bondage but to Anglo-Americans' "slavery" under Great Britain—would become established in America soon. His confidence could not hide the historical logic that eventually America would grow old and, like any organic and man-made artifact, experience the pains of corruption and dissolution. The "analogy of things" of "rise, progress and declension" did not stop short of America's step.

"One of the People," another South Carolinian writing in July 1775, brought to the fore an additional explanation for the demise of the Roman Republic.[20] His explanation began with surveying a golden age in Roman annals, in which "Rome—the Great Queen of Earth—Imperial Rome—flourished secure of intestine commotions." However, "absorb'd in contemplation on the Rise and Fall of Empires," "One of the People" followed the decline of the empire to the time when "luxury and ambition gave birth to the invidious distinction of Patrician and Plebeian, a distinction which never ceased to foment eternal discord in the state; and terminated but with the empire." If Rome indeed suffered from corruption and personal ambition, "One of the People" pointed out, those were not final causes of its fall. Luxury, rather, created such a social discord that liberty could not stand for long. Once again, America had a lesson to learn from the awesome historical experience of the Roman Empire. "O! May America never adopt such distinctions that must sap the vigour of her constitution, now in bloom," "One of the People" announced, reiterating the organicist analogy of polities. What were America's prospects of escaping the dangers in establishing social ranks and thus reenacting the failures of the Romans? The author's tone and implicit conclusion were grave. If America was currently blooming, it was unlikely it could avoid decay and escape the historical movement into old age.

Another gloomy prediction was published in South Carolina three months later, in November 1775. An anonymous author engaged in a historical account that began with conveying a state of nature that combined Aristotelian assumptions about political societies and Rousseauian notions of natural liberty: "In the early ages of the world mankind enjoyed an uninterrupted liberty and a perfect independence. Each family was as a little state of which the father was the chief, and which acknowledged no other superior. They lived without ambition, for every one was contented with his inheritance and they had no other needs than their homes and their herds which supplied them with food and protection."[21] Unfortunately, that golden age did not last long, and societies were obliged "to bear the yoke which a Caesar or Alexander has introduced by violence," reducing them "into slavery." Yet, the argument continued, "it must be allowed that necessity and the importation of foreign vices . . . was [decline's] parent."

The author was relying here on the notions of a prominent school of Scottish conjectural historians who posited a stadial theory of history. This cluster of Scottish "sociological historians," among them Adam Smith and Adam Ferguson, gained wide influence in the eighteenth century. They recognized that societies were progressing in time, but they interpreted this progress as a mixed blessing. The movement from simple, "rude" societies to complex ones was usually seen in terms of a "four-stage theory," consisting of hunting, pasturage, agriculture, and commerce.[22] Commerce was habitually associated with corruption and decay. Thus, "the necessity to import," or the loss of an Edenic agrarian self-sufficiency, was a manifestation of human societies' entry into the final stage of commerce, in which an economy is complex and entangled in profitmaking webs of imports and exports. Such "modern" societies were believed to harbor luxury and corruption, and were consequently exposed to a usurper such as "a Caesar or [an] Alexander." This ambivalence toward modernity, the fear of the juggernaut of emerging impersonal market forces and commercial societies, was a mainstay of the republican discourse. America, under this analysis, was not exempt from the eventual malign influences of "commerce."[23] Hence, the prospect of the present age was gloomy: "We are said to grow wiser; but I fear we are not more happy than were our ancestors. Riches have corrupted us, and luxury will complete our ruin. We are said to be more polished and reformed, but I fear only in the arts of cunning and ambition, in the thirst of power, and the love of universal dominion." In the final phase of commerce, nothing of the prehistoric purity was left. The depressing conditions of "the principal states of Europe at this period" could only confirm such notions. The anonymous author turned his attention to America and found "the prospects . . . terrifying." If British "tyranny and oppression have opened the scene," then "blood and slaughter will close it."[24] Nothing in this analysis indicated that America could postpone its advancement to a commercial stage and avoid another Caesar who usurped Rome as it lost its virtue.

Another formulation of Roman decline was elaborated in the *Virginia Gazette* in May 1776. According to this interpretation, the "natural decay and death" of republics occurred from the insidious effects of "the contaminating poison" of despotism.[25] Once again we come across the assumption that polities proceed according to organic cycles of birth and decay and that as such they contain the poison of their decline. "The first kings of Rome," the author pointed out, "were generals and chief magistrates, not monarchs. The great rights of sovereignty were avowedly acknowledged to belong to the people." Thus, "when Tarquin attempted to become a monarch, he was expelled [from] the state, and an end was put to kingly rule, by the establishment of a republick." The republic thus evolved from attempts at despotic encroachments on popular sovereignty. Not long after, however, "the next evil sprang from the attempts of the patricians to establish an oligarchy. The people moved slowly to opposition." But finally, Romans, who "had for some time endured poverty, stripes, chains, and imprisonment," established "a plebeian party . . . to oppose the patrician." This narrative conformed to that of "One of the People" examined earlier, as it interpreted the social strife and endless contentions of the Plebeians and Patricians as weakening the republic "till both were swallowed up in despotism of the Caesars." The moral of this well-known tale seemed straightforward: "Monarchy or oligarchy are the customary and fatal diseases of republicks." Indeed, the "probable rise" of "these great causes of mischief" were, the Virginian writer reassured, "indefinitely remote" in the American colonies, still colonies for yet another month. America lacked a feudal past and enjoyed "the absence of hereditary distinctions of rank," and "the peaceable and humane character of the people" promised a virtuous future. Furthermore, unlike in Europe, "no man's blood hath yet stained our continent but that of open enemies." In short, the Virginian concluded, "We seem to be aptly circumstanced for the best republics, upon the best terms that ever came to the lot of any people before us." Nevertheless, were such optimal conditions enough to postpone ad infinitum the "fatal diseases of republicks"? However remote the "probable rise" of despotism in America may have been, this writer, like other southerners, could not, and did not, deny that even America would eventually succumb to the unbending laws of time and decay.

In William Henry Drayton's *A Charge on the Rise of the American Empire,* delivered to the grand jury in Charleston, we encounter a mature and elaborate theory of the rise and decline of political entities. Drayton conveyed in his *Charge* a picture of an overwhelming natural law that allegedly subdued not only diminutive humans but also colossal empires: "It is just to glance an eye over the historic page, to be assured that the duration of empire is limited by the almighty decree." Reiterating the organicist metaphor, Drayton mused: "Empires have their rise to a zenith—and their declension to a dissolution; the years of a man, nay the hours of the insect on the bark of the Hypanis, that lives but a day, epitomize the advance and decay of the strength and duration of dominion." Hence, "One common fate awaits all things upon earth"—empires, humans, and even insects. Having laid his organic conceptual framework, Drayton turned (unsurprisingly) to the Roman example: "We see, that from the most contemptible origin upon record, Rome became the most powerful state the sun ever saw: the world bowed before her imperial fasces! Yet, having ran through all the vicissitudes of dominion, her course was finished. Her empire was dissolved, the separated members of it might arise to run through familiar revolutions."[26] England, no longer a province of the Roman Empire, in turn was incarnated as Great Britain and "extended her dominion: arrived at, and passed her zenith." Drayton now turned to elaborate historical comparisons:

> Three and thirty years numbered the illustrious days of the Roman greatness—eight years measure the duration of the British grandeur in meridian luster! How few are the days of true glory! The duration of the Roman period is from their complete conquest of Italy, which gave them a place whereon to stand, that they might shake the world; to the original cause of their declension, their introduction of Asiatic luxury. The British period is from the year 1758 when they victoriously pursued their enemies into every quarter of the globe; to the immediate cause of their decline—their injustice displayed by the stamp act.[27]

Drayton's interpretation of Britain's slide from glory to corruption as a consequence of its imperial policy—namely, its attempt to extract revenue in America—has already been discussed. However, Drayton also believed in super-structural foundations that explained the British decline. He concluded that, "like the Roman empire, Great Britain in her constitution of government, contained a poison to bring on her decay; and in each case, this poison was drawn into a ruinous operation, by the riches and luxuries of the East." These significant similarities were no coincidence. The workings of "natural causes and common effects" also propelled the American states to be "dissolved from the British dominion." Drayton asserted to his listeners that no one should wonder why "Britain has experienced the invariable fate of empire." Are we "surprised when we see youth or age yield to the common lot of humanity?"[28] The answer to that question was obvious to contemporaries who thought of political artifacts in terms of living things. Accordingly, the answer to the natural corollary of that question should have been evident, too: What would happen when America came of age? Could one acknowledge the "invariable" pattern of the rise and fall of empires and not worry about the future lot of the emerging, most western of empires?

Two years after laying out his *Charge*, Drayton was even more explicit. While Roman "consuls, senate and people" constituted "one of the best [governments] of antiquity," and "the king, lords and commons erected [in Britain] the most perfect system the wit of man ever devised," those regimes had a fatal flaw: "Both, as is the case with all things temporal, lost their capability of action, and changed their very nature." In America, Drayton knew, "we are about to establish a confederated government," one, he hoped, that would "last for ages." In 1778, however, Drayton did not find reason for optimism. The proposed Articles of Confederation did not seem "to be formed upon those principles, which the wisest men have deemed and which long and invariable experience prove, to be the most secure defenses of liberty." Indeed, Congress seemed to "have lost sight" of a wise mode of government.[29] Decline may have started even before America reached its Roman-like zenith.

Northern patriots, to whom we will now turn our attention, were not as historically inquisitive as their southern compatriots. Cultured southerners delved into the reasons for Rome's decline in an attempt to extract from that awesome historical experience patterns and meaning—if only to recognize the pitfalls that awaited them. Northerners showed little similar inclination. In a stark contrast to their fellow Americans, northerners, while making extensive use of classical narratives, rarely analyzed the Roman fall or provided an overarching scheme of historical change. When Americans residing north of the Mason-Dixon Line, especially New Englanders, turned—rarely—to investigate the reasons for the decline of the Roman Empire, they typically did not provide a sophisticated or nuanced historical analyses of the fall. Rather, their interpretations tended to be one-dimensional and instrumental. Thus, "Cato of Utica," a pseudonymous Bostonian writer in May 1774, blamed "the ill policy of the [Roman] imperial ministry" for the demise of the republic. This "Cato" asserted that "the conflagration that devoured the Roman world was kindled in the provinces," implying boldly that Britain might itself fall as a result of its miscalculated colonial policy.[30] Commenting on Rome's decline, "Cato" characteristically explained that fall in epiphenomenal terms, such as mistaken policy, and not as a manifestation of larger historical patterns or forces.[31]

When cyclical notions of time were expressed in the north, they were communicated by loyalists, not by patriots. "Americanus" declared in the

Boston Post-Boy that "governments, like all other things, have their periods; the extinction of a free government arises from the anarchy of the people." This polybian formulation was followed by the example of Carthage, where "the encroachment of the people upon the senate, brought anarchy and ruin"; and of Rome, which "flourished in her glory . . . [but] the influence of plebeians produced confusion, and from thence the tyranny of dema- gogues commenced."[32] "Americanus" forwarded these ancient historical examples as warning posts for colonists to demonstrate the acute danger in shaking standing political orders. Through his conservative rhetoric, he unveiled a cyclical understanding of history that was not to be found in northern patriot language. Declension was not part of the northern patriot intellectual framework.

It was not the case, to be sure, that northern patriots were not aware of the republican cyclical view of history and of the relevance of the Roman decline to such a historical outlook. As early as 1755, a full decade before the Stamp Act, John Adams wrote a lengthy entry in his journal regarding Roman decline.[33] Many other northerners, as shown in chapter 2, elabo- rated on Roman decline in relation to Britain's apparent fall. However, when it came to extending the logic of corruption to America, the view expressed by Jonathan Austin in the Boston Massacre commemoration oration of 1778 seems to have been common to northern writers. "Specu- lative writers may indeed tell us," Austin pointed out, "that the seeds of dissolution exist in every body politic—that like the body natural, it must decay and die." However, Austin disagreed with this historical truism. "I am not a fatalist," he asserted. What "speculative writers" considered the poison of polities—namely, corruption and luxury—Austin considered mere consequence: The cause of political decline, in his view, was the use of standing armies.[34] In other words, decline was a consequence of political measures, not a meta-historical force exerting its sway on the body politic. America, Austin implied, could avoid decline by maintaining its militias. The Southern writers who worked under the sway of the cyclical persua- sion, as we have seen, did not provide such an escape from decline.

In the remainder of this chapter I explain how, in the north, a herme- neutic scheme I refer to as "classical typology" replaced the need to make sense of, or even to refer to, decline—Roman or American—because its implication was that America would avoid the downturn of the historical cycle. This unique exegesis was the intellectual structure through which northern patriots understood their relation to the classics and which suggests the millennial nature of their attitudes toward history and time.[35] Remarkably, this pattern was seldom expressed south of the Mason-Dixon Line, just as the cyclical view was not elaborated in the north. Classical typology demonstrates how Americans in Pennsylvania and New York, but especially in New England, employed reformed Protestant categories in their figurative interpretations of history. Hence, classical typology culminated not in predictions of decline but, rather, in classicized millennial expectations.[36] Northerners' fusion of Christian sensibilities with classical narratives convinced them that America could—and, indeed, would—escape the cycle that had plagued human societies through recorded time. In other words, they engaged in a classicized, "exceptionalist" historical interpretation.

Typology is a system of exegesis developed and practiced by the fathers of the early Christian church.[37] A type, or *typos* in Greek, in its primary and literal meaning simply denotes a rough draft, a less accurate model, from which a perfect image is made. These theologians saw types as anticipating and prefiguring Christ, endowing earlier events and persons from the Old Testament with a deeper, more complete significance. Types thus denoted symbols designed by God to prefigure Christ, the antetype, who fulfilled the type, or *figura*. Typology is in essence, therefore, a theory of anticipation and recurrence in history, a method of understanding the correspondence of events separated by time. It is a series of signs that works through a recognizable code of types and antetypes and operates on the principle of metaphor: Two events or objects are distinct in a certain sense but are at the same time similar in some other way; the meaning of the one determines the meaning of the other. Like metaphor, typology "represents more than literary ornamentation or deviation from the normal rules of linguistic practice," because it constitutes "coherent systems in terms" of which thinkers conceptualize their experiences.[38] Unlike metaphor, however, typology traces the connections and similarities between two unique events, each of which is equally real, or historical. As Erich Auerbach explains, "The fact that a figural scheme permits both its poles, the figure and its fulfillment, to retain the characteristics of concrete historical reality, in contradistinction to what obtains with symbolic or allegorical personifications, so that figure and fulfillment although the one 'signifies' the other, have a significance which is not incompatible with being real. An event taken as a figure [i.e., type] preserves its literal and historical meaning. It remains an event, does not become a mere sign."[39]

The first primary pole of typological interpretation is therefore the literal meaning as recorded in the Hebrew Bible; the other pole consists of the events in the life and teachings of Christ that correspond to the events in the Old Testament. If in metaphor and allegory the signifier can be cast off once its meaning has been understood, in typology both signifier and signified bear equal ontological weight. Typology thus differs from metaphorical and allegorical forms by the historicity of both the sign and what it signifies and by the relation of promise (or prophecy or shadow) and fulfillment (or incarnation) between type and antetype.[40]

For most of its history, typology has been a method of encoding and interpreting the relationship between the Hebrew and Christian testaments. The typology of Old Testament figures had been established by centuries of exegesis, based on the belief in the unity of the two testaments. In mid-seventeenth-century England, however, typology demonstrated extraordinary dynamism, changing and expanding, becoming increasingly secular in its applications, more subtle, and more involved in genres not strictly religious, ranging from myth and political writing to poetry and prose narrative.[41] By the end of the seventeenth century, typological references and structures had become common poetic materials and began appearing in most genres of literature. In the political realm, analogizing of kings and other rulers to Christ, an act familiar during the Middle Ages and the Renaissance, reached a culmination in seventeenth-century England. Charles I, for example, was commonly described as the martyr king, while Cromwell was portrayed as the Davidic king, both figures typifying Christ. Typology, originally a single weapon in the armory of biblical scholarship, by the seventeenth century had become an elaborate system of reference and literary historical code that "was a tremendously popular method of exegesis with Catholic, Anglican, and Puritan theologians alike."[42] Scholars even see secular European cultural unity as rooted in a uniquely religious mode of representing reality—the Christian tradition of figural interpretation of the Bible.[43]

This remarkable change in the nature and application of typology was driven to a large extent by Protestant reformers who found typology an effective method for using the facts of salvific history to emphasize the rectitude of their cause and their independence from Rome.[44] If the European Reformation added new contexts to typology, American Puritans recast it anew. Applied more broadly, typology enabled Puritans to read biblical types as forecasting not just the events of the New Testament but also their own historical situation and experiences. In the words of Perry Miller, "By the nature of their enterprise and by the example of Scripture they had been again and again obliged to subject more than the Bible to the rules of interpretation."[45] Puritans made sense of their spiritual struggles and achievements by identifying with biblical personages such as Adam, Noah, and Job, who in earlier typologies would prefigure only Christ. This extension of typology was in no way restricted to individual typing; the Puritans also interpreted their group identity as the fulfillment of Old Testament prophecy, identifying their community as the "New Israel." The Atlantic crossing of the Puritans became an antetype of the exodus of the Israelites, while New England was typed as a new Zion. After conservative, cautious typological beginnings, New England's sacred errand into the wilderness and the approaching apocalypse were soon accepted as antetypes of sacred history. Claiming to strive for plainness, Puritan writers created instead a subtle and complex linguistic system of shadows, types, and prefigurations.[46]

The literary historian Sacvan Bercovitch demonstrates how, in developing the errand into the wilderness as part of the final stage of history, Puritans distorted traditional forms of exegetical typology, weaving their historical narratives into extensive schemes of figural interpretations. In this process, typology took on "the hazy significance of image and symbol; what passed for the divine plan lost its strict grounding in scripture." The eighteenth-century clergy, foremost Jonathan Edwards, took advantage of this movement and expanded Bible history to encompass the whole of American experience. In effect, Puritans "substituted a regional for a biblical past."[47] Not only did such revamped typology free Protestant America from the regionality of New England, and was thus imagined as another, greater Mountain of Holiness, but the Bible was now "only one among several manifestations of the typical system."[48]

The power exercised by reformed Protestantism in shaping American political culture at the time of the Revolution was remarkable.[49] Patricia Bonomi emphasizes the growing influence of religion in eighteenth-century America, particularly "the increasing interpenetration of religion and politics."[50] Indeed, scholars have noted how easily during the Revolution religious and political images were "joined in the public realm as the colonists sought to legitimate their break with England and articulate their vision of the future."[51] The historian Nathan O. Hatch demonstrates how revolutionary Whig clergymen began reading republican conceptions of religious and civil liberty backward to the Puritan founding.[52] However, the theo-political elements of "traditional covenant theology of Puritanism [that] combined with the political science of the eighteenth century into an imperatively persuasive argument for revolution" may have come together in unsuspected and overlooked ways.[53]

The classical typology offers yet another mode through which Samuel Adams and his comrades may have realized a "Christian Sparta."[54] By fusing the distant intellectual spaces of Protestant hermeneutics of history with classical narratives, typology provided an additional venue where religion could penetrate and affect the intellectual frameworks of revolutionaries. Consequently, not merely doctrine and theological-ideological content was transferred between the realms of the sacred and the secular, the Christian and the pagan.[55] Classical typology brought together a Christian mode of historical interpretation and republican narratives. Indeed, Protestant Americans' extensive conditioning in figural interpretation may well have trained them by the Revolution "to look instinctively for 'likeness' or foreshadowing of republican liberty."[56] Eighteenth-century Americans' conditioning in typology, I will argue, drove northern revolutionaries to expand their figural readings to the realms of classical history. The remainder of this chapter will demonstrate how, once the exegetical door was opened, the classical world was incorporated into a typological structure. This intellectual fusion created a unique revolutionary hermeneutics, a classical typology.

By the last quarter of the eighteenth century, the Greco-Roman world had a long relationship with typological hermeneutics. The explanation of pagan mythology in Christian terms dates from patristic times, when early Christian apologists perceived similarities between some of the major figures of the classical pantheon and central characters in the Bible.[57] By the seventeenth century, it was clear that mythical figures such as Hercules, Pan, Orpheus, Achilles, and Aeneas could be regarded as types foreshadowing Christ. In the Anglophone world, poets and men of letters, political apologists, and historians introduced figures from Greco-Roman mythology into their writing with prefigurative intentions, in search of Christian meanings in the classical canon.[58]

In revolutionary America, patriots typologized not the mythical world of the Mediterranean civilizations, however, but the histories of classical Greece and especially of Rome. As the expansion of the uses of typological methods during the seventeenth century took place, the argument from design—asserting that an orderly universe must entail a rational creator—encouraged still more adventurous typologizing within the Anglophone world of ideas. If the Bible, which was of divine authorship, contained hidden prefigurative relationships, it followed that one might find similar links not only in godly inspired texts, but also in natural phenomena or historical events.[59] The "book of nature" had thus become a legitimate source of figural scavenging. Revolutionary Americans employed their classical typology in an age that rarely doubted that the world was ordered according to a rational code. Within such an intellectual atmosphere, the typological correspondence between America and the classics reflected confidence in the existence of a cosmic, divine order. Such an order implied temporal aesthetics that inter-correlated "shadows" and "fulfillments" within historical time.

Classical typology, it should be clear, was not a theological exegetical device but a mode of historical interpretation through which Americans classicized their secular experiences. Freed from its scriptural foundation, classical typology could concern itself with events and relationships that had little or nothing to do with the conventional origins of the exegetical interpretation associated with it. Perhaps the classical typology's prevalence during the Revolution was related to the fact that many eighteenth-century Americans were conditioned by a theological doctrine that was steeped in typological thought. That seems to explain the ubiquity of typological patterns in New England, where Americans were especially exposed to such modes of biblical exegesis. In any event, the notion of classical typology allows us to recognize the significant sway the classics had on Americans' historical consciousness as typological readings penetrated the structures of their interpretation of the relations between the classical past and the revolutionary present. Biblical means were thus able to serve classical ends.

Unlike the Bible-oriented typologies that tended to focus on justifying the connections between the two testaments, classical typology was introspective in nature, articulating current experiences, and focused on the present. In other words, it was a typology in the use of politics. Patriots, like exegetical typologists, perceived a complex network spreading across secular events, making reality seem charged with classical value and meaning. When they unveiled historical parallels, patriot writers reacted as inspired exegetes uncovering the meaning of a hazy passage in the Bible. Hence, William Hooper was excited to unveil the decline of Rome and Britain in terms of "picture" and "original," using a common trope of typological thinking, and Josiah Quincy marveled at finding the relationship between Britain and America prefigured by that of Caesar and Rome.[60] Such expressions were no coincidence. Numerous writers and orators who contemplated the nature of the relationship between the classics and America established significant connections between narratives and persons that belonged together as earlier and later portions of a single sequence of events. In a hermeneutic sense, the patriot typologists discovered America in Rome—or, rather, Rome in America. America, patriots believed, had "in her store her Bruti and Cassii," while others were confident that America would boast its own "Scipios, Solons, Catos"; it was a place where the natives reincarnated the heroes of antiquity, where "each one's a Cato."[61] Like biblical exegetes justifying the New Testament on the basis of the Old Testament, American patriots could represent America as a better incarnation than its ancient forerunners. Unlike the metaphors invoked throughout the Revolution, describing and explaining the American polity in terms such as the human body (the "body politic"), the family, or the theater, classical typology correlated types and precursors that bore equal historical significance.[62] Typology supported a reading of history that linked the past and the present while furnishing significance to, and connections between, persons, places, and events millennia and oceans apart. By correlating the classical world to the present, typology enabled northern patriots to reaffirm America's superiority in light of ultimately unsuccessful classical predecessors. Typology, in short, provides the context in which many of the appeals to antiquity in the colonies-turned-states north of the Mason-Dixon Line, especially in New England, may be best understood. However, like its biblical counterpart, it worked against historicist sensibilities toward the past, for it depended on taking persons and events out of their historical contexts.[63]

The orator celebrating Cornwallis's defeat in Yorktown juxtaposed the great Roman General C. Scipio Africanus (185–129 BC) and the American General Nathaniel Greene: "The Roman Scipio, instead of opposing the Carthaginians in Italy, fought them in Africa: General Greene, as if divinely taught that the earl Cornwallis's ruin should crown the glory of Washington, instead of opposing him in Virginia, pushed his conquest to the south."[64] Read out of context, such a passage may indeed be perceived as a metaphor in which Greene is understood in terms of Scipio. However, this juxtaposition, I argue, ought to be read typologically, in which the antetype, Scipio, served as parallel and model that the type, Greene, fulfills. Typology, as opposed to metaphor or allegory, establishes a connection between two historical events or persons, the first of which signifies not only itself but also the second, while the second encompasses or fulfills the first. The author of this juxtaposition observed and described a relationship between what might otherwise appear to be unrelated entities. Scipio served as a discrete historical person who existed independently of his typical attributes, and his historical reality was not annulled but confirmed and fulfilled by a deeper meaning derived from the American Greene. Seen together, Scipio and Greene fortified, enhanced, and fulfilled each other's meaning. The similarity discerned in otherwise incongruent historical events bears witness to the singularity of the identity and purpose that permeates these two historical persons.[65] Scipio's and Greene's typological significance consisted in the intelligibility discovered in the relation between two events that made up a single performance in history.

Following the Intolerable Acts and the gathering of the Continental Congress in 1774, patriots began wholeheartedly to depict themselves as classical actors in what can be seen as a "Catonian moment" of classical self-recognition. Those rebelling Americans who organized their political world around typological hermeneutics constructed a network of interrelated events, an impressive tapestry in which contemporary occurrences seemed related to and intertwined with antiquity. Indeed, northern writers and orators took pains to portray the connections between the classical and American narratives, commonly, in accordance with typological exegesis, in which America surpassed and exceeded its classical precursors.

The battles of Lexington, Concord, and Bunker Hill accelerated the process of classical hero formation. The intensification of the classical language, manifested through utterances depicting America's "young Senates," "new Catos," "Brutii," and "Cassii" pointed not necessarily to a quest for national independence but, instead, to the historical meaning that might be ascribed to such independence. Once hostilities broke out, Americans showed a persistent tendency to perceive their campaigns, battles, and commanders in classical terms, as shown in chapter 1. War and military valor were a major component in most classical narratives, and the Roman Republic's irregular militias composed of arms-bearing citizens imprinted a lasting impression on eighteenth-century political sensibilities. For an embattled people like revolutionary Americans, especially during the bleak years of the prolonged war, the annals of virtuous, warlike republics were a fertile source of analogies, models, consolation, and hope. If Rome began as a minuscule city-state that ended up conquering most of the known world with its virtuous armies, America could also be depicted as a young republic that still had its promise to fulfill. The repeated losses, war weariness, lack of supplies, long winters, and inadequate commanders all took a heavy toll on the American farmer-soldiers and perpetuated a continuous feeling of crisis and despair. Understanding the American war in classical terms could make historical sense of the agonies of war and redeem the persistent feeling of inadequacy that the young United States suffered while confronting the most formidable of armies. The warlike classical allusions that came from north of the Mason-Dixon Line, however, did not merely perform a rhetorical role to produce a sense of purpose and boost morale. That classical language typologized the ongoing hostilities, soldiers, and commanders, collapsing the temporal distance between *figura* and fulfillment, Rome and America.

The early textual treatments of the Canadian campaign of 1776 indicate the development of typological sensibilities in a revolutionary context. Americans repeatedly described the futile expedition to conquer Quebec on New Year's Eve of 1776 in terms of Hannibal's invasion of Italy on his way to besiege Rome during the second Punic War (218–202 BC). At the beginning of that war, the Carthaginian leader pressed his army through the wintry passage of the Alps, losing more than half of his men and most of his war elephants to cold weather as he marched into Italy. Although Hannibal was able to imperil the city of Rome, he was eventually defeated because of his extended lines of supply and lack of political support back in Carthage. During his long stay on the Italian peninsula, however, Hannibal inflicted on the Romans some of their greatest defeats, including the brilliantly perceived and executed battle of Cane. To understand their undertakings in such epic terms appealed to Americans. They gladly found parallels between Hannibal's Italian campaign and the American incursion into Canada. These campaigns indeed shared two structural similarities: the wintry hike of both armies into the enemy's land, Hannibal's across the Alps and Benedict Arnold's through the Maine wilderness; and their ultimate failure, Hannibal's inability to conquer Rome and Arnold and Montgomery's defeat at Quebec's gate.

Much of the textual outpouring commemorating the Quebec battle outlined the events of late 1775 in parallel to Hannibal's War. William Smith's *An Oration in the Memory of General Montgomery,* delivered in front of the Continental Congress early in 1776, was steeped with classical allusions and references, especially to Rome, where "the praise of public virtue was wrought into the whole texture of Roman polity."[66] The occasion of the oration was the death of General Richard Montgomery, conqueror of Montreal, who had joined forces with Benedict Arnold's army and was killed during the futile attack on Quebec. Smith, in what would become a mainstay of the portrayals of this campaign, compared the bitter marches of Hannibal across the Alps and Benedict Arnold's march through Maine. That comparison, considered a great honor because of Hannibal's admired generalship, demonstrated that "even the march of Hannibal over the Alps, so much celebrated in history, allowing for the disparity of numbers, has nothing in it of superior merit, to the march of Arnold; and in many circumstances there is a most striking similitude."[67] Smith's interpretation conforms to the Auerbachian understanding of figural hermeneutics, in which "often vague similarities in the structure of events or in their attendant circumstances suffice to interpret in a certain way."[68] The two wintry hikes sufficed as a structural resemblance to read the Canadian campaign typologically, "allowing for the disparity in numbers" between Hannibal's massive army and the small American invasion force and indicating that Americans were aware of the potential dissonances in this historical comparison. Smith did not merely point to the similarities between the two exhausting winter hikes, however; he also compared the American execution favorably to the Carthaginian. Here we encounter a significant characteristic of this historical mode of interpretation: Patriots linked classical and American narratives, but they repeatedly judged the American incarnation as superior to the ancient.

If authors identified similarities in the structures of the ancient and contemporary campaigns, they also established a relationship between the two American commanders and the ancient protagonists. Barely two months after Montgomery fell, the *Virginia Gazette* commemorated him, recalling how, "When Cato fell, Rome mourn'd the fatal blow."[69] In the north, however, pamphleteers declared upon Montgomery's death that "no Roman or Spartan chief ever fell with greater glory," demonstrating a characteristic of typological interpretation by concluding how well Americans compared in their eyes to the ancients.[70] Another dialogue, delivered in New Haven, declared the American commanders of the campaign "heroic warriors, Roman souls enthron'd / In breasts of patriots; leaders like to those / Whom ancient Rome named 'Thunderbolts of War.'"[71] This writer typologized Montgomery and Arnold, described as the Scipio brothers, as the "thunderbolts of War" incarnated in American bodies. That dialogue further depicted the fallen Montgomery as "cover'd with glorious wounds. So fell this chief, That whom, a brave Rome could never boast."[72] This writer represented Montgomery as a realization and fulfillment of a Roman promise and as greater than the warriors of antiquity ever were.

Time and again, writers compared Benedict Arnold, the surviving commander of the Canadian disaster, to Hannibal, the greatest, if ultimately defeated, general of the Punic Wars. Some of those readings were typological. In a typological context, writers expected readers who came upon the figure of Hannibal to realize that the Carthaginian's military qualities suggested something about Arnold's martial skills. Writers repeatedly compared Arnold and his Maine hike to Hannibal's, as in *America Invincible,* where the poet depicted Arnold as "Amilcar's son [i.e., Hannibal, the son of the Carthage's king Amilcar]," who "with deathless rage / Against the Roman's furious conflicts wage" and portrayed his troops as the marching Carthaginian army: "With Cartaginian strength / Through woods and forests pass's Hisperia's length; who crossed the snowy alps, and try'd their fate / even thro' Campania to the Roman gate."[73] Such seamless blending of classical and American narratives and persons were elaborated to a considerable level of classical sophistication, which is evident in the counterfactual descriptions of Arnold's army, as if it were marching through Italy toward Rome.

"[Arnold's] march reminds me how that mighty chief/Of warlike Afric [Carthage], once renowned in arms, Fam'd HANNIBAL, led o'er the craggy Alps/His sturdy troops; struck terror into Rome, And flew her armies," mused an unknown author of a dialogue published in Connecticut in 1776.[74] "Reminded" of Hannibal's march to Italy, the author went on to describe the nature of the correlation between the ancients and moderns: "Those ancient heroes your's [America's] re-animate, Whose souls the same heroic ardor fires." Readers were supposed to understand the existence of a literal reincarnation of ancients in American actors, a connection established through sharing transcendental, timeless attributes. By conflating two real historical events, the author found a clear structural similarity between them. Discerning this correspondence, the dialogue suggested that Hannibal's crossing was a figural foretelling of Arnold's march. To complete the picture of an ancient revival in America, the author posed a perplexing question: "Doubt your brave leader, and his warlike hosts, Once cros'd the Alps; split seas of Roman blood; And made Rome's empire totter to its base?" The answer by now should be expected: "Our's excel in nobleness of soul; In sense of honour and humanity; In zeal for public more than private good."[75] Americans were, in short, better republicans than the paragons of classical republicanism. In these lines, then, we encounter more than mere comparisons between antique and modern histories and characters; the ancients were depicted as "re-animated," or fulfilled in America. Such notions culminated in the representation of Benedict Arnold in classical settings, and these counterfactual depictions of Americans—always concluding with favorable appraisals—became a mainstay among classical typologists.[76]

Hannibal, however popular a type of the Arnoldian antetype, was not the only *figura* employed to prefigure the American general. In the tragedy *The Death of General Montgomery, at the Siege of Quebec*, Montgomery's ghost describes Arnold's march and his army's suffering in classical terms, which diverge from the standard Hannibal trope: "A Sacrifice more rich . . . was never offer'd up . . . not even when Cato died at Utica, or many a Roman brave, with noble Brutus, on Pharsalia's plain."[77] Cato and Brutus both ultimately lost to Caesar, paying with their lives in a futile attempt to redeem the noble cause of liberty. Arnold's sacrifice, although he had not paid with his life, was portrayed as equal to these ultimate republican surrenders.

Although no scholar has ventured to conduct a systematic survey of Washington's classical representations, historians and biographers have recognized the extent to which George Washington, the most thoroughly classicized figure of his generation, was represented as an ancient hero.[78] A comprehensive study of the extensive classicization of Washington is out-side the scope of this study, as well. However, I will underscore how many of Washington's representations as a classical hero during the years of the war (Washington's classical representations were even more intense during the post-Revolution years) conformed to the logic of classical typology.

Washington's classical representations from 1775 to 1783 ranged through a large variety of classical heroes, from Cato, for republican firmness, to Fabius, for employing stalling tactics during the war; Scipio, for superb generalship; Cicero, as the "father of the country"; and Cincinnatus, for submitting military power to civil authority.[79] At times, Washington was represented as outshining all of his ancient types: "A Hannibal could cross the Alps at the head of a brave and determined army—a Scipio could de-fend Rome while his soldiers loved liberty—and a Caesar could conquer . . . but it was reserved to a Washington alone to conquer without these means, and to save a country," asserted "Theophilus" in the *New Hampshire Gazette* on March 24, 1778. One of the rare examples of classical typology originating in the south was tellingly concerned with Washington, whose stature as a native southerner as well as a larger-than-life commander was vital for the struggling union. A writer in the *Virginia Gazette* thus ad-dressed his readers: "Should any one among you require the force of ex-ample to animate you . . . let him turn his eyes to that bright luminary of war in whose character the conduct of Emilius, the coolness of Fabius, the intrepidity of an Hannibal, and the indefatigable ardour and military skill of Caesar, are united." The writer continued: "Let not the name of Brutus or Camillus be remembered whilst that of Washington is to be found in the annals of America. Great in the Cabinet as in war, he shines with un-rivalled splendor in every department of life."[80] By the end of the war, it was clear that the "second" had outdone his "firsts": Rome's boasted chiefs, who "proved the worst scourages of the human race" and who were "born to enslave, to ravage, and subdue . . . , return to nothing" when compared to Washington.[81]

The typological nature of the classical representations of Washington, which are sketched here only briefly (such representations are beyond counting), has gone largely unrecognized by historians. Even conspicuous typological expressions such as, "And what Timoleon was, thy Washington shall be," in which Timoleon, the classical type—a Greek statesman and general noted as "the scourge of tyrants"—prefigured Washington, the American incarnation, have not elicited analysis of the use and meaning of the classics in terms of typology.[82] However, northern patriots perceived the Revolution through classical typological structures of an ancient promise fulfilled by an American incarnation. To recognize fully the extent of figural perceptions of history during the Revolution, I will take a close look at one of the most fascinating and revealing typological texts of the era: Jonathan Mitchell Sewall's *Epilogue to Cato, Spoken at a Late Performance of That Tragedy.*

It has been known for a long time now that the classics, at least to a certain extent, were handed down to American colonists through the filter of British Whigs, a phenomenon that was part of a burgeoning "vernacular classicism" in late-eighteenth-century America.[83] The prominence of Cato the Younger—the Roman tribune who opposed Julius Caesar throughout his stormy path to power, who marched through the African desert to flee the dictator, and who shut himself up within the walls of Utica to commit suicide when the enemy was in range—throughout the Revolution is a case in point. Americans were acquainted with this symbol of republican martyrdom through three main sources, only one of them an original classic. Plutarch's *Lives,* which was immensely popular in the colonies, presented the figure of Cato as it came down in Western memory; John Trenchard and Thomas Gordon's series of oppositional tracts from the 1720s titled *Cato's Letters,* another tremendously popular text in the colonies, have further memorialized the image of the staunch republican through their choice of pseudonym; and Joseph Addison's tragedy *Cato,* which described Cato the Younger's last hours besieged in Utica by Julius Caesar, and his dilemma before choosing to commit suicide once the Roman republic was doomed, was arguably the most popular play in the colonies and was central to the dissemination of classical Roman semiotics in revolutionary America.[84]

Addison aimed his play at eighteenth-century audiences immersed in a public sphere defined by its polite sensibilities. As such, he intended the play both to delight and to instruct in the realms of manners and character building, without necessarily conveying political overtones.[85] However, scholars writing about eighteenth-century American political culture have widely acknowledged the influence of the image of Cato on radical Whigs.[86] The stern republican, faithful to his ruined republic until the bitter end, seemingly influenced many patriots through close knowledge with Addison's play. As Fredrick Litto pointed out in a seminal essay from the 1960s, that tragic drama was transformed during the Revolution from a piece of polite entertainment into a patriotic "instrument of political propaganda."[87] Both Nathan Hale before his execution and Patrick Henry in his "Liberty or Death" oration appealed to their audiences through rephrasing the immortal lines of Addison's ancient hero.[88] Washington's lifelong intimacy with Cato, and especially the staging of Addison's play in the dire winter of 1777 at Valley Forge, is a well-known instance of the influence exerted by the image of the belligerent Cato on Americans amid their own civil war.[89]

Jonathan Sewall's *A New Epilogue to Cato, Spoken at a Late Performance of That Tragedy* was first performed and published in 1778 together with the play to which it served as a concluding section. The literary historian John Shields speculates that this American *Epilogue* was performed many times during the Revolution, possibly even for Washington and his men at Valley Forge.[90] Sewall, a lawyer and occasional poet (not to be confused with the loyalist Jonathan Sewall, his great-uncle), became well known as a Revolutionary War versifier. His *Epilogue* replaced the older British ending written by Dr. Garths in four out of five printings of *Cato* in America between 1778 and 1793. Sewall obviously intended to Americanize the timeless Addisonian allegory. However, although scholars have had fleeting interest in the *Epilogue*, they have tended to overlook the importance of the American *Epilogue* to the naturalization of the British play and thus have not extracted its full meaning beyond Washington's image in the text.[91] The *Epilogue*, however, is evidently not about Washington, as large as the general might loom in the text. By merely appealing to Washington's figure, we not only overlook the *Epilogue*'s richness, but also the significance of the classics in forming a revolutionary discourse of historical time. Thus, although the popularity of *Cato* in eighteenth-century America has been universally acknowledged, Sewall's *Epilogue,* the most significant text in the acculturation of that tragedy, has been narrowly read, and thus misread, if read at all.

In the *Epilogue,* Sewall presented a Manichean worldview in which he contrasted "heroic fortitude" and "patriotic truth" with "tyrannic rage" and "boundless ambition" in a cosmic battle that "mark'd all periods and all climes." It is a specific, American, climate that preoccupied the *Epilogue,* however. During the Revolution, Britannia occupied the role of the wicked, while "what now gleams with dawning ray, at home,/ Once blaz'd ... at ROME."[92] Sewall thus identified the protagonists of the *Epilogue* and established the link between America and Rome. Employing the trope of a ray, which once blazed in Rome and currently dawned in America, Sewall meant to convey a metaphysical bond that tied the histories of the two polities together. Like the Roman senate, the American "senate," the Continental Congress (the "aristocratic" branch of its successor legislature, soon to be significantly named the U.S. Senate), had armed a "virtuous few" to fight the "British Caesar." America has found a worthy candidate to reenact the Catonic role in the face of a British Caesar: "for a CATO" she has armed "a WASHINGTON." The identification of the two leading antagonists marked the beginning of an elaborate effort to assign Roman signifiers, all characters from Addison's play, to contemporary American figures.

While Sewall represented Washington as a Cato and the British monarch as a Caesar, he portrayed William Howe, the British general, as the cunning Decius, one of Caesar's cronies. On America's side, "in Franklin and in generous DEAN shine forth/ Mild Lucius' wisdom, and young Portius' worth." He assigned Marcus, Cato's son, to another American general, as his image "blazes forth in [John] SULLIVAN!" In General Nathaniel "Greene ... we see ... Lucius, Juba, Cato, shine." The list, however, went beyond the *dramatis personae,* extending to Roman heroes who did not take part in the play: to Joseph Warren, the fallen hero of Bunker Hill, who "like Pompey ... fell in martial pride," as well as to the "great MONTGOMERY [who] like Scipio dy'd!"; to Benedict Arnold, repeating a commonplace type discussed earlier, who crossed "Canadia's Alpnie hills—a second

HANNIBAL!"; and finally, to the traitor Benjamin Church and the Roman traitor Sempronius, whom Sewall linked only to jointly condemn them.

The matchmaking list is extraordinary and shows the length to which Americans could go to explain their revolution as a reenactment of a classical spectacle.[93] To understand the nature of the relation between the classical "original" and American "representation," one must, however, pay close attention to the ways in which the connection between signifier and signified, Roman and American, were established. The *Epilogue* asserted the relations between ancients and moderns in a string of prepositions, adjectives, verbs, and indefinite articles: "for a Cato," America has "arm'd a Washington"; "in [General Nathaniel] Greene . . . we see . . . Lucius, Juba, Cato, shine in thee"; "Montgomery like Scipio died"; "Arnold . . . a second Hannibal"; "Marcus blazes forth in Sullivan,"; and "We've had our Decius." Naming Americans the "second," "western," or "like" classical heroes was a trademark of classical typological thinking, conveying the notion of incarnation and latter-day fulfillment. While the revolutionaries were not actual Romans, they were meant to reanimate and reenact those ancients on an American stage. By now, the pattern of typical thinking, where Roman history was "the original" through which the annals of the American "picture" could be read, should be clear.

Sewall, however, went beyond matching ancient and modern pairs in constructing a portrait of a classicized, prefigured America. He further entangled the ancient and modern narratives by importing his American heroes into the streets of beleaguered Utica. "When Rome received her last decisive blow,/Had'st Thou, immortal [General Horatio] GATES! Been Caesar's foe," Sewall lamented; "thy superior conduct [would have] won the day!" Sewall continued to fantasize other heroes' probable achievements in the ancient world: "In Caesar's days, had such a daring mind [as Benedict Arnold's], with Washington's serenity been join'd,/The tyrant had bled—great Cato liv'd,/And Rome, in all her majesty, surviv'd!" We have already met such counterfactual language in attempts to wed American and Roman histories and to emphasize the superiority of the American fulfillment over the Roman types. Americans, in short, came to be seen as better than the Roman originals. If only they had been allowed to conduct the battles of antiquity, "FREEDOM had triumph'd on Pharasalian ground," where Caesar has won his conclusive battle, "Nor SARATOGA's heights been more renown'd!" Sewall even read the Italian expanse of antiquity figuratively by imprinting classical geography onto the North American continent: "See persevering ARNOLD proudly scale / Canadia's Alpine hills." In Sewall's depiction Arnold fully played out his role as "a second Hannibal" as he crossed the "American Alps."

By drawing a laminated map of American champions overlaying Romans, Sewall provided a key to understanding *Cato* as an American play. Such a legend, which affixed to each classical persona an American protagonist, developed the complexity of typological readings of America to an extraordinary degree. Sewall fused classical and American narratives by applying the play point by point to American actuality. Such an attitude demonstrates the nature of the typological mindset that vigorously searched for classical equivalents and parallels in American narratives. Eighteenth-century audiences, possessing more attuned typological sensibilities than modern readers, would have been familiar with the hermeneutic mode of this *Epilogue* that deciphered American reality as a recurring classical enactment. As in Mercy Warren's revolutionary play *The Adulateur,* which described revolutionary Boston in classical terms, American admirers of Addison could use Sewall's *Epilogue* to imagine their experiences and leaders operating in a classical-like drama, deriving the meaning and historical significance of their actions from the struggles of Rome of the first century BC.[94] Sewall's *Epilogue* transformed *Cato* from a timeless allegory into a typological plot structured along the lines of a Roman promise and an American fulfillment.

Remarkably, as opposed to the tragedy that it scrupulously retold in American terms, Sewall's *Epilogue* ended optimistically. "No pent-up Utica contracts your Pow'rs," Sewall encouraged Americans, "but the whole boundless continent is Yours." In this couplet, which marked the most lasting legacy of the *Epilogue* as the *New World* newspaper adopted it as the motto in 1840, Sewall abandoned his strict attachment to Addison's play, as well as to the historical plot. If Cato typified Washington, Caesar prefigured George III, and the rest of the play's figures foreshadowed modern actors, America was no Utica, which Addison portrayed in its last days before it fell; nor was it Rome that succumbed to Caesar. The *Epilogue* portrayed America as it was understood through the classical typology: as a fulfillment, an improved incarnation of classical polities.

Classical typology, like its Christian counterpart, involved a belief in the fulfillment of the type, of America surpassing its ancient prefiguration.

Only when the War of Independence was over did Americans begin to contemplate averting decline by replacing time with space, by expanding westward to "the whole boundless continent" as a way to conserve America's yeomen agrarian virtue and to defeat *fortuna*. This solution would ripen only during Thomas Jefferson's presidency.[95] During the Revolution, decline was forestalled through notions of typological fulfillment. Belief in the American fulfillment of a Roman promise gone askew was omnipresent and may explain the ease with which northerners co-opted a classical history that led to corruption and decline as their *exemplum*. Southerners, nevertheless, could merely be content with the present direction of the cycle, with America's present youth. Youth, however, as it was widely known, would eventually succumb to old age and decline.

The classical typology practiced throughout the war years was a dynamic framework of exegesis, an interpretive mode through which revolutionary Americans expressed a particular attitude toward time and history. This attitude prescribed that Americans and America (they usually praised the nation as a whole, not their respective states or regions) were perfections of classical models, however glorious the ancients might be deemed. Such notions are evident in cases in which they deemed that virtue was quantitatively more abundant in America ("each one is a Cato"), or that America was qualitatively endowed. Thus, if "most nations have been favoured with some patriotic deliverer: the Israelites had their Moses; Rome had her Camillus; Greece her Leonidas . . . these illustrious heroes . . . did not, like Washington, form or establish empires, which will be the refuge or asylum of liberty."[96] The structure of classical typology, like its scriptural counterpart, promised that the American latter-day manifestation would prove superior to its classical precursor. Hence, expressions that asserted America's superiority were not merely an apologia on behalf of a fragile polity. Such statements expressed a confidence prevalent in the north in the American republic's promise. That confidence was founded in the structure of an interpretation of history that ensured that America would surpass the classical "original."

Revolutionary Americans expressed through classical history distinct views regarding the relevance of the past to the present, as well as of the ways in which the past and the present affected their expectations of the future.

The different dialects revolutionaries employed in the north and the south demonstrate, however, that they held contrasting attitudes toward historical time. Indeed, two distinct conflicting historical consciousnesses emerged from the respective geographies. In the southern colonies-turned-states (and occasionally in the middle colonies), the repeated analysis of the theme of imperial decline, especially that of the Roman fall, and the virtual absence of the rhetorical practice of classical typology, points toward a prevailing conventional republican understanding of time. In such a scheme, time was corruptive and baneful to political, as it was to organic, entities. Within this conceptual framework, the forming American republic was experiencing its phase of youth and vigor, just arriving at a golden age of—usually fleeting—prosperity. While southerners saw the United States as a member of a heroic lineage of great polities, the scheme prescribed a complicity with the eventual decline of America, like that of all past and future political bodies. Understanding the past could perhaps ameliorate— possibly even postpone—decline. Yet since southerners understood America as a historical artifact subject to historical laws, they could not, and did not, deny that America eventually would have to fall.

This strain of American historical consciousness, anxious and pessimistic, was anything but innovative. A cyclical understanding of time perpetuated as a well-established tradition of thought and was shared by an Atlantic community of Anglophone commonwealth men. As J. G. A. Pocock points out, historiographical conventions conditioned people in the early modern period to understand decline as commencing from the zenith of power, followed by revolutions that were rotations of fortune's wheel.[97] Elaborating a republican cyclical view of time, southerners lacked the vocabulary—or, perhaps, the intellectual flexibility—to exempt themselves from the invariable hand of corrupting time; they had to acknowledge that America eventually would decline.

Manifesting distinctiveness from the early modern Anglo-American norm in so many other spheres, New Englanders' attitude toward time was unique, as well.[98] Earlier in this chapter, we saw how northerners, especially New Englanders, throughout the Revolution elaborated a classical typology that expressed their distinct rhetoric of history; how that typology invested their actions with meaning and significance; and how it revealed a particular understanding of historical time. Classical typology provided a structure through which patriots could attach grand historical

significance to their revolutionary deeds. That framework oriented northern patriots to articulate a theory of history in which the classics were
believed to typify, foreshadow, and "pre-rehearse" the young American republic and its heroes; Americans, in this scheme, were superior reincarnations of the ancients.[99] This typology entailed a distinct rhetorical view of
the past and represented an attempt to articulate particular relationships
within history—namely, the affinities across time of the republics of antiquity and the United States.

Classical typology, operating in a regional culture dominated by reformed Protestantism, provided an interpretive framework to correlate the
histories of Greece and Rome to the revolutionary present. Through that
framework the future would often bear specific characteristics. Northerners (especially New Englanders) embedded in typological thinking, unlike their southern counterparts, demonstrated in their attitude toward the
future anticipation, optimism, and millennialism. Philip Freneau proph-
esied as early as 1772 that America's Alexanders and Pompeys were kept
"in the womb of time yet dormant lye/waiting the joyful hour for life
and light."[100] A few years later, as war and independence were imminent,
at least some of his compatriots believed that this prophecy was on the
verge of being fulfilled. Consequently, they began to articulate a millennial
view of America painted in classical colors. The south had no counterpart
of similar visions to provide. Southerners did not represent themselves as
reincarnations of past heroes; rather, they understood a shared common
fate to bind them with the republics of antiquity. Such a perceived shared
fortune consisted of experiencing a—still unfulfilled—rise to republican
glory, which would be followed by inevitable decline. Typological exegesis, by contrast, induced northern patriots to expect nothing less than to
surpass their ancient predecessors and to succeed where those predecessors had failed—that is, they expressed time and again their expectation to
escape history and time.

Their self-representation as reincarnations of a classical promise painted
northern millennial predictions in classical colors; the millennium, conceived either as a worldly golden age or as a metaphysical reign of Christ,
was often portrayed with reference to and in terms of classical empires and
republics. An anonymous Bostonian poet writing as hostilities were about
to commence in 1775 provided a useful example of how northerners tied
together the ends of classical history and an American millennial future:

"Caesar, Sylla, or old Phillip's son [Alexander; all ancient tyrants] plunderers of man I'll greatly scorn"; instead, he looked to the future, to "sing of nations, Empires, yet unborn," and

> view the glories of the op'ning morn!
> when justice holds her scepter o'er the land
> and rescues freedom from the tyrant's hand
> when patriot states in laurel crowns arise
> and only merit bears away the prize.

This millennial picture conveying an empire (or, rather, empires, alluding to the separate colonies) crowned in classical laurels continued: "Commerce revives, and arts and science rise," until finally "this common Wealth [America] arise," as a "bright Millennial [light] greets my eyes."[101] While the poet saw the classical past of empires that fell prey to violent usurpers as inherent in the explanation of the present situation of America, he suggested that the emerging American "empire" would break out of this nefarious cycle. The northern view of America's future was from its inception "exceptional."[102]

Similarly, John Trumbull's *An Elegy on the Times* reiterated the typological conventions that Boston reanimated Rome and that Americans were braver than the Spartans, more virtuous than the Romans, more judicious than the Greeks, and the noblest of them all. They were, in short, perfections of classical types. Trumbull went on optimistically to ask his readers to "attend the flight of days, view the bold deeds, that wait the dawning age, where time's strong arm, that rules the mighty maze, shifts the proud actors on this earthly stage!" Here, human actors were feeble, unable to resist time, just like in the cyclical view. However, while Britain "trembles on the verge of death," unable to escape the downturn of the cycle, Trumbull attempted to "look thro' time, and with extended eye, pierce the deep veil of fate's obscure domain." What the poet found in America's future defied classical decline: "Beneath the cloud of days" are "throng'd cities . . . tow'ring armies," a seagoing empire that rules the "dread dominons of the wave." The "virgin-clime unfolds her brighter charms, and gives her beauties to thy fond embrace!" In exulting, biblical language, Trumbull described how America would "rise her vallies in perpetual prime, and ages blest of undisturb'd renown, beam their mild radiance o'er th' imperial clime." He expected no decline in the coming "flight of days" and "dawning age" of the Western fulfillment and perfection of antiquity's republics; only millennial, history-defying prospects awaited America.[103]

"A Dialogue on the Success of Our Arms, and the Rising Glory of America" further elaborated this classical–millennial fusion. This essay, too, demonstrated a remarkable classical typology in which Americans exceeded the ancients in "nobleness of souls"; unlike in Rome, however, in America there were "no civil broils, dissentions, party rage, no strife or faction disunite or rend that concord, compact, unity of soul . . . no envious Hanno seeks a rival's fall [a jealousy that supposedly cost Carthage in her loss of the Punic Wars]; or dare's oppose his country's greatest good . . . no haughty Caesar aims at regal sway, or arms against his country's sacred rights." Defying our contemporary view of revolutionary America as experiencing a divisive and brutal civil war, this poet depicted America as a Rome without the latter's faults, such as internal schism and strife. The young republic seemed to have learned from the experience of classical civil strife; "madmen" such as Caesar and the other feuding warlords who had brought the demise of the Roman republic "make us wise. Their vices, errors, and tyrannic schemes, such signal ruin to their countries brought, that we are warned, and stand upon our guard." Still, danger loomed: Americans must "withstand the shocks, and devastations of devouring time. Where now is Greece? Where Athens once extol'd; the nurse of science, and the source of arts? Can Rome be found; she is now an empty name . . . [Even Rome, who] was once the mistress of the earth . . . who rode triumphant, o'er the spacious main, and bow'd the nations to her haughty will . . . her grandeur, pow'r and wealth, are lost, are buried in the gulf of time."[104]

Time was admittedly detrimental and could subdue even the greatest of the ancient empires. America, however, operated under different historical rules. "Here on this land these orbs begin to shine, with brighter beams, and vivifying rays, here now an empire rises to our view; which far in pow'r and glory, will exceed the mighty empire of the eastern world." America, in short, was about to surpass Rome. What was the origin of such utter assurance in America's ability to defy *fortuna* and decay? "On what sure grounds you build your sanguine hopes? how can you now, with confidence assert, what future ages will revolve to view, which now are buried in the womb of fate?" It was providence that assured the young republic's victory in its quarrel with time. "Here, here the golden era will commence;

the age long promis'd to the church on earth, the blest millennium." This millennial prophecy, which was supported by a classically inspired view of America, was literal: "Here will Jesus fix his sapphire throne, his golden scepter sway, and rule the nations with the wand of peace." The American "grand republic," surpassing the republics of old, "shall sway her way, from sea to sea . . . give law to Europe, rule the swelling main; 'till she, illumin'd by a light divine, first view the dawning of these glorious days, of pure religion, liberty and peace . . . . rise mighty empire, rise on western shores, for ages far surpass all former empires, and unrival'd shine in virtue, freedom, grandeur, wealth and pow'r." Indeed, the poet reassured his readers that in the American empire, a polity that was perfecting a classical promise, "Messiah Reigns."[105]

After eight long years of fighting, and only two months before the formal conclusion of the war in September 1783, John Warren (the younger brother of the toga-wearing Joseph Warren, who will be discussed in chapter 4) provided yet another remarkable example of the way in which northerners amalgamated traditional republican notions of time with millennial logic. Warren expressed in his July 4 oration in Boston, delivered at a time when cynicism and doubt were much more prevalent than during the early years of the Revolution, notions that have been associated mostly with revolutionary southern writers. Warren, like southerners examined earlier in this chapter, referred to Polybius's "incontrovertible axiom, that every State must decline . . . in proportion as she recedes from the principles on which she was founded." Such decline would occur, according to the civic-humanistic paradigm, when a state's citizens lost their virtue, "the true principle of republican governments."[106] Warren continued to analyze at length the reasons for the rise and decline of "those famed Republics of antiquity, which later ages have considered as the models of political perfection," from Sparta and Thebes to Carthage and Rome. When he considered the reasons for those polities' horrific "level[ing] with the dust," Warren provided a strikingly similar account to his southern counterparts: The ancient republics lost their public virtue and subsequently collapsed by means of a "most shameful prostitution of wealth to the purposes of bribery and corruption." Indeed, so "southern" was Warren's account that he made use of fatalist language, concluding that corrupted conditions "must produce" the destruction of even the most venerable states.[107]

Yet Warren was no southerner. History may have involved "incon-

trovertible" Polybian laws, but America, he argued, could escape those de-
crees. Americans, he asserted, "may learn wisdom by the misfortunes of others . . . by tracing the operations of those causes which have proved ruinous
to so many states and kingdoms." Hence, they could "escape the rocks and
quicksands on which [the ancients] have been shipwreck'd." Indeed, Americans would have to work extremely hard to defy history by "retain[ing] the
spirit which gave our Independence birth," by "sacrifice[ing] our dearest
interests in our country's cause," and by "enjoin[ing] upon our children a
solemn veneration for her laws, as next to adoration of their God." Once
this "glorious work is done," Warren told his audience, America would
evade the republican snare of corruption and ruin. At this point, Warren's
language becomes unmistakably millennial. Even "the remotest corners of
the globe [would] resound with acclamations of applause, 'till even the
inanimate creation shall join the concert . . . for heaven has opened a new
asylum" in America. Warren resorted to visionary scenes, unmistakenly
derived from Luke 2:14, in which seraphs prophesize the birth of Christ:
"Rejoice ye inhabitants of this chosen land! Let songs of joy dwell long
upon your thankful tongues . . . 'till angels catch the sound, and echo back,
Peace and good will to men." Warren finally predicted that the American
republic, guided by the heavens and unnaturally retaining its virtue, would
succeed where no polity had done so before. America would thrive "'till
stars and suns shall shine no more, and all the kingdoms of this globe shall
vanish like a scroll."[108] America, a republic carved along the contours of
the "famed Republics of antiquity," would not suffer from their malaise but
would instead escape history and witness the end of time. To northerners
such as Warren, America was not just a Rome: It was a Rome upon a hill.

Classical antiquity was a major intellectual arena for formulating the perceived significance and meaning patriots attached to their Revolution. Yet
two opposing attitudes toward time and history emerged from the classical discourse when the break from Britain was imminent: While in the
south—and occasionally in the middle colonies-turned-states—time was
perceived, particularly among the landed gentry, as a cycle through which
political societies revolved, repeatedly spawning and perishing, northerners
contemplated time through a classical framework of typological exegesis.
Thus, to paraphrase Sherlock Holmes, we have encountered not one but

two dogs that did not bark: Not only did southerners and northerners articulate opposing attitudes toward time, but neither cultivated or made use of the other's paradigms. Southerners rarely, if ever, engaged in classical typology, while northerners did not elaborate cyclical schemes of history. In the following chapters, we will examine the ways in which these contrasting attitudes toward time played out in different contexts and how they were reformulated and reconfigured in changing historical circumstances.

These opposing temporal understandings reveal how inadequately "revolutionary consciousness" has been described in modern scholarship. For a variety of ideological, methodological, and political reasons, New England tends to dominate the historiography of the American Revolution.[109] The result of this tendency was the production of works that, while attempting to examine American revolutionary consciousness, have actually focused on the New England mind writ large. One obvious example will suffice to demonstrate how scholars have discarded southern patterns of thought in attempts to convey the Revolution as an intellectually coherent movement, and how this chapter attempts to provide a corrective to such tendencies. In *Visionary Republic,* an admirable monograph in many respects, Ruth Bloch argues for the significance of millennial ideas to the formation of revolutionary consciousness. Although she refers repeatedly to "American patriots," Bloch's argument seems to deserve merit only when applied to New England and, to a certain extent, to the middle colonies. Her argument has little explanatory power when applied to the southern colonies, because the majority of her evidence originates in New England and virtually none originates in the south. Bloch claims that "an animating ideal of the future was necessary to propel American colonists to make their decisive break from tradition."[110] However, southerners—at least, as far as the classics-related discourse is considered—depicted a tenuous, if not outright pessimistic, future as they worked within an intellectual tradition in which the only certainty was that of a looming decline and fall. According to the findings in this chapter, which have been derived from an evidentiary base restricted to the classical discourse, southern revolutionaries express virtually none of the northern exegetical practices and millennial impulses. This discrepancy may support claims to a tentative long-term influence of the Great Awakening in the south and demonstrates that Americans' understandings of their revolution were by no means monolithically millennial, as one may assume from reading *Visionary Republic.*[111] The American

Revolution, this chapter demonstrates, accommodated more than one "revolutionary consciousness."

Recognizing these two distinct historical sensibilities, manifested through the respective classical idioms practiced in the north and in the south, has important implications to understanding American national culture as it evolved in the Early Republic and the antebellum decades. The fact that at its moment of inception America had two governing concepts of history and time may, for example, alter our understanding of the origins of "the burden of Southern history." C. Vann Woodward has argued that this "burden"—namely, the South's perceived "un-Americanness," its economic flagging, its lack of a myth of success, its disengagement from the belief in human perfectibility, and its lack of the notion that problems have attainable solutions—originated in the region's real and alleged "frustration, failure, and defeat . . . in the provinces of economic, social and political life."[112] Woodward attributed the South's "basically pessimistic . . . social outlook and . . . moral philosophy," to its collective experience with the institution of slavery and defeat in the Civil War. The findings of this chapter, the identification a pathetic strain of southern historical interpretation already present in the wake of the Revolution, suggests that this "burden" may have had roots that preceded the nineteenth century. Upper-class southerners may have been contemplating their future within a pessimistic framework as early as the Revolution, preparing the intellectual groundwork for a burdened history that would mature during the coming decades in a variety of intellectual arenas.[113] These early origins, of course, had nothing to do with slavery being under northern siege and the military defeat the region would experience a century later.

Was revolutionary America engaged in an elaborate discourse about the similarities and parallels between its own and ancient histories, carrying out the "last great pre-modern efflorescence" of the Renaissance? Or was it instead forward-looking and thus "liberal"?[114] The answer may be a matter of geography. As viewed from the south, the classical language supports pre-modern notions of time and history. America was rising in a perpetual cycle that had degraded the great empires of the past, including Britain. However, when we turn our attention to the north, we realize that republicans broke there with cyclical understandings of history and imported biblical exegesis as a means to correlate past and present republics. It was, as we have seen, New England that diverged from standard republican notions with its millennial and exceptional impulses toward the understanding of the inapplicability of historical laws to America. Hence, both Pocockian republicanism, an antique-oriented and anxious doctrine, and Paul Rahe's modernity-embracing republicanism that spawned during the crises of the seventeenth century, seem to have correspondence in America.[115]

Typological hermeneutics, which allowed northern patriots time and again to express the belief that they were finer incarnations of the classics, reflected notions that were compatible with, and akin to, "progress," with its characteristic confidence in improvement. Thus, northerners manifested during the Revolution proto-progressive notions that were poised to conquer the American intellectual stage of the nineteenth century by spreading the north's governing narratives and worldviews to the entire nation by means of its intellectual institutions.[116] In this process, cyclical understandings of history were relegated to the back of the American intellectual discourse.

Nonetheless, as Dorothy Ross points out, "progress" did not automatically translate to historicism.[117] To the contrary, practitioners of classical typology seem to have rejected understandings of history as self-contained and self-explanatory. As Erich Auerbach has noted, "In the figural interpretation the [historical] fact is subordinated to an interpretation which is fully secured to begin with."[118] In other words, historical contingency and indeterminacy were regulated by the practice of classical typology, which drew its interpretation from a strict pattern of promise and fulfillment.[119] Consequently, a commitment to viewing history as anticipating the present as well as the future did not accommodate the development of perceptions of historical change. It would be hard to understand history through a typological lens as a succession of singular and discrete events. Classical discourse—in both its northern and its southern modes—thus represented America in teleological terms, either of "realization" and "fulfillment" or of rise and fall. Under these circumstances, classical discoursers would look constantly backward in time for models, parallels, and meaning. American understandings of history as self-contained and self-explanatory would develop later than in Europe, when they would develop at all.

4

TAKING THE TOGA

American Patriots
Performing Antiquity

O N THE MORNING OF March 6, 1775, according to *Rivington's Gazette*, Joseph Warren burst into Boston's swarming Old South Church dressed in a Ciceronian toga to deliver the fifth annual oration to commemorate the Boston Massacre. Even in a period of extraordinary obsession with Roman antiquity, this episode was remarkable. Only a few years later, toward the conclusion of the War of Independence, however, Americans had become accustomed to representing themselves as heroic Romans in ancient civic regalia. Indeed, in August 1782 Alexander Hamilton could effortlessly appeal to his friend John Laurens to quit his sword, "put on the toga," and "come to congress."[1] This chapter will focus on incidents in which patriots acted out, or were perceived as performing, revolutionary roles while dressed in borrowed, albeit frequently metaphorical, togas. These episodes underscore the remarkable performative potential of the classical discourse during the critical months leading to independence. However, these performances provide further insights into the patriots' historical imagination and their attitudes toward time: William Pitt, Earl of Chatham, who defended America in the British Parliament and was consequently represented as a Roman senator in a toga; Joseph Warren, who delivered the fifth Boston Massacre oration allegedly dressed in a

Ciceronian toga; Mercy Warren's neo-Roman dramas, which resurrected the revered Romans of the republican pantheon in the streets of Boston to lead the Revolution; and, finally, Patrick Henry, deriving the concluding line of his celebrated speech to the Virginia Convention of March 1775, "Give me liberty or give me death," from Addison's *Cato,* and subsequently imagined as a Cato preaching to the Roman senate.

The toga, a billowing cloth wrapped around the male body, was the principal garment of a freeborn Roman citizen. A single piece of material of irregular form—long, broad, and flowing, without sleeves or armholes, and covering most of the body—the toga provided a stark contrast to late-eighteenth-century fashion. As opposed to the customary stiff, heavy woolen breeches and waistcoats that embodied sartorial politeness, the toga stood for ancient virtue, freedom, and the lack of artifice by merit of its flowing cloth and historical resonance. The togas considered in this chapter, both material and metaphorical, will deepen our understanding of the various ways in which patriots articulated through classical performances a multiplicity of attitudes toward historical time. We will see how patriots transcended the textual confinement of the classical discourse by performing embodied Roman spectacles or by producing texts and representations that were intended to promote classical performances or the imagination thereof.[2] By looking closely at such revolutionary classical performances, we will analyze the rhetorical strategies through which such performances attempted to affect spectators—or, alternatively, we will consider spectators' reasons for, and the consequences of, describing contemporary performances in deeply classicized terms.[3] Thus, we shall deepen our understanding of the historical imagination that animated American patriots, and especially of the nature of the intense and complex relationship they perceived between antiquity and revolutionary America.

The classical performances that this chapter follows will reinforce, but also nuance, conceptions of the patriots' understanding of time as a negotiated, meaningful medium that enabled revolutionaries to conflate, merge, and juxtapose their contemporaneity with the ancient annals. These performances will bring to the fore additional dimensions of the revolutionaries' attitudes toward time and will reveal the extent to which perceptions of historical time in the years and months leading to the War of Independence could be elastic and fluid. By negotiating and perceiving time as a pliable medium, patriots could enact and make sense of representations that suggested a union of Roman and American annals. Hence, by adding to the varieties of the patriots' temporal experience, this chapter intends to provide a richer understanding of the classical imagination and attitudes toward history and its meaning that underlay the "Spirit of '76." Seen through these performances, that revolutionary spirit will appear not like a world created anew but, rather, as a reenactment of millennia-old republican narratives in which the American actors were clad—or, rather, imagined—in togas.

As soon as the imperial contention broke out in 1765, but before the final escalation of those tensions in the mid-1770s and before the fashioning of an independent classical American persona, Americans could still glorify Englishmen with classical imagery and represent them as Roman heroes. Such language was naturally preserved for those who befriended the colonial position. Indeed, the American representations of William Pitt as a Roman senator, pleading for America before the British "senate," and the reproduction of his image dressed in a toga provide a useful starting point for exploring classical performances in revolutionary America. Colonials chose to represent William Pitt, who stood by America during the Stamp Act, as an illustrious Roman orator. Thomas Hopkinson, for example, described Pitt in the aftermath of the Stamp Act crisis preaching to "the British senate," better known then and today as Parliament, as a Roman senator demonstrating "a Cato's firmness and a Tully's Zeal, And every Worth that grac's the Roman sires."[4]

Hopkinson was not the only American portraying Pitt as a Roman hero in the wake of the Stamp Act. The gentlemen of Westmoreland County, Virginia, commissioned Charles Wilson Peale to paint a portrait of "the great commoner" and subsequently created a remarkable likeness that was sent across the Atlantic to Richard Henry Lee late in 1768. The mezzotint engraving depicted Pitt "in a Consular Habit" dressed not in British aristocratic fashion but, rather, in full Roman attire, which included a toga, a Roman tunic, and Roman sandals. The classicized earl, which at least one modern scholar believes was meant to represent Caesar's assassin Marcus Junius Brutus and thus symbolize American resistance to British tyranny, was situated in a heavily emblematic setting surrounded by republican symbols.[5] There is little need to ponder the meanings of those symbols, however, because Peale published a broadside explanation that interpreted his painting's allegorical references.[6] The classical aspects of the allegorical setting consisted of a Roman column in front of which Pitt stood. Beside him stood a classical pedestal on top of which rested a "civic crown." Pitt was depicted pointing at a figure of liberty, holding a *pilleus* and a Phrygian cap, a bonnet worn during antiquity by former slaves who had been emancipated by their master and whose descendants were therefore considered citizens of the Roman Empire. The cap became a symbol of liberty from antiquity to revolutionary Boston. Peale scattered other non-classical republican symbols in the background, such as a copy of the Magna Carta and an altar on which sat busts of Hampden and Sidney. (A banner hanging between them carried the Latin inscription "Sanctus Amor Patriae Dat Animum," or "Holy love of the fatherland gives the spirit.") The most striking feature of the picture, no doubt, was Pitt's outfit. Standing in an oratorical position—or, rather, "in a Consular Habit"—Pitt was wearing full Roman dress.

Remarkably, when Josiah Quincy described Pitt a decade after Peale drew him, it may have seemed as if he had described Peale's painting. Quincy's description was written during the epistemological transition that took place in the years immediately preceding independence, in a context that had become more radicalized since Peale had represented Pitt as a Roman. Quincy, who traveled to the British Isles to present America's case, watched Pitt denouncing imperial policy toward America in Parliament. Quincy wrote that Pitt rose "like Marcellus," the Roman war hero who defeated Hannibal and saved Rome from Carthaginian rage, to denounce Britain's conduct in America. To Quincy Pitt seemed "like an old Roman senator, rising with the dignity of age, yet speaking with the fire of youth. The illustrious sage stretched forth his hand with the decent solemnity of Paul, and rising with his subject, he smote his breast with the energy and grace of Demosthenes."[7] Quincy produced an elaborate and rich depiction in which he classicized Pitt's appearance and explained his character in ancient terms, situating Pitt in a classical context and conflating him with three classical-age figures. Like Peale had done a decade earlier through a different medium, Quincy described an imaginative scene that hurled the

Fig. 1. *William Pitt*, Charles Willson Peale, 1768, oil on canvas. (Courtesy of the Maryland State Archives)

English statesman back in time and depicted his performance as a classical spectacle. If Quincy had been an artist, his Pitt no doubt would have been clad in a toga.

The mid-1770s, which witnessed the enactment of the Intolerable Acts, the convention of the Continental Congress, and the commencement of hostilities, were crucial for the colonies' eventual rise to independence. Those years were also the last in which it was still a practical convention to identify an Englishman, such as Pitt, as a classical hero; in fact, it is very hard to find such instance after Quincy's description of Pitt in 1775. Patriot Americans in the independent and embattled United States soon abandoned the classical glorification of Englishmen. After independence, they depicted only American protagonists, such as Joseph Warren, as Romans.

On March 6, 1775, at Boston's Old South Church, Joseph Warren delivered the annual commemoration oration of the incident impressed on American collective memory as the Boston Massacre. During the event that Warren's oration commemorated, British soldiers shot and killed five Bostonians. The massacre was probably not the result of murderous intentions of the British sentries, as Americans claimed, or of an American plot, as some English charged.[8] The traditional Whig fear of standing armies, combined with the ominous ratio of four thousand armed Redcoats to fifteen thousand Bostonians, led to the fateful clash, almost immediately named by the town's Whig leadership a "Massacre," which in the imminent revolutionary years became an important icon in the Whig vocabulary. The Boston leadership used the massacre to manipulate and instigate further opposition to British presence in the city and to compel attention to the question of what British power was doing in America.

In March 1771, the year following the massacre, a committee on which Joseph Warren sat suggested an oration to commemorate the fateful event. James Lovell, a distinguished Bostonian, was chosen as the orator. Thus began a sequence of annual orations, remaining unbroken until its suspension after the July 4 celebration of the year 1783. The annual oration, administered by "eloquent orators" who, according to contemporaries, kept the revolutionary fire "burning with an incessant flame" for thirteen years, was always published in pamphlet form soon after its delivery and given wide circulation.[9] The commemoration orations became "a glorious recital of the myth of the Revolution. Often they would begin with a lofty declamation on the ideals of government with frequent citation of Greek and Roman models. . . . Ultimately, the orations aimed at the renewal of mythic innocence, ever under the threat of corruption, through action in the public cause."[10] John Adams remarked that the orations were read by nearly everyone who could read, "scarcely ever with dry eyes."[11] However, the orations had a crucial role as a spectacle, not merely a text at a time when oratory emerged as a major revolutionary medium. As a student of early American oratory recently pointed out, "The Boston Massacre orators established the authority of the Whig leadership through their display of physical courage in the face of hostile auditors and through their figures of memory and mediation."[12] These speeches manifested the ideologies of Boston's foremost citizens, selected and designated as speakers by special committees. Indeed, there were "few men of consequence," as Adams further pointed out, "who did not commence their career by an oration at the 5th of March."[13] The orators included illustrious names such as John Hancock and Benjamin Church; only Joseph Warren was chosen twice, in 1772 and 1775, to deliver the annual speech.

The chain of annual commemoration orations, which produced "some of the most sensational rhetoric heard in the Revolutionary era," had several functions in the sociopolitical economy of revolutionary Boston.[14] The series of orations molded collective memory and perceptions at the precise time of the founding of an American nation. As Sandra Gustafson points out, the orations presented an alternative model of power and order in a time of revolution; they established hegemony over the local populace; they demonstrated the courage of the Whig leadership; and they constructed the people's distinctive colonial identity out of the experience of suffering and death at the hands of British soldiers.[15]

When Joseph Warren took the podium in 1775, he drew on newly established rhetorical conventions to mold a classical identity. During the 1750s and '60s, a host of English rhetoricians who were widely read in America proposed a redefinition of the function and nature of the art of rhetoric.[16] This proposed rhetorical framework was consciously drawn from the model of classical Roman rhetoric, with the aim to form and sustain a public consensus, intellectual and moral, as the basis of civil action.[17] This old–new style, seeking to recover classical rhetoric, was "broadly understood as the active art of moving and influencing men, of galvanizing their passions, interests, biases, and temperament."[18] The new oratorical style, elaborated in the British North American colonies by orators such as George Whitfield, "posing, gesturing, and acting out Biblical scenes," provided a setting in which patriotic sacrifice was not merely verbally inculcated but directly acted out.[19] This rhetorical context underlay Warren's staged, Roman-inspired performance.

Joseph Warren was born in Roxbury, Massachusetts, in 1741, the second generation of Roxburites. He descended from a family that had settled in America nearly a century before his birth. He was educated in his hometown school; his father furnished him with "200 shillings worth of Latin books," reflected in his later command of that language. After graduating from Harvard in 1759, he became "one of the outstanding doctors of Boston." He revealed his inclination toward politics when resistance to the Stamp Act led him to contribute articles to the public prints. His polemics, mainly written under pseudonyms such as "Paskalos" and "True Patriot," sharply attacked Governor Francis Bernard, forcing (with the help of Samuel Adams and others) his eventual return to England. After becoming a member of the Committee of Safety, Warren delivered the second (and his first) commemoration oration in March 1772. Writing and reading out the Suffolk resolves in September 1774, and becoming chairman of the Committee of Safety early in 1775, Warren had firmly established himself as "the symbolic executive of the revolutionary government" in Boston.[20] In March 1775, Warren for the second time took on the burden of delivering the commemoration oration. A physician who reached the top of the leadership of the American Revolution, a patriot martyr who died only three months after his second oration on the slopes of Bunker Hill, Warren was a lead actor in one of the puzzling episodes of the Revolution.

After Lovell had set an impressive precedent in 1771 on the occasion of the first oration, Warren, chosen to deliver the 1772 oration, drew four thousand spectators in bad weather to the Old South Church. Apparently, the thirty-five-minute speech "did much to shape the ideas of later generations of Americans on the Boston Massacre."[21] Employing classical antiquity in reference, metaphor, and allusion was certainly very common in contemporary rhetoric and in no way particular to Warren. Indeed, the 1772 oration, like twelve of the thirteen massacre commemoration orations from 1771 to 1783, began with classical mottos; in 1772, Virgil and Cicero adorned Warren's speech. In his first commemoration oration, Warren discussed the nefarious effects of standing armies in a free society ("You have appointed this anniversary as a standing memorial of the bloody consequences of placing an armed force in a populous city," Warren reminded his audience), the rise and decline of Rome with reference to contemporary Britain, and the republican Roman spirit that "inspired the first settlers" of America. In 1772, few Americans, if any, imagined that independence was a mere four years away; accordingly, the focus of the classical discourse was still on comparisons of the rise and fall of the Roman and British empires in a process that I earlier called "Nerofication." Warren elaborated on this topic in 1772, illustrating the extent to which the classics were fundamental to the Boston Massacre sermons, arguably the most important public events in revolutionary Boston. Acknowledging the central role of the classics in his 1772 oration may help us understand and contextualize Warren's togaed oration of 1775:

> It was this noble attachment to a free constitution, which raised ancient Rome from the smallest beginnings, to that bright summit of happiness and glory to which she arrived and it was the loss of this which plunged her from that summit, into the black gulph of infamy and slavery. It was this attachment which inspired her senators with wisdom; it was this which glowed in the breasts of her heroes; it was this which guarded her liberties, and extended her dominions, gave peace at home, and commanded respect abroad: and when this decayed, her magistrates lost their reverence for justice and the laws, and degenerated into tyrants and oppressors—her senators, forgetful of their dignity, and seduced by base corruption, betrayed their country—her soldiers, regardless of their relation to the community, and urged only by the hopes of plunder and rapine . . . whereby the streets of imperial Rome were drenched with her noblest blood, thus this empress of the world lost her dominions abroad, and her inhabitants, dissolute in their manners, at length became contented slaves; and she stands to this day, the scorn and derision of nations.

Following this awesome description of Roman decline, Warren concluded by pointing out that it was Americans' Roman-like attachment to a constitution, "founded on free and benevolent principles, which inspired the first settlers of this country."[22]

"The fervor" of the orator, remarked the antagonistic Thomas Hutchinson about Warren's 1772 speech, "could not fail in its effect on the minds of the great concourse of people present."[23] The *Boston Gazette,* from the other side of the political divide, mentioned "the unanimous applause of [Warren's] audience," and the town voted Warren its thanks and requested a copy of the speech for the press in a ritualistic gesture that followed each and every oration through 1783.[24] Warren's 1772 oration was, no doubt, a great success.

America, Warren made clear in 1772, was like Rome in its inhabitants' capacity for civic virtue. The implication was clear: The emerging American people were re-creating a virtuous, Roman-like society. Could this line of reasoning culminate in the adoption of Roman garb three years later? Warren's second oration, in 1775, was given in a much more troubled time: The oration of March 1772 was delivered during a relatively tranquil period when the wind had apparently deserted the revolutionaries' sails; the beginning of 1775, by contrast, showed unmistakable signs of a coming storm. After the Tea Party in Boston Harbor in December 1773, relations between Massachusetts and Britain deteriorated swiftly, and the Intolerable Acts declared the colony to be in a state of rebellion. Warren staged his oratorical performance at a time when a spark was enough to ignite revolutionary dynamite.

The 1775 oration, we now know, was delivered in the most rebellious of the colonies a mere month before hostilities commenced at Concord and Lexington, at a time when Warren's death on the slopes of Bunker Hill was imminent. Yet regardless of its dramatic potential, the oration remains a forgotten moment in the Revolution's chronology. His biographer points out that Warren's place in the collective memory declined from a nineteenth-century stature similar to that of Samuel Adams to virtual anonymity in the twentieth century. Perhaps his effacement from historical memory was caused by his untimely death, depriving him of a justified ranking in the American pantheon "together with Adams as one of the two most important revolutionary leaders in the Massachusetts revolutionary movement."[25] Warren's second, theatrical oration, which might have become a proto-Gettysburg Address, is known today only to specialists.

A careful examination of the oration of 1775 demonstrates, if one needs such demonstration, the virtual impossibility of reconstructing even an apparently clear-cut episode. Everything, it seems—including the issue of Warren's apparel—was politicized and contested in revolutionary Boston. "This day," the *Boston Evening Post* informed its readers in its March 6, 1775, issue, "an Oration will be delivered by Joseph Warren Esq., in commemoration of the bloody tragedy on the 5th of March 1770."[26] Yet that year's commemoration, the political actors believed, might follow a different path. It was clear to all that the Redcoats were likely to "take the occasion to beat up a Breeze," Samuel Adams predicted, which could easily lead to a new massacre.[27] Later accounts report that a "threat [was] uttered by some of the British officers, that they would take the life of any man who should dare to speak of the massacre on that anniversary."[28] Indeed, with Boston full of British troops, trouble could be expected.[29]

The presence of a large crowd, including British soldiers, seems one of the few undisputed facts regarding the oration. Even if the claim that "many people came to town from the country to take part in the commemoration," as a nineteenth-century biographer of Warren claims,[30] cannot be verified, it is safe to assume that an "immense concourse of people" assembled at the Old South building, where the town was to meet.[31] Both patriots and Tories acknowledged the presence of Redcoats in the crowd, each party assigning different numbers and motives to British attendance.[32]

The hall was overcrowded, the audience filling the aisles while the soldiers occupied the stairs, perhaps, as a nineteenth-century historian claimed, to "overawe the orator, and ... prevent him by force from proceeding,"[33] if he dare say "anything about the king."[34] Whether they were many, a party, or a great number, the presence of fuming British Redcoats in the packed crowd waiting for the annual diatribe against standing armies and British tyranny must have added an ominous sense to the impending drama. The aggressive presence of the British soldiers and the fact that the pulpit was covered with black cloth as a sign of bereavement are relatively undisputed, but little else is.[35] Even the time of the oration is uncertain: Was it given at eleven o'clock or eleven thirty? Or did the orator keep the audience waiting more than an hour, "gaping at one another ... expecting," finally showing up at twelve thirty?[36]

The difficulty of reconstruction begins in earnest when we come to the crux of the examination: the toga. From this point on, several alternative narratives emerge. "A Spectator" tells us in elaborate detail how Warren stopped his "one-chair carriage" in front of the meeting house, entered the apothecary's shop across the street from the Old South, followed by a servant holding "a bundle, in which were the Ciceronian toga, etc."[37] After donning the toga, "A Spectator" wrote, Warren crossed the street and entered the building. Remarkably, although several later authors repeated this story, the account by "A Spectator" is probably the only firsthand source that mentions a toga. Did Warren, presumably wearing a toga, simply come in "and ascend the Pulpit," or did he enter "from the rear by the pulpit window," or did he enter by "a ladder at the pulpit window" to avoid pushing through the crowd, especially the soldiers?[38] The conduct of the speech, too, is disputed: "A Spectator" noted Warren's "Demosthenian posture, with a white handkerchief in his right hand, and his left in his breeches,—[he] began and ended without action."[39] Watching this classical performance, Samuel Adams noted, the British officers "behaved tolerably well till the oration was finished," while Frederick MacKenzie reported that "the oration . . . was delivered with out any other interruption than a few hisses from some of the officers."[40]

Portraying Warren in a "Ciceronian toga" and as standing in a "Demosthenian posture" was significant beyond merely associating the American with classical antiquity: Both ancients were legendary orators and widely considered, respectively, Athens's and Rome's greatest speakers. When Cicero attacked Mark Antony in the Roman Senate in a series of fierce speeches he called "Philippics," he was honoring his inspiration, Demosthenes, who some three centuries earlier had damned Philip II of Macedon in fiery addresses. Warren's passionate oration then supposedly embodied and re-performed immortal classical speeches condemning tyranny. His outfit and posture were associated with a classical and eloquent setting of opposition to tyranny. So were the words he spoke. Indeed, there is little cause to dispute the actual text that Warren read to the crowd, and his words conspicuously alluded to classical history. Beginning once again by citing classical authorities, this time Virgil and Horace, Warren declared that England, which once had "boasted a race of British kings, whose names should echo . . . Cyrus, Alexander, and the Caesars," was now decaying under the yoke of 'an avaricious minister of state, [who] has drawn a sable curtain over the charming scene."[41] Next, Warren turned to urge his fellow Americans in their difficult hour to adopt the "maxim of the Roman people, which eminently conduced to the greatness of that state, never to despair of the commonwealth."[42] If England in the past played the part of a Roman proxy, it was now America's task to replace it in that salutary mission. What a difference it would make to hear such proposals from an orator in a toga, turning a mere speech into a performance, transmuting him from a Bostonian physician into a pseudo-Cicero, a spurious Demosthenes. Even the conclusion of the commemorative event was disputable, described by some as orderly and by others as a farcical pandemonium with people swarming down the gutter "like rats" after cries of "fire" had been called.[43]

The contradictions and uncertainties of the events at the Old South Church on March 6, 1775, demonstrate the explosive situation in Boston and leave a trail of possible counter-accounts of what actually happened. Nevertheless, investigating the question of Warren's peculiar garb may be profitable to better understanding the political culture and historical imagination of revolutionary Bostonians. "A Spectator" seems to have been the only contemporary to mention Warren's toga. Yet "A Spectator" was not an impartial reporter. His faceless identity, itself a pseudonymous disguise of a mere onlooker, functioned as a tool of Tory propaganda (*Rivington's Gazette* was a Tory newspaper published in New York) meant to undermine Warren's ideology and, perhaps, his person. Why, then, did no one else write about Warren's peculiar costume? Did Warren actually wear a toga? If not, why did not any of the thousands of people present protest and expose the untruth in the account by "A Spectator" after its publication? And if "A Spectator" did indeed fabricate the toga, why did he do so? Finally, why have historians uncritically assumed that Warren wore a toga?[44]

Three possible alternative plots emerge. The first possibility, "the *Rivington's* narrative," follows the account by "A Spectator" literally. The toga, there attributed to Warren, was the principal garment of a freeborn Roman male citizen in time of peace. It consisted of a single piece of material of irregular form, long, broad, and flowing, without sleeves or armholes, and covering the whole body with the exception of the right arm. Because it was worn without a fastening, the wearer had to keep his left arm crooked to support its voluminous drapery.[45] Stressing that Warren had on a "Ciceronian toga" might have distinguished his garment from the Greek rectangular mantle, the *himation* (*pallium* in Latin), which was thrown over the left shoulder and fastened either over or under the right. Most likely, though, it called attention only to the classical nature of the garment. What, then, does the "etc." in the "Ciceronian toga, etc." in the description by "A Spectator" indicate? It could have meant that Warren had on a classical tunic (*chiton* or *tunica*) beneath his toga, which was the normal combination for civilian dress in antiquity. Perhaps the toga was covering Warren's contemporary apparel during the chill of a Bostonian March. However, if Warren indeed wore a toga, we have only one, Tory, account that mentions this unusual dress.

A second possible explanation would follow a narrative that took the use of the toga figuratively. Such an explanation would take "toga" for a robe of office, a cloak, a mantle, or perhaps some kind of professional or academic gown. Indeed, one of Warren's nineteenth-century biographers followed such reasoning and described him wearing "a robe."[46] Warren's wearing of a toga-like garment offers a viable explanation of the seeming excesses of a Bostonian performing in a toga: The orator may have worn classical-like dress yet not a classical garment per se. Such an approach may also explain why no other accounts bothered to mention it. However, if indeed Warren wore a toga-like robe, a possibility that set fire to "A Spectator's"—and only his—imagination, we have no evidence to support such speculation. Further, "A Spectator" left no doubt in his description of Warren's garment: It was a Ciceronian toga, not an article of clothing resembling a toga, that he described.

The third option is a narrative that would discredit the actual use of the toga or a toga-like garment altogether and treat the story as an attempt to deceive. "A Spectator" as a politically motivated Tory writer, according to such an account, invented the toga to mock and harm Warren and the patriot cause. The spiteful and derisive language of "A Spectator" sustains such a hypothesis. He alludes to the Bostonian "mob" that fled from the fear of fire, swarming down the gutters "like rats." "A Spectator," we may then assume, fabricated the toga to ridicule Warren and Boston's select-men. Such a theory sounds surprisingly likely in a time full of conspira-cies and pseudo-conspiracies.[47] Alas, it, too, has crippling faults. If Warren indeed never wore a toga, the account by "A Spectator" did not draw angry denials from any members of the large patriotic audience at the Old South Church.[48] However, if "A Spectator" invented the toga to belittle Warren, his choice of words did not suggest mockery. Describing Warren putting "himself into a Demosthenian posture, with a white handkerchief in his right hand, and his left in his breeches," would not sound derogative in any sense to a contemporary. If "A Spectator" intended to scorn Warren, he did a hesitant, ineffective job.

Since we cannot decide among the three options, the appropriate ques-tion to ask should not concern Warren's actual dress but, rather, whether he *could* have worn a toga, bearing in mind the cultural setting in which he was acting. The "could," then, is a question of coherence and consistency. Would it be culturally sensible in revolutionary Boston to host a speech by an orator wearing a toga? The underlying assumption for such an inquiry is that the report by "A Spectator" in itself—the fact that he chose to portray Warren as clad in a "Ciceronian toga," in a "Demosthenian posture"—is no less important than the question of Warren's actual apparel. The detailed account by "A Spectator," like any cultural product, became part of the revolutionary reality as it was impressed on the cognition of thousands of *Rivington's* readers.

In one of the few speculations on the meaning of Warren's performance, the historian James McLachlan argues that the toga must have conveyed a "cultural code" between the orator and his audience; this semiotic discourse, according to McLachlan, reflects the dominance and diffusion of the classical tradition in 1770s America.[49] Yet as we have seen, we need to evaluate revolutionary Boston's cultural context to establish whether it was so deeply steeped in the classics that an orator could deliver a performance in a toga. Warren's toga should serve not as an explanation but, rather, as a metaphor, a possibility, and a logical consequence.

From the start, analysts treated the Boston Massacre, the subsequent trial of the British soldiers accused of committing it, and the major players in the unfolding events in terms of antiquity. An admirer told Robert Treat Paine, the prosecutor, that his court performance was "Ciceronian like."[50] John Adams, for the defense, heard on a different occasion that his court acts were "equal to the greatest orator that ever spoke in Greece or Rome."[51] The commemoration orations of 1773 and 1774 were among the most important communal ceremonies of Boston; between Warren's first and second performances, classical themes dominated the orations. In the oration of 1773, for example, Benjamin Church said: "The citizens of Rome, Sparta, of Lacedemon, at those blessed periods when they were most eminent for their attachment to liberty and virtue, could never exhibit brighter examples of patriot zeal, than are to be found at this day in America."[52] These rhetorical patterns indicate the extent to which the massacre and the emerging rebellion came to be conceived and depicted in Boston in classical colors. One can only imagine the effect a performance in classical attire would have had on a crowded concourse of patriots.

The intense looking backward to antiquity was not incompatible, however, with the novelties that American society, especially its northern region, was experiencing. Among those changes was the prolonged but sure transition from the superiority of the spoken word to that of the printed word. Reading practices, tastes, and objectives were changing dramatically, creating a new republican culture of print.[53] Nonetheless, through a "heightened attention to the significance of language and performance,"[54] political oratory emerged as a highly politicized and mobilizing genre, not yet submitting to the power of print. "The headless ghost of orality," a new oratorical public sphere in which the patriot voice sounded clearly, was still a crucial factor within the political arena.[55] American political orators incarnating the ideal patriot, an ideal derived from classical models, created novel modes of national identity based on their public performances.[56] Formed by Virginian raconteurs such as Patrick Henry (the "Forest-born Demosthenes") and the Bostonian James Otis, this sphere combined two genres of revolutionary oratory: that of secular politicians and that of the patriotic clergy.[57] This politicized oratorical sphere was intended to be heard by a live audience; it aimed to induce changes of heart and to stimulate and intensify attitudes. Joseph Warren's presentation took place in the context of these cultural transformations and exemplified those novel styles and procedures.

The literary historian Jay Fliegelman maintains that an "elocutionary revolution" took place early in the Revolution and introduced a new language composed not of words, but of tones, gestures, and the countenance with which a speaker expressed his formulations.[58] Indeed, contemporary political discourse emphasized the theatricality, metaphor, imagery, myth, and body language that moved Americans' passion.[59] An orator's primary obligation, according to Fliegelman, was no longer to communicate thought and feeling, but also to display the experiencing of those feelings, resulting in a greater theatricalization of public speaking.[60] Set in a period in which the performative aspect of speech was elevated over the argumentative, Warren's "Demosthenian posture" would have played out through the theatricality of language and body.[61] A toga would not only be acceptable in such a cultural ecology; it would have harmoniously suited the occasion.

Parallel to such developments in oral performance, a genre of pseudonymous writing emerged as a vehicle through which the ancients were brought into American politics.[62] These ventriloquized print performances, many of them classical in reference, provided a venue for the embodiment of ancient heroes. Through those texts, Americans were accustomed to the ancients' joining in their daily political discourse. From the Boston

Massacre in March 1770 until Warren's second oration in March 1775, Bostonians read in the *Boston Gazette* alone more than one hundred and twenty articles signed with names alluding to antiquity. Those names ranged from "Cato of Utica," "American Solon," "Scavola," and "Brutus" to "Civis," "Junius Americanus" and "Veritas." Warren may have been responsible for some of them.[63] Such texts helped to condition local crowds to imagine, and eventually accept, their Whig leaders donning togas, metaphorical or otherwise.

Colonial culture also emphasized disguise and masquerade, which would have helped make Warren's costumed performance digestible to contemporaries.[64] The Revolution was not only a struggle for republican independence; it was also a culmination of a century-old tradition of popular rebellion in which colonial crowds "acted out their political and economic discontent in Indian disguise."[65] In their attempts to solve the dilemmas stemming from their unfixed national identities, Americans engaged in a discourse of disguise correlating to the traditions of carnival and misrule. An example of such an embodied and disguised act was the Boston Tea Party, in which participants dressed as Indians overpowered a British ship and threw its load of tea into Boston Harbor. Even if Warren himself was not a leader aboard that ship, as his biographer claims, he and his fellow citizens were well acquainted with (literary as well as literal) disguise as a means to attain political goals.[66] The transformative qualities of costume and disguise could enable Warren to experience and perform the identity of a virtuous, classical citizen.[67] "Playing ancient" was an expression of metaphorical sensibility that breached the cultural rules governing normal dress. A speech delivered by an orator in a toga represented the logical conclusion of the convergence of the oral republican sphere with the classical pseudonym and culture of disguise in a new kind of embodied performance.

Art, too, was politicized and classicized in the city that Samuel Adams tellingly described as a "Christian Sparta."[68] The portrait of that Christian Spartan, the master agitator Samuel Adams, engraved by Paul Revere and published (ironically) in the April issues of the *Royal American Magazine* of 1774, demonstrates how classical motifs referred to and surrounded the revolutionary sitter, and how Revere "exhibited both interest and understanding in his subtle alteration of the classical devices . . . an ability to relate them to the needs of political portraiture in America."[69] In the

Fig. 2. *Mr. Samuel Adams,* Paul Revere, 1775. (John Carter Brown Library at Brown University)

portrait, adapted from a portrait of Adams by Copley, Revere surrounded Adams's figure with the classical figures of Liberty, Fame, and War. Liberty was robed and raised a Phrygian cap, while Revere dressed War in classical armor and a Roman soldier's helmet, altering the Renaissance armor that he had painted in earlier portraits.[70] Hence, visual representation, like textual depictions, portrayed and imagined the Whig leadership of Boston as virtuous ancient heroes.

Revealingly, contemporaries memorialized Major-General Joseph Warren, killed at Bunker Hill a mere three months after his second commemoration oration, in terms of an ancient hero. The many eulogies dedicated to Warren's memory situated the fallen hero in the company of Cato, Cicero, and Scipio. A eulogist in the *Pennsylvania Packet,* for example, admitted Warren two weeks after his fall to a pantheon that included "each Roman, every Greek, whose name glows high recorded in the roll of fame."[71] Similarly, another eulogy envisioned "this early victim in fair Freedom's cause" surrounded by "each Roman, Every Greek whose name / Glows high recorded in the roll of time."[72] Again and again, writers depicted Warren in celestial settings, thronged by the heroes of the republican tradition, ancient and modern, and described as embodying "Scipio's martial flame, a Cato's firmness, Tully's eloquence."[73] They compared his death to that of the Spartan general confronting his few soldiers against the massive Persian army in Thermopylae: "So fell Leonidas, the Spartan chief." A lengthy eulogy in the *Virginia Gazette* portrayed Warren as having "the integrity and the eloquence of a senator" and as "unlike the Spartan general [likely referring to Leonidas once again] only in not expiring in the arms of victory."[74] Mourners read those eulogies, which represented Warren as a modern reincarnation of an ancient hero, throughout the Atlantic seaboard, from north to south.[75] A full generation after Warren's death, the drama *Bunker Hill* (1798) narrated Warren's final hours and last stand as a classical-age episode in which the playwright, John Daly Burk, represented America as an ancient republic and Warren as an epic, heroic, classical American.[76] In the dramatic climax of the fateful battle, Burk likened his protagonist to the Spartan King Leonidas, who fought with a band of three hundred men at Thermopylae in a vain and admired stand against overwhelming Persian forces. Like the eulogies soon after Warren's death in 1775, the tragedy recounting Warren's final stand did not mention the toga Warren did or did not wear during the fifth Boston Massacre commemoration oration.

Joseph Warren's 1775 oration did not become a "historical moment" in collective American memory. Had it only become the starting point of war, Warren's second Boston Massacre oration had all the essential elements to become a founding event in American history. That potential did not materialize. Was, however, Joseph Warren's performance unique? Can we match it with any contemporary precedent or parallel? We shall now proceed to examine yet another remarkable manifestation of the extent to which pre-war Bostonian contemporaneity could be classicized and of the patriot imagination's ability to conjure images of Americans performing in togas in the years leading to armed resistance. Indeed, Mercy Otis Warren's dramas *The Adulateur* (1772) and *The Defeat* (1773) further place Joseph Warren's oration within a performative—and Bostonian—context through which revolutionaries could imagine and envision classical spectacles. In Mercy Warren's plays, however, we come across actual Romans, concrete historical figures conjured to act in a contemporary American setting and to perform American roles in the impending American Revolution.

Mercy Warren Otis, sister of the patriot James Otis and wife of James Warren, wrote *The Adulateur* and *The Defeat*, which were in many ways conventional literary dramas and products of their time, participating in an established eighteenth-century genre, the neo-Roman play.[77] That genre consisted of five-act tragedies set in a classical setting, usually the Roman past. Those dramas commonly domesticated and adapted the harsh principles of Roman stoicism to contemporary Whig sensibilities, thus making the classical world more meaningful and digestible to early modern Anglophone appetites.[78] The fact that Mercy Warren eventually wrote a conventional neo-Roman play, *The Sack of Rome* (1785), and inserted some five lines concerning "Roman bravery" from Addison's *Cato*, the flagship of neo-Roman plays, as *The Adulateur*'s motto, leaves little doubt that her early plays were consciously engaging in discourse with the neo-Roman genre. Unlike in the case of Addison's *Cato* and the other generic plays, however, Warren did not intend *The Defeat* and *The Adulateur* to provide audiences with a neoclassical allegory in which a Roman past was to be understood through contemporary bearings.[79] Mercy Warren's plays were not literary depictions of events from ancient history; rather, her plays imported Roman heroes into contemporary settings to act in eighteenth-century America—specifically, in revolutionary Boston. Warren's neo-Roman dramas did not follow standard literary convention and make classical history contemporary by updating Roman history for the sake of modern audiences. Alternatively, her plays classicized contemporary history. Giving the lead roles to a cluster of Roman republican heroes, Warren achieved the opposite effect from the standard neo-Roman play: Rather than adorning Rome with a Boston-like appearance, Warren Romanized Boston.

The Adulateur was Mercy Warren's first published work and consisted of a thinly disguised attack on Massachusetts's governor, the high Tory Thomas Hutchinson. Issued anonymously, like all of Warren's pre-1790 work, *The Adulateur* and its successor *The Defeat* were written in blank verse and published in installments in Boston newspapers.[80] Warren set the plays in "Servia," a subdued province that had been encroached on by "the adulateur," its governor Rapatio. Warren's intentions were anything but to conceal the real-life referents of Servia and Rapatio, which readers easily recognized, respectively, as Massachusetts and Hutchinson. Rapatio first appeared in *The Adulateur* reflecting on the Stamp Act while sitting in the remains of his ransacked house and resolving to destroy Servia and its inhabitants in reprisal. The setting was one that no American could misinterpret in that it referred to Thomas Hutchinson's ordeal, which involved the destruction of his mansion by a Bostonian mob during the Stamp Act crisis. Most readers could also easily identify Deputy Governor Andrew Oliver under the cover of the name of another character, Limpet.

With the identity of Warren as the author unavailable to the general readership, it seems that most readers would not have been able to identify the characters that Brutus, Rusticus, Hortensius, and the other Romans Warren resurrected to play the part of the heroic Whigs in the familiar Tory-controlled Boston. The fact that the identity of the author of *The Adulateur* and *The Defeat* is no longer concealed allows modern scholars to confidently recognize James Otis Jr. in Brutus and James Warren in Rusticus, among others.[81] Most contemporary readers of the plays, who were deprived of the knowledge that those eminent Bostonians were the playwright's brother and husband, respectively, may have recognized other eminent Whigs in the Roman figures. Alternatively, they could read the plays without making a correlation between the Romans and specific Americans at all. Hence, while the Tories, especially the governor and his alter ego, the leading villain Rapatio, could be easily correlated to the real-life figures they represented, the Roman Whig leadership remained unattached to specific contemporaries; throughout the plays, Romans vicariously replaced Boston's patriot leaders. I will return to the significance of this point shortly.

Warren's goal in *The Adulateur*, as her biographer points out, was simply "to warn citizens of the evil, insidious intentions of the new governor."[82] The apparent motive of *The Defeat*, a shorter and even more fragmentary piece than its scrappy predecessor, was similar. *The Defeat* made use of many of the characters introduced in *The Adulateur*, including Rapatio–Hutchinson, but also, significantly, employed a similar, if not identical, array of the Roman–Bostonians initially introduced in *The Adulateur*. Warren meant for *The Defeat*, like its precursor, to mobilize public opinion against Hutchinson and his circle of cronies and in favor of the Whig leadership. Both pieces were tightly connected, sharing themes and *personae dramatis*; both also highlighted the Roman characters and virtues of Bostonian

patriots and satirized and exposed the ludicrous corruption of British officials in Massachusetts. In both dramas, the Romans roused their American countrymen to expel tyranny and restore liberty. The two plays were
evidently written while Warren held a similar political as well as literary
frame of mind and could arguably be seen as making up one larger intellectual whole.

In both *The Adulateur* and *The Defeat*, the American–Romans lamented
the death of liberty in Servia, a Latinized name that alluded not only to
the servile state of Massachusetts but also to the tyrannical, Roman nature
of its enslavement. Both plays pitted righteous, freedom-loving Roman–
Americans (or, rather, Bostonians) against evil, despotic, and thoroughly
corrupted Tories in a Manichaean world in which good and evil, Whig
and Tory, were unmistakably opposed. The plays rendered crown representatives, though not the crown itself, as adulating and corrupting Servia's
citizens through "honor, places, [and] pensions," while the patriot heroes
were immune to such vices. To subdue the colony he governed, for example, Rapatio ordered his henchmen to murder innocent civilians, alluding to the Boston Massacre. Rapatio–Hutchinson's ultimate goal was
to "throw the state in dire confusion, nay, . . . [to] hurl it down and bury
all . . . in one common ruin." As opposed to the evil, hysterical Tories, the
Roman–Bostonian protagonists called, in light of such murderous machinations, for "cool, sedate, and yet determin'd" action in opposition to Rapatio's measures.[83] Warren resurrected "Whig" heroes of antiquity—Brutus,
Cassius, Junius, and other well-known and adored heroes of the Roman
republic—in both plays to fulfill the role of leaders in the emerging American rebellion and to destroy Toryism. Finally, both plays—tragedies, by
Warren's own definition—ended optimistically. *The Adulateur* concluded
millennially, "Thou, my country, shall again revive, Shake off misfortune,
and through ages live. See through the waste a ray of virtue gleam, Dis-
pel the shades and brighten all the scene. . . . Till time expires, and ages
are no more," and *The Defeat*, following its title, ended with the Patriot
Whigs winning a battle against their Tory enemies.[84] Servia significantly
did not gain independence in either play, reflecting the still limited goals of
American resistance during 1772–73. At the close of *The Adulateur*, Rapatio
captured the high position he sought, however; in *The Defeat*, he fell from
power and was removed from his gubernatorial position.

Rosmarie Zagarri points out in an illuminating biography of Warren that as a political satire *The Adulateur* "was a masterpiece," yet she finds the shortcomings of both *The Adulateur* and *The Defeat* in their lack of "a full-fledged plot, character development, and dramatic resolution"—unsurprising and, perhaps, inevitable, given Mercy Warren's lack of experience in theater culture.[85] "Although she had read many plays," including those of Shakespeare and Molière, Warren "probably had never seen a play performed on stage." *The Adulateur* and *The Defeat* would never be produced, either, because Boston had laws against staging plays and did not even host a theater before 1794. Setting aside the generic question of whether these plays were in fact satires, as Zagarri points out—or, rather, "tragedies," as Warren represented them—one may wonder why Warren chose to convey and promote her ideas in the form of dramas in the first place. Warren actually discussed that very question more than fifteen years after the publication of her early neo-Roman plays in the introduction to the 1790 edition of *The Sack of Rome*. Although "theatrical amusements may, sometimes, have been prostituted to the purpose of vice," Warren stated, "in an age of taste and refinement, lessons of morality and the consequences of deviation, may perhaps, be as successfully enforced from the stage, as by modes of instruction, less censured by the severe." Indeed, she thought "lessons of morality" well fitted to the stage, because "the exhibition of great historical events, opens a field of contemplation to the reflecting and philosophic mind."[86] Such perceptions complemented Warren's humanistic and exemplary views of history, as they underlay the playwright's historical contemplation and reflection in *The Adulateur* and *The Defeat*.[87]

Warren probably chose to render her radical Whig propaganda as classical dramas in an attempt to unsettle her audience by exposing Hutchinson's machinations in a familiar, yet estranged Bostonian setting roamed by Romans. The playwright achieved powerful rhetorical effects as she placed the American struggle in the context of an established continental literary genre—namely, neo-Romanism—and thereby linking American Whig ideology with classical republicanism or, rather, actual classical republicans. Warren was thus able to provide a historical context and significance to the radical events Boston was experiencing in its testing years of resistance. The unusual fictional means of translocating Romans into contemporary Boston nevertheless had implications beyond the propagandistic and literary.

The Roman names with which Mercy Warren chose to adorn Boston's

Whig leaders were striking enough; the fact that she alluded throughout *The Adulateur* and *The Defeat* to classical history demonstrates that Warren's choice of nomenclature was anything but epiphenomenal. Warren deepened the classicization of her plays by naming council members "Senators" at a time when the obvious referents of that word were members of the Roman assembly, not that of non-existent United States. She meant for the Romans not merely to adorn an American setting but to carry over a classical reality to revolutionary Boston. Warren translocated more than characters; she also imposed the plots in which those classical figures were involved and for which they earned their fame. Warren's plays repeatedly alluded to the original regicidal feat committed by Brutus and Cassius on Julius Caesar. In late-eighteenth-century America, the mere names of Brutus and Cassius were enough to evoke what radical Whigs understood as the noblest of republican acts, tyrannicide, which concluded with the martyred deaths of the failed redeemers of the republic. Warren provided an additional dimension of significance to Brutus's and Cassius's struggle against Rapatio by repeatedly referring to Servia's governor in terms of a Caesar, especially as the Caesar who provided his name to the institution of the principate and fame to his murderers: Julius Caesar. Indeed, Warren depicted time and again Rapatio, if not as a Roman despot by name, then as a conscious follower of the example of the Roman emperors. In Rapatio, Warren tells us, "breath'd the soul of Caesar," as he himself exclaimed, "Nero, I tower above thee!" Indeed, to secure Servia's liberty from Roman tyranny, the Roman–Americans swore to "dare, what men can dare, and with our daggers force a way to freedom," alluding to Caesar's murder by a group of senators at the Roman Senate.[88] In yet another play that Warren published in 1775, *The Group*, she revived Rapatio's figure once more and further elaborated the allusions to Caesar's regicide. In this last of her pre-war plays, "every patriot [was heroic] like old Brutus," while they were resolved "to die, or set their country free" as "the shining steel half drawn," ready to destroy tyranny.[89] Warren was imposing classical narrative on her Roman–American heroes.

Although Thomas Hutchinson's physical well-being was indeed threatened in the years preceding the war, the ransacking of his house in 1765 attesting to the imminence of the physical threat, neither in real life nor in Warren's dramas was "governor-cide" proposed. Rapatio–Hutchinson, whom Warren depicted as having the ambition of a Roman Caesar, apparently lacked the ruthlessness of a true tyrant. Hence, in *The Defeat*, as Rapatio and his loyalist circle were defeated, their lives were spared. As Warren fused the ancient and modern dramatis personae of the historical drama, she altered the classical narrative. Thus, the fate of Roman Cassius and Brutus, regicides who eventually paid with their lives in the aftermath of the extra-judicial execution of Julius Caesar, was not shared by their American namesakes, who refrained from killing their American "Caesar." Although a horrified Rapatio complained that "the hated Cassius . . . calls for my destruction," that destruction was political, not physical. Ultimately, Rapatio evaded the destruction by the hands of his Whig–Roman enemies by capitulating to the victorious patriots. Warren perhaps engaged in pragmatic self-censorship, wishing to avoid the consequences of calling for a royal governor's murder and not following the ancient narrative through.

Warren may have altered the classical plot, but by classicizing their protagonists and keeping close connection with the ancient narrative, *The Adulateur* and *The Defeat* achieved much more than merely rendering and explaining reality in vivid, heroic colors. These plays enticed readers to visualize the events they were witnessing in their daily lives and to understand the instigators involved in those events as classical heroes. We will never know whether the actors would have worn Roman attire to complement their Roman identities had Warren's plays been acted on stage. However, the literary, metaphorical togas in which Mercy Warren donned Brutus and Cassius were striking enough, making it seem as if the heroic actions depicted were carried out by Romans.

Both plays demonstrated a significant imbalance in the characters' nomenclature: Not only were the villains not given Roman names (certainly not a consequence of the lack of Roman rogues), but, as I noted earlier, if one could easily identify Thomas Hutchinson in Rapatio—and, of course, Massachusetts in Servia—it was impossible for most of the plays' readers to reveal with certainty the identities of the Whig heroes in the characters of Brutus, Cassius, Lucius, and the rest of the Romans. Thus, while the villains held specific American referents, the protagonists' identities remained Roman through and through, a fact that increased the realism of the Roman resurrection and participation in the American rebellion. Warren's plays reveal the ease with which Boston's patriot intellects could perceive fellow patriots as Romans operating in American settings and project such perceptions into a burgeoning revolutionary public sphere.

The use of classical characters infused historical meaning into the American revolutionary movement. However, it also expressed an intriguing attitude toward history. Unlike the typological patterns examined in chapter 3, in Mercy Otis Warren's dramas the heroes did not fulfill an ancient promise but virtually carried antiquity into the American present. In other words, Warren did not ask readers to recognize similarities between Americans and Romans; rather, she asked them to perceive their leaders *as* Romans. The ontology implied in such overlapping temporal sensibilities, in which two societies separated by two millennia were united, was different from that of a typological time dimension. While typological time drew connecting lines between the past and the present, signifying related but separated events, Warren's plays rendered historical time as a fused medium that translocated actors between two historical settings. In Warren's rendition, Romans acting in revolutionary Boston shrank the temporal expanse between antiquity and the present, eliding for all practical purposes eighteen centuries of history. When Bostonians *were* Romans, fighting on behalf of republican virtue against sinister, despotic forces, Warren undermined time as a substance separating what was, is, and will be.

Mercy Warren's plays engaged wholeheartedly in the revolutionary classical discourse and articulated that discourse to an extraordinary level. Warren could feel comfortable with the genre of dramatic plays for several reasons: Confined by gender boundaries, she could not appeal to the public through oratory, as her brother James Otis did so effectively. Instead, she had to choose a literary genre and maintain her textual anonymity. Indeed, she found a genre that suited her purpose: Her unperformed plays, which appeared in newspapers as well as in pamphlet form, were liminal transcripts that functioned in a dramatic space between their textual and performative attributes. As plays, which were written to be staged and to be read aloud yet destined never to be acted, those tragedies maintained dramatic qualities that prompted readers to visualize and imagine them acted out. Although they were fated to remain an unfulfilled outline of a classical performance, the dramas cultivated historical sensibilities that enabled patriots to accept their leaders as Romans. Indeed, situated in the context of revolutionary Boston, Warren's neo-Roman dramas were no aberration of the classical idiom. Like other manifestations of that language, her plays transcended the volatile American present while understanding the here and now through the terrain of well-recognized and venerated classical patterns and narratives. The genius of Warren's plays is that, unlike most other manifestations of the classical discourse, they represent the revolution's leaders not as Americans transformed into Roman heroes, but as Roman republicans transformed into Americans. Since Warren's revolutionary plays were never staged, we do not know whether her Roman–American heroes would have performed in modern outfits or as ancients in togas; both possibilities seem plausible. Whether the characters wore actual or metaphorical togas, however, Warren conjured heroic Romans to participate in the American rebellious venture. During such moments in which the stakes were so high, the Revolution may have seemed Roman as much as American.

Surveying Boston's classical landscape of the mid-1770s, we may revisit Joseph Warren's togaed performance and ask whether the inhabitants of that city could have made sense out of a public sermon delivered in Roman garb. "A Spectator" no doubt wanted his readers to believe that Joseph Warren indeed had worn a toga, a fact not less important than the issue of Warren's actual garb. The style and language of "A Spectator" suggest that he was not engaged in satire but that he was serious when he reported that Warren wore a toga. Thus, even if "A Spectator" made up the toga tale to undermine Warren, we have no reason to doubt the possibility of such an event, because *Rivington's* readers were supposed to believe that it had indeed occurred. Finally, the fact that many modern historians adopted unquestioningly the notion that Warren donned a toga to deliver his speech may reveal much about our own modern perceptions of the excesses and symbolic inventory of revolutionary America.[90] Hence, the cultural landscape of revolutionary Boston—its vigorous classical discourse and symbolism, the fact that Americans time and again wore borrowed, if imagined, togas, and the fact that "A Spectator" at the very least conveyed a plot that he believed would be credible—all seem to confirm the possibility of such an event.[91]

Like Pericles long before, and Lincoln four score and eight years later, Warren lamented his dead in front of the same public he would soon lead on Bunker Hill. His oration, delivered in the face of his opponents, soon to become bitter enemies, mobilized the universe of republican symbols, juxtaposing America and its pristine youth against British corruption. Joseph Warren's metamorphosis, real or imagined, from a modern to an ancient by adopting the dress, tone, and ideology of a Roman transcended time and civilization and simultaneously reaffirmed both his own and his crowd's sense of being at the same time Americans and an extension of Roman history. Whether "A Spectator" meant it or not, his depiction of Warren delivering his oration in a toga gave the orator legitimacy within an American context that supposedly flowed from a classical past and was illuminated by it. Only after the Revolution did wearing togas become popular in America, not necessarily in live performances in the style of Joseph Warren, but on numerous white marble busts and statues of national leaders.

Revolutionary classical performances were by no means a Bostonian, or even a northern, phenomenon. Indeed, the classical dimensions of Patrick Henry's "Give Me Liberty or Give Me Death" oration demonstrates the extent to which classical spectacles, or performances interpreted as such, could take place south of the Mason-Dixon Line. Henry's oration was repeatedly recounted and interpreted in striking classical terms. One of the most celebrated episodes of the American Revolution, Henry's oration took place less than three weeks after Joseph Warren's Boston commemoration oration, hundreds of miles to the south. The "Give Me Liberty or Give Me Death" oration, unlike Warren's, was enshrined in the American psyche as a glorious revolutionary moment and has been retold and analyzed on numerous occasions and in numerous contexts.[92] Here, however, I intend to focus on the interplay of American contemporaneity and classical history, both in Henry's performance and in the reactions to it. As in Joseph Warren's oration, intricate classical communications passed between the political performer and his audience during the crucial months preceding the War of American Independence.

As the literary historian Sandra Gustafson has pointed out, most contemporary descriptions of Patrick Henry began with acknowledgments of his social and physical limitations. After meeting Henry at the Continental Congress, for example, John Adams said of him, "He had no public education. At fifteen he read Virgil and Livy, and has not looked into a

Latin book since." Thomas Jefferson contemptuously argued many years after the Revolution that Henry "was a man of very little knowledge of any sort, he read nothing and had no books. . . . [H]e could not write." In the culture of southern elites, such lack of formal education could be crippling. St. George Tucker recalled that, when he first observed Henry, he looked at him "with no great prepossession." Nevertheless, none of Henry's contemporaries failed to acknowledge his mesmerizing oratorical skills. Even his detractor Thomas Jefferson classicized Henry's rhetorical ability, musing that he spoke "as Homer wrote," while others observed an even more extraordinary change that occurred when Henry addressed audiences: "that almost supernatural transformation of appearance, which . . . [was] invariably wrought by the excitement" and manipulation of his oratorical genius.[93] It was Henry's oratorical genius, his talent for captivating his audiences by transforming his mundane self, that brought him lasting fame. In his "Give Me Liberty or Give Me Death" speech, Henry managed to stimulate his viewers to imagine him as a classical Roman, and more specifically, as Cato of Utica.

Henry was a rising star in the American revolutionary movement, one of the few truly national figures recognized across the colonies. The imperial strain provided up-and-comers like Henry a space in the public sphere in which they could demonstrate their zeal and talent and mold a new revolutionary consciousness. Henry, despite his scant education and superficial knowledge of the classics, nevertheless became in the eyes of his audiences deeply implicated with Greco-Roman images throughout his career. Henry's dramatic, transformative talent made him appear to his peers as a Plutarchian figure as early as the Stamp Act crisis, a decade before his noted speech to the Virginian Convention. In the classics-saturated public sphere of the Old Dominion, Henry was arguably the most deeply classicized figure of his day, at least until Washington took command of the Continental Army.[94] As a young and relatively unknown member of the House of Burgesses, Henry showed a polemic genius that was bold enough to warn the British monarch in May 1765 against collecting taxes in America, ending his speech with the memorable phrase: "Caesar had his Brutus—Charles the First, his Cromwell—and George the Third—may profit by their example."[95] In his own mind, and perhaps in the minds of his audience, as well, Henry may already have situated himself as the third potential tyrannicide, the epic follower of Brutus and Cromwell.

Throughout Henry's political career, his image as an unusually charismatic speaker attracted comparisons to ancient orators. He was repeatedly referred to in tropes such as "the Demosthenes of America" or the "forest-born Demosthenes."[96] The Continental Congress was said to have listened to him "in the spirit of Aeneas' audience at Dido's palace,"[97] contextualizing Henry as the Virgilian Aeneas about to embark on the colossal mission of founding Rome. His Virginian compatriot George Mason went further and said, "Had he lived in Rome about the time of the first Punic war . . . Mr. Henry's talents must have put him at the head of that glorious common wealth."[98] Visualizing Henry in the third century BC, leading the Roman republic at the finest periods of that revered polity, Mason reversed the common figurative measure of understanding Henry as a reincarnation of an ancient in an American setting by imagining Henry as a Roman–American, a contemporary thrown back in time to antiquity. Mason's historical imagination practiced the opposite of what Mercy Warren did in her plays—that is, import the Romans to America. Historical time, conveyed through a scene in which a Virginian was acting in ancient Rome, functions as a malleable and flexible medium in which actors may shift back and forth from America to Rome and from Rome to America.

By the time he delivered the "Give Me Liberty or Give Me Death" oration, Henry was thus already recognized, and would continue to be recognized, in classical terms. These depictions of Henry, which conditioned his audiences to interpret his dramatic performances of March 1775 in terms of an epic and ancient history, culminated in envisioning him delivering his speech to the Virginia Convention as a reincarnation of Cato the Younger of Utica. Modern scholarly treatments of the "Give Me Liberty or Give Me Death" oration tend to emphasize Henry's evangelical style. Historians have demonstrated that Henry's oration resembled a secularized sermon, akin to a religious conversion. Hence, they have found much significance in the fact that, in describing Henry delivering his oration, Edmund Randolph compared him to St. Paul preaching to and converting the Greeks in Athens.[99] Tellingly, Charles Cohen, who in an illuminating essay underscored Henry's Pauline image, ignored the classical overtones in Randolph's description. Not only did Randolph describe Henry as preaching in Athens, but a few lines later, describing the same occasion, he alluded to Henry and Richard Henry Lee as "Demosthenes [who] invigorated the timid, and Cicero [who] charmed the Backward."[100] The "Give Me

Liberty or Give Me Death" oration and its performer must be understood and contextualized through largely overlooked classical aspects of the text, its performance, and the reactions that it has elicited.

Returning from the Continental Congress, Henry delivered his speech in a Virginian delegates' meeting in Richmond on March 23, 1775. In his oration, Henry, taking his usual bold patriot's position, advocated that the provincial convention assume the functions of government, called for the establishment of a militia and the development of a plan of defense for the colony, and unflinchingly urged resistance against Britain. Thomas Marshall, a member of the convention, remarked to his son, future Chief Justice John Marshall, that the speech was "one of the most bold, vehement, and animated pieces of eloquence that had ever been delivered."[101] Imploring the delegates to support the radical resolutions he had presented, Henry probably elicited classical interpretations of his performance not only through his renowned classical rhetorical style but also through his choice of concluding words.[102] Henry's powerful and memorable ending— "Is life so dear, or peace so sweet, as to be purchased at the price of chains and slavery? Forbid it, Almighty God! I know not what course others may take, but as for me, give me liberty, or give me death!"—was derived directly from Cato's words in the second act of Addison's tragedy: "My voice is still for war. Gods, can a Roman senate long debate which of the two to choose . . . but chains or conquest, liberty, or death."[103] As in the "Caesar–Brutus" speech he had delivered a decade before, Henry posed in front of his audience as a classical republican figure: During the Stamp Act controversy, he postured as a modern-day Brutus, threatening George III with regicide; he now chose to act out an embattled Cato. The importance and omnipresence of Addison's *Cato* in revolutionary America—notably, its influence on Virginians who lacked college educations, such as Henry and Washington—is well known.[104] Indeed, some of Henry's viewers described him not only as a classical orator but specifically as a Cato fighting Julius Caesar. Henry once again had his way with his spectators, eliciting the exact images he intended.

Henry's paraphrasing of a neoclassical work of commanding eminence such as Addison's *Cato*, an enormously popular and influential "instrument of political propaganda" in the colonies, solicited classical allusions from his patriot audience.[105] At least three commentators on Henry's speech portrayed Henry in vivid, classical terms. In *The History of Virginia*,

Randolph described how "Henry moved and Richard Henry Lee seconded it. The fangs of European criticism might be challenged to spread themselves against the eloquence of that awful day. It was a proud one to a Virginian, feeling and acting with his country. Demosthenes invigorated the timid, and Cicero charmed the backward."[106] Randolph's description, however, written after the Revolution ended, paled in comparison to Judge St. George Tucker's account of the same occasion. To describe the glory of the moment he had witnessed, Tucker invited his readers to immerse themselves in a fantasy in one of the most remarkable classical allusions of an era steeped in such flourishes: "Imagine to yourself this speech delivered with all the calm dignity of Cato of Utica; imagine to yourself the Roman Senate assembled in the capital when it was entered by the profane Gauls, who at first were awed by their presence as if they had entered an assembly of the gods. Imagine that you had heard that Cato addressing such a Senate . . . and you may have some idea of the speaker, the assembly to whom he addressed himself, and the auditory."[107]

Five times in these few sentences, Tucker invoked the imagination of his readers, creating a fictive classical setting to convey the essence of the historical moment in which the American was Cato and the British played the role of the barbarians. Tucker surely conflated space and time, lumping together Henry in eighteenth-century Virginia, Cato in Utica of the first century BC, and the invasion of Rome by the Gauls during the fourth century BC. He depicted Henry, the "forest-born Demosthenes," while paraphrasing the dramatic words of Cato (or, rather, Addison's version of Cato), as a modern-day Cato in front of the Roman senate, defying Rome's enemies.

A third account, by John Roane, described Henry's body language while delivering the speech as if his arms had been shackled: "After remaining in this posture of humiliation long enough to impress the imagination with the condition of the colony under the iron heel of military despotism . . . he looked for a moment like Laocoon in a death struggle with coiling serpents."[108] Laocoon, a Trojan priest who warned the Trojans not to accept the Greeks' wooden horse, inserted his spear into one side of the Trojan horse to see if it was empty. To prevent Laocoon from discovering the Greeks inside the legendary wooden horse, the gods immediately sent two serpents, who killed him and his sons.[109] Henry, in Roane's account, was fighting colossal obstacles, revealing the dire situation of his country.

"Then the loud, clear, triumphant notes, 'give me liberty' electrified the assembly," Roan wrote. "The sound of his voice, as he spoke these memorable words, was like that of a Spartan paean on the field of Platea," the battleground where the Spartans heroically defeated the Persians. Roane embedded all of Henry's being in his classical imagery, employing Greek mythology and Greek history to describe Henry's body movements, his voice, and his general comportment in classical similes. For the centerpiece of his description, however, Roane turned to Roman annals: Henry "stood like a Roman Senator defying Caesar, while the unconquerable spirit of Cato of Utica flashed from every feature; and he closed the grand appeal with the solemn words 'or give me death!'" This conclusion was a worthy ending to the string of classical allusions and metaphors that Roane employed.[110] In Roane's remarkable description, Henry's stance was once again that of a "Roman Senator defying Caesar." However, his being could not be mistaken for that of Brutus or Cassius, Caesar's notable opponents; it was that of Cato the Younger. With Henry's final words, derived from the literary image of Cato so well known to the revolutionary generation, Roane saw in Henry Cato's "unconquerable spirit" flashing "from every feature." This remarkable transformation of an American into a Roman, a Henry into a Cato, demonstrates not only the historical similarities that Americans found between their own and the embattled Roman republic. It demonstrates how their historical sensibilities played out similarly and led them to perceive, even if just "for a moment," their compatriots as classical reincarnations.

Henry, aided by "the uncontainable and transformative power" of his speech, was evidently able to create the Catonic aura for which he wished, which is evident through his paraphrasing of Addison's Cato.[111] Manipulating his crowds with the force of his voice and oratorical charisma, Henry transcended his lack of formal education and achieved a remarkable accomplishment. At least three reporters of his celebrated oration described him in classical terms; remarkably, two of the attendees described him specifically as a Cato defying Caesar in front of a Roman senate, terms that, as we have seen, were facilitated by his powerful choice of a concluding phrase. Both Tucker and Roane placed Henry in the Roman senate, perceiving his Roman-like attributes flashing "from every feature." Indeed, this not a transformation that originated in Henry's use of a "secularized variant of the evangelical sermon," which several scholars have underscored.

Rather, Henry provided the Virginia Convention with a spectacle that had a strong classical component. Henry's impressive symbolic and metaphorical transformative abilities, then, should be understood in the context of the classical hermeneutics of the emerging Revolution.

Henry's oration further underscores the classical idiom's significance to revolutionary worldviews. Indeed, one must acknowledge the importance of the heavily classicized representations of an event that instantly became central to the emerging revolution. However, to truly understand the profundity and radicalism of the classical discourse, we should further identify the meta-historical and spatial assumptions that enabled contemporaries to produce and make sense of descriptions that may seem outlandish to modern historical sensibilities. Henry's speech synthesized several cultural strands, which helped an American "born in obscurity, poor, and without advantages of literature" to rouse "the genius of his country" and bind "a band of patriots together to hurl defiance at the tyranny of so formidable a nation as Great Britain."[112] Revolutionary oratory and the revolutionary classical discourse allowed Henry's words to be transformed into that of a Roman and allowed Henry, in the imagination of his spectators, to be cast back into the ancient world. Henry's text, gestures, and posture thus elicited expressions of the revolutionary classical imagination, which provided historical meaning to the emerging battle with Britain and thus expressed a unique historical consciousness. The imaginative connection between Cato and Henry, established by the orator as well as by commentators on his performance, demonstrates how patriots could collapse eighteen centuries of history and thus temporarily reverse, and abolish, what we understand as "historical time," a progressive, irreversible chain of causality and change. The temporal distance between the American master performer and the Roman republican martyr shrank—or, rather, was annulled—to enable representations of Henry–Cato depicted as preaching to the Roman senate. This image carried its own corollary as it further transformed Henry's foe into the historical Cato's nemesis, Caesar.

The toga-draped performances of the Revolution, real and metaphorical, provide an opportunity to unearth the classical semiotics of revolutionary America. Specific incidents and their symbolism enable us to grasp the possible range of the meanings and contexts of classical performances (or texts intended to be performed symbolically).[113] The images of American patriots wearing borrowed togas—literary or actual—demonstrate the ways in which the classics were embedded in a culture of performance and oratory in revolutionary America and point at the hermeneutic range these spectacles offered.

These classical spectacles shed new light on the social ecology and cultural context within which they occurred. They provide examples of the ways in which classicized attitudes toward time worked on specific occasions, but they also complicate our understanding of the temporal map of revolutionary Americans. Hence, deciphering the conceptualizations of time underlying these performances emphasizes the cognitive and historical dimensions of American resistance. Classical history, we come to realize, did not merely assist in rejecting Britain or simply provide an "invented tradition," which as prominent historians have pointed out in the past decades is vital for the development of national movements.[114] Antiquity furnished new stages and venues on which revolutionary Americans could express their vigorous political energy and dissenting ideologies. Patriots performed in those arenas what it meant for them to be classical republicans and for their society to be an extension—or, rather, an embodiment—of ancient civilizations.

Clifford Geertz famously asked how, when a man winks, we can identify whether he is merely "rapidly contracting his right eyelid" or "practicing a burlesque of a friend faking a wink to deceive an innocent into thinking conspiracy is in motion."[115] Accordingly, in explaining the meanings of patriots' classicized performances, we need to be attentive to any clandestine communiqué passing between performers and writers to their audiences. We need to interpret circumspectly the performance as well as its representations: Should we perceive them literally or as a burlesque? And are we mistaking a meaningful wink for a mere contraction of the eye? What, for example, did it take for a respectable physician and political leader to wear a toga while delivering a speech steeped with classical allusions at a town meeting, where all of the participants were well acquainted with his everyday self? Or, alternatively, what kind of social atmosphere supported a reporter and his readership in imagining the classical dimensions of such an event?

Time, an agent of contingent and continuous change in contemporary historicist understandings, which presumably underlies the sequential and irreversible unfolding of secular events, emerges through patriots' performances as a malleable, flexible, and negotiable medium. Perhaps most striking, at certain moments, from Patrick Henry's oration to Mercy Warren's resurrection of the Romans in Boston, revolutionary time took on an elastic and reversible quality. To modern observers, such performances may violate historical sensibilities and appear as stark anachronisms, a view that may have led historians to see the relations of the American Revolution and classical antiquity as superficial and as "intellectual window dressing."[116] The classical performances of American patriots, however, reveal once again the depth—not the superficiality—of this relationship, if only by articulating a complex and multifaceted understanding of time.

Patriots engaged in a complex discourse about a revered past that they projected onto their present. Their acting out of classical events, however, forced the past on the present, as in Mercy Warren's Roman–Americans, and America on Rome, as in the representations of Patrick Henry as a Cato in front of a Roman senate. For that to take place, time was bent over, folded, and reversed, as Roman and American histories merged. Hence, when revolutionaries "played Roman," they blurred the contours separating eighteenth-century America from Roman antiquity. Think of Patrick Henry, a Cato preaching to a Roman senate in defiance of tyranny; of Joseph Warren clad in a toga in front of his admiring audience; of Cassius, Brutus, Hortensius, and the rest of the Roman protagonists participating in the American Revolution. Such episodes indicate that patriots, in the very moment in which they were articulating their discrete political consciousness, understood time as something other than a medium of irreversible advance. They treated time as a condition that not only could accommodate repetition and fulfillment (as in cyclical and typological frameworks), but could alternatively accommodate the unification of the classical past with the revolutionary present. We may not be able to extract a unified statement from these performances about their expectations of time to come: Mercy Warren's plays expressed millennial overtones; the other cases we have examined, however, do not provide clear evidence of any expectations they might have held from the future. But all demonstrate the extent to which time was represented as malleable and flexible at the very moment of rebellion. These performers and their audiences saw classical antiquity, which gave patriots a stage on which classical virtues could be performed publicly, not only as bound in a cycle of periodical repetition with America or merely as making a promise that America was intended to fulfill. Rather, classical antiquity, and especially Rome, could be imposed on the American present, and America could be imposed back on Rome, rendering time an act that could be performed both forward and backward.

"The object will be to make Independence a blessing," young Alexander Hamilton wrote to his close friend John Laurens in the summer of 1782. He predicted that such a mission would require "all of the virtue and all the abilities of the country." Hamilton then pleaded: "Quit your sword, my friend; put on the toga. Come to congress."[117] He phrased his tripartite request to Laurens to relinquish his military post, become a civilian, and engage in national-level politics in figurative language, as a classical act. The sword, the toga, and congress were objects from a different, classical world (although swords were still part of a vanishing aristocratic martial universe, and "Congress" was consciously adopted by Americans to signify their Roman-like assembly). Hamilton's wished, then, that Laurens would perform a concrete political act in the physical world, but also that he would carry that act out as a Roman performance of disinterested patriotism. The toga would transform a routine act in what was seen as the final stages of a waning war into a marvelous, Roman spectacle. (Unfortunately, less than two weeks after Hamilton wrote the letter, Laurens was killed in one of the war's concluding skirmishes.) The white, broad, rectangular dress symbolizing virtuous ancient citizenship and freedom stood once more for a script for classical performances. Revolutionary Americans followed that script by envisioning themselves taking the toga, entering a white-columned building in which an assembly of virtuous leaders was seated, and performing acts of immortal statesmanship. That Congress could be a Roman assembly as much as an American one.

5

CATO AMERICANUS

Classical Pseudonyms and the Ratification of the Federal Constitution

O N SEPTEMBER 27, 1787, Cato spoke: "You have already, in Common with the rest of your countrymen, the citizens of other states, given to the world astonishing evidence of your greatness—you have fought under peculiar circumstances, and was successful against a powerful nation." He admonished, "Beware of those who wish to influence your passions . . . in principles of politics, as well as in religious faith, every man has to think for himself."[1] Caesar furiously replied within three days: "If that demagogue had talents to throw light on the subject of Legislation, why did he not offer them when the Convention was in session? . . . [T]here is no virtue nor patriotism in such conduct. . . . [I] urge you to behave like sensible freemen."[2] Cato sharply retorted on October 11, "For what did you open the veins of your citizens and expend their treasure? . . . [T]his Caesar mocks your dignity."[3] A mere week later, Brutus joined the dispute. "A free republic cannot succeed over a country of such immense extent" he claimed. "The Grecian republics were of small extent; so also was that of the Romans."[4]

Cato? Caesar? Brutus? Did they not die centuries before the last decades of the eighteenth century? They did, yet their voices clamored in the debates over the ratification of the federal Constitution throughout 1787–88. The widespread use of classical names as textual alter egos for lesser and greater American writers in changing historical circumstances stand at the center of this chapter. In earlier chapters, we saw that revolutionaries conceived their endeavors with a remarkable classical intensity that produced a variety of sensibilities through which they came to terms with time and history. In this chapter, we will see how, during the process of ratifying the new Constitution, participants in the political discourse plundered classical history to support their arguments and partisan points of view. The long and contentious months of ratification witnessed not only an extensive and calculated exploitation of the ancient example, but also the zenith of a particular genre: the classical pseudonym. Numerous essays, mainly in newspapers printed and reprinted up and down the Atlantic coast, were signed with classical names, preaching for and against the adoption of the proposed Constitution. The following pages examine the texts of writers who assumed classical masks on an unprecedented scale as they pitched themselves into political battle and analyze the changes and continuities the classical language endured in the wake of the Critical Period.

We thus continue tracing the different modes through which late-eighteenth-century Americans conceived of, and represented, historical time through the histories of Greece and Rome. We shall come to see how the intense use of classical pseudonyms in numerous squibs, fillers, commentaries, and pamphlets published throughout 1787–88 articulated yet another nuanced temporal mode in which history was understood in the exact moment of the forging of the American federacy as a stage for embodiment and reenactment. Here we will recognize an additional venue through which citizens of the young United States represented the classical polities—first and foremost Rome—and America as occurrences that were part of a single historical momentum. The classical pseudonyms used in the debate over the ratification of the federal Constitution demonstrate how time and history were conceived and represented as stages for modern performances of scenes that took place in a long-gone classical past. The actors in those scenes were, once more, Americans clad in borrowed, if literary, togas.

Although pseudonyms and their subset, classical pseudonyms, were a common rhetorical strategy in the early modern Anglophone world, the semiotic profundity of the literary act of posing as ancients in the American context has received surprisingly little scholarly attention.[5] Scholars have tended to mention classical pen names briefly, usually when referring to the pamphlets and essays selected as texts to be analyzed.[6] Much less attention has been paid to the reasons for, and consequences of, adopting classical pseudonyms. The following inquiry into the meanings of the pseudonyms used during ratification will provide a thicker description of the complex and obscure phenomenon of moderns' conversing through the totems of the past. This description will demonstrate the complex relationship of rhetoric and history—and, hence, the rhetoric of history—extensively elaborated during the process of ratification.

Focusing on classical pseudonyms brings to the fore overlooked issues in literary and political history. For example, this chapter may suggest possibilities for further exploration of meaningful connections between pseudonymity and political rhetoric. Furthermore, the findings of this chapter will enrich our knowledge of the processes that were involved in the adoption of the Constitution and thus deepen our understanding of intellectual aspects of ratification in general, about which we still seem to "know so little."[7] The following pages demonstrate how the original acts of constitutional interpretation, the debates over ratification, were performed to a significant extent by Americans posing as classical oracles. Analyzing the extensive use of this rhetorical strategy, which had been a common weapon in the Whig arsenal since the early eighteenth century, will illuminate the ways in which Americans worked out their relation to time and history during the fateful months of 1787–88, at the dawning of the Federal era.

False names, aliases, noms de plume, and pen names all signify authors assuming fictitious or spurious names. However, pseudonyms, anonymity, and forgery should not be lumped together. Interpolation, mistaken ascription, and textual alteration also differ from pseudonym. A text will be considered pseudonymous here only when "the author is deliberately identified by a name other than his own" and thus detaches the signature from the signatory.[8] Pseudonyms as a topic seem only recently to have attracted the attention of literary scholars and historians.[9] "Pseudonym" entries are still hard to find in literary dictionaries, and there is no standard textbook on the subject of pseudonyms in the English language (although compilations attributing pseudonyms to authors are abundant).[10] The *Encyclopaedia Britannica* devotes a very short entry to pseudonyms: "The same end [as with pseudonymity] is gained by publications without any name, or anonymously."[11] The *Encyclopaedia Britannica* could not have gotten it more wrong: The prefix "pseudo" entails the sense of falsity and pretension, of something that is apparent but not real. Unlike anonymity, which screens the author, leaving the reader in a void, pseudonymity is inherently deceptive.[12] Although a writer is evidently present, only an assumed identity is encountered. The reader, trying to visualize the writer whose words are perceived, is barred by a wall of deceitful pretense, of false existence, of impersonation.

I consider a pseudonym "classical" if it can be assigned to one of two generic groups, each with its own literary characteristics: pseudonyms borrowed from the names of ancient historical figures (e.g., Cato) and abstract, Latin augural, predictive pseudonyms (e.g., Sincerus). Subdividing further, we can distinguish three types of augural names. The first is drawn from a classical republican virtue (e.g., Candidus); the second reflects on, and actually summarizes, the thrust of a text (e.g., Benevolus to imply a condemnation of the hardships of poverty); and the third consists of a position in the Roman magistrature (e.g., The Censor). These augurative names have in common the quality of dealing with concepts and allusions to antiquity rather than with any specific individual. The borrowed pseudonym, by contrast, is either a Roman or a Greek name (the majority were Roman) that posed a challenge to readers, a cipher that had to be cracked to understand the essay's inner meaning. One had to grasp the writer's intention to understand the thematic relation between pseudonym and text. This could explain why Alexander Hamilton did not choose the best-known historical characters as his noms de plume. He expected his readers to invest some effort in recognizing them.[13]

Pseudonyms as literary measures go back to biblical times and canonical writings and became popular in early modern Europe in political pamphlets and newspaper proclamations.[14] The main reason for writing anonymously and pseudonymously in seventeenth-century and eighteenth-century Europe was the harsh censorship imposed by absolutist regimes. In England, "authorial anonymity . . . was, essentially, an officially tolerated form of sanctuary, for even in the cases where the printer was successfully prosecuted, the author could not always be found."[15] In the political culture of the ancien régime, the government considered heretical any set of ideas that competed with those it held. Political debate existed more easily under forms of mediation that would not expose writers to the severity of the censor.

By the end of the seventeenth century, English Whigs had made the custom of anonymous and pseudonymous political writings common, occasionally using classical references. Various writers who took Latin names, such as "Vindex Anglicus (England's Guardian)," published pseudonymously in the seventeenth century. But it was Milton's prose (such as *Areopagitica* [1644]), laden with Greco-Roman allusions and exercising an "authority rarely granted" in the colonies, that captured the minds of Americans.[16] Like Americans a century and a half after him, Milton was responding to a contemporary crisis by turning back to the classics. During the century after Milton, other English authors, especially but not exclusively those writing in the Whig persuasion, expanded this tradition. Thus, in the pseudonymous *Cato's Letters,* published in Britain in 1720–23, John Trenchard and Thomas Gordon produced one of the most popular, quotable, and esteemed sources of political ideas throughout the contemporary Anglophone empire. These writers' pseudonym commemorated Cato the Younger, the great Roman patriot who committed suicide when his beloved republic fell into the hands of Julius Caesar; he was a symbol of public liberty and virtue, the merits most esteemed by Whig writers. By linking a radical Whig ideology with classical pseudonymous writing, Trenchard and Gordon, writing in England, participated in and contributed enormously to a widespread tradition of signing political essays with classical pseudonyms.[17] "Cato" would remain one of the most popular pseudonyms in the Anglo-American world throughout the eighteenth century.

Though it by no means has been fully studied, this phenomenon no doubt extended to all parts of the Anglophone world, including Ireland, Scotland, and the American colonies in the West Indies and North America. When revolutionary turmoil arose in the New World, the tradition was already well developed. At least since the 1720s, colonial British Americans, inspired by the authoritative example of *Cato's Letters* and other British works, had been publishing political essays, social commentary, and pamphlets under classical noms de plume. Yet the use of classical pseudonyms in revolutionary America underwent certain permutations as it evolved in response to developments after 1764. This chapter, while concentrating on the uses of classical pseudonyms during the ratification debates of

1787–88, is also intended as a first step in providing a functional analysis of Americans' use of classical pseudonyms throughout the revolutionary era.

As was the case throughout the Anglophone world, the last decades of the eighteenth century in North America marked a turning point in the distribution of information and in the transition, long under way, of American society from one less dependent on oral communication to one more dependent on print. Yet the political sphere still separated the worlds of the said and the published by prohibiting stenographical and verbatim accounts of assemblies' sessions, necessitating channels through which wider political discourse could be elaborated.[18] Reading practices, tastes, and objectives were expanding dramatically and were increasingly receptive to the creation of a new republican culture of print.[19] According to the literary historian Michael Warner, the novel republican universe understood texts to be normally impersonal, written by an unknown writer to a readership that was anonymous; readers received printed communications as part of a network of potentially limitless unknown and unknowable others who might also be reading the same texts and participating incognito in the politically oriented discourse. The impersonality of public discourse became both a trait and a norm of this republican sphere, propagating a "distinct preference for fictitious personae."[20] Through "heightened attention to the significance of language and performance," issues became public—for an abstract community—not by establishing an interaction between particularized persons, but through the printed representation of fictitious figures.[21] In parallel to the ascent of a new oratorical public sphere, formed by orators such as Patrick Henry and James Otis, in which the patriot's voice clearly sounded, the ventriloquized performances of the ancients provided an agency for the elaboration of colonial objections to metropolitan behaviors, the articulation of arguments over the shape of new republican regimes in the states, and the creation of a national government.

The historian Dror Wahrman points out that in their attempts to solve the dilemmas stemming from their unfixed national identities, Americans engaged in a discourse of disguise and masquerade.[22] Such discourse included not only textual masks, but also veiled embodied acts, such as the Boston Tea Party, carried out by Bostonians dressed and painted as Indians.

Writers frequently used cognomens, those fancy epithets bestowed on individuals, to serve as alter personae by which they were known in literary exchanges. Thus, in private societies that lay outside state control, the frequent use of neoclassical cognomens "aestheticized conversation by distancing it from mundane talk of familiars." By the end of the eighteenth century, belletristic circles were accustomed to the ancients' serving as fictitious guises. Yet the explanation for the use of pseudonyms during the first half of the eighteenth century does not account for their prolific use by the century's end. Writers may indeed have retained their social cognomens when they contributed to public print in a wish to increase salability by the use of exotic identities.[23] Such reasoning, however, cannot elucidate the ideologically driven practice of the classical pseudonym, which intensified with the unfolding of the American Revolution.

As the quarrel with Britain intensified, American writers generated a spectacular amalgam of pseudonymous essays and pamphlets, many of them classical in reference. The names used in these years seem mostly to have been restricted to the augurative: In Boston in 1764, "Philo Publicus," the "public friend," lamented the decline of American society, which had "grown more and more luxurious every year";[24] "Britannus Americanus" rejected his mother country in 1766 and provocatively called on Americans to "tax their fellow subjects in England";[25] "The Tribune," assuming the populist title of defender of the Roman plebs in Charleston in 1766, exclaimed that "security of freedom can only be in public virtue."[26] The total number of classical pen names used in the revolutionary era and in the early republic is unclear, because no full compilation as yet exists. Some believe that it is "beyond counting."[27]

The colonists who used classical pseudonyms in the early 1760s still thought of themselves as aggrieved Britons and provincials, not as the voices of a rising republic. As such, they made use of a common rhetorical device, introduced by Whigs in Britain. But such notions were changing rapidly: Together, the expansion of print culture, the contest with Britain, the formation of state governments, the war, and the struggle to construct a national government and identity encouraged the further use and alteration of the nature of classical pseudonyms. To take one small example, between the years 1750 and 1753, eleven classical pseudonyms appeared in the pages of the *Boston Gazette,* and a mere eight appeared between 1760 and 1763. But during the four years of 1770–73, when patriotic sensitivity ran high and propagandists wished to maintain the momentum of the revolutionary movement, the same newspaper contained one hundred and twenty one classical pseudonyms. When "Spartanus" (after Sparta, which was known for its frugality and militarism) argued in 1776 that the colonies must have the right "to alter their form of government," he was already part of a flood of pseudonymous writings.[28]

This dramatic expansion of the genre, which in the case of the *Boston Gazette* saw a rise of more than three orders of magnitude (1,000 percent) from pre-revolutionary levels, could be accompanied by a qualitative transformation: By the end of the Revolution, classical pseudonyms were no longer a mere stylistic gesture but had emerged as a vehicle for the expression and working out of the American political imagination. A noticeable shift occurred from the predominance of abstract (augural) classical pen names to the frequent use of the actual names of honored ancients as pseudo-writers of political texts. In shaping their republic, writers chose ancient masks enabling them to convey their arguments through a more authentic and intimate performance, which reflected the ideological anxieties and aggressions that poured out of those tracts. This change seems to have taken place after the expansion of the early 1770s: thus, again to take a limited example, a mere 20 percent of the classical pseudonyms employed throughout the years 1768–71 in the *Boston Gazette* were names of people (augurative pseudonyms made up the remaining 80 percent). Between 1786 and 1788, the period during which classical semiotics fully developed, approximately 50 percent of the classical pseudonyms in the same publication were borrowed names.[29] Yet not only do the borrowed pseudonyms seem to have been employed to a wider extent; they also appear potentially to have carried more symbolic significance than their augural predecessors. Writers chose to personify and embody their arguments by identifying themselves and their ideology with ancient figures that carried powerful semiotic depth. The evolution of the classical pseudonym from the augurative to the borrowed, from the abstract to the person, placed the pseudonymous texts in a position to elucidate the American situation in the light of antiquity. What follows will trace the dramatic unfolding of this transformation.

Many factors encouraged the popularity and wide use of classical pseudonyms. English literary historians have pointed out that anonymity in England, which was "at least as much a norm as signed authorship," was motivated by aristocratic or gendered reticence, religious self-effacement, anxiety over public exposure, fear of prosecution, hope of an unprejudiced reception, and the desire to deceive.[30] Circumstances were quite similar in the American colonies. First, American authorities were extremely sensitive, in rapidly changing political contexts, to anything that looked like agitation.[31] An explanation for preferring pseudonyms over anonymity might have been the belief that a worthy cause would be better served by the reverberation of many voices while maintaining the impression that the newspaper essays and pamphlets were spontaneous expressions of American public opinion.[32] Thus, Benjamin Franklin approved the blanketing of the colonies with anonymous and pseudonymous writings, because they would "render the discontents general . . . and not the fiction of a few demagogues."[33] Further, the use of pseudonyms indeed "enabled men of honor to behave dishonorably," making responses to such attacks challenging: A reply might have given undeserved weight to a pseudonymous (or, for that matter, to an anonymous) confrontation, while overlooking it could considerably harm a reputation.[34] Still, even if good general reasons can be found for the use of pen names, the fact remains that writers choose many of their pseudonyms from the Greco-Roman world, with a preference for the Roman.

Antiquity provided the rhetorical high ground in an argument, for several reasons. To begin with, it supplied writings with a classical charm, an air of disinterestedness that rose above particular interests of time and place, displayed the writer's education, and suggested his social rank in an act that can be referred to as "intellectual window dressing."[35] Further, references to antiquity, whatever the content, carried the weight of wisdom and tradition two millennia old, providing a sense of security and continuity, of custom and usage. An identified personage was not essential; "The Censor," assuming the role of the Roman official in charge of morality, endorsed industry, frugality, virtue, and religion.[36] Moreover, as Pierre Bourdieu notes, if "linguistic relations are always relations of power" and "utterances are . . . signs of authority, intended to be believed and obeyed,"[37] then the power of words to perform is the function of the authority and appropriateness of their speaker. The classical pseudonyms possessed such rhetorical power as a result of the conditions of their reception and authorization. Changing the narrator via a pseudonym at once altered the force imposed by the utterance on the audience and the way it was received and enacted claims for authenticity and power through the semiotic use of speech and text.[38]

Nevertheless, the main reason for mobilizing antiquity, especially Roman, to promote republican ideals (and not, for instance, another source of enormous intellectual stimulation such as the Bible) was that the ancients were seen to embody and epitomize those ideals. Whigs identified the Greco-Roman tradition with republicanism and civic virtue and saw it as the origin of those concepts. Appeal to the ancients and to their political science, and history supplied much needed trustworthiness, positioning the emblems of the past as guardians, validating pamphlets and pamphleteers by their mere presence.

The decision to adopt a pseudonym was obviously a crucial moment in the making of such a text, and so was the choice of what pseudonym to employ. Although distance denies us the knowledge of whether writers chose their alias before actually putting their convictions in writing or as an afterthought, essays in which the pseudonym was a dominant factor interlocked tightly with the text and its message, and essays in which the pseudonym was a mere fleeting allusion can be distinguished through close readings.[39] It is also obvious that many authors chose their classical pseudonyms to engage and refute their textual rivals; a telling instance is the New York "Caesar," who chose his nom de plume to battle his contemporary "Cato," his namesake's historical nemesis.[40] However, whether imperative to the content or not, the sheer quantity of classically signed essays must have made writers feel at ease under such signatures (and readers comfortable reading them). So common did the tactic become that classically masked figures spilled over into private discourse. James McLachlan points to the popularity of the habit of giving college students during the 1770s classical aliases, and a cipher proposed by Alexander Hamilton in 1792 further demonstrates the acceptance of this classical nomenclature.[41] In Hamilton's cipher, out of twenty-four politicians to whom he attributed a code name (including the president and several ministers and senators), twenty-two were classical: among them, Washington was Scavola; Adams, Brutus; Jefferson, Scipio; and Madison, Tarquin.[42] Thus, the ancients had seized America's reins of power, at least in Hamilton's mind. Moderns could easily be thought of as ancients and bear their names, evinced by the popular habit of Americans' calling each other by such names as "Demosthenes," "Cincinnatus," and "Catiline."

Although the themes covered by the masked writers included social, moral, and even scientific topics, the dominant themes were political. Men such as Benjamin Franklin—who was "not out of childhood before he was struggling with the issue of personhood and written discourse"[43]—published an antislavery satire under the pseudonym "Historicus"; an unknown "Academicus" published an article in honor of the newly founded Virginian Society for the Promotion of Useful Knowledge. Yet the majority of noms de plume were adopted to enhance political platforms in polemical essays. The whole spectrum of partisan politics appeared in the pamphlets and newspaper essays signed with classical pseudonyms; they were polemical vehicles intended to convert readers to a political position. Numerous partisans exploited the literary means that resurrected the past and the glorious dead.

Pseudonymous essays appeared mostly in newspapers, as well as in pamphlets and broadsides, which seem to have exercised "a vital influence on the minds of the reading public."[44] Thousands of political essays and readers' letters proved vehicles of propaganda, meant not only to inform but also to persuade. By 1775, forty-four newspapers were being published in colonial America; that number grew to sixty-three in 1784 and to well over two hundred by 1800.[45] Furthermore, historians find that a decline in the production of political pamphlets during the 1780s was offset by a remarkable expansion of political writing published in American newspapers, which proved far more effective than pamphlets as instruments of political communication.[46] Of 797 federalist and anti-federalist commentaries published between February 1787 and September 1788, only 22 percent appeared at any time as pamphlets, broadsides, or books, while 98 percent were published in the nation's newspapers. No more than 2 percent of the commentaries were printed exclusively as pamphlets, broadsides, or books, while 78 percent appeared solely in newspapers.[47] This apparent dominance of "the press" in commentary on the Constitution referred not to a large corporate newspaper establishment, however, but to the many independent printers who circulated small newspapers or published a writer's pamphlets for a fee. Like the pseudonym genre, American newspapers derived and copied from English models and developed in a distinct fashion within the American context. Each paper was designed primarily to be read in the town and province in which it was printed and became an instrument of self and world awareness.[48] However, since most newspapers' content was a reproduction of articles from other newspapers, supplied by the "impressive postal network [that] had been built in the first quarter century of the federal government," the pseudonymous essays repeatedly reprinted in different newspapers and districts eventually reached wide audiences.[49]

The ratification debates took place on the local, state, regional, and national levels. Local and state debates were conducted in town, city, and county meetings; in political and social clubs; in state legislatures; and in ratification conventions. However, the national debates were conducted almost entirely within newspapers, magazines, broadsides, and pamphlets.[50] Therefore, newspapers are key sources for the study of the public debate over the Constitution. Roughly ninety-five newspapers were published in the United States in 1787–88, of which at least seventy-five published the Constitution in less than two months and commented on its nature and argued for and against its adoption in items that ranged from squibs or fillers to lengthy and sophisticated political treatises. Most newspaper printers pursued policies favorable to the new Constitution, and some refused to publish anti-federalist material unless authors submitted their names with their writings. Only six newspapers clearly opposed the Constitution, while several others, though not anti-federalist per se, reprinted a significant amount of anti-federalist material.[51]

Although historians point out that writers may have "found it increasingly difficult by the late 1780s to preserve their concealment in a society intent on public discourse" and that early Americans saw during the battle over the adoption of the federal Constitution "the practice of concealed political writing [come] under direct attack," the popularity and acceptance of the institution of pseudonymity was still remarkable compared with any later standard. Even under pressure to reveal themselves, 75 percent authors of political pamphlets during the years 1787–88 were anonymous or used a pseudonym.[52]

Pseudonymous writers using classical masks had several strategies by which they chose to address their own fictitious identities, as well as their fellows' assumed classical identities. Perhaps the most common strategy was not to elaborate on the classical name at all. Authors who chose this course plainly signed their classical name at the beginning or at the end of the essay, frequently with all of the name's letters capitalized, without any further reference to the classical identity of the author.[53] A variation on this strategy was to add to the classical signature a personal touch, thus elaborating the illusion of a classical identity. Such was the manner of "Portius," who assumed the middle name of the revered republican Marcus Portius Cato; he ended his essay with "the earnest and unfeigned prayer of Portius."[54] Some writers chose to elaborate their classicized identities. "P. Valerius Agricola" proclaimed himself "a Citizen of America, concealed in the shades of obscurity, unconnected with party, and uninfluenced by power."[55] Such self-stylization highlighted the tension between the American and the assumed classical identities. Similarly, "Timon," adopting the name of the skeptic Greek playwright, described himself as "a man who is embarked with you in the same bottom, and who is bound to you by the strong ties of interest and affection," emphasizing his American presence rather than the classical absence implied by his choice of name.[56] "Anti-Cincinnatus," replying in a classical rhetorical fashion to the anti-federalist New Yorker "Cincinnatus," elaborated on his adversary's choice of name: "Under the signature of Cincinnatus . . . our author had a design in the choice of signature, to fasten a stigma on the worthy patriotic [Cincinnati] society." However, "Anti-Cincinnatus" assured his readers that "this is by no means the wish of 'Anti-Cincinnatus.'"[57]

The Virginian "Valerius" posed an interesting case. His piece was addressed "to Richard Henry Lee, esq." and was meant to attack Lee for "disdaining the clandestine mode of conveying information under a fictitious signature," among other issues. Lee, "Valerius" argued, had "boldly given . . . [his] name to the public, and with a peculiar air of importance, . . . thought the channel of a pamphlet was more respectable and better suited to the dignity of [his] letter, that that of a news-paper." "Valerius," however, was determined to fight the presumption of his rival, which he identified in Lee's signing his true name instead of a pseudonym. "A great name, on many occasions, makes up for a deficiency of argument," "Valerius" went on. Regarding his own classically concealed identity, he added that he was "a plain, unlettered man; I pretend not to an extensive knowledge in the many sciences of government. I have, scarcely, the reading of an obscure individual." "Valerius" concluded by hoping that "error, though supported by dignified names [such as Lee's], will never be adopted; and that truth . . . will always prevail."[58] Failing purposely to sign his real name, "Valerius" apparently assumed that adding the name of the founder of the Roman republic would not harm his cause. However unlikely, he employed classical symbolism not to exclude the "common sort" but, instead, to attack Virginia's elites.

Another way in which authors extended the credibility and classical resonances of their metaphorical names was by discussing events their ancient namesakes had witnessed and in which they had participated. Thus, "Brutus," when discussing the untenability of large republics, warned Americans that when "the Grecian republics and . . . [the republic] of the Romans . . . extended their conquests over large territories of country . . . the consequence was, that their governments were changed from that of free governments to those of the most tyrannical that ever existed in the world."[59] The Roman Brutus had memorably taken part in the drama of the destruction of the Roman republic and the emergence of the Caesars. Similarly, "Valerius" discussed "the expulsion of the Tarquins," the last Roman kings, an act for which the historical Publius Valerius Publicola was responsible.[60]

Classical pen names frequently functioned within the texts they signed in ways that leave no doubt about their rhetorical significance. Classical pseudonyms, which involved distinct textual tropes stemming from a discourse in ancient names, encouraged further elaboration of their authors' classical imagination. Writers addressing other writers who used classical pseudonyms, for example, regularly extended the illusion of a conversation among ancients. Hence, "Cassius" scolded, "blush and tremble, Agrippa! Thou ungrateful monster!" while "Cato" asked, "Are you to have Caesar's principles crammed down your throat with an army?"[61] Both were referring to their contemporary political rivals, the pseudonymous authors "Agrippa" and "Caesar," and employed a layered discourse, enriched with the classical overtones derived from the names of the author and his textual adversary. By extending the classical simulacrum created by their choice of names, authors produced multilevel texts that, if taken out of context, could be read as genuinely "classical." One, indeed, must read contextually—and carefully—to distinguish between the American and classical signifiers.

Such use of history and pseudonym brings to the fore an additional peculiarity of the genre: the curious use of language in the discourse of classical pseudonyms. The repetitive use of pen names, allusions, and metaphors of antiquity constructed a *Sprachspiel* (language game) that permitted an alternative reading of those texts.⁶² The classical *Sprachspiel* offered Americans a frame of reference in which statements and arguments that otherwise would not have made sense acquired coherence and meaning. A discourse in which long-dead men play an active role is in danger of being considered unintelligible or even comic. Only a conceptual frame, a language game, with implicit but clear rules of what may and may not be meaningfully said could enable such a discourse to pass as coherent.

So imbued with the *Sprachspiel* did readers become that they might have referred to the three writers of the "Publius" essays (which came to be known as *The Federalist Papers*)—as Washington in fact did in a letter to Hamilton—as "Your Triumvirate,"⁶³ reviving the Roman notion of an association of three magistrates for joint administration. Washington spoke to Hamilton in terms of antiquity by extending Hamilton's own metaphor of calling himself and his fellow writers by the name "Publius."⁶⁴ This kind of language reflected the way the classical discourse was internalized. The use of pseudonyms, itself part of a larger phenomenon of bestowing classical nomenclature on slaves, towns, political institutions, and one's peers, helped to accustom Americans to making their daily lives and the people inhabiting them meaningful in terms of antiquity. Contemporaries could talk about Washington as an American Fabius, the Roman general who defeated Hannibal by his cautious tactics (alluding to how Washington had won the War of Independence) and of Jefferson as a Demosthenes, the great Athenian orator. Accordingly, an American "Solon" could claim in 1771 "to write a system of government . . . for the united provinces in America," repeating the great Athenian legislature he chose as a namesake.⁶⁵ Such semiotic logic, which made Solon the creator of a modern constitutional proposal, merged past and present through an effective code of classical representation. The notion of America as a latter-day embodiment of a classical polity was not an empty cliché but, rather, a meaningful figurative mode employed by Americans at the turn of the eighteenth century.

Not everyone in the eighteenth century took part in this particular classical language game. Women typically avoided the use of classical masks to obscure their gendered identities. Elite white women used classical pen names in their private correspondence, the best-known case of which was Abigail Adams's self-fashioning as "Portia" in her correspondence with her husband, John.⁶⁶ Occasionally elite women wrote anonymously or under a pseudonym as newspaper dramatists, pamphleteers, and commentators, with both men's and women's names.[67] Those names were frequently not classical. Indeed, the most celebrated pseudonymous pamphlet written by a woman during ratification was Mercy Otis Warren's *A Columbian Patriot*, an anti-federalist tract that bore a vigorous, yet non-classical, pseudonym.[68] Hypothetically, female American writers could have assumed republican guise and embodied classical virtues in the public sphere. This classical feminine silence stemmed from the vigorous engagement of the discourse of antiquity in a grammar of virility. Early American political discourse was male-centered, steeped in a "culture of manhood" that ignored women as potential public figures.[69] Women, not supposed to engage actively in the *res publica*—neither in ancient Rome nor in early America—found it incongruous to perform as classical personae.[70] When they did choose to participate pseudonymously in the political discourse, they rarely did so under (feminine or masculine) classical masquerade.[71]

In 1775, John Adams and the Tory Judge Daniel Leonard were still exchanging augurative pseudonymous blows in their struggle over the issue of how far to go in resisting Britain. Leonard assumed the name "Massachusettensis," and Adams replied with "Novanglus"—literally, the Latin New England. In those early revolutionary years, ideological arguments were less personal than in years to come, a fact reflected by the dominance of augurative, non-personal masks.

After the conclusion of the War of Independence, Americans completed the process of bastardizing the European pseudonymous gesture by extensively transforming their bond with antiquity into a symbolic space of classical emblems. Pseudonymous texts functioned as metaphors explaining America in terms of antiquity and mediating between the American mind and the world. They selected, organized, and transformed daily experiences into manageable and intelligible data, providing authors as well as readers with a vehicle for synthesizing their experiences. Americans' transference of present-day problems into terms of antiquity was an active undertaking, involving the vigorous search for, and eventually construction of, parallel lines in the histories of antiquity and of the states to be united. They invoked history, which served as an organizing structure, to displace the ambiguities involved in present situations still lacking narrative and moral coherence.

Antiquity was helpful in the process of constructing a viable republican tradition as a means of envisioning the infant republic as connected to and embodying the glorious republics of the past. The age-old theory of the westward movement of learning, the *translatio studii,* which in America became "an assumption," particularly reinforced the ancient drama, which took place in public print, with notions of the rising glory of the new nation.[72] Authors conveyed classical morals and predications through the prism of pseudonyms, justifying and explaining the acts of the modern–ancients. The reflective distancing, achieved by the affiliation of the revolutionary generation with the ancients and demonstrated by their repetitive assumption of fictitious personae, was imperative in the creation of a linguistic space through which contemporaries crystallized their historical perceptions and social visions, the fundamental constituents of political imagination.

Once it was no longer satisfactory to define itself as merely non-English and post-revolutionary, Americans started to reflect on the meaning of their union, and politics acquired a confrontational and vituperative character. In the 1780s, Americans had not yet established a unitary definition of what it meant to be an American and developed "two parallel imagined communities, proclaiming themselves in print, celebrating the same rituals, appropriating the same symbols."[73] The two political parties, which during the 1790s would be named Federalists and Republicans, however, denied each other's legitimacy, forming a political culture governed by a grammar of political combat, which entailed a "politics of anxious extremes."[74] This temperament, already manifested in the late 1780s, fostered the intense employment and further construction of the classical semiotic space of political culture, as many texts began appearing as duels between classical personae, responding to and disputing with their pen rivals.

Many of the contests derived their intellectual energy from personal animosities as they became "personifications of the larger conflict."[75] No deadly weapons were wielded in those textual duels, and many more than two witnesses were involved, but the lethal language of the antagonists was sharp enough to draw blood (figuratively in the public sphere, if not literally).[76] Indeed, the masked rivalries made the ancients such lively images

within the American political arena that one may wonder at the symbolism inherent in the death of Alexander Hamilton, the master pseudonymous duelist, after being shot in a duel on a deserted New Jersey shore.

In independent postwar America, the context in which the classical symbols operated fundamentally changed as the classics, no longer exclusively
employed to elaborate on America's promise and legitimacy, became a
weapon in a bipartisan political system. An early example of this novel
political atmosphere demonstrates the transformed classical semiotics of
the use of pseudonyms. The debate about the Society of the Cincinnati
can be seen as a prelude to the pseudonymous debates on the Constitution as it manifested itself similar dynamics and thus demonstrated the
transforming nature of pseudonymous disputations as well as the political
atmosphere in America. That debate, conducted over core republican issues such as the extent of the equality that should prevail in America and
hereditary rights and status in a republic, offers a glimpse of the role the
ancients played in early national politics.

The Society of the Cincinnati was founded in 1783, after the war ended,
as a hereditary "society of friends." The exact aims and motives of its
founders were the reason for the cause célèbre that ensued. The society's
symbolic name was consciously and carefully selected. "The officers of the
American army," the Cincinnatis declared, "having generally been taken
from the citizens of America, possess high veneration for the character of
that illustrious Roman, Lucius Quinctius Cincinnatus, and [are] resolved
to follow his example by returning to their citizenship."[77] The retired officers of the Continental Army declared that they, like the legendary Roman patriot, left their fields and ploughs to answer the call to defend their
republic. Like the Roman, they capitulated when the war was over in front
of the civil authorities, only to return to their sylvan shades. However, the
society, fashioned around civic republican values and aimed at aiding veteran officers, aroused much public hostility. Because of its apparently aristocratic and hereditary tendencies, a quarrel broke out about its legitimacy
that manifested the growing rivalry between yet unformed political parties
that would define American politics in the coming decades.

The fact that the president of the society was the ultimate Cincinnatus,
the modestly retired General George Washington, did not suffice to check

the attacks against it.[78] The opponents of the society, in their attempts to gain public support for their cause, found a popular spokesman in a pamphleteer who called himself "Cassius," drafting a revered Roman to compete with Cincinnatus's patriotism—namely, C. Cassius Longinus—who with Brutus led the conspiracy to slay Julius Caesar in 44 BC and committed suicide after being defeated by Mark Anthony. Like Cincinnatus, Cassius was perceived as one who magnificently attempted, albeit unsuccessfully, to save the Roman republic from its enemies. In American collective associations, the two Romans embodied public virtue and patriotism. The "Cassius" pamphlet was originally published in Charleston, was reprinted in several other states, and its writer was later identified as Aedanus Burke of South Carolina.[79]

The symbolic significance of the dialogue between two great Roman patriots could not be ignored. Both Cincinnatus and Cassius were pivotal figures in the republican tradition adopted and incorporated by Americans; through the narratives of the Roman republic, the situations that Americans faced appeared bound for republican significance. The discourse involved "Cincinnatus" on one side, as the symbolic figure of the society bearing his name, and "Cassius" on the other, attempting to expose the concealed aristocratic intentions of the Society of the Cincinnati. The choice of these two figures was not coincidental. The historical Cincinnatus stood for unpretentious retired army men returning to the vine and fig tree, while Cassius represented the defense of the republic from tyrannical ambition. "Cassius," attacking the hereditary nature of the Society of the Cincinnati, asked in his pamphlet, "Did that virtuous Roman [Cincinnatus], having subdued the enemies of his country, and returned home to tend his vineyard . . . , confer an hereditary order of peerage on himself and his fellow soldiers?"[80] His strategy was to destabilize the connection between the name of the society and its perceived essence.

Once the Revolutionary War was over, the battle for the souls of the American people had to be won. Was postwar America to remain a loose league of former colonies, or should it become a federation of united states? Republican reality was articulated in light of ancient history during the debate over the Constitution. Scholars see the Constitution itself as "self-consciously republican" and based on the Polybian Roman example.[81]

However, throughout the period of ratification in 1787–88, numerous pseudonymously written newspaper articles and pamphlets for and against the proposed constitution expressed a symbolic dimension of a classical sensibility that went beyond any ideological meanings of the Constitution as a text that derived from ancient political wisdom. Relating the constitutional endeavor to classical republican tradition provided not only an intellectual space for conceiving and framing the Constitution, but also a classical medium through which Americans could be imagined as reenacting Rome's greatest generation.

After Delaware, New Jersey, and Connecticut, all small states that had strong commercial interests and economic prospects—and thus, stakes in a stronger union—had expectedly ratified it by January 1788, the Constitution appeared to have gotten off to a flying start. Even the early debates in the press had gone well for the Constitution's supporters. The first and one of the most decisive tests for the Constitution came, however, in Massachusetts. Badly divided and buffeted by disorder in the wake of Shays's Rebellion, Massachusetts in the late 1780s was a politically unpredictable entity. During the ratification debates, twelve newspapers were printed in Massachusetts, where the public debate took a peculiar course: Local newspapers printed many original squibs and short pieces, but no lengthy, substantive pieces on the Constitution emerged during the first weeks of the public debate. Rather, many federalist and anti-federalist items from other states, particularly Pennsylvania and New York, were reprinted in Massachusetts in the first two months after the Constitutional Convention adjourned. Most of the early Massachusetts newspaper items did not discuss the nature of the Constitution; rather, they reflected the bitter, personal nature of factionalized and popular politics at the local and state levels.[82] Not until mid-November did Massachusetts writers contribute substantially to their own state's newspapers. Once they did, however, they demonstrated the impressive extent to which they were involved in a discourse about their assumed classical identities.

In the debate over the Constitution in Massachusetts, which lasted from September 5, 1787, to February 12, 1788, twenty-nine original (Massachusetts-based) writers who signed using classical pseudonyms can be discerned. Of this total, twelve were anti-federalists, while seventeen were federalists. However, the number of classically signed pieces that appeared during ratification in Massachusetts was vastly larger than twenty-nine:

Authors wrote multiple pieces (such as the sixteen essays by anti-federalist "Agrippa"), and most of the essays were reprinted in several Massachusetts newspapers. In addition, the influx of essays signed with classical pseud-onymous from out of state that appeared in Massachusetts, as well as in all of the other states, was continuous. To see how salient the classical pseudonyms were in the Massachusetts debate, one need merely read an occasional federalist commentary: "'Helvidius Priscus'... sentiments will go off 'by the grits'—Agrippa has expired ... 'Brutus'... still fumbles on with his discordant farrago—'Candidus' gasp'd out a few broken and pite-ous expressions."[83] Even if the classical pseudonyms during ratification were not "beyond counting," as one scholar of the classical tradition in America claimed, their quantity and significance throughout ratification were momentous.[84]

Early in the debate in Massachusetts, two federalist authors took names of ancient lawgivers: the Athenian "Solon" and the Spartan "Lycurgus." Those writers implied the similarities between the American Constitu-tion and the ancient constitutions of the Greek polis. "Lycurgus," however, took the metaphor a step further by addressing the participants of the Constitutional Convention as "our Solons."[85] "Lycurgus" thus extended his classical identity and bestowed it on the delegates to Philadelphia, as well. Another author who explicitly addressed the connection of the classics to America was the federalist "Cato," which, as we shall soon see, was one of the most popular pseudonyms used by both federalists and anti-federalists in several states.[86] While "Foederalist is of pure Roman extraction," Cato wrote, conjuring a classical parable, as "antifoedus came along, in a very short time after, Julius Caesar was emperor of Rome." Warning Ameri-cans from the dangers of "antifoederalism," "Cato" pointed out that the descendants of the Roman "foederalists" were the American federalists "who lately emigrated to America, and inherit[ed] all the republican vir-tues." In this bizarre historical narrative, American federalists were virtual descendants of an imagined Roman "Foederalist" tradition, and therefore of the Bostonian "Cato" himself, and the anti-federalists were adherents of Julius Caesar and harbingers of republican destruction. Roman history was reenacted in America.

Other Massachusetts authors, if not as eccentric, still interrelated American and ancient history. "Helvidius Priscus" is a case in point. An anti-federalist who named the Constitution a "Draconian Code," alluding to the harsh laws of the Athenian Draco, summoned "the Patriots of old" to come forward to aid America and begged Americans not to fear "the arbitrary frown of either Otho, Galba, or Vitellius," the notorious Caesars, "nor the fate of Helvidius Priscus," the stoic philosopher and republican statesman who was banished and killed under Vespasian Caesar, Vitellius's successor.[87] "Helvidius Priscus" made sure his readers would understand his pose of a classical martyr. His grim tone continued in a second letter. In a lengthy discussion of "the Roman usurper" Caesar and alluding to Caesar's affinity to his federalist adversaries, "Helvidius Priscus" predicted that the anti-federalists, "instead of sinking into contempt, [would] stand distinguished in the annals of fame, for opposing [the Constitution] with the magnanimity of genuine patriotism." The federalists, in the meantime, should beware that the specters of the fallen revolutionary heroes "should appear as the evil genius of Brutus, and summon them to the shades, though not to die like the Phillippian Hero, in the last glorious struggle for freedom, but in the ignoble effort to consign posterity to the manacles of slavery." Like "Cato," "Helvidius Priscus" summoned the revered Romans to participate in his contemporary discourse. His appeal to an ancient persona, however, was a double-edged sword: "Portius," a federalist assuming one of Cato's middle names, addressed "Hevidius Priscus" as a "modern Catiline."[88]

The anti-federalist "Brutus" was obviously disappointed with the re-tired General Washington's endorsement of the Constitution. Although the Massachusetts-bred "Brutus" admittedly entertained "a high opinion of that illustrious commander," he believed that the Constitution insulted the country "with a military arrogance" and asked: "Is this what the illustri-ous General [Washington] fought for? Are these his Laurels? If they are, he borrowed them from Caesar."[89] Nothing could have been more insult-ing to a republican general such as the self-assumed Cincinnatus George Washington than a comparison to Julius Caesar, especially when such de-rision was mouthed by Brutus, the hero who destroyed Caesar after Caesar had established himself as dictator for life. Here we encounter once more the great potential for reenactment and role playing in the classical pseu-donyms, which created rich layers of textual meanings. That potential would materialize repeatedly throughout the debates.

Three Massachusetts federalists were quick to respond to this outrage by co-opting Brutus's republican identity. "Junius" chose his name to defy

"Brutus'"s claim to being Brutus: It was he, Marcus Junius Brutus who was the "real" Brutus. "Junius" exclaimed, "The fame of the American Fabius [George Washington] can never be wounded by the shafts of wretches [such as Brutus], however well skilled in ribaldry and defamation."[90] An anonymous writer asked "whether there was any necessity for the signature of Brutus to the piece of scurrility upon the American Fabius in the In-dependent Chronicle . . . ? Does not this wretched performance carry the mark of the Brute upon the face of it?"[91] Addressing Washington as Fabius, the famed ancient general, the anonymous author claimed that "Brutus" was actually "a Brute," not a true Brutus. "Cato," too, was quick to attack "Brutus," although the two Romans were real-life allies in their tragic war against Caesarism. Addressing his piece "to Brutus," "Cato" called: "Oh! Brutus—how it grieves the ingenious heart, thus to see thee prostitute thy sense and thy honesty . . . to the vile practice of falsehood and deceit! . . . Blush, Brutus! Blush! Wrap thyself again in thy native insignificance— retire from the world."[92] This clash of classical Americans would repeat itself in New York.

New York, not less than Massachusetts, was a primary center for the national debate over the ratification of the Constitution. Its newspapers, filled with essays overflowing with personal invective, produced a flurry of major original essays and may have offered the largest number of es-says published under classical pseudonyms. Between July 21, 1787, and July 26, 1788, anti-federalist New Yorkers put eleven different classical pseud-onyms into use, while their local federalist adversaries employed fifteen such names. However, in New York, as in Massachusetts, the number of local authors who wore ancient masks was no indicator of the total number of classical pseudonyms appearing in the local public sphere. New York witnessed many more than twenty-six classicized pieces; the "Publius" es-says alone (which later became known as *The Federalist Papers*) consisted of eighty-five installments, which were frantically reprinted in New York newspapers, as well as in those of most of the other states.[93] Eighty-five installments for a single series was an exceptionally high number; several other series of pseudonymous essays in New York, however, also were pub-lished in quite a few installments. "Brutus" published sixteen essays, while "Cincinnatus" published nine, and "Cato" published seven, many of which were reprinted across and beyond the state. Thus, hundreds of pseudony-mous essays were printed and reprinted in New York newspapers written both by New Yorkers and by out-of-state authors, and hundreds of essays that were written by New Yorkers were published elsewhere.[94] New York, in short, was a major hub for production and consumption in the burgeoning economy of classical pseudonyms.

"Cato" fired the opening salvo in what was to become an extraordinary quarrel of ancients in the State of New York. His first letter, published on September 27, 1787, elicited a furious reply from "Caesar" after a mere five days.[95] The two antagonists of the late Roman republic, Marcus Porcius Uticensis Cato and Gaius Julius Caesar, were reenacting their age-old battle. Cato was admired as the Roman republic's defender. His suicide in Utica when his cause was finally lost symbolized the death of the republic. Although his generalship and dynamic personality were acknowledged, Julius Caesar was remembered as the republic's ambitious death dealer. No one would likely assume "Caesar" as a pseudonym except to resuscitate an ancient battle, this time in the *New York Journal* and the *Daily Advertiser.* One need not wonder that it was a federalist promoting a strong national government who chose Caesar as his alter ego, and not a republican seeking the diffusion of central power.

The rhetoric of "Caesar" was full of classical allusions. "Cato," he cried, is "an ally of Pompey, no doubt." Washington was "the American Fabius," the Roman general who had defeated Hannibal by strategies of delay. "Caesar" ridiculed "Cato" as "this prudent Censor" and "demagogue"; both epithets would suit a (derogative) description of the historical Cato. "Caesar" warned that "Cato, in his future marches, will very probably be followed by Caesar," undertaking to stalk "Cato" as Julius Caesar had hunted Marcus Procius Cato, eventually driving him to suicide.[96] The symbolism of the discourse created by the classical pseudonyms thus unfolded. The two historical arch-enemies came to blows again, this time in the arena of the American newspapers. They reenacted the drama of the first century BC, intensified by the fact that few readers knew or guessed the writers' true identities.[97]

In his rebuttal, "Cato" referred to "this Caesar," alleging that he was the same as "his tyrant name-sake" and claiming that "Caesar" objected to free deliberation just as Julius Caesar had in Rome. Taking names seriously for the ideas behind them, "Cato" identified the contemporary "Caesar" with the historical Caesar by attributing tyrannical aspirations to him. "Cato" continued to refer to his contemporaries through the medium of the ancients: "The American Fabius [Washington], if we are to believe Caesar, is to command an army."[98] In referring to the historical Cato and Caesar and their contemporary namesakes, the contenders were exploiting the metaphorical and symbolic possibilities of the situation. Indeed, a formal debate on the matter of federalism was in progress, but historical knowledge was necessary in order to capture the symbolism embedded in these texts. The debate was embodied through Roman annals by bringing the contexts and actors of antiquity onto the American stage.

"Curtius," assuming the name of the hero who was memorably condemned, together with Helvidius Priscus, for treason under Nero, joined the ancient choir on the federalist side, citing Addison's *Cato* (perhaps to retake Cato's memory from the anti-federalists). "Curtius" asked, "But who is Cato," referring to the American author, "whose elegant diction and long spun argumentation would lead us to suspect him both the scholar and the sophist?" He concluded: "The virtuous [historical] Cato is forgotten!"[99] Only a week had passed when "Brutus" spoke for the first time. The Roman Brutus stood for patriotism and virtuous disinterestedness. He, even more than Cassius, was considered a man who dared commit regicide for the sake of his beloved republic, ridding it, he hoped, of Julius Caesar's tyranny. The American "Brutus" agitated fiercely against the Constitution, unsurprisingly aligning himself with his historical ally "Cato": "The Grecian republics were of small extent; so also was that of the Romans. [When their size extended,] their governments were changed from that of free governments to those of the most tyrannical that ever existed."[100] "Brutus" joined "Cato" in opposition against their nemesis: "Where was there a braver army than under Jul. Caesar? . . . That army was commanded generally by the best citizens of Rome . . . , yet that army enslaved their country."[101] Anti-federalists were thus warning that their political adversaries would take seriously their tyrannical Roman role.

In his fifth letter, published a month later, "Cato" presaged: "Great power connected with ambition, luxury, and flattery, will as readily produce a Caesar, Caligula, Nero or Domitian in America, as the same causes did in the Roman empire."[102] "Cato," witness to the fall of one republic, was issuing a warning that the fate of his ancient patria was imminent in America with the return of tyrants to the American shores. Hailing the writing of "Brutus," he also appealed to the historical alliance between the two men. During the first month of 1788, "Brutus" again confronted the (historical) Caesar, accusing him of being the man who transformed Rome "from a free republic . . . into that most absolute despotism."[103] "Brutus" identified with his namesake's rage, which had led him to regicide, by acting out his Brutus role, attacking the real-life enemies of his assumed character. Yet a new, vituperative contender emerged: "Mark Antony," who assaulted "Brutus," contending that his "patriotism is pretension; his zeal is suspicious" and that he had "sacrificed the truth." "Mark Antony" played up his rebuttal by quoting the immortal monologue of Shakespeare's Antony, in which he lamented Caesar and ironically denigrated Brutus: "For Brutus is an honourable man; so are they all, all honourable men."[104] The great drama of the last days of the Roman republic was unfolding week by week in the New York newspapers, staged by American actors.

When "Americanus" (literally, "Latin American") first attacked "Cato" at the end of 1787, he estranged himself, via his pseudonym, from European politics: "Away with this Spartan virtue."[105] He did so without excluding himself entirely from the republican tradition, though, still styling himself "Americanus." Later to be identified as John Stevens Jr., "Americanus," in his third address in late winter of 1787, drew on the histories of Greece and Rome: "The Grecians and Romans have infinite merit in subjecting themselves to so severe a discipline . . . for the sake of liberty."[106] In his fourth essay, he declared, "Should an angel come down from heaven and present us with a constitution . . . spotless . . . would there not be Cato[s] and Brutus[es] ready to disseminate groundless jealousies and vain fears?"[107] The Latin form of expressing "American" was Stevens's way to confront those who assumed the visages of the great men of Rome, Cato, and Brutus. He claimed to be no less—and, perhaps, more—a patriot than his rivals, if only in converting the classical tradition into his "Americanus" mode.

The case of the multiple addresses by "Publius," published in New York during the winter of 1787–88, exemplifies the quintessential characteristic of the classical pseudonyms. Acknowledging a tripartite connection among the pseudonym (the "text"), the words it signed (the "context"), and the classical history it suggested, allegorized, and turned into metaphors ("hypertext") helps to identify the semiotic profundity of the appeal to the ancients, which developed fully in the constitutional debate. Publius Valerius, who established the Roman republic after the last king of Rome had been expelled in 509 BC, was the pseudonym adopted by Alexander

Hamilton, James Madison, and John Jay in a series of essays supporting the proposed constitution in 1787–88. The three adopted "Publius," a nom de plume commemorating the Roman's act of banishing a king and founding a great republic, for their own founding mission. Publius's persona pervaded the essays, which appeared regularly in the New York newspapers and were published at surprisingly short intervals. The mere name of Publius enriched the arguments presented in the essays with supplementary contexts, illuminated meanings and goals, and entrenched the notion of republican virtue within the many classical allusions deployed throughout the essays. When "Publius" compared America to the "vast projects of Rome" and spoke of the "glory of the Achaeans," the writing acquired an aura of tradition and authenticity.[108] Hence, each essay was signed "Publius," a textual act that contextualized the constitutional arguments with what could be described as a "hypertext" of classical allusions and appeals to ancient history. *The Federalist Papers* were thus defined by the conspicuously false pretense of having been written by the founder of the Roman republic. By July 26, 1788, "Publius" and his federalist allies were able to persuade enough New Yorkers to ratify the Constitution.

Ten weekly newspapers were printed in Virginia at one time or another from September 1787 to June 1788. Unfortunately, many issues of those papers no longer exist, a fact that causes "considerable uncertainty about how much and what actually appeared" in Virginia during ratification.[109] The extant essays on the Constitution, advocating both its ratification and its rejection, do demonstrate a well-versed use of classical pseudonyms. Nevertheless, in the debate in Virginia, a state that may have been "the greatest problem" for ratification because of its huge territorial extent (it included West Virginia and Kentucky), its agrarian ethos, and its importance as a southern leader, we do not find the same intertwining classicization as in the pseudonymous articles published in Massachusetts and New York. Pseudonyms may have not appealed to southern culture, a world that, in the words of the historian Kenneth Greenberg, "placed a high value on appearances as asserted and projected through the words of honourable gentlemen." Indeed, in the south the connection between a man's real character and the character projected by a pseudonym was extremely problematic, "dangerous," since it announced that one's appearance differed from one's true nature.[110] Still, at least nine Virginian authors used classical pseudonyms, four of them federalists (among them "Cassius," who published three letters); four, anti-federalist; and one a virtually impartial commentator on the Constitution. This might be an unimpressive number when compared with the situation in Massachusetts and New York. Nevertheless, one should remember that Virginian newspapers were busy printing out-of-state commentaries on the Constitution, among them numerous pieces signed by classical authors. For example, Virginian editors chose to reprint at least ten of the early "Publius" essays.[111] Those Virginian authors whose essays have survived and who did choose to write under classical pseudonyms indeed showed an inclination to repeat the classicized battles of their northern compatriots.

Two writers, "Valerius" and "Cassius," chose the heroes of the Roman republic—one, its founder (Publius Poplicola Valerius, the "Publius" of *The Federalist Papers*) and the other its tragic tyrannicide (Gaius Longinus Cassius), to fight the anti-federalist Richard Henry Lee. Both authors addressed Lee in their respective essays from classical stances. Citing the letters by "Cato," another Virginian, "Brutus," came to Lee's help and struck "Cassius" from the anti-federalist side: "Men that are above all fear, soon grow above all shame . . . says Tacitus of Tiberius. Even Nero had lived a great while inoffensively and reigned virtuously. . . . I would advise you, Cassius, to read Cato's letters." By invoking Roman authorities as well as villains, this reanimation of the three long-dead defenders of the Roman republic did not follow the alignment of the historical narrative, where Cassius, Brutus, and Cato all fought for the same noble cause. Virginians separated the historical allies along the lines of federalism and anti-federalism.

Many more ancients were conjured throughout the debates in the other states of the union, for and against ratification. Massachusetts, New York, and Virginia, however, representing the three cultural and geographical cores of the late-eighteenth-century United States, demonstrate well the nature, breadth, and depth of the discourse under classical pseudonyms. On July 2, 1788, as the Constitution was ratified by nine states' conventions, the great debate had ended. The chapter of ancients' debating a modern Constitution came to a conclusion.

Of forty-four authors signing under classical pseudonyms in the debates raging in Massachusetts, New York, and Virginia, thirty-four (77 percent) chose names of Roman origin; six (13 percent) adopted Greek names; and four (10 percent) preferred hybridized Greek and Latin names (see table 1). Twelve (27 percent) of the names were augural; twenty-seven (61 percent) were borrowed; and five (such as "Anti-Cincinnatus") do not fit this taxonomy. Five of the names were used by both federalists and anti-federalists—"Cincinnatus," "Senex," "Cato," "Portius," and "Poplicola," the last three used by both sides in the same state—while seventeen were used exclusively by federalists, and twenty-two were used exclusively by anti-federalists. "Brutus" and "Cato" were the only names used by authors in all three states. Unsurprisingly, the republican duo "Brutus" and "Cato" were particularly popular pseudonyms throughout the eighteenth-century Anglophone world.

Because authors published multiple installments under the same pseudonym in their own state, as well as in other states, and editors incessantly reprinted essays originating in other local newspapers as well as .essays produced in other states, the forty-four discrete classical pseudonyms that originated in Massachusetts, New York, and Virginia shown in table 1 appeared numerous (possibly thousands of) times throughout the thirteen states during ratification. Classically signed essays infested the political discourse throughout ratification. For example, the number of classically signed essays printed in New York from February 1 to July 26, 1788, which included essays originally produced in New York as well as texts reprinted from other states, reached a remarkable one hundred forty nine. Many more were published before that date, from the adjournment of the Philadelphia convention in September 1787 and February 1788. Some five hundred essays that originated in New York during the debates were printed and reprinted throughout the thirteen states.[112]

This plethora of pseudonyms did not express exclusive or stable political positions during ratification. The majority of names could be used by both sides, although only five were in fact employed by both federalists and anti-federalists, as the two sides relied on a common pool of ancient figures known mostly through the classical canon to provide pseudonyms.[113] The classical space constructed via pseudonyms provided a shared medium and framework within which Americans could articulate their disagreements and reach consensual assumptions. American writers, witnessing daily the resurrection of the ancients through textual harangues and diatribes, were conditioning themselves to participate in the bitter struggles of the first

TABLE I. Classical pseudonyms used in Massachusetts, New York, and Virginia during ratification

Name	Origin	Federalist	Anti-Federalist	State
Agrippa	Roman		x	MA
Amator-Patriae	Roman	x		MA
Americanus	Roman	x		NY
Anti-Cincinnatus	Roman	x		MA
Anti-Defemationis	Roman		x	NY
Aristides	Greek		x	NY
Atticus	Roman	x		MA
Brutus	Roman		x	MA, NY, VA
Caesar	Roman	x		NY
Cassius	Roman	x		MA, VA
Candidus	Roman		x	MA
Candidus (Spurious)	Roman	x		MA
Cato	Roman	x	x	MA, NY, VA
Cato-Uticensis	Roman		x	VA
Cincinnatus	Roman	x	x	MA, NY
Civis	Roman	x		MA
Civic-Rusticus	Roman	x		VA
Cornelius	Roman		x	MA
Curtiopolis	Hybrid		x	NY
Curtius	Roman	x		NY
Democritus	Greek		x	NY
Denatus	Roman		x	VA
Fabius	Roman		x	NY
Helvidius-Priscus	Roman		x	MA
Junius	Roman	x		MA
Mark Antony	Roman	x		MA
Honorus	Roman	x		MA
Marcus	Roman	x		NY
Numa	Roman		x	MA
P. Valerius-Agricola	Roman		x	NY
Philo-Musae	Greek	x		MA
Plebian	Roman		x	NY
Poplicola	Roman	x	x	NY
Portius	Roman	x	x	MA
Publius	Roman		x	NY
Republicus	Roman		x	VA
Rusticus	Roman		x	NY
Senex	Greek	x	x	NY
Solon	Greek	x		MA
Timoleon	Greek		x	NY
Timon	Greek		x	NY
Valerius	Roman	x		MA
Vox Populi	Roman		x	MA

Source: Compiled from Merill Jensen, ed., *A Documentary History of the Ratification of the Constitution,* 20 vols. (Madison: Wisconsin Historical Society, 1976–), vols. 4–10, 19–20.

party system. Hence, this nomenclature may have reinforced centripetal political forces and drawn on an intellectual "middle ground" that provided a common language. However, the ideological stances that were worked out through those discussions were soon to diverge even more bitterly.[114]

Indeed, examination of the pseudonyms that appeared during the tumultuous months of ratification reveals that federalists and anti-federalists employed only a few pen names that their opponents were unlikely to use. New York federalists could make use of some of the more authoritarian-inclined ancients, such as Julius Caesar and Mark Antony, to advocate the kind of strong national government they endorsed; no anti-federalist would use those powerful Romans as a disguise. However, it seems that even the New York authors employed those controversial—not to say, notorious—ancients when responding to compatriot rivals such as "Cato" and "Brutus," Caesar's and Antony's real enemies. Furthermore, because anti-federalists could call on unlikely ancients such as Agrippa, the powerful deputy of Augustus Caesar, as one of the most outspoken opponents of the Constitution, most pseudonyms were indeed eligible as armor for both sides of the debate.[115]

Such use of a common pool of names could not and did not bridge opposing views about the nature and meaning of time and history. Federalists under classical guises, such as "Americanus," the literal Latin American, tended to express convictions regarding the uniqueness of America in historical time—namely, that Americans were establishing a *novus ordo seclorum*, a new order of the ages, that placed them "in a situation totally new."[116] Anti-federalists, the "men of little faith," were much more skeptical about the novelty of the Constitution's promise.[117] "Are we so much better than the people of other ages and of other countries, that the same allurements of power and greatness, which led them aside from their duty, will have no influence upon men in our country?" asked "Brutus" in an attempt to explain the dangers of a strong executive such as the proposed presidency.[118] Apparently, anti-federalists thought they were not. "Philadelphiensis," styling himself as a Hellenic Philadelphian, excitedly admonished that "the days of a cruel Nero approach fast; the language of a monster, of a Caligula, could not be more imperious."[119] "Philadelphiensis" was not alone among the anti-federalists who predicted a second coming of the age of the Caesars to America once the Constitution was adopted.[120] The fact that federalists chose pseudonyms such as "Caesar" and "Mark

Antony" did little to abate such fears. In fact, anti-federalists depicted federalists as potential Roman-like tyrants, targets of the Nerofying language used to attack the British a mere decade before.[121]

Despite adopting numerous Roman pseudonyms, Americans on both sides of the debate had begun by 1788 to question the relevance of Roman history to their situation. Federalists questioned Roman antiquity as a meaningful precedent, because they believed that "the path we are pursuing is new, and has never before been trodden by man."[122] Anti-federalists doubted the Roman example for different reasons. "Agrippa," for example, believed that Carthage, not Rome, set the appropriate model for America to follow: "Carthage, the great commercial republic of antiquity, though resembling Rome in the form of its government and her rival for power, retained her freedom longer than Rome, and was never disturbed by sedition during the long period of her duration." This, "Agrippa" argued, was "a striking proof that . . . the spirit of commerce is the great bond of union among citizens." He concluded, "Our great object therefore ought to be to encourage this [Carthaginian] spirit."[123] The fear of a strong executive, and the perceived incompatibility between an extended territory and a republican form of government, the mainstay of anti-federalist argumentation, added force to the misgivings contemporaries had regarding Rome as a potential historical example for the American federation.[124] Furthermore, while questioning the relevance of the Roman *exemplum*, both sides of the debate looked back to the ancient Greek leagues for precedents, to make sense of their present and to score rhetorical points.[125] The size of those ancient confederations, their purpose, and their conduct all seemed appropriate to the American situation.[126]

However irrelevant Roman history may have seemed to become, the vast majority of the classical names with which both sides chose to adorn their public writings were still of Roman origin (see table 1). Rome obviously played a unique role in the Americans' consciousness that transcended its immediate relevance as a political model. American authors made clear the direction in which their historical imagination was inclined by persistently adopting Roman names to identify their authorial personae. Americans were lured by Rome's civic example, as well as by its balanced mixed-government and the power and glory of the republic that once ruled the world. Authors' choices of Roman names reflected the traditional inclination toward the Latin world as well as the perceived historical significance and character of their political endeavors and aspirations. Donning the (metaphorical) Roman toga appealed to Americans to a great extent, as they could position and represent themselves as the great republicans they admired so much.

The pseudonymous writers may not have intended to create an illusion of classical authenticity. By signing as ancients and by participating in a discourse that referred to other Americans posing as if they were the ancients they claimed to be, however, they revealed a peculiar attitude toward time and history. The temporal sensibility revealed by drawing on classical pseudonyms was dictated by the use of the first person, the donning of an ancient mask that extended the fantasy of reenactment and embodiment. "Caesar" of New York threatening to follow and destroy his compatriot "Cato" and the Boston-bred "Brutus" and "Junius" arguing over whether Washington was an encroaching Caesar or a virtuous Fabius are examples of the role-playing traced in this chapter. The ancients were repeatedly conjured in an act of necromancy, their roles reenacted on an American stage.

The classical language during ratification reflected a transformed historical context. The situation Americans confronted was not one of war and the fortification of an unstable notion of independence but, rather, the necessity to generate a coherent political system that would satisfy the needs and aspirations of its thirteen discrete members. Such altered circumstances generated and reflected novel ways in which Americans represented and conceived of time through the prism of the classics. The extensive use of classical pseudonyms and the subsequent elaboration of a classical discourse through conscious fictions of historical reenactment thus reflect a peculiar understanding of the relation between the past and the present. The attitude toward time revealed through the use of classical pseudonyms demonstrates how the past could provide a stage on which modern ancients would play a new and spontaneous script. Unlike the texts that earlier revolutionaries produced, these exchanges were not conceived by a single classically inclined intellect. Rather, they were produced by several authors posing as ancients. Hence, they created a partisan, impromptu dialogue written by a plurality of ancient voices. This unplanned and unstructured quality of the pseudonymous discourse was one of its remarkable qualities, and it allowed—perhaps dictated—a high degree of freedom to alter the classical narratives. Finally, by adorning their textual judgments with classical names, writers suggested the different ways in which events unfolded, related, and reflected on each other in historical time. The bearers of classical pseudonyms represented history as a recurring series of episodes, a stage upon which modern actors reenacted ancient scripts.

At the transitional moment of crystallization of ideologies during ratification, a cyclical sensibility of time seemed to dominate classical expression in America. The proto-progressive view inherent in classical typology, for example, receded to the background of political discourse. The repeated warnings of the fate of the republic, whether the Constitution would or would not be adopted, attest to such a change. Thus, even though anti-federalists may eventually have lost the political campaign—the Constitution was indeed adopted—the partisans fought the historical battles on temporal terms that complemented the anti-federalist stance.[127] Federalists, prone to millennial understandings of time (to which classical typological patterns would conceivably have been compatible) fought their battles as masked ancients fully conscious of the imminence of republican corruption. The federalist "Mark Antony," for example, described his rival "Brutus" as urging "conscious fallacies upon the public mind" and as one for whom "the investigation of truth is not [an] object; his patriotism is pretension; his zeal suspicious and as he writes with design, we ought to read with caution."[128] Even optimistic federalists such as "Antony" saw America as severely threatened by cunning anti-federalist Catilines. Decline, corruption, and pessimism were ever present even in the minds of members of the Federalist Party, who "welcomed the prospect of change" and tended to invoke millennial visions of America's future.[129] It is indeed impossible to find millennial visions under classical pseudonyms. Federalists, like anti-federalists, were anxious about the possible subversion of the American republic. America, at this strategic point, was *in* history.

A functioning Constitution could not solve all of the problems of the inchoate American nation, and neither did it put an end to the habit of wearing ancient masks in the printed public sphere. The substance of national life was destined to be fiercely debated between supporters of Hamilton and Jefferson during the 1790s, clashing bitterly throughout Washington's presidency. Such a match, for example, materialized between "Aristedes" and "Catullus" regarding Secretary of State Thomas Jefferson's alleged pro-French inclinations; the "Pacificus–Helvidius" debate drew

Hamilton and Madison to skirmish under classical pseudonyms regarding Washington's proclamation of neutrality in 1793. Americans witnessed such sparring even during the first decade of the nineteenth century, when "Phocion" and "Aristedes" clashed over the Louisiana Purchase.[130] However, never again would Americans transmute their troubles and fears into those that struck the great republics of the past to the extent they did during the battle over ratification.

Robert Darnton says, "When you realize you are not getting something . . . that is particularly meaningful to the natives [i.e., the historical subjects of inquiry], you can see where to grasp a foreign system of meaning."[131] The practice of using classical pseudonyms seems to offer such an encounter. Indeed, more than two hundred years after the height of the use of that literary device during ratification, the widespread habit of adopting classical noms de plume may at first glance appear obscure.

The extensive use of classical pseudonyms during ratification points to the dynamism of the classical discourse in America, which adapted impressively to changing historical circumstances. Classical pseudonyms, a common genre throughout the eighteenth century, gained spectacular momentum during the debates over the federal Constitution. That masked discourse demonstrates the extent and depth to which classical self-representations of participants in the post-revolutionary print culture could reach. Because those commentaries on the Constitution had a clear purpose—namely, to draw converts to the respective sides of the political battle—we may assume that authors addressed their audiences using a language they judged effective for such ideological conversion. Pseudonyms provided writers with a powerful rhetorical device and created a semiotic space in which the American present could be debated in terms of antiquity. Donning their borrowed togas, Americans could cope better with their anxieties, explain the volatilities of their republican world, and construct a coherent and meaningful narrative out of their daily experiences. Once the intimacy between authors and their ancient masks, demonstrated by their choice of names and words, is acknowledged, a novel perspective of the conception and construction of history and time in the young American republic emerges.

The extended episode of ratification demonstrates the extent to which the relationship between America and antiquity was complex and multifaceted. The nuanced historical rhetoric of pseudonyms, which peaked during ratification, became the dominant enunciation of the classical idiom of the defining years of 1787–88. The preceding chapters showed how the classics enabled revolutionary Americans to articulate and express novel understandings of the meaning of time and history. Once the war was over, as the American citizenry experienced the Critical Period during the perceived failure of the Articles of Confederation, the political situation took yet another volatile and anxious path as the American union was no longer engaged in justifying a rebellion and establishing national independence. It was, instead, engaged in casting meaning on the fragile and recently won sovereignty.[132] The discourse of the postwar years could not be constrained in a promise-fulfillment pattern, which, as we have seen, was a significant pattern north of the Mason-Dixon Line during the Revolution. Unlike the classical typology, the embodiment and role playing involved in the use of classical pseudonyms during ratification harbored a discourse that questioned the durability of the American republic and articulated its potential dangers as those that confronted the polities of antiquity.

Classical pseudonyms, a rhetorical strategy involving first-person classicization, the personification of a writer as an ancient figure, open a window onto the construction of a dimension of time in which history was perceived as a stage for reenactment and role playing. Americans became ancients through numerous acts of signing classical names throughout 1787–88 and extended the classical illusion by debating with other "classical" Americans as if they were reliving a long-gone historical act. Under pseudonyms, now employed in the political context of an independent republic, both supporters and opponents of the Constitution expressed fears and anxieties that were mostly subdued and implicit during the war. Such use of classical pseudonyms expressed anxieties over the fact that America was not immune from the fate of Rome, the republic that lost its republican soul as it became an empire. Both sides predicted that either an age of tyrannical Caesars (typically an anti-federalist claim) or an age of anarchy (a claim made mostly by federalists) was imminent. As they "played ancient," northerners and southerners realized that they could no longer be Rome without experiencing—or, at least, contemplating, that great republic's fate. As writers under classical guises struggled fiercely against other American ancients, the antique-role playing provided a rhetorical medium through which they came to realize their republic's frailty, a political moment that has been famously referred to as "Machiavellian."[133] Such language had seldom been expressed in such blunt terms since the Nerofication of Britain during the 1770s, and even then it was never aimed at fellow patriots. Americans did not present time as a dimension of unmitigated betterment within such a discourse. Rather, political players of all parties and all regions expressed an understanding of time as an agent of corruption. Embryonic notions of progress were momentarily shunned.

Within the broad context of the late-eighteenth-century classical discourse in America, the pseudonymous texts acquire their full meaning and significance as a means through which writers conveyed, defined, explained, and narrated their political experiences to their newspaper-reading audiences. Seeing the pseudonymous texts as symbolic and performative forms of language, rather than as discrete entities, opens up understandings of the ways that language generated claims of historical authenticity and history was understood as a dimension of epic reenactment. The numerous pseudonymous calls formed a great chorale of ancient voices that imagined the American republic repeating historical endeavors of classical glory and corruption. The linguistic universe in which such performances took place made the patriots of the past referees of the present, defining and redefining the relationships of the dead and the living.

6

"THE PEN OF THE HISTORIAN, OR THE IMAGINATION OF THE POET"

The Revolution's History Classicized

As the first histories recounting the Revolution were surfacing during the late 1780s and the following decade, Americans were worried how posterity would remember them and their endeavors.[1] John Adams, conveying his characteristic insecurities, predicted that "the history of our revolution will be one continued Lie from one end to the other." Indeed, Adams was persuaded that "the essence of the whole will be that Dr. Franklin's electric Rod smote the earth and out sprung General Washington. That Franklin electrified him with his rod—and henceforth these two conducted all the Policy, Negotiations, Legislatures and War."[2] Adams's sarcasm was accurate on two counts: The Revolution would be remembered to a large extent, in those early days and after, as a drama played out by great men, the Founders. Further, the Revolution would be memorialized in these early histories as a mythic, fabulous event. Indeed, the Revolution was presented in many of the histories produced during the American nation's early years as a larger-than-life event in which great, classical-like heroes were responsible for marvelous endeavors on an epic scale.

From the vantage point of the early post-revolutionary years, the revolutionary era seemed a world apart. A rupture appeared to have occurred after the Revolution, separating two distinct epochs, the present and the recent revolutionary past. While revolutionary America was represented as a Livian world of republican heroes and deeds, the America of the 1790s in which these histories were written was more easily conceived of as a Tacitean world of parties, power struggles, and intrigues.[3] As soon as the Revolution ended, America appeared to have experienced a fall into history, opening an unbridgeable gap that separated the present and the preceding decades, America of the 1790s and revolutionary America. Within this frame of mind, the Revolution and its champions were enshrined as a classical episode hosting classical heroes, unreachable and, like the revered ancients, carved of cold white marble. Indeed, with the historians alluding and referring throughout their treatises to Greece and Rome, the Revolution seemed more like an epic event of classical annals than an episode related to the reality of contemporary Federal America.

By the closing decade of the eighteenth century, Americans had already gained a century-old tradition of history writing.[4] One might have guessed, as some modern historians argue, that once the Revolution was concluded Americans would recall Lexington and Concord instead of Salamis and Thermopylae as their historical foundations.[5] The absence of classical ruins on the American landscape should have created an American history undetermined by the past, a history that could actually begin at the beginning, with the founding of the nation.[6] Hence, the success of the Revolution should have marginalized the role of the classics in the American historical imagination. Instead of referring to events two millennia old, Americans could have committed during the 1790s to their most recent shared past of sacrifice, patriotism, war, and state building. Nevertheless, early American historical imagination continued to rely heavily on the classics to come to terms with the Revolution.

The early accounts of the American Revolution were not modern histories. They were unabashedly patriotic, teleological, partisan, and propagandistic. The world of revolutionary America seen through the first patriotic histories of the Revolution, published during the late 1780s through 1790s, would not have been strange to readers accustomed to the Plutarchian and Livean tradition of history writing, as they, like their classical precedents, attempted to give back to their readers a sustaining image of their deepest values.[7] Indeed, the world of the Revolution was constructed, represented, and remembered as a mythic one that in many ways resembled the venerated polities of the ancient past, especially of early republican Rome.

Many of these histories reconstructed and represented the revolutionary years as an extraordinary, outstanding period in human annals, comparable only to classical history. In the words of David Humphreys (1752–1818), whose biography of General Israel Putnam is considered the first revolutionary biography, the Revolution was "an era singularly prolific in extraordinary personages, and dignified by splendid events."[8] The revolutionary era seemed so extraordinary to the early historians that, as an advertisement for the 1793 edition of David Ramsay's *History of the American Revolution* stated, there was "no portion of modern, or perhaps ancient history, more worthy of the attention of readers at large."[9] Mercy Otis Warren concurred, writing that the revolution ought to be "marked in the annals of time, as one of the most extraordinary eras in the history of man." Jedediah Morse, the historian geographer, deemed the Revolution "one of the most remarkable scenes that ever commanded the attention of the world."[10]

Early historians concurred that monumental tasks and enormous difficulties distinguished the revolutionary era. In *The History of Virginia* (1804), John Daly Burk was impressed with how revolutionary Americans "resisted the encroachments of the mother country . . . broke the fetters of colonial subjection . . . [and] defied the armies and navies of Britain."[11] Mercy Otis Warren concluded that "the objects that employed the abilities of the congress at this period, were of such magnitude, as required the experience of ancient statesmen."[12] With its undertakings so great, the revolution's spectacular success seemed even greater. "Within this short period," wrote Burk, "generals and statesmen were formed without any previous discipline or instruction; orators and poets sprang up as it were by magic; whilst inventive and experimental wisdom were successfully employed in advancing in all directions the boundaries of human knowledge."[13] That was not all. The Revolution, Burk ruminated, was "the cradle of the American Hercules," an era characterized by "Justness of design, correct conception, elevation of sentiment, honor, virtue, courage." Indeed, during the Revolution the world witnessed the unfolding of a "representative system in the midst of the waste" and of Americans "confounding the malice and the power of their enemy by their wisdom and courage."[14]

Historians deemed the Revolution so extraordinary because it was one of those rare occasions on which a society as a whole seemed to display public virtue. In the words of John M'Cullough, author of *The Concise History of the United States* (1795), "Many [Americans] sacrificed their property to the public cause [and] voluntarily suffered hunger, cold, nakedness, disease, and death, rather than betray the cause they had espoused." Even "ladies of the greatest delicacy voluntarily left their house, and followed their husbands into prison ships and exile, exhorting them to fortitude and perseverance, and setting them examples of heroism, and love of their country."[15] Certainly, in the words of Mercy Otis Warren, there was "no age which bears a testimony so honorable to human nature; as shews mankind at so sublime a pitch of virtue."[16] Burk believed that the Revolution formed "the most luminous portion of the line of duration."[17]

Subsequently, early historians viewed and represented the Revolution and the gigantic challenges it set, as well as the spectacular way in which America's virtuous citizenry resolved these tests, as an episode as worthy as classical annals. However, the present in which they were writing their histories did not appear to stand up to those glorious epochs. Objective circumstances had indeed changed after the war and made the 1790s different from the preceding decades. The conclusion of the war and the completion of the process of state building significantly narrowed the possibilities of achieving military glory and of manifesting republican virtue. If, as M'Cullough pointed out, "the virtues of patriotism, of domestic and conjugal tenderness and fidelity, shone forth with a peculiar luster" during the war, the years following the Treaty of Paris of 1783 witnessed the embarrassing financial and diplomatic weakness of the United States. Further, the unexpected formation of the first party system and the rise of opposition politics on the national level exacerbated the feeling that something fundamental had changed after the Revolution.[18] Indeed, it seemed to the historians that "a spirit of selfishness, and a want of unanimity among states" instantly replaced the characteristic virtue of the war years.[19] The plunge into the mundane after the success of the Revolution was harsh and bitterly disappointing.

The Revolution and the reality of the 1790s seemed a world apart. Yet to understand the origins and nature of the disappointment with the present that the historians repeatedly expressed, we need to understand the extent to which the Revolution was constructed and understood as an episode in classical history—especially, once more, as Roman history. They were commenting not only on America of the revolutionary years, but also on their disenchantment regarding the America that was born out of those years.

David Ramsay (1749–1815), one of the most acknowledged and respected historians of early America, expressed such notions in his histories of both revolutionary South Carolina and the United States. Ramsay may have not referred incessantly to the classics in his histories, as other historians did, yet for what he lacked in explicitness he compensated in subtlety. Indeed, Ramsay's work leaves no doubt as to which societies and ages he had in mind when he described revolutionary America.[20]

Ramsay himself attracted classical references: His contemporaries described him both as the "Tacitus of America" and the "Polybius of America."[21] Indeed, such descriptions may have been encouraged by the classical representations of the processes, events, and individuals that he described. "Everything in the colonies," Ramsay wrote, "contributed to nourish a spirit of liberty and independence." American plantations were "communities of separate independent individuals, for the most part employed in cultivating a fruitful soil, and under no general influence, but of their own feeling and opinions." The liberty, independence, and pastoralism that Ramsay saw as the essence of the American settlement were equally characteristic of the Roman republic during its heyday. Not only in their socioeconomic conditions—that is, their dependence on the backbone of a virtuous yeomanry—did American societies resemble Rome. The unique geographical conditions of America, too, were a necessary component of such similarities. "The large extent of territory gave each man an opportunity of fishing, fowling and hunting without injury to his neighbor. Every inhabitant was or easily might be a freeholder. Settled on lands of his own, he was both farmer and landlord. Having no superior to whom he was obliged to look up, and producing all the necessaries of life from his own grounds, he soon became independent. His mind was equally free."[22]

Paradoxically, the exceptional condition of America—namely, its seemingly indefinite supply of fertile and unoccupied land—was what gave it such a strong resemblance to Rome in Ramsay's account. Its inhabitants were "at liberty to act and think, as [their] inclination prompted" due to the endless amount of available arable land. Indeed, Americans, economically independent and politically autonomous, according to Ramsay, "disdained the ideas of dependence and subjugation." They were acculturated, he believed, in what Quentin Skinner has dubbed neo-Roman liberty, the anxious aversion to any form of perceived dependence.[23]

As in Rome's republic of the third century BC, so in America, luxury made "but very little progress among their contented uninspiring farmers." This incorruptibility was vital, for it enabled Americans, like Romans, to transform themselves "into an active disciplined military body, and a well-regulated self-governed community."[24] America's agrarian-martial character was unmistakably classical in its origin. The perceived similarities between America and Rome had their downside, as well. During the Critical Period, while Ramsay was chairman of the Congress of the Confederation, he warned that body's legislators that "anarchy or intestine wars would follow [in America] till some future Caesar seized our liberties."[25] Ramsay restated his anxieties in *The History of the American Revolution* (1789) when he described the prevailing fear "that after much anarchy some future Caesar would grasp . . . [American] liberties, and confirm himself in a throne of despotism."[26]

Like Ramsay, David Humphreys depicted America as a society that closely resembled the revered Roman republic. Writing in a Plutarchian tradition, a convention that, according to his modern editor, took "the truth about a biographical hero to be moral rather than circumstantial or factual," Humphreys also placed civic virtue as the central attribute of American society. Indeed, his biography of the Massachusetts-born Revolutionary War General Israel Putnam commemorates a larger-than-life, mythic hero in the model of Plutarchian protagonists. Arguably the most memorable part of Humphreys's biography is the fantastic (and unverified) story of Putnam's slaying of a dangerous she-wolf in a dark cavern, making his county safe again for farming. Humphreys described Putnam crawling twice into the wolf's den, holding a torch and tied to a rope held by his companions who waited anxiously outside. Only at the second attempt was Putnam able to kill the beast, after which he emerged victorious from the dark grotto—indeed, a story worth telling even by the revered Plutarch.

The most obvious allusion to Roman history in Humphreys's biography, however, was the description of Putnam as a modern-day Cincinnatus, rising from the field to gain command of an army and returning to his pastoral abode once the battle had been won. One ought to pay attention, however, to the fashion in which Humphreys constructed Putnam as an American Cincinnatus through nuances, without actually mentioning the Roman hero by name. At the end of the French and Indian War, Humphreys recounted, Putnam, like Cincinnatus of old, "having seen as much service, endured as many hardships, encountered as may dangers, and acquired as many laurels as any officer of his rank, with great satisfaction laid aside his uniform, and returned to his plough."[27] This archetypical pastoral retirement was enough to invoke in contemporaries' minds the image of Cincinnatus. Humphreys, however, continued to describe "Putnam, who was plowing when he heard the news" of the British raid on Lexington and Concord, abandoning "his plough in the middle of the field, unyok[ing] his team, and without waiting to change his clothes, sett[ing] off for the theatre of action."[28] The modern editor of the biography, in an insightful introduction, reminds us how unlikely it is that this story represents what actually occurred when Putnam heard of the commencement of hostilities. Nevertheless, what matters may indeed be that "a society lives by its myths," and Putnam's representation as a Cincinnatus should be understood in the context of the construction of the Revolution and its participants as alienated from the early national culture that represented them as such.[29] Both Cincinnatus and Putnam belonged to mythologized ages that were very different from what Humphreys's readers could identify in their contemporary America.

Historians who chose to represent revolutionary America as an agrarian society uncorrupted by luxury, as an Arcadian space of fields and vineyards that could keep its inhabitants uncorrupt and virtuous, were commenting on their own rapidly modernizing society, which they perceived as increasingly egotistic. Such perceptions aggravated the frustrating feeling that the world of the Revolution was long lost. The Revolution in their minds became a time in which larger-than-life heroes acted and achieved unfathomable accomplishments, from subduing hellish wolves to taming the most powerful of empires. Even as Americans gained a "history of their own," they still relied heavily on the classical narratives and on the structures and patterns of classical history. Antiquity dominated the reconstruction of America's most recent history.

Historians had different ways to bring the worlds of America and antiquity together. There were more direct variations than those of Ramsay and Humphreys, who projected the recent history of the Revolution as a chapter in ancient history. In *The History of Virginia*, Burk recounted once more the daunting tasks that confronted Americans, from organizing governments and containing anarchy to rousing "the genius of the nation, and direct[ing] its eagle flights to purposes of grandeur and utility." The statesmen who led the young nation had to manage "the horrors and waste of battle, the patient suffering and determined courage of the oppressed, and the temporary triumph of the oppressor; to mourn the death of the brave, to consecrate their memory by the balm of public gratitude." Yet America's Founders stood up to these disheartening expectations so nobly that it appeared as if they were "animated statues of clay or marble." Clearly, the revolutionaries seemed to Burk to be similar to the other figures carved in marble—those of classical antiquity. It is no surprise, then, that Burk deemed revolutionary orations worthy of "such as might have been spoken to the Roman senate when Pyrrhus of Hannibal had entered Italy." Indeed, by producing "orators, poets, heroes, statesmen, philosophers," Americans realized "by their manners and actions the history of ancient sages."[30] In other words, the American Revolution was a reenactment of classical history.

Mercy Otis Warren's celebrated *History of the Rise, Progress, and Termination of the American Revolution* (1805) provides another striking example of the ways in which the early historians constructed the relationship of the classics and the Revolution.[31] Warren's history was distinct from contemporary American histories on several counts. Not only was she the only women among the group of gentleman historians who produced the early revolutionary histories, but she was also the only staunch Jeffersonian Republican among a group of predominantly Federalist nationalists, and hers was the only history that was published more than a decade after its completion. Warren had finished writing her history by 1791 but published it only in 1805, most likely laying it aside because of "the virulence of party spirit" of the Federal era.[32] However, Warren's history stands out also in its intense construction of the relationship between America and the classics. Warren's dramas *The Adulateur* and *The Defeat* fused revolutionary contemporaneousness and classical history by placing Roman characters in revolutionary Boston's Whig leadership, thus constructing the American

Revolution as a stage on which Roman history was reenacted. *History of the Rise, Progress, and Termination of the American Revolution*, written more than fifteen years after her neo-Roman dramas and published some thirty years later, still demonstrated her characteristic and peculiar historical sensibilities, and particularly toward classical history.[33]

In *The Rise, Progress, and Termination of the American Revolution*, Warren made the classical ancients once more central to explaining America and its Revolution. Now narrating events that already belonged to the past, rather than writing in their midst, Warren understood and projected the recent history of the Revolution as a chapter in classical history. The Revolution that emerged from Warren's *History* seemed in many ways closer to Roman annals than to end-of-the-eighteenth-century America. In her attempt to construct the past rather than to mold the present, as she had sought to do in her plays from the 1770s, Warren intertwined Roman history in her narration of the American Revolution. Once more, she discerned more than structural similarities between the two historical epochs.

Warren's treatise consisted of a civic-humanistic narrative that understood history to be constructed of a set of moralistic and exemplary plots. Like other, similar interpretations of the eighteenth century, Warren's outlook and meta-historical assumptions consisted of what modern scholars consider Whig interpretations of history, an eighteenth-century British historiographical mode that understood the course of human events as progress toward greater freedom.[34] This pejorative label—Whig historians are accused of submitting to the fallacies of teleology and to presentism— definitely suits Warren's account of liberty's advance toward its fulfillment in the United States. Warren saw in clear Whig fashion "freedom, long hunted round the globe by a succession of tyrants," to appear "at this [revolutionary] period, as if about to erect her standard in America."[35] Indeed, it was Warren's Whig assumptions, the imminent relation she discerned between the ongoing march of liberty from antiquity to the present, that tied so closely the classical and American societies.

Warren understood history as a "tragic theater" and, hence, classical antiquity and the American Revolution as acts participating in a vast drama that unfolded over millennia.[36] As in other contemporary Whig narratives, Warren detected two antagonistic, battling forces that dominated history: On the one hand were ambition, avarice, and the lust for power, "the leading springs which generally actuate the restless mind" that lead to luxury and corruption; on the other were civic virtue, frugality, and disinterestedness. This dichotomous view inevitably led Warren to interpret history as a succession of battles between evil, tyrannical forces and benign, virtuous ideals. Warren located the historical origins of her account of that momentous battle in the Roman revolution, when the republic was cataclysmically transformed into a principate. Even Caesar's death could not save the republic, since "specious Augustus [had] established himself in empire by the appearance of justice," and "the savage Nero shamelessly weltered in the blood of the citizens." The Roman republic's dissolution had cosmic consequences that extended far beyond the Italian border. "From the dictatorship of Sylla to the overthrow of Caesar, and from the ruin of the Roman tyrant to the death of the artful Cromwell, deception as well as violence have operated to the subversion of the freedom of the people," according to Warren. Indeed, ever since Rome's fall, luxury and corruption had caused "all the rapine and confusion, the depredation and ruin, that have spread distress over the face of the earth from . . . Caesar to an arbitrary prince of the house of Brunswick." The march of corruption that Warren artfully articulated, from the Roman Caesars to the British monarchy, was stated boldly and demonstrated how Britain and Rome shared "the love of domination and an uncontrolled lust for arbitrary" power. These poisonous traits "have been equally conspicuous in the decline of Roman virtue, and in the dark pages of British story. It was these principles that overturned that ancient republic. It was these principles that frequently involved England in civil feuds."[37]

Where did America fit into this tragic tale of overpowering vices that topple even the greatest of empires? Warren believed that the same despotic powers that Britain had inherited from Rome repulsed at least part of the inhabitants of the British Isles and "drove the first settlers of America from elegant habitations and affluent regions of the western world." The first settlers' flight from the continent was thus an ocean crossing by radical Protestants in search of religious liberty, an attempt to retain in America their civic purity, which stood opposed to the perceived corruption and oppression of the Anglican church, and to avert political decadence. Unfortunately, Warren believed, "the corrupt principles which had been fashionable in the voluptuous and bigoted courts of the Stuarts soon followed the emigrants." Not only did these excesses find a footing in America, but also, "unhappily for Great Britain and America the encroachments of the crown had gathered strength by time." Indeed, it was this lineage of corruption, from Rome to Britain and America, that eventually "involved the thirteen colonies in the confusion and blood" of the Revolution.[38]

The Revolution, according to Warren, was America's attempt to retain its virtue in light of the frightful advance of corruption in history. In fact, Warren depicted the Revolution as an era during which Americans manifested virtue on a scale rarely witnessed in history. The patriots displayed devotion, self-denial, prudence, and industry to an astounding degree. "Happily for America," its "inhabitants in general possessed not only the virtues of native courage and a spirit of enterprise, but minds generally devoted to the best affections . . . [bearing] the costly sacrifices of health, fortune and life." Indeed, so commendable were American revolutionaries that there was "no age which bears a testimony so honorable to human nature; as shews mankind at so sublime a pitch of virtue."[39] If Britain attempted to corrupt America, America fought back with its admirable stock of virtuous citizens. It was nothing less than astonishing to Warren that through the boycotts that left Americans devoid of many necessities, and the dissolution of government that reduced them almost to a state of nature, their virtue prevailed and that they "did not feel the effects of anarchy in the extreme."[40] American patriots, in short, "rivaled the admired heroes of antiquity."[41]

Warren's rendition of a Manichaean struggle between luxury and virtue, corruption and disinterestedness, was anything but an original theme. Indeed, it was a mainstay of Whig histories. What was distinct in Warren's philosophy of history was the way in which she understood Rome and America to be related. Warren, we have seen, depicted Britain as a debauched Rome and America as a reincarnation of republican Rome. What shall we make, then, of her remarkable conviction that during the trying years of the Revolution, America raised her "Caesars and her Catilines, as well as her Brutuses and her Catos"? Lucius Sergius Catilina (108–62 BC) was arguably the most infamous of Roman conspirators who attempted to subvert the republic, a conspiracy memorably foiled by Cicero's Catiline orations, in which the orator exposed the villain's crimes. Unfortunately for the ancient republic, although Catilina failed in his attempts at subversion, his legacy paved the way for Julius Caesar, who finally dealt the republic its death blow. Hence, being labeled a "Catiline" was the most denigrating of all epithets; Caesar, at least, was successful in his mischief. Warren, searching for American Catilinas, found her saboteur once again in Thomas Hutchinson, Massachusetts's last civil governor. As noted earlier, Warren had already devoted her energy to defaming Hutchinson in *The Defeat* and *The Adulateur,* when the American Tory was still in power. The decades that had passed since Hutchinson had sailed to England in 1774, never to return, did not weaken her venom toward him. In her history, she spared no grim words to describe the man she deemed "an adulator." Placing Hutchinson at the level of the worst villains the world has known, Warren concluded that "few ages have produced a more fit instrument for the purposes of a corrupt court." Warren went on to describe Hutchinson's sinister character: "He was dark, intriguing, insinuating, haughty and ambitious, while the extreme of avarice marked each feature of his character." Like Catilina of old, Hutchinson was driven by the love of luxury and the lust for power. Like Catilina, he attempted to elevate himself to a more powerful position by subverting his country's constitution. It is no wonder, then, that Warren accused Hutchinson of urging "the creation of a *patrician rank,*" referring to the Roman elite caste, "from which all officers of government should in future be selected."[42] In choosing to describe Hutchinson's scheme in terms of a patriciate, and not of an aristocracy, Warren demonstrated the extent to which she understood not merely Hutchinson but also America's revolutionary past in general in Roman terms. Hutchinson fulfilled Warren's prediction that America would find her Catilinas. Who, then, would fulfill the other half of that prediction by becoming America's Cato?[43]

A number of Catos emerged during the Revolution. Warren believed that the American people in general—or, at least, the patriots, like the Romans of the early republic—"possessed not only the virtues of native courage and a spirit of enterprise, but minds generally devoted to the best affections." It was not a coincidence that in both virtuous societies, "freedom, long hunted . . . by a succession of tyrants, appeared." In describing America, however, Warren did not confine herself to the Roman paradigm. Thus, southerners could be described as "ready to swear, like Hannibal against the Romans, and to bind their sons to the oath of everlasting enmity to the name of Britain."[44] The classical world harbored a store of *exempla,* and Warren did not hesitate to take full advantage of the Carthaginian classical fortitude, which during the second century BC demonstrated the epitome of devotion to one's republic.

While the American populace demonstrated such collective virtue, their leading exemplars matched those of antiquity. Warren perpetuated the comparison so popular in the revolutionary days: that of Benedict Arnold's march on Canada in the dead of winter in 1775 to "the celebrated march of the renowned Hannibal." As in her revolutionary plays, Warren did not shy away from complimenting her close circle of Bostonian patriots. Her brother James Otis, for example, demonstrated, among a long string of virtues, "patriotism marked with the disinterestedness of a Spartan." While Otis demonstrated Lacademonian impartiality, the arch-revolutionary Samuel Adams possessed "stern manners, a smooth address, and a Roman-like firmness, united with that sagacity and penetration that would have made a figure in a [ancient] conclave." As close as one could possibly be to an American Cato, Adams "exhibited on all occasions, an example of patriotism . . . and virtue honorary to the human character."[45] Brutus and Cassius of Warren's revolutionary plays were described once more as American classical protagonists.

A staunch Jeffersonian Republican, Warren was not as adulating as most American authors toward George Washington, the Federalist father of his country. Nevertheless, she repeated the conventional appraisal he received for exhibiting "the caution of Fabius" and "the energy of Caesar" (perhaps intentionally alluding to the problematic symbol of the ruthless Julius Caesar in relation to Washington, although underscoring Caesar's merits and avoiding his crippling shortcomings with relation to the future American president). Even when she described men who were not in her opinion wholly capable of rising to ancient heights, Warren still employed figurative ancient comparisons. Hence, General Lee "emulated the heroes of antiquity in the field, while in private life he sunk into the vulgarity of the clown."[46]

Warren did not restrict herself to individuals; in her writing, American collective bodies could enjoy ancient glory, as well. Hence, the Continental Congress was, according to Warren, "composed of men jealous of their rights, proud of their patriotism and independence, and tenacious of their honor and probity." Indeed, the states' representatives demonstrated "the most pointed indignation, against such daring attempts to corrupt their integrity." We have already seen how Warren repeatedly tied a combination of stern patriotism and fear of corruption together with the classical cosmology. Indeed, she described the revolutionary congressmen as holding "genuine *amor patriae,*" leaving no doubt as to the classical nature of that revolutionary body's patriotism. Finally, by dubbing Congress "the Amphyctions of the Western world," referring to the ancient Greek league of city-states, Warren sealed her representation of the Congress—the name in itself being a stark reminder of Roman nomenclature—as an institution to be perceived as a gathering in the revered tradition of classical leagues.[47]

As in her neo-Roman plays, Warren represented the Revolution in the *History* as a drama and history in general as a "tragic theatre." In this drama, players were assigned recognized roles of historical figures, according to which they followed their assigned parts. Warren's exasperation was evident when Americans did not act according to their ascribed historical roles. The retired officers of the Continental Army who formed the Society of the Cincinnati—taking the name of Cincinnatus, the retired dictator who capitulated and returned peacefully to his oxen and plough—provided Warren with an occasion for such frustration. Indeed, the Cincinnati did not retire "satisfied with their own efforts to save their own country," as their ancient namesake has done. Rather, Warren believed, the American Cincinnati "ostentatiously assumed hereditary distinctions, and the insignia of nobility." What they should have done was to "have imitated the humble and disinterested virtues of the ancient Roman" Cincinnatus.[48] The historical stage, in Warren's perception, was a space that invited—or, rather, imposed—reenactment, role playing, and imitation.

Indeed, Americans during the long Federal decade could easily perceive their recent history as a reenactment of classical narratives. Recall how in 1805 John Adams could perceive "the history of all ages and nations in every page" of a Roman history he was reading at the time, "and especially the history of our country for forty years past. Change the names and every anecdote will be applicable to us."[49] Adams did not express an outlandish stance with regard to constructing the Revolution as a reenactment of classical narratives. The American preface to an Italian treatise, *The Romans in Greece, an Ancient Tale, Descriptive of Modern Events,* translated and published in America in 1799, expressed similar sensibilities. Indeed, American readers were expected to apply the ancient tale, which, according to its original title, was "descriptive of modern events," to current events. As Adams did, the preface assumed that "the historical facts . . . only want the names of persons, of places and of nations changed, to be the faithful record of the present times."[50] History in the early republic consisted of a classical outline that needed only to be filled with modern content.

Richard Snowden's *American Revolution; Written in the Style of Ancient History* (1793) did not conceive of "ancient" in terms of "classical antiquity." Indeed, the subtitle of Snowden's peculiar history, "Written in the Style of Ancient History," referred not to the historiographical tradition of the classical historians but, rather, to biblical style. Nevertheless, by writing American history in biblical, or "ancient," style, Snowden did not provide his readers, as might be expected, with a sacred history of the Revolution laden with divine intervention or with a providential history. To the contrary, like in other biblically styled contemporary texts, God is virtually absent from Snowden's "ancient" history, a curious fact not only because such use of biblical style might create such an expectation, but also because most other historians—who were not committed to biblical style— indeed assigned providence a more significant role in their histories than Snowden did.[51] However, through the arcane prism of biblical style, and like the other works examined in this chapter, Snowden's *American Revolution* presented the history of the Revolution and the creation of the United States as a chapter of a distant, revered, and mythic occurrence. The narration of the American Revolution in biblical style and language makes the Revolution appear as if it had taken place ages before the early American republic was created. Snowden told the Revolution in the rhythm and tone of an ancient text, not as an event that took place only several years before his account. His stylistic preference made readers construct the Revolution as a distant event on epic scale.

Snowden's history of the Revolution targeted schoolchildren as its intended audience. Indeed, Snowden confessed, "The style of ancient history was chosen, both for its conciseness and simplicity, and therefore the most suitable to the capacities of young people."[52] One suspects, however, that Snowden's idiomatic style did not simplify matters for young readers. Conversely, his frequent use of notes to explain the cumbersome descriptions he provided testifies that readers, especially the young, would find it difficult to decipher his idiosyncratic "ancient style." Snowden's use of ancient style was an ideological choice that was meant to render the Revolution exotic and to set it apart from contemporary America. Indeed, his treatise seemed to describe a world of legendary happenings long gone by. Snowden, however, did not shun classical history altogether; he did, for example, describe Washington as following "the footsteps of Fabius, who went out against the Carthaginians, and by his wisdom saved the Roman people from falling a prey to their enemies."[53] But it was his commitment to a biblical style that distinguished Snowden's history.

Throughout the history's two volumes, Snowden used relatively short and numbered verses, just as in biblical writing. But the versed staccato was hardly all of his antique armor. Snowden also employed old English throughout the history to provide further authenticity to his temporal claims, using constructions such as "spake" and "thou." Throughout his peculiar history, he replaced the names of modern cities and nations with ancient names; hence, London became "Lud" (an ancient Hebrew city), while Spain and France were alluded to by their Roman names "Hibernia" and "Gaul." Even when the author employed a modern name, he attempted to provide it with an antique flavor. Snowden thus referred to "that ancient river, the river Rhine."[54] Snowden also applied this treatment to American names. Hence, the town of Concord became "Concordia," and Virginia became "the state of the Virgin," and he named America the "Land of Columbia." These names, used consistently throughout Snowden's narrative, gave an antique feel to the mental geography of the landscape of the American Revolution.

Yet an antiqued geography was only a small portion of Snowden's "ancient style." Nations, too, would be rendered exotic: the French were Gauls, and blacks were Ethiopians. Even more striking, the author identified the actors in his treatise almost solely by their first names, as in the Bible and as opposed to modern identification by family names: "And the names of the captains [i.e., generals] were these, Artemas, Charles, Philip, Israel, Horatio, Seth, Richard, David, William, Joseph, John" (referring to generals Ward, Schuyler, Putnam, Gates, etc.). In the absence of family names, Snowden frequently had to revert to footnotes to clarify exactly who he was referring to. Indeed, he often combined this stylistic device with other measures to further the fantasy he elaborated. Hence, capitalizing on Franklin's biblical name, Benjamin, Snowden referred to "Benjamin their brother," alluding to Franklin's biblical namesake, the youngest son of Jacob. Introducing the Marquis de Lafayette, Snowden announced that "Fayette, he was a nobleman from the kingdom of Gaul."[55]

Snowden extended this treatment to institutions (Congress became "the great Sanhedrin," with an explanation that he was referring to the ancient Israelite assembly), disease (smallpox was "the leprosy of uncleanness," alluding to the Bible's most cursed ailment), and alcohol (rum was "the strong water of Barbados)," among others. Snowden also used the exact wording of the Bible to describe situations in America: Americans were, according to Snowden, "as sheep having no shepherd, every man doing that which was right in his own eyes," exactly like the Hebrews of old. Snowden also made use of biblical figural language. Lord North's counsel was "as the counsel of Achitophel in the days of David king of Israel," alluding to Achitophel, the adviser who counseled the king against his own interest, and American courtiers as "the locusts of Egypt, they devoured every goodly thing."[56]

Narrating events in revolutionary Virginia ("the land of the Virgin") Snowden concluded in the known and repeatedly used words of the biblical canon: "and the rest of the acts of Dunmore, and all that he did . . . are they not written in the book of Ramsay the scribe?" Here David Ramsay, arguably the most recognized of the early American historians, was himself portrayed as a biblical chronicler. This implied that the events that Ramsay, as well as Snowden, recorded were distant and of epic scale. Similarly, concluding another chapter, Snowden stated rhetorically, "And the rest of the Acts of the people of the [American] provinces, how they warred . . . are they not written in the Second Book of the Chronicles of the wars of the king of Britain with the people of the provinces; and recorded by the Scribe of Columbia, in the books of the great Sanhedrim?"[57] This quote demonstrates the extent to which Snowden merged the pseudo-reality he was presenting—that of the American Revolution as a chapter in ancient history—through the use of biblical language and phrases ("written in the Second Book of Chronicles"), and of ancient names ("the great Sanhedrin" and "the Scribe of Columbia").

Remarkably, to complete his ancient vision, Snowden wrote as if he actually were an ancient author writing in antiquity. Indeed, since he had committed himself to his ancient fantasy, he found it necessary to reconcile eighteenth-century novelties with his biblical narrative. Hence, he repeatedly described British ships of war as "armed with engines," meaning guns, "as were not known in the days of old: fire and balls issued out of their mouths . . . they were inventions of Satan." Snowden further delved into and wondered about these "engines." He described, astounded, how these demonic devices were cast: "The men heated the furnace seven times hotter than it was wont to be heated, and they cast the iron into the furnace seven times hotter than it was wont to be heated, and they cast the iron into the furnace, and lo! It became an engine to destroy men!" Continuing to show amazement at inventions that were already hundreds of years old by the late eighteenth century, Snowden described gunpowder as "black dust which they put into their engines . . . without it the engines could do nothing." To complete the estrangement from the present, Snowden referred to "those days" when alluding to the Revolution, as if he were actually discussing a distant and fundamentally altered reality.[58] The present of 1793 never seemed so remote and distant from a past that was barely two decades gone.

Since his idiosyncratic system of encoding events and people only made comprehension of the Revolution more cumbersome (as opposed to his claim in the preface), this peculiar literary mode must have served an important ideological end. Snowden's was a treatise that presented recent American history as a chapter in the history of a long-gone world of heroes and sacrifice in mythic proportions. The present of the 1790s could not, of course, provide any reason for understanding contemporary reality in similar terms. Indeed, the sense of the past that emerged from Snowden's history was similar to the other early revolutionary histories we have examined thus far. They all understood the present as fundamentally different from whatever had happened before they were written, be it the recent American Revolution or millennia-old occurrences; in all of them, the Revolution resembled antiquity much more than the present; they all implied that the period following the great events and achievements of the Revolution experienced a disenchantment, while America settled into an unexciting, mundane reality.

An investigation of American historical consciousness during the Federal decade should not be restricted to strictly defined "histories." Indeed, throughout early modernity, historical plays and dramas drew on the same styles, images, tones, and techniques that shaped narrative historiography. As the literary historian Paulina Kewes points out, even if many of these genres are no longer recognized as history, contemporaries treated them as such. History's generic status in the period could thus be treated as "hybrid," consisting of a much wider variety of works than would be considered "history" today.[59] Hence, John Daly Burk's drama *Bunker Hill* narrated that early revolutionary battle as a classical-age episode, in a similar fashion to his unfinished magnum opus, *The History of Virginia*. It should thus be considered another manifestation of the temporal sensibilities we are tracing.

Burk's drama *Bunker Hill, or the Death of General Warren* (1798) was another extraordinary instance of a writer conveying revolutionary reality as a tale of a distant era. Although *Bunker Hill* presents yet another classicized view of revolutionary history, it differed from the works examined thus far in several respects. First, generically, it was not a work of history per se but a "historical tragedy," a drama highly influenced by the neo-Roman tradition of Addison's *Cato* (as were Mercy Otis Warren's revolutionary dramas). Like Addison's *Cato*, Burk's *Bunker Hill* described a relatively short time span (with the battle of Bunker Hill at its center), placing a virtuous, unflinching, and unfortunately moribund character as its protagonist. Like other revolutionary dramatic texts we have examined, *Bunker Hill* provided a partisan, sentimental, Whig history. Like Mercy Otis Warren a generation before him, Burk portrayed the British military leaders as an anxious, frightened, diffident, and arrogant group and used the highest praise to describe unflinching, virtuous American rebels.[60]

Remarkably, this popular drama of the American Revolution involved Rome and its heroes as much as America or the battle in Boston;[61] equally remarkable, the play mentions more Romans by name than Americans. The preoccupation of *Bunker Hill* with Roman history is so intense that ancient history seems as relevant and vital to the drama as the American history it intended to depict. The opening section of the play situates the American Revolution in a mythical time dimension. The emerging "American Empire" is represented as Noah's Ark, fighting the deluge until "secure on freedom's Ararat," Burk's metaphor for the United States. Burk quickly turned from a biblical to a classical time dimension, however, as he situated himself as "the poet," a Homeric figure that was about to recount a tale—we need remind ourselves a mere—two decades old. This American

Homer—or, rather, Virgil (as we shall see, the tale Burk was about to tell was Roman rather than archaic)—elaborated on the worthiness of his story. "If Rome her Brutus and her Cato [could] boast," America not only had worthies such as Washington and Warren, but a "thousand names beside, the least of which would swell the Roman pride."[62] American audiences were about to hear a tale towering alongside, if not above, Roman history.

The drama itself followed the hours before and during the British attack on Breed's Hill in June 1775 (the battle was mistakenly called Bunker Hill, named after another nearby mound), an assault that succeeded only after several bloody charges had failed at the astonishing cost of more than two thousand Redcoats. The battle proved to both sides that American irregulars could and would fight the British professionals effectively and was thus considered an important psychological watershed. Almost thirty years later, Burk chose to retell the story of the battle by concentrating on its fallen hero.

The protagonist was Joseph Warren, the physician-turned-rebel described in detail in chapter 4, pictured in the play three months after his Boston Massacre oration on March 6, 1775, and a few hours before his death in battle. In an early monologue, Warren expressed the conventional wisdom about the universal significance of the emerging Revolution: "At length the sun of [American] freedom 'gins to rise upon the world." Such standard Whig readings of history, in which America's cosmic mission was to relieve the world of tyranny, were common. "Too long the world has groan'd beneath the yoke of frantic despotism," Warren exclaimed in the opening monologue. Burk continued to connect America's undertaking to classical history in the play as Warren announced, "The spirit of old Rome inspires the [American] land." In a land inspired by Rome, it comes as no surprise that Warren's compatriots could see in him the greatest of Romans: Like Warren, "so Cato, the great Roman, us'd to act." Burk made sure that Warren matched the high expectations of a Roman republican. "I never heard that Brutus was content, that he had done just so much, and no more," the American exclaimed as he expressed his urge to serve his country. Brutus, the revered tyrannicide, was not Warren's only model. He recalled how the unyielding Cato led the fleeing Roman Senate "thro' Numidia's burning sands . . . in pursuit of freedom; preferring pain and every ill to bondage." Another admired Roman whom Burk's Warren wished to emulate was Cincinnatus, who "from the plough [was] call'd by his country's voice . . . [and] flew to battle." Warren, holding these Roman models in front of him, promised America his ultimate sacrifice, as a true Roman should: "I devote myself, my services, my life to freedom." Unsurprisingly, as he contemplated while his life in the balance, Warren could "think of nothing but of souls, who in contempt of death their country sav'd, of Curtius, of Scoevola, and of Brutus, of Cato, Cassius, Decii and Camilli." The American hero's only wish was to add to this revered train of ancient patriots "the name of Warren, and hand them together down in succession to posterity." If his morbid wish were to come true, Warren claimed, he would "gladly meet their hardest fate." Warren expressed his will to die and to add his mark to the millennia-old brotherhood of virtuous Roman republicans. Republican history emerged in Burk's drama as a glorious succession of sacrifices, and time emerged as the medium of repeated republican martyrdoms.[63]

When Warren exclaimed "Liberty or Death" before his final battle, Burk consciously repeated Cato's call in Addison's famous drama.[64] It was not merely Cato, however, that Burk imitated. He also echoed American revolutionaries who imitated the Catonic motto. Indeed, Burk echoed Patrick Henry, who modeled himself on the Addisonian Roman during his finest moment in March 1775, some three months before Warren's final battle. When Warren anguished about having but "one poor life to give my country" and wished he had "ten thousand, it should have them all," it is, again, not clear to what degree his words echoed Addison's Cato and to what degree they echoed Nathan Hale's.[65] Indeed, both Patrick Henry and Nathan Hale, who consciously played out Catonic roles during the Revolution, had become Roman-like figures in late eighteenth-century America upon whom Americans gazed in reverence. When Warren's death wish was finally fulfilled at the end of the climactic battle, his demise was drawn according to the Roman code of honorable death. "The patriot Warren died," Burk made sure his audiences knew, "without a groan . . . midst the agonies of death, his darling country occupied his thoughts."[66] In his death, as in his literary life, Warren has become a Roman.

Warren was not the only Roman in Burk's drama. All of the Americans at Bunker Hill also "fought with Spartan valour . . . like the Romans." America itself was "a pure Republic . . . whose glory shall eclipse the Roman and the Grecian commonwealths." Indeed, Warren believed that "if every trifling hill be . . . ennobled" in battle and sacrifice as Bunker Hill in

America's "vast continent's Geography; Columbia may with Rome hold up her head and move along with empires." The low Bunker Hill was itself classicized, likened to the Greek and Roman volcanoes "Aetna or Vsuvius," from which the American troops poured fire on the ascending British like "scalding lava o'er the works of men." Boston, the "glorious town," Burk predicted, "shall long survive the fall of monarchies, the sack of states" to live on with "Rome and with Athens" in the pages of history.[67]

Americans aspired to become American Romans and, by and large, they succeeded in doing so, according to Burk. Their British enemies, however, entertained classical aspirations, as well. General Gage imagined to himself "the Roman legion, or Grecian Phalanx rang'd in battalia; [t]he furious aspect of the ancient Gaul, or painted Briton our brave ancestor." If the British likened themselves to the Romans and Greeks, they naturally dreaded the "barbarian" Americans raging at their rear, "like the incursive Parthians." If the British were Romans in Burk's drama, however, they were, unsurprisingly, the retreating Romans of the cumbersome and flailing empire. Indeed, in the first act, the British already forecast that their nation would fall "a prey to hungry courtiers . . . like ancient Rome when she had lost her rights." Once again, if Britain was to be a Rome, it would be the corrupt Rome that was already past its zenith. When the chaste American Elvira reprimanded her British suitor Abercrombie, she reminded him "how differently did Cato think of honor!" than he had.[68] Burk thus returned to the discourse of the 1770s that juxtaposed the virtuous American–Romans with the corrupt British–Romans.

Burk represented the climactic battle in *Bunker Hill*, the scene of carnage at the end of which Warren perished, as a classical moment, in which his protagonist was likened to the Spartan King Leonidas, who fought with a band of three hundred men at Thermopylae in a vain and admired stand against overwhelming Persian forces. "So Leonidas (I'm vain of the example) with proud disdain his mighty soul resigned. . . . [Bunker] hill shall be America's Thermopylae; hence shall her little band of patriot sons oppose those modern Persians." Bunker Hill was Thermopylae; the British were the despised Persians; the American Continentals were the Spartan "band of patriots"; and Warren was the Spartan King Leonidas. Like the Spartans, the Americans ultimately failed to defend their post, but also like the Spartans, Burk wished, they would be remembered as the most honorable of soldiers fighting unbeatable odds. When Burk called Warren to "led'st thy Grecians out" toward America's "Thermopylae, or Salamis," he promised his protagonist he would "arise thy self a temple more superb than Rome's proud Capitol."[69] Defeat was thus transformed into an opportunity to demonstrate America's glory and the classical virtue of the fallen leader.

George Washington's death at the close of the eighteenth century, on December 14, 1799, must have been a shaking experience for many Americans. The "Father of His Country" who had led the young nation during its forming decades left his compatriots abruptly at age sixty-seven. Washington's death symbolized the biological limits of the aging generation of the American Revolution. Indeed, Washington's death may have generated an "existential crisis" for the fledging nation.[70] A remarkable manifestation of the admiration of and affection for Washington, and of his centrality to American life, was the outpouring across America of hundreds of eulogies, orations, prayers, and songs in his memory in the months that followed his death. This textual flood was, in the words of the historian François Furstenberg, "a major media event."[71] In hundreds of eulogies, which often lapsed into hagiography, the man who was admired during his lifetime was transformed into a Founding Father carved in marble.[72]

Many of Washington's eulogists, in the words of the literary historian Michael Gilmore, were eager "to present the first president as the equal, if not indeed the superior, of any ancient."[73] To Washington, remarked George Minot, "public labor was amusement, suffering in the cause of freedom was a luxury, and every hour as it flew carried an offering to his country." Indeed, his personality was "so impartial . . . so moderate . . . so magnanimous . . . so philanthropic . . . unexampled virtue!"[74] Eulogists needed not to refer directly to Washington as a classical hero to represent him as one. Indeed, by referring to his classical virtues—his patriotism, martial prowess, civic altruism, disinterestedness, self-effacement, sincerity, and humility—Americans knew that the eulogies presented them with a Roman.[75]

They were not shy, however, about explicitly comparing "the Patriot without reproach" with the ancients.[76] Eulogists such as Pastor Thomas Paine perpetuated the common revolutionary-era comparisons between Washington and Fabius, who "like thee, could 'save a nation by delay,'" and Cincinnatus, "who, like thee, in the vigor of Roman heroism, could return from the conquest of his country's enemies, to his humble Mount Vernon beyond the Tyber."[77] Others, such as Fisher Ames, found less canonical ancients to whom to compare Washington, such as the Theban Epaminondas, whom "Washington resembled . . . in the purity and ardor of his patriotism."[78] It is remarkable how eulogists universally represented Washington, in the words of George Richards Minot, as "superior to ancient or modern examples."[79] Further, Washington's eulogists seemed to agree that "neither the annals of ancient or modern times afford a parallel of the character we are contemplating," according to Charles Atherton, and that "his deeds of merit have surpassed all the human efforts of past and modern ages." Hence, it seemed to Benjamin Orr "vain" to "extend our enquiries to the earliest date of civil government . . . for the character of our illustrious Washington stands alone."[80] Atherton pointed out that, though both Alexander the Great and Washington were magnanimous, while the Macedonian "was greatly wicked . . . Washington was greatly good."[81] But even when compared to less controversial ancients, eulogists found Washington superior. Unlike the wisely cautious Fabius, Washington could "seize victory by enterprise"; unlike the virtuous Cincinnatus, he could "protect from faction the liberties he had wrested from invasion"; and unlike the victorious Julius Caesar, Washington did not cross "the banks of a Rubicon," and thus did not succumb to his personal ambitions.[82] Washington's memorialists concurred that the president was better than his classical models, that "Rome with all her heroes—Greece with all her patriots, could not produce his equal."[83] Such hyperbole led the eulogists almost inevitably to mythologize and deify Washington.[84] Indeed, they represented him through celestial metaphors, as "moving in his own orbit," imparting "heat and light to his most distant satellites," and as "a newly-discovered star, whose benignant light will travel on to the world and time's farthest bounds," as sparkling "in one of the constellations of the sky."[85] It is no wonder that one could conclude that Washington's glory would shine until "earth itself sink into chaos."[86]

These eulogies shed light on a cultural ecology larger than the mere cult of Washington and the way the "man and monument" was remembered after his death.[87] These post mortem acclamations illuminate significant aspects of American society, its anxieties, and its political culture at the commencement of the nineteenth century. Washington was certainly greatly admired by large segments of the American people. Yet the image that appears through the eulogies that were spoken and printed in the months after his death was not merely of Washington but of an idealized America. As Michael Gilmore points out, "The true subject of the eulogy is the speaker and his community rather than the character and career of the person nominally portrayed."[88] The Washington that emerged from the eulogies was meant to instruct Americans and to serve as an ideal collective biography of the American people.

The era that seemed to have abruptly ended with Washington's death was a time of great deeds, of great men, of war, and of nation building. Washington's days, according to the most famous of his eulogies (which coined the phrase "first in war, first in peace, first in the hearts of his countrymen"), delivered by Charles Lee in front of the two Houses of Congress, consisted of the greatest "political, as well as military events."[89] It seemed clear to Fisher Ames that Washington's "presidency will form an epoch, and be distinguished as the age of Washington." This celebrated "age of Washington" will be viewed by future generations "through the telescope of history" as a unique era in which "so many virtues blend[ed] their rays." Since great deeds required great historians, to capture Washington's grandeur America would need "some future Plutarch."[90] Indeed, America led by Washington, eulogists seemed to agree, was favorably comparable to the classical societies in their greatest moments.

Yet if the age of Washington, "a theatre of glory unrivalled in the annals of time," had ended, a new era was about to commence.[91] How would the new era compare with the Revolution, a "memorable period of our annals and of [Washington's] glory?"[92] It seemed questionable whether America could endure another trying period, since Americans were not "a race of Washingtons." The great man was one of a kind.[93] The tasks that confronted America on the verge of the nineteenth century, however, were much less daunting than those of its immediate, revolutionary past. If the undertaking of the Revolution was titanic, a "moment in the existence of nations and men, on which the destinies of both are suspended," the challenges confronting post-revolutionary America were mundane.[94] As one eulogist admitted, all that was left was only "to perpetuate to our country that prosperity, which his goodness [Washington] has already conferred."[95] Another eulogist understood the difference between the eras in terms of plantation and nourishment. Since America had been planted by

Washington, the task now left was for the young nation to be "nourished by [John] Adams."[96]

Washington's death, then, underscored once more post-revolutionary America's fall into history. With the American Cincinnatus who won the war, founded the country, and presided over it during its first decade gone, the tasks of merely maintaining what Washington had founded seemed commonplace and trite. American eulogists and their audiences thus mourned not only George Washington in their tributes, but also the passing of a glorious era. If these texts were indeed forward-looking, focusing relentlessly on the future, as François Furstenberg has pointed out, they only made the Revolution seem more remote and less accessible.[97] As the early histories of the Revolution did, Washington's eulogies signified and symbolized the ushering in of a new era. The Revolution and its leader were transformed into a primordial if proximate past, while the present appeared very different. Once more, Washington and the Revolution he headed seemed closer to classical antiquity than to the present.

Americans during the 1790s found themselves in a precarious situation. Their Revolution was considered a spectacular success. They had established against all odds a nation among nations and founded a *novus ordo seclorum* that defied the truisms of history and political science. Nevertheless, many felt uneasy about the evident shortcomings and viability of that success. The rise of political parties, the financial distresses, the precarious international situation, and the apparent yielding of the republican-communitarian ideal to the market forces all contributed to their apprehensions.[98] Americans' uneasiness is apparent in the first histories they produced after the Revolution, into which, as the historian Lester Cohen noted, they wrote their anxieties.[99] Reacting to, and commenting on, their apprehensions, Americans attempted to freeze the Catonic moment of the Revolution by idealizing the Spirit of '76 and its heroes. Indeed, by depicting the American Revolution as a shining moment of classical performance, the early historians were expressing their discontent with the world that was born out of that Revolution.[100]

Scholars have recently underscored the ways in which early revolutionary histories functioned as tools of national identity building, a view most recently elaborated by Peter Messer.[101] Further, it seems that these

American treatises participated in what the historian Philip Hicks has called the contemporary European "neoclassical project," an attempt to attain a classical tone, mode, and standards in history writing on modern subjects.[102] Yet if some of these works indeed attempted to take part in a cosmopolitan historiographical tradition, they could not, almost by definition, also participate in the imposing project of the "Enlightened narrative," history writing on the grand scale that, according to J. G. A. Pocock, took an intensely Latin, "western" emphasis and concerned itself with the medieval histories of the successor states formed within the old frontiers of the Roman Empire.[103] The American histories were, to a large extent, a parochial, proto-exceptionalist affair.

Yet the early histories that represented the American Revolution as an episode in classical history were poised halfway between the old and the new and in their peculiar way were innovative and groundbreaking. Early American histories did manifest historical sensibilities that scholarship commonly affiliates with pre-modern intellectual sensibilities.[104] These histories remained "more exemplary than explanatory," and "the republican version of the jeremiad" may have led to the time-honored notion that virtue was liable to be lost as soon as it had been found.[105] Nevertheless, the works we have examined in this chapter constituted a major, if unwitting, step toward the acceptance and establishment of modern historical sensibilities. Cohen pointed out in a seminal monograph more than a generation ago how providence was transformed in the "revolutionary histories" from an explanatory factor into a conventional metaphor, forwarding a modern theory of historical causality.[106] A secular theory of causality was not the only innovation of these texts. The fact that the Revolution seemed through the lens of these histories much closer to classical Rome than to the world of the 1790s may have had an additional and unexpected result. If the 1790s seemed so mundane and dull compared with marvelous events that took place in a mythic world that existed only a few years before, a dramatic transformation must have occurred immediately after the Revolution. This American fall into history, the conclusion of the epic age of the Revolution and the commencement of a new and worldly one, drove Americans unwittingly toward historicist understandings of the nature and consequences of historical time. Such understandings implied, perhaps for the first time in American historiography, that the past has indeed become a foreign country.

The revolutionary histories took a major step toward a modern understanding of history and the processes it entails. The texts we have examined, and others that the space of a mere chapter do not allow me to cover, employed the classics both as a strategy and as a mode of thought and hence shared a unique sense of the "pastness" of the past. They understood the past—indeed, a very recent past—as fundamentally different and alienated from an altered present. Such understandings implied, however, that time governed history or that profound change did occur in time. Henceforth, the road to the understanding of history as a continuous interaction of forces of continuity and change, of contexts and structures, was open.[107] In the nineteenth-century world that was becoming less and less like that of antiquity by the minute, those histories were jeremiads for a revolutionary classical American world. That world may have never existed, but Americans felt that they had lost that world nonetheless.

EPILOGUE

From Republic to Empire: Beyond 1776

His country sav'd
Proud Briton's sons did he subdue;
Like Cincinnatus then withdrew,
Content like him to take the plough,
In VERNON's shade.

—*An Ode, on the Occasion of George Washington's
Birthday,* 1790

What the Founding Fathers feared has indeed come
to pass; the President of the United States has become an uncrowned king . . . the Julius Caesar of
the American Republic.

—HANS MORGENTHAU, "The Colossus of Johnson
City," 1966

"ARE WE ROME?" asks a trendy book that compares the United States
and the Roman Empire. In light of the return of classical Rome as a
common metaphor for the United States this question does not seem as
odd as it would have only a few years ago. After a long-term decline in the
perceived aptness of Rome as an explanatory model for America, the trend
seems to have reversed, with a plethora of comparisons between America's
position in the opening of the third millennium as a sole superpower and
the mighty Roman Empire of old.[1] Representations of the United States
in terms of that ancient republic-turned-empire, which were a mainstay
from the revolutionary era until well into the antebellum period, seemed

to have receded by the end of the nineteenth century. Although classical allusions occasionally resonated thereafter, the classical societies, with their store of heroes and villains, seemed less and less adequate to explain the modern—not to mention, postmodern—American democracy. All of this changed, however, with the inception of the new world order at the dawning of the third millennium and America's leading role within the transformed geopolitical situation. It is too easy to forget not only that these allusions to imperial Rome have eighteenth-century origins, but also that this classical idiom demonstrated a remarkable stability throughout the existence of the republic. Acknowledging the roots of the twenty-first-century identifications of America as the overextended, declining "Roman Empire" may help to frame the current vocabulary of America as Rome in its historical context. It also demonstrates that the republic's historical imagination has changed less over the past two centuries than we might have expected.

A striking continuity between eighteenth-century and twenty-first-century classical discourse is the fascinating and complex role that Julius Caesar and Lucius Cincinnatus have played in American political self-fashioning. While Cincinnatus, the retired senator who was called from his plough to save Rome, subsequently retired peacefully from his dictatorship and returned contentedly to his farm, Caesar sealed Rome's fate by subordinating the republic's interests to his burning ambition, initiated a civil war, and transformed the republic into an empire. From the early days of the Revolution, Americans looked back at these antithetical models to define the immensity of the perceived danger that certain individuals—"American Caesars"—posed to the republic and identified those who could potentially redeem the United States as "American Cincinnati." The continuous crowning of American Cincinnati and the condemnation of American Caesars is especially illuminating in light of the radical changes the American republic has endured throughout its existence. While this discourse has involved questions of the first magnitude, it has been carried on within the context of a political culture whose conceptual framework has changed little in more than two centuries. These two classical paradigms have helped Americans throughout the existence of the republic to make sense of their nation's fears and hopes and to define, and come to terms with, contradictory ideas about leadership, citizenship, politics, and society.[2] The continuity in the use of classical discourse demonstrates how similar anxieties have haunted America since its inception and still fuel its apprehensions about the Roman-like appearance of the world leadership it has achieved. The presence of homegrown Caesars and Cincinnati gave, and still gives, rise to fears that, like that of Rome, the empire America has gained will consume the republic it so badly wishes to preserve.[3]

Throughout most of the eighteenth century, Julius Caesar loomed large as one of history's most compelling figures, whose consuming ambition doomed the Roman republic. Since Caesar's undeniable merits were acknowledged, from his superior generalship to his literary genius, Americans could occasionally turn a blind eye to his pernicious role in history. The overwhelming attitude toward Caesar was nonetheless negative, and contemporaries regularly portrayed him as being liable for opening the door to the tyranny of the notorious Roman emperors, a position that henceforth bore his name. Indeed, from the early days of their rebellion, American revolutionaries selected Caesar as a popular epithet to slander British officials. By independence, not only magistrates and ministers but also King George III himself was regularly referred to in America as "the British Caesar."[4] Nevertheless, Caesar's function in the American imagination changed as the war ended. After 1783, the British monarch was no longer on Americans' minds. However, the harmful Roman, still remembered as the executioner of the republic, continued to preoccupy and horrify Americans. After the War of Independence was won, Americans would imagine not the British but their own compatriots on the other side of the ideological divide as potential Caesars.

Although Marcus Porcius Cato "the Younger," the stern republican martyr who opposed Julius Caesar throughout his stormy path to power, was arguably the Revolution's most popular and admired Roman hero, his role, like Caesar's, transformed once the Revolutionary War in America ended. Cato's morbid and uncompromising struggle, and his eventual defeat, was of little use in the hustle and bustle of postwar American realities. Once the war ended, another Roman, Lucius Quinctius Cincinnatus, replaced Cato as the embodiment of the ideal American republican figure. If Cato was the perfect inspirational model in times of war, Cincinnatus symbolized demobilization, subordination of the armed forces to the civil powers, and the moral superiority and virtuous simplicity of those who toil the land. This transference of favor from Cato to Cincinnatus can be seen at its clearest with regard to George Washington, the "American Cato" who led the Continental Army during the long war years, emerged victorious, retired to his Potomac estate, and was quickly hailed as America's Cincinnatus.[5]

According to tradition, Lucius Quinctius Cincinnatus was called from the plough and appointed dictator when the Aequi surrounded the Roman Army in 458 BC. After defeating the Aequi, he gave up his office and returned to his farm. His voluntary and disinterested acts of sacrifice were universally admired. Cincinnatus's actions further connoted a frugal resistance to temptation and the superiority of peasants to city dwellers, of Country to Court. It was not so much Cincinnatus's historical importance (he is a rather indistinct figure in ancient historiography) as his combination of virtues that turned him into a significant symbol in American minds. Encapsulating the republican ideals of civic humanism—of a disinterested, agrarian, virtuous citizen—Cincinnatus epitomized the integrity that could sustain a republic. His frugality, agrarianism, patriotism, and military fortitude were important. But it was mainly his marvelous surrender to civilian power and lack of personal ambition that made him the perfect standard to apply to George Washington, as well as to a train of later Americans.

Even before the war ended, juxtapositions of Washington and Cincinnatus had commenced. Both military leaders were believed to have left the plough to save their countries and to have surrendered their power to civil authority and return to their farms. Washington, like Cincinnatus, claimed Charles Henry Wharton in *A Poetical Epistle to His Excellency George Washington* (1781), rose "when of old, from his paternal farm / Rome bade her rigid Cincinnatus arm; Th' illustrious peasant rushes to the field, Soon are the haughty Volsii taught to yield. . . . His country sav'd, the solemn triumph o'er, He tills his native acres as before."[6] References to Washington's Cincinnatian image during the war were systematically elaborated once the fighting ended. After the Revolution, Washington's retirements as commander of the Continental Army in 1783 and from the presidency in 1796, and his return to the public eye when presiding over the Constitutional Convention in Philadelphia in 1787 and when he assumed the presidency of the United States in 1789, provided meaning to the perceived relationship between the American and Roman leaders.

Contemporaries repeatedly addressed Washington as "like," "the modern," the "second," and "the American" Cincinnatus. Captain Josiah Dunham described in private correspondence how Washington "great, like CINCINATUS, returned to the plough."[7] Characteristically, the Georgian William Pierce elaborated during the framing of the federal Constitution that Washington, "like Cincinnatus . . . returned to his farm perfectly contented with being only a plain citizen after enjoying the highest honor of the Confederacy, and now only seeks for the approbation of his countrymen by being virtuous and useful."[8]

Similarly, on Washington's fifty-sixth birthday, the citizens of Wilmington, Delaware, drank a toast to "Farmer Washington—may he like a second Cincinnatus, be called from the plow to rule a great people."[9] Throughout his political career, Washington's suppression of his personal wishes for the sake of the public good were represented as the shared virtues of the Roman and the American and were hailed as the noblest qualities of a republican citizen. Even Washington's bitter antagonists, such as the republican *Philadelphia Aurora*, were aware of his Cincinnatian appeal and did not neglect the opportunity to use it against him. The *Aurora* remarked ironically on October 20, 1797, that "Mr. Washington, the Cincinnatus of America," did not "follow the plow like the Venerable Roman of that name."[10]

The vast majority of allusions to Cincinnatus were not ironic, however, but revering and sincere. Washington's Cincinnatian image became vastly popular in diverse genres, from patriotic poetry (Philip Freneau's poem "Cincinnatus," for instance, describes the American general and the Roman dictator as one and the same, both retiring from war to their "sylvan shades") to visual and plastic arts, such as paintings by Charles Wilson Peale and John Trumbull that show Washington as Cincinnatus (which unfortunately have been lost, although descriptions remain).[11] The epitome of such artistic representations was Jean-Antoine Houdon's magisterial statue of Washington, now placed in the Virginia Capitol Building in Richmond, a magnanimous example of the cultivation of the Cincinnatian symbol in America in which the retiring president rests his arm on the Roman fasces standing in front of his plough.[12]

A lasting effect of Washington's enactment of the Cincinnatian role was that it generated a formulaic posture of retirement for a whole generation of revolutionary-era leaders who ritualized their retreat to the countryside as a Cincinnatian performance.[13] The list of self-proclaimed Cincinnati contains the names of great men as well as of lesser figures who have been all but forgotten over the years.[14] By 1776, John Adams had already expressed his desire to "retreat like Cincinnatus . . . and farewell Politicks. . . . [I]t seems the mode of becoming great is to retire."[15] Once he had retired, Adams was indeed compared to Cincinnatus (among other ancients).[16] Thomas Jefferson idolized "my family, my farms, and my books"

Fig. 3. *George Washington,* Jean Antoine Houdon, 1788, marble. (Courtesy of the Library of Virginia)

and never stopped redesigning his remote Monticello retreat. In 1809, as his second presidential term came to a conclusion, he wrote, "Never did a prisoner, released from his chains, feel such relief as I shall on shaking off the shackles of power."[17] Relieved of his duties, he spent his final years in stoic leisure at Monticello. John Jay, "the Cincinnatus of New York" and the nation's first secretary of state, was preoccupied in his retreat with his own Roman virtue, while James Madison's retirement to his Montpellier estate closely resembled Washington's retreat to Mount Vernon and Jefferson's withdrawal to Monticello.[18] Many other, lesser figures followed that Cincinnatian example.

Nothing was further than that ideal from the store of vices for which Julius Caesar was remembered. Caesar (100–44 BC) left his mark on Roman— indeed, on world—history by claiming a series of brilliant victories, notably in conquering Gaul, that dramatically expanded the Roman Empire. Returning to Rome after the Senate refused to extend his proconsulship in 49 BC, he decided to cross the Rubicon and march on Rome with a legion and thus ignited civil war. The rest, as they say, was history, as afterward Rome remained a republic in name but devoid of its former meaning. Caesar ever since has been the shibboleth of republicans for subversion and corruption of civic virtue.

Americans, who were used to identifying the British (especially George III) with Caesar during the Revolution, perceived a new set of Caesarean threats after the war ended. Mercy Otis Warren's prediction that it would not take "many years, before America discovered she had in her bosom, her Caesars and her Catilines" seems to have been prophetic.[19] David Ramsay, chairman of Congress of the Confederation during the Critical Period, warned that body's legislators that "anarchy or intestine wars would follow [in America] till some future Caesar seized our liberties."[20] The specter of an American Caesar haunted the young republic, and the fear such a figure would usurp and subvert the republic did not stay abstract for long. Americans repeatedly found compatriots undermining republican principles and identified them as "Caesars." Many of Secretary of the Treasury Alexander Hamilton's enemies believed that he, with his high-handed policies, posed the danger of Caesar. Jefferson's famous, if suspect, anecdote about Hamilton's inquiries regarding portraits on Jefferson's wall in 1791 reveals sensibilities of those days. The men in the portraits "are my trinity of the three greatest men the world has ever produced: Sir Francis Bacon, Sir Isaac Newton, and John Locke," Jefferson claimed to have told Hamilton. Hamilton supposedly replied, "The greatest man that ever lived was Julius Caesar," divulging his shocking admiration of the destroyer of republics.[21] John Adams, too, connected Caesar with the ambitious secretary of the treasury. The "intrigues and cabals" of both Roman triumvirates, of which Caesar was a proud member, Adams believed, were as malevolent as "Hamilton's schemes to get rid of Washington, Adams, Jay, and Jefferson and monopolize all power to himself."[22] An accusation made in 1798 by a Republican lawyer summed up the case of likening Hamilton to Caesar: "Like Caesar you [Hamilton] are ambitious and for that ambition to enslave his country Brutus slew him. And are ambitious men less dangerous to American than Roman liberty?"[23] After an "American Brutus" materialized in the form of the unlikely Aaron Burr and slew Hamilton–Caesar, John Adams commented, "When Burr shot Hamilton it was not Brutus killing Caesar in the Senate–House, but it was killing him before he passed the Rubicon."[24]

Hamilton himself believed that it was the Republicans, not he, who were "the Catilines and the Caesars of the community."[25] Becoming more personal, he claimed that if the United States had "an embryo-Caesar," it is Jefferson's future vice president (and his own future killer) Aaron Burr. Indeed, later generations concurred with Hamilton, judging that "Aaron Burr . . . resembled Caesar very much, in character, and he certainly did very much in manners."[26] Jefferson saw in Hamilton a Caesar for his centralizing, arch-federalist ideology; Hamilton found in Jefferson a Caesar for different reasons. Writing in 1792 under the Roman pseudonym "Catullus," Hamilton likened Jefferson to "Caesar coyly refusing the proffered diadem," wishing to be seen as "Caesar rejecting the trappings, but tenaciously gripping the substance of imperial domination."[27] Likening Jefferson once more to Caesar, this time under the Greek pseudonym "Phocion," Hamilton proclaimed himself a Cincinnatus. "How different was the conduct of the spirited and truly patriotic HAMILTON?" he asked, rhetorically, in the third person. "He wished to retire as much as the philosopher of Monticello. . . . He had a large family and his little fortune was fast melting away in the expensive metropolis. But with a Roman's spirit he declared that, much as he wished for retirement, he would remain at his post as long as there was any danger of his country being involved in war."[28] Hamilton's self-portrayal did not depict a Caesar, as his opponents repeatedly accused, but a disinterested, self-effacing Cincinnatus. His simultaneous rendition of these two antithetical paradigms was an early manifestation of a tradition that would characterize and, to a large extent, define American political culture in centuries to come.

The next round of American Caesars and Cincinnati commenced with the rise of the Tennessean "military chieftain" Andrew Jackson to national attention. When Jackson carried out his campaign in 1818 to punish the obstinate Seminoles and ended up seizing Spanish forts in Florida and executing British citizens as spies, he encountered severe censure from federal congressmen. In a speech in early 1819, Henry Clay hurled Caesar's "Veni, Vidi, Vici" at Jackson for his allegedly unauthorized action. In the same speech, Clay further alluded to Jackson as Caesar and to himself as Brutus: "If a Roman citizen had been asked, if he did not fear the conqueror of Gaul [Caesar] might establish a throne upon the ruins of the public liberty, he would have instantly repelled the unjust insinuation. Yet Greece had fallen, Caesar had passed the Rubicon and the patriotic arm even of Brutus could not preserve the liberties of his country."[29] The fear of Caesar has re-emerged in America.

After 1818, Jackson's rivals represented the "military chieftain" time and again as a "New Caesar" who succeeded "so well in copying the first of that name."[30] Jackson's enemies eventually consolidated in 1832 to fight the supposed threat he posed to the republic under the banner of the Whig Party. The name "Whig" conjured up the memory of Anglo-American resistance to tyranny, most recently by revolutionary Americans (some of them, including Jackson, still acting as living memories) who threw off the yoke of the British monarch (George III, as we have seen, was himself understood in terms of Julius Caesar). American Whiggism thus became a symbolic stage on which to fight a succession of Caesars. Henry Clay believed that he was protecting American liberty against the aggrandizing Caesarian Jackson. South Carolinian nullifiers who opposed Jackson from the other side of the geopolitical divide also represented themselves as followers of Cato, resisting the Caesarian Jackson.[31] Thus, John C. Calhoun pointed out how Julius Caesar, like Jackson, invaded the public treasury on his way to destroying the Roman Republic.[32] In 1837, after Jackson's successor, Martin Van Buren, was elected president, a writer in the *Connecticut Courant* wrote sarcastically that "Caesar [Jackson] was a great man. Tiberius [Van Buren]," however, was "a pitiful rascal."[33]

Acting out historical roles could have harsh consequences, however. Largely forgotten is an incident in which staunch opponents of the bank veto threatened Jackson and his closest advisers with assassination on the Ides of March of 1834, the celebrated date of Julius Caesar's murder. Nothing came of that supposed threat. In fact, the *New-Bedford Mercury* dismissed the entire episode as a hoax. Although a letter did seem to threaten the president, the pseudonymous author ("A Democrat") thought it fit to address Jackson as "dear sir" and complimented him as "one of the best presidents and generals that has been known in America." No wonder most readers and historians conjured images of a buffoon and not of a Brutus and condemned the letter to the trash bin of history.[34] However, when Jackson eventually endured a real assassination attempt on January 30, 1835, an editor suggested that the attacker, Richard Lawrence, might have "become infatuated with the chimeras which have troubled the brains of the disappointed and ambitious orators who had depicted the president as a Caesar who ought to have a Brutus."[35] Nineteenth-century newspaper editors understood the symbolic power of Caesar. Another Brutus aspirant, John Wilkes Booth, would bring that power to its logical conclusion some thirty years later.

"They talk of us of Caesar, and of Rome," Representative Balie Peyton of Tennessee declared. Yet "when Caesar won his battles, he crossed the Rubicon, and marched at the head of his Gallic legions to a throne. When Andrew Jackson had won for himself imperishable renown . . . he disbanded his soldiers and retired to his farm."[36] Peyton's comments revived Caesar's historical antithesis: If Jackson was seen by his enemies as Caesar, to his partisans he was Cincinnatus reincarnated. Indeed, Jackson was long seen as a benefactor, and symbol, of farmers. His followers, among them the newspaper editor Amos Kendall, cultivated and perpetuated his image as a farmer-soldier. Supporters toasted the "farmer of Tennessee," while others publicly admired his disinterestedness in leaving "his farm . . . and his plough," two essential symbols in the Cincinnatus myth.[37] Hence, it was easy for Jackson's admirers to make the short step and appropriate classical legend by anointing him an American Cincinnatus, a symbol that became as effective as that of Jackson the Caesar. The Caesarian Cincinnatus—or, rather, Cincinnatian Caesar—was an American novelty.

As early as 1823, a Democratic meeting in Philadelphia celebrating Jackson's candidacy referred to him as an "American Cincinnatus" who had retired to his Tennessee farm, the Hermitage, "cultivating with his own hand the soil that he defended from the grasp of a foreign foe."[38] Although the chances are that Jackson's "own hand" never cultivated the land (both he and George Washington, another worker of the land, had many slaves who toiled on their estates), the Cincinnatus theme resonated with constituencies across the nation. Jackson's opponents understood the power of the farmer-soldier image and answered during the 1828 elections: "'The modern Cincinnatus,' 'the Second Washington' . . . what an abuse of language!"[39] Jackson's Cincinnatian image was perpetuated after his retirement. In 1838, a year after Jackson departed from the presidency after making the Cincinnatian decision not to run for a third term, a Democratic newspaper called him "a Cincinnatus to whose simple and honest patriotism any degree of even irresponsible power might with safety have been entrusted."[40] After their leader's retirement and even after his death, Jacksonians were still in dialogue with the charges of Caesarism laid by Whigs and continued to cultivate Jackson's Cincinnatian image.[41]

William Henry Harrison, the victorious commander at the Battle of Tippecanoe in 1811, was yet another antebellum Cincinnatus. Harrison, the "Farmer of North Bend," Ohio, attempted to win the presidency twice: in 1836, when he lost to Martin Van Buren, and in 1840, when he was victorious. During those campaigns, Harrison was repeatedly compared to Cincinnatus. All components were present: a victorious general—Old Tippecanoe—subservient to the civil politics of the republic, who modestly preferred farming to politics but yielded to popular demand and resumed power when the republic stood in danger. An election poem titled *Harrison Song* recounted his perfect Cincinnatian stance: "When grim war arose, he buckled on his armor, to meet his country's foes . . . and when he'd served his country well . . . he turned to his home again, and sought a farmer's toils." Adjusting the Cincinnatus narrative to Jacksonian American politics, the poem continued, "Though he'd filled the offices, he never took the spoils," and concluded compellingly that Harrison was "another

Cincinnatus . . . the Hero of North Bend."[42] Processions were another venue through which Harrison's Cincinnatian image was cultivated. During the national Whig Party's convention in Baltimore in May 1840, Ohioans inscribed on their banner the motto: "She Offers Her Cincinnatus to Redeem the Republic."[43] The title of a partisan pamphlet published in Harrison's home state during the 1840 campaign succinctly summed up the case for Cincinnatus: "William Henry Harrison, the Farmer of North Bend. The American Cincinnatus. The People Called Him from the Plow and Will Sustain Him."[44] After the intense campaigning, President-elect Harrison opened the longest, and most classical, of inaugural speeches as a disinterested, virtuous Cincinnatus "called from a retirement which [he] had supposed was to continue for the residue of [his] life."

Unfortunately, Harrison did not have the opportunity to retire in the style of Cincinnatus due to his untimely death after only thirty days in office. Zachary Taylor, nominated by the Whigs and elected president in 1848, was like Harrison a veteran of the War of 1812 and one of the heroes of the recent Mexican War. The "Hero of Buena Vista," as Taylor was known, was a career army officer and a novice politician who supposedly was "untrammeled with party obligations," who owned a large cotton plantation in Mississippi. As one of only a few American presidents who did not serve in a civil post before election, Taylor counted as his assets his notable military achievements and his political aloofness. A letter by Taylor dated 1847 regarding his candidacy for the presidency reveals the significance and articulation that the Cincinnatian image had achieved in American politics by the mid-nineteenth century. "For the high honor and responsibilities of the Presidency," Taylor wrote in true Cincinnatian form, "I have not the slightest aspiration. A much more tranquil and satisfactory life awaits me, I trust, in the society of my family, and particularly fields, and in the occupations most congenial to my wishes." The unattractiveness of power and the longing for pastoral life were the hallmark of true American Cincinnati, from Washington to Taylor. So was the involuntary nature of the decision to commit to politics. "If I have been named by others and considered a candidate for the Presidency," Taylor wrote, "it has been by no agency of mine in the matter." Taylor made clear that he would "go into the office untrammeled, and be the Chief Magistrate of the nation, and not of a party." Indeed, he vowed to serve as "a 'no party' President," a fiction stemming from the paradox of republican politics, that was nonetheless imperative for a Cincinnatian image.[45] Taylor–Cincinnatus, like the Roman of old, would rise from his farm to serve and save his republic.

Thus, by the mid-nineteenth century the Cincinnatian path that Washington had trod was established, as retired military officers who turned to politics, as well as their constituencies and audiences, chose to perpetuate the presence of Cincinnatus in America. At the core of that mold stood the military hero who wanted to have his cake and eat it: the nonpolitical politician who wanted to be drawn by a thankful citizenry to a position of power he did not seek.

The Cincinnatus model may have been molded by the mid-nineteenth century, but Caesar's was still unstable: The Caesar of the American republic in the second half of the nineteenth century was not a military commander. Further, he seems to have had a personality as far removed as possible from former American Caesars such as the feisty and combative Andrew Jackson. Indeed, this "Caesar"—Abraham Lincoln—was remembered from his youth as a storyteller, not as a fighter. And because he was not a planter of any magnitude and held minimal military experience as a militia-company commander who never saw combat, his supporters never seemed to have considered anointing him as a Cincinnatus. Lincoln was a self-made lawyer who ascended to the premier position of the nation through the Whig-turned-Republican political platform, nominated as a default candidate of rival factions within the Republican Party.

It is too easy to forget how deeply Lincoln was hated during his presidency, not only by southerners, but also by many northerners. His scorning opponents accused him of trampling over the Constitution and civil liberties and of "loving negroes," and saw him as a self-serving tyrant who was committed to the destruction of the South in order to serve his personal ambition. Americans felt that once they spotted dictators they knew how to deal with them. An editorial in the *Richmond Dispatch* probably spoke for many southerners: "Assassination in the abstract is a horrid crime . . . but to slay a tyrant is no more assassination than war is murder. Who speaks of Brutus as an assassin?"[46] A U.S. senator wondered, "Is this an American congress or a roman senate in the most abject days of the roman empire? . . . [H]ow much more are we to take?" The warning was clear when a speaker at a New York rally echoed the words of the Virginian revolutionary Patrick Henry while admonishing a perceived Caesar and reminded Lincoln "that Caesar had his Brutus."[47]

Brutus, Americans knew, slew Caesar. And Lincoln, like Julius Caesar, had won a Civil War by using dictatorial powers and declaring martial law. John Wilkes Booth knew how to treat a Caesar—theatrically, at least—since he and his brothers (one of whom was named Junius Brutus, after his father) had played the roles of the chief conspirators who eventually rid the republic of the tyrant in Shakespeare's *Julius Caesar*. Booth, fueled by hatred and anguish over the South's defeat, felt that he might be saving the American republic from a Caesar whose ascendance, if history were to repeat itself, would be followed by the demise of the republic and an appalling succession of Caesars. Indeed, he staged the assassination as a symbolic reenactment of Brutus's historical act. Lest anyone misunderstand his point, as Michael Kaufman, a diligent student of the assassination, points out, Booth decided to perform "his own act in conscious imitation of the killing of Caesar . . . strike down the president in public . . . use a derringer made in a place called Northern Liberties . . . carry a dagger ornately etched with 'America, Land of the free' on its blade . . . commit the act in full view of an audience, with an accompanying message, in Latin [*sic semper tyrannis*], that would explain it all: Thus always to tyrants."[48] The Latin phrase, embedded as the state motto on the Great Seal of Virginia, left no question as to the meaning Booth attributed to his act: It was the phrase Brutus used when slaying Julius Caesar. Abraham Lincoln seemed to have realized his role as a Caesar when he was murdered by an ideologically driven self-proclaimed Brutus. But if for much of the South, Lincoln was a slain Caesar, to the rest of the nation, he instantly became a martyred, "Redeemer President."[49]

The Civil War left Americans devoid of Cincinnati. Lincoln, we have seen, lacked the military credentials and the qualification as a toiler of the land. George B. McClellan, the brilliant but flawed general, also did not seem to fit the role for contemporaries. An editor apologized, tongue in cheek, "on behalf of McClellan why he is not a Cincinnatus: He had not been called from the plough, like Cincinnatus, but he had been summoned by the war from a railway office to take command of the army in the field."[50] This ironic statement did not refer to McClellan's unsatisfactory achievements on the battlefield or to his ambition and lack of respect for the civil authority, all imperatives of the Cincinnatus model that McClellan had breached during his command. The deficiencies might have contributed to McClellan's unsuitability, but it was his commercial, clerk-like position as a railway engineer and his disconnectedness from the land that made the editor decide that the Young Napoleon was unfit to serve as a Cincinnatus. Ulysses S. Grant, McClellan's eventual successor as commander of the Union Army, seemed a more likely Cincinnatus. In 1865, as the war concluded, a news reporter described the victorious Grant as "a pure republican . . . worthy of the best days of ancient Rome." As to Grant's future as a public figure, the reporter concluded, "It may be doubted whether he would not, like another Cincinnatus, prefer to follow his plow or his tanning again."[51] Grant decided to stay in the military; he eventually led the Republican Party and settled in the White House. Nevertheless, the presidents of the first half of the nineteenth century may have been the last true farmer–Cincinnati; Grant and later Cincinnati were no longer "farmers." The pastoral aspect of post–Civil War Cincinnati was thus marginalized and eventually disappeared altogether. The central element of the transformed Cincinnatian image was that of the retired, apolitical soldier who appeared to be drafted as if against his will into politics. Frequently, such soldiers' wartime experiences enabled them to take dovish, peace-seeking stances as civilians. (Hence Grant, known during the war as "the Butcher," was elected because he returned the nation's swords to their sheaths, famously saying to the divided nation, "Let us have peace.")

Grant was the first of a string of Union generals to enter the political fray and win the presidency. His successor, Rutherford B. Hayes, a major-general in the Union Army during the war, stretched the Cincinnatus logic to its extreme. Hayes vowed not to seek reelection after he was elected president in 1878 and further proposed in his inaugural address to limit the presidency to one six-year term. Hayes kept his pledge and did not run for a second term, although he was unable to constrain his successors constitutionally from following his example.[52] This strand of the Cincinnatian tradition, which emphasized the subordination of personal ambition to the good of the republic, was—unsurprisingly—set by Washington and exercised by subsequent presidents, including popular ones like Washington himself and Andrew Jackson, who easily could have won third terms. The custom of not pursuing a third presidential term was broken only by Franklin Delano Roosevelt, who served four consecutive terms, when the republic was more than one hundred fifty years old. After Roosevelt's four-term presidency, the Cincinnatian ideal was formalized in the Constitution's Twenty-second Amendment, which declared that "no person shall be elected to the office of the president more than twice."[53] Thus, the Cincinnatian tradition was ultimately formalized in the republic's governing document.

The twentieth century, too, saw its share of American Caesars and Cincinnati. Dwight D. Eisenhower's aloofness (which fooled Democrats into thinking they might recruit him to their party before he committed himself to the Republicans) and his peace-seeking strategy based on his experience with war (to resolve the Korean conflict) should be seen as yet another link in the Cincinnatian strain we are tracing. Eisenhower's fierce attack in his farewell address on the "immense military establishment and . . . arms industry" only added to his image as a peace-seeking warrior.[54] If Eisenhower was a Cincinnatian president, his generation's Caesar was doubtless General Douglas MacArthur, who publicly challenged President Harry Truman's strategy of "limited war" in Korea. This challenge to civil authority, so foreign to the Cincinnatus–Washington mold, was, according to a recent account of American imperialism, "perhaps the only moment in its history that the American Republic came close to meeting the fate of the Roman Republic." The man who "play[ed] the part of Caesar" in this account was MacArthur.[55] Truman himself seems to have understood MacArthur's behavior in Roman terms. He wrote: "MacArthur thought he was the proconsul for the government of the United States who could do as he damned [well] pleased."[56] Consequently, Truman dismissed MacArthur from active duty, and MacArthur returned to America after eleven years of absence, reinforcing the image of a proconsul in the Roman style. In challenging the president publicly, MacArthur crossed a line—"the Rubicon," according to Niall Ferguson—that few military men have dared to cross in the American republic's history. Indeed, a biographer, dubbing MacArthur an "American Caesar" and titling his book that way, elaborately compared the ambitious Roman and American generals: "Both were bold, aloof, austere, egotistical, willful. The two generals surrounded themselves with servile aides-de-camp; remained long abroad, one as proconsul and the other as shogun, leading captive peoples in unparalleled growth; loved history; were fiercely grandiose and spectacularly fearless; and reigned as benevolent autocrats."[57]

Military conflicts and their aftermath bred many of America's leaders and its store of Roman-like heroes. The recent War on Terror seems not to be an exception. By replicating the Caesar–Cincinnatus tension, this struggle has brought to the fore a new class of Cincinnati and Caesars. For a short moment, it seemed that General Wesley Clark would be the next American Cincinnatus. Clark, a four-star general who commanded the North Atlantic Treaty Organization (NATO) forces in the Kosovo conflict in 1999, worked after his retirement as a military analyst for large television networks when an Internet grassroots movement under the banner (and website) www.draftwesleyclark.com proclaimed that it was able to "engage tens of thousands of volunteers . . . [to] spur hundreds of thousands of supporters . . . [to] raise $2 million in pledges . . . [to] be covered by every national TV network, cable news network and national newspaper [and] most importantly—[to persuade] General Clark to jump into the race."[58] Finally, Clark "capitulated" to this popular pressure and joined the Democratic primary race. Clark's seemingly reluctant move, which was staged as the result of his acceptance of the citizen's will, is—as we have seen throughout this chapter—a vital component of the Cincinnatus pattern. America has seen plenty of victoriously retired generals who were similarly "drafted" on a platform that denounced an ill-fated military policy. Accordingly, authors in cyberspace were quick to elaborate on Clark's Cincinnatian appeal. The historian and journalist David Greenberg, in a piece published in *Slate* titled "Cincinnatus for President," pointed out that "by playing Cincinnatus, Clark . . . can radiate purity and appeal to the public's distrust of power-grasping career politicians."[59] In an essay posted a day later, Greenberg added that Clark "has played the Cincinnatus role beautifully" by refusing "to identify with either party, outing himself as a Democrat just this month" and appearing "to revel in the 'Draft-Clark' outfits that have emerged at the grassroots, as if he were capitulating to public demand."[60] Clark's Cincinnatian appeal was further developed in Democratic websites, one of which called Clark "a modern-day Cincinnatus called to duty in September by a grass-root draft movement."[61] Generals since Washington have repeatedly fashioned themselves as nonpolitical public servants, posing as if others have drafted them into public office rather than advertising their ambition, and made it clear that, if not altogether sad about it, they would have happily retired from public attention. Cincinnatus, if you will, still (reluctantly) rules.

Once Clark dropped out of the race, the Democratic Party lost its first twenty-first-century Cincinnatus.[62] The opposition to the Republican administration was quick nonetheless to enthrone a new Caesar. George W.

Bush, like other "Caesarian" presidents, reigned during a stormy period, with his presidency overshadowed by the events of September 11, 2001, and their military, geopolitical, and constitutional consequences.[63] As in the case of Clark–Cincinnatus, much of the debate over Bush's Caesarism took place in the cyber arena of the Internet. The new computerized technology of photomontage, for instance, allowed a proliferation of realistic representations of Bush as Caesar. From book covers published by prestigious academic presses to mainstream websites, personal home pages, and radical political venues, Americans were exposed to the image of their president in Roman toga and breastplate, crowned with laurel leaves. Bush as Caesar flourishes in the democratic anarchy of the virtual world in opinion essays as well. In an article titled "American Caesar," for instance, Ralph Nader declared that "in the name of fighting stateless terrorism, George W. Bush is looming as the American Caesar running roughshod over the civil liberties of the American people."[64]

The charges that Nader laid before the president do not differ much from the Caesarism of which former presidents were accused. The second Iraq War and the proliferation of the comparisons between the "new American Empire" and Rome, however, brought new dimensions and focus to the traditional understanding of presidential Caesarism. Maria Wyke has outlined the remarkable burst of comparisons of George Bush to Julius Caesar that emerged in the wake of the second Iraq War. After the United States declared on September 12, 2002, that it would employ military force against Iraq with or without an international coalition, Robert Fisk of the *Independent* newspaper asked, "What was the name of that river which Julius Caesar crossed? Was it not called the Rubicon? Yesterday, Mr. Bush may have crossed the very same river."[65] The journalist Brad Warthen remarked, after the invasion of Baghdad, that "this Rubicon [the Tigris and Euphrates] is wider than the one Caesar crossed."[66] In those and numerous other comparisons, the main accusations against Bush did not focus on the traditional charges of accumulation and subversion of domestic powers. Rather, Bush was attacked for his alleged imperialistic, Caesarian foreign policy. This was the context, then, in which a *Charleston Gazette* editorial accused Bush of assuming "the mantle of Julius Caesar. He is in the process of ruining the American republic and establishing an American/corporate empire," and in which Gary Trudeau has been depicting the president in his famed comic strip *Doonesbury* as an empty Roman military helmet.[67] Hence, the war gave Bush's antagonists an opportunity to accuse him not only of usurping constitutional powers and rights, but also of turning "in time of crisis to dictatorship, the illegitimate declaration of war, [and] for the march blindly across forbidden borders into an invasion which will bring with it historic, potentially disastrous, consequences."[68] In the eyes of his opponents, George W. Bush has become the Julius Caesar of the day.

The American republic was conceived through the fear of Caesarism, the capitulation of the republic to a power-hungry, ruthless, and potent leader. Cincinnati have risen ever since to counter the imminent danger of the usurping Caesars. This dialectical pendulum of threatening Caesars and redeeming Cincinnati, which still resonates, reveals much about the enduring anxieties and hopes, realities and ideals that pervade American politics and culture. The long history of these emblems in America should not persuade us, however, that they did not undergo change over the centuries. A central Cincinnatian attribute of Washington and of following Cincinnati, for example, was their perceived connection to the land. A century later, with Cincinnati such as Ulysses S. Grant, the pastoral attributes of the model were marginalized, and twenty-first century Cincinnati, such as Wesley Clark and John McCain, are professional soldiers with no connection to the land whatsoever. Late accusations of Caesarism, we have seen, have also acquired novel meanings in light of the discourse of the "new American Empire." Nevertheless, the continuity of the Cincinnatus–Caesar discourse in America is much more impressive than the change it has endured, especially when taking into account the enormous transformations that have taken place in America since the late eighteenth century. The American Republic, whether an early modern diminutive entity composed of thirteen coastal states or a postmodern continental giant composed of fifty, has maintained throughout its existence a stable cosmology of political rhetoric.

The longevity of the Caesar–Cincinnatus discourse reveals more than an intriguing continuity in American political culture, however. That neoclassical idiom points to peculiar historical sensibilities that seem to be out of line with the main current of American historical consciousness— namely, of "American exceptionalism."[69] The belief that America is not progressing toward a contingent, historical future and that, instead, encourages interpretations of America as unyielding to the "normal" laws of history is traced to colonial-era notions of the place of the New World in God's redemptive plan. Yet, Americans believe, the success of the American Revolution and the rise of the federal system, which "appeared as a radical break in the old cycles of history," have created "a new kind of democratic republic."[70] The United States, it seemed, can avoid the snares that trapped past republics.

Historians seem to agree that a-historical, exceptionalist understandings of America became "a presumptive consensus in American political discourse" during the nineteenth century; indeed, such notions seem still to influence America's tendency to "escape history."[71] While the cluster of attitudes toward time we name "exceptionalism" tends to interpret American history as a linear, progressive, and millennial-like (conceived either in religious or in secular terms) advancement toward a blissful future, the Cincinnatus–Caesar dialectic suggests alternative attitudes Americans have held throughout the republic's history toward time and its workings. Indeed, we need to rethink the focus on exceptionalism as a sole paradigm for interpreting American historical consciousness, since there apparently were other approaches to the same problematic.

The consistent hope for, and the repeated identification of, a Cincinnatus was ambivalent in terms of its attitude toward the future: Even though it was at its core an optimistic pattern—Cincinnatus will rise, save the republic, and retire peacefully—a Cincinnatus could eventually prove to be a disguised Caesar (as many of Jackson's opponents could attest), and, more important, Cincinnati could also maintain the purity of the republic and its institutions only temporarily. A Cincinnatus could merely postpone, not eliminate, the possibility of decline. Cincinnatus thus adhered to a classico-cyclical mind frame that was out of step with exceptionalism. Caesar poses an even more radical break with exceptionalist views: The threat of an American Caesar signifies the imminent danger of the collapse of the republic. Caesar as a historical paradigm makes very little, if any, sense within a linear-progressive view of the historical process. A Caesar, by definition, could destroy only a destructible entity. Hence, in times in which Caesars threatened America, the cyclical view of history seemed to resurface in public discourse. During the Revolution, when Americans rebelled against the monarchical British Caesar, as well as in Jacksonian America, another era of threatening Caesarism, cyclical interpretations of history were abundant.[72] In such times, anxious Americans contributed remarkable cyclical interpretations of American history, such as Thomas Cole's series of paintings *Course of Empire* (1834–36), a five-part visual allegory of the rise and decline of an empire, which few could fail to identify as a Roman America.[73]

Students of empires from Polybius to Pocock have recognized the dynamic processes that cause those structures eventually to dissolve. It should not surprise us, then, that much of the present-day discourse of the American Empire is devoted to reflections not only on its rise but also on its possible fall. Indeed, the discourse of American imperialism is saturated with reflections on, and warnings of, the approaching end of American imperial hegemony. Niall Ferguson, a notable historian of imperialism, points out that America is "a Rome in which the Senate has *thus far* retained its grip on would-be emperors."[74] If "unlike Rome, [America's] republican constitution has withstood the ambitions of any would-be Caesars," it has done

Fig. 4. *The Savage State,* from *The Course of Empire,* Thomas Cole, 1834–36. (New-York Historical Society)

Fig. 5. *The Pastoral State*, from *The Course of Empire*, Thomas Cole, 1834–36. (New-York Historical Society)

Fig. 6. *Consummation*, from *The Course of Empire*, Thomas Cole, 1834–36. (New-York Historical Society)

Fig. 7. *Destruction*, from *The Course of Empire*, Thomas Cole, 1834–36. (New-York Historical Society)

Fig. 8. *Desolation*, from *The Course of Empire*, Thomas Cole, 1834–36. (New-York Historical Society)

so only "*so far.*" Ferguson adds, in a revealing parenthetical statement, that we are still witnessing America's "early days [as an empire]. The United States is 228 years old. When Caesar crossed the Rubicon in 49 BC, the Roman republic was 460 years old."[75] This remarkable historical calculus brings to mind William Henry Drayton's revolutionary-era computation of the life span of empires. "Three and thirty years numbered the illustrious Days of the Roman Greatness," he counted. "Eight Years measure the Duration of the British Grandeur."[76] America, if this logic is followed, would experience even shorter glory. William Henry Drayton in 1776, and Niall Ferguson 230 years later, attempted to calculate the span of the cycles of empire. We have yet to see whether America's downward turn on the historical cycle has arrived. At the very least, however, we have completed a cycle in American historiography.

NOTES

Introduction

1. John Adams, quoted in Richard, *The Founders and the Classics*, 84.

2. John Adams to Nathan Webb, letter, October 12, 1755, in Taylor, *The Papers of John Adams*, 1:5.

3. John Adams to Abigail Adams, letter, September 18, 1774, in Smith, *Letters of Delegates to Congress*, 1:80.

4. Letter 35, in Adams, *A Defence of the Constitutions of the Government of the United States of America*, 3:210.

5. *Rome Reborn on Western Shores* points to the usefulness of thinking beyond political culture and ideology when contemplating national identities and nationalism. Hence, my hope is that this book will contribute to the growing sophisticated historiography on the variable ways in which one could imagine "nationhood" in early modernity: see, e.g, Bell, *The Cult of the Nation in France;* Calhoun, *Nationalism;* Colley, *Britons.*

6. Edmund Pendleton, quoted in Gummere, *The American Colonial Mind and the Classical Tradition*, 18.

7. Peter Burke defines "the sense of history" as a combination of factors that correlate with "historical consciousness": a sense of anachronism; an awareness of evidence; and an interest in causation. Here I am interested mainly in anachronism, or the sense of historical perspective and of the "differentness" of the past, and to a lesser degree in causation. See Burke, *The Renaissance Sense of the Past*, 1.

8. To that end, I focus on classical "language" as a discrete and lasting intellectual universe through which revolutionary Americans construed their political predicament. My use and conceptualization of "language" is indebted to John Pocock's definition and usage of that term. For a theoretical exposition of political languages, see "Introduction: The State of the Art," in Pocock, *Virtue, Commerce and History*, 1–36; idem, *Politics, Language and Time.*

9. Including contributions such as Richard, *The Founders and the Classics;* Winterer, *The Culture of Classicism;* idem, *The Mirror of Antiquity.* For other works that have expanded our knowledge of the classics in early America, see Eadie, *Classical Traditions in Early America;* Gummere, *The American Colonial Mind and the Classical*

Tradition; Rahe, *Republics Ancient and Modern;* Reinhold, *Classica Americana;* Sellers, *American Republicanism;* Wood, *The Radicalism of the American Revolution.*

10. By referring to "civic humanism" instead of "classical republicanism," John Pocock and others underscore the importance of early modernity in the reformation of that language.

11. Richard, *The Founders and the Classics,* and Winterer, *The Mirror of Antiquity,* provide numerous and fascinating examples of the ways in which American revolutionaries derived models from antiquity.

12. Rahe, *Republics Ancient and Modern,* 571.

13. See pp. 10–13.

14. For the extent of the influence of the cult of classicism, see chapter 1. For the European context, see Honour, *Neo-classicism.*

15. Charles Lee, quoted in Reinhold, *Classica Americana,* 41.

16. Charles Lee, quoted in Sellers, *American Republicanism,* 77. Seller notes that Lee's was "a wholly conventional claim."

17. For the standard account of the republican synthesis, see Shalhope, "Republicanism and Early American Historiography"; idem, "Toward a Republican Synthesis."

18. For the original introduction of the concept of "classical republicanism," see Fink, *The Classical Republicans.* The magisterial analysis of that creed remains Pocock, *The Machiavellian Moment.*

19. For the changing notions of "democracy" and "republic" in eighteenth-century America, see Adams, *The First American Constitutions,* 96–114.

20. William Hooper to James Iredell, letter, April 26, 1774, in Saunders, *The Colonial Records of North Carolina,* 9:985.

21. "Anticipation of the Literary Fame of America," quoted in Eadie, *Classical Traditions in Early America,* 115–16. Drayton, *Memoirs of the American Revolution,* 2:386.

1. A Revolutionary Language

1. Hicks, "Portia and Marcia," 275. On eighteenth-century American attitudes toward history, see Colbourne, *The Lamp of Experience.* For the English historiographical context, see Hicks, *Neoclassical History and English Culture.*

2. Thomas Jefferson to J. Hector St. John de Crevecoeur, January 15, 1787, quoted in Kaminski, *The Quotable Jefferson,* 10.

3. Jonathan Boucher, quoted in Reinhold, *Classica Americana,* 25.

4. Cremin, *American Education.*

5. Reinhold, *Classica Americana,* 29.

6. Breen, *The Marketplace of Revolution;* Greene, *Pursuits of Happiness.*

7. David D. Hall and Elizabeth Caroll Reilly, introduction to Amory and Hall, *A History of the Book in America,* 378. See Monaghan, *Learning to Read and Write in Colonial America.* For the late-eighteenth-century American printing scene, see Pasley, *The Tyranny of the Printers.*

8. Clark, *The Public Prints*, 8.

9. Kielbowicz, "The Press, Post Office, and the Flow of News in the Early Republic," 274.

10. Clark, *The Public Prints*, 251.

11. Sloan, *The Early American Press*, 209.

12. Michael Warner calls the new culture of print "ideology of print," in which print and republicanism were integrated: Warner, "Franklin and the Republic of Letters," 112. For reading and circulation in the new "republican public sphere," see idem, *The Letters of the Republic*. See also Amory and Hall, *A History of the Book in America*.

13. Reinhold, *Classica Americana*; Winterer, *The Culture of Classicism*.

14. Winterer, *The Mirror of Antiquity*, 26.

15. Monaghan, *Learning to Read and Write in Colonial America*, 238.

16. Winterer, *The Mirror of Antiquity*, 12, 68.

17. Idem, "From Royal to Republican."

18. On this new literary polite culture, see David Shields, "Eighteenth Century Literary Culture," in Amory and Hall, *A History of the Book in America*, 434–76.

19. Winterer, *The Culture of Classicism*, 29.

20. Silverman, *A Cultural History of the American Revolution*, 76; "A Black Whig," *A Sermon*.

21. Winterer, *The Mirror of Antiquity*, 22.

22. Johnson, "Hellas in Hesperia," 143.

23. Richard, *The Battle for the American Mind*, xviii.

24. Nelson, *The Greek Tradition in Republican Thought*.

25. Winterer, *The Culture of Classicism*, 19.

26. Warren, *An Oration*.

27. Cohn-Haft, "The Founding Fathers and Antiquity," 145.

28. Reinhold, *Classica Americana*, 214.

29. The exception was Americans' interest in the various Greek leagues, especially during the debate on the Constitution during 1787–78: see, e.g., Hamilton et al., *The Federalist Papers*, nos. 4, 18, 43.

30. The "Age of Jacksonian Democracy" led to a reexamination of the reputation of Athens, which became a more attractive model, though it never reached equality with Latin.

31. Winterer, *The Mirror of Antiquity*, 23.

32. Reinhold, *Classica Americana*, 214.

33. Schlesinger, *The Cycles of American History*, 5.

34. Samuel Adams's "Christian Sparta" is the notable exception to this rule: see Winterer, *The Mirror of Antiquity*, 73.

35. Commager, "The American Enlightenment and the Ancient World," 10.

36. *Virginia Gazette* (Rind), March 3, 1768. For the influence of Plutarch in early America, see Reinhold, *Classica Americana*, 250–64.

37. Brackenridge, *The Death of General Montgomery*, 64.

38. Quentin Skinner names this uncompromising ideology "neo-Roman" liberty: Skinner, *Liberty before Liberalism*, 1–58.

39. "Cato of Utica," *Boston Gazette*, May 30, 1774.

40. "Boston," *Newport Mercury*, June 27, 1774.

41. "Cato," *South Carolina Gazette*, July 25, 1775.

42. "A Commonwealth's Man," *New Hampshire Gazette*, August 24, 1776. South-erners similarly disliked symbols of tyranny: see "Strictures in a Pamphlet Called 'A Friendly Address to All Reasonable Americans,'" *South Carolina Gazette*, December 26, 1774.

43. Cited in Richard, *The Founders and the Classics*, 119.

44. Jones, *Revolution and Romanticism*, 134.

45. For the cultivating role of the *Letters* in British America, see Bushman, *The Refinement of America*, 36–37.

46. *Virginia Gazette* (Dixon and Hunter), February 17, 1776.

47. "Charles Thomson's Note of Debates," in Smith, *Letters of Delegates to Congress*, 1:233; "Fragment of a Speech in Congress," in ibid., 1:427.

48. D'Andrade, "A Folk Model of the Mind."

49. Sellers, *American Republicanism*, 11–19. For similar manifestations of classical imagination during the English Puritan Revolution, see Kelsey, *Inventing a Republic*.

50. Winterer, "From Royal to Republican," 1265.

51. For late-eighteenth-century Americans' investment in fame and honor, see Adair, *Fame and the Founding Fathers*; Freeman, *Affairs of Honor*.

52. "Rusticus," *Remarks on a Late Pamphlet Entitled Plain Truth*, 11.

53. *An Impartial History of the War in America*, 388.

54. For a similar example of a thorough juxtaposition of American and classical arms, see "To the American Soldiery," *Virginia Gazette* (Dixon and Hunter), December 23, 1775. See also "Military Anecdotes," *South Carolina Gazette*, April 24, 1777, May 1, 1777, for narratives of the Battle of Marathon and of Xenophone's retreat during the early months of 1777.

55. George Washington to General Burgoyne, letter, quoted in Gummere, *The American Colonial Mind and the Classical Tradition*, 18.

56. "Worcester," *Massachusetts Spy*, October 23, 1777.

57. "Cato of Utica," *Boston Gazette*, May 30, 1774.

58. Brackenridge, *The Battle of Bunkers-Hill*, 16.

59. Otis, *A Vindication of the British Colonies*, 22.

60. "To the Inhabitants of the Colony of Massachusetts Bay," *Boston Gazette*, March 6, 1775. For similar notions, see "Mr. Edes," *Boston Gazette*, March 3, 1777.

61. "To the Worthy Committee Correspondence in the Town of Boston," *Boston Gazette*, January 23, 1775.

62. William Henry Drayton, in Ramsay, *The History of the Revolution of South Carolina*, 1:61.

63. "Coloni," *New Hampshire Gazette*, August 8, 1775.

64. "An Elegy to the Memory of Charles Lewis, Esquire, Who Was Slain at Point Pleasant," *Virginia Gazette* (Pinckney), May 25, 1775.

65. Christopher Gadsden, "Letter to Samuel Adams," April 4, 1779, in Walsh, *The Writings of Christopher Gadsden*, 164.

66. In what has become the shibboleth of students of the classics in America, Bernard Bailyn has argued that the classics were "intellectual window dressing . . . not determinative of thought": Bailyn, *The Ideological Origins of the American Revolution*, 23.

67. Quincy, *Observations on the Act of Parliament Commonly called the Boston Port-Bill*, 81.

68. Adams, quoted in Richard, *The Founders and the Classics*, 57.

69. Ibid., 67.

70. Smith, *An Oration in the Memory of General Montgomery*, 9.

71. *Pennsylvania Gazette*, May 10, 1775.

72. Witherspoon, *The Humble Confession*, 2.

73. Hicks, "Portia and Marcia"; Winterer, *The Mirror of Antiquity*, 12–67. The quote is in Brown, *Knowledge Is Power*, 160.

74. Warren, *The Adulateur*, *The Defeat*, in idem, *Poems*. For an extensive examination of these works, see chapter 4 in this volume.

75. James Wilson, "Of the Natural Rights of Individuals" (1790), in McClosky, *Works of James Wilson*, 2:600.

76. Hicks, "Portia and Marcia," 289; Winterer, *The Mirror of Antiquity*, 47.

77. For more detail, see Linda Kerber's concept of republican motherhood in Kerber, *Women of the Republic*; Lewis, "The Republican Wife."

78. Kann, *A Republic of Men*, 16–18.

79. "Aurelia," *Boston Gazette*, July 27, 1778.

80. "A Friend to Liberty," *Newport Mercury*, March 13, 1775.

81. "A Black Whig," *A Sermon*, 9, 11.

82. Pocock, *Barbarism and Religion*, 3:127. See also Guyatt, *Providence and the Invention of the United States*, 100–101.

83. Pocock, *Barbarism and Religion*, 3:127. Pocock argues that the idea of *translatio* was eventually replaced by Gibbon's notion of decline and fall.

84. Otto Bishop of Freising, quoted in Zakai, *Exile and Kingdom*, 80.

85. Ibid., 82.

86. Berkeley, quoted in Tuveson, *Redeemer Nation*, 93–94.

87. Adams, quoted in Silverman, *A Cultural History of the American Revolution*, 9.

88. Quoted in Bercovitch, *The American Jeremiad*, 114.

89. Nathaniel Ames, *Astronomical Diary* (1758), quoted in Zakai, *Exile and Kingdom*, 83.

90. "Non Quis Sed Quid," *South Carolina Gazette*, July 4, 1774.

91. "A Dialogue between the Ghost of General Montgomery and a Delegate," *Virginia Gazette* (Purdie), supp., March 8, 1776.

92. For the emergence of a proto-nationalistic commonality of interests in the colonies, see Breen, *The Marketplace of Revolution.* For the classical statement of "imagined communities," see Anderson, *Imagined Communities.*

93. "From the Original Letters of Caspipina," *New Hampshire Gazette,* October 2, 1774.

94. Cited in Aldridge, "The Concept of Ancients and Moderns," 105.

95. "Rising Glory of America," in Clark, *Poems of Freneau,* 1:7, 12.

96. Quincy, *Observations on the Act of Parliament Commonly called the Boston Port-Bill,* 82. After independence, the British Commonwealth tradition and its store of heroes would be pushed to the back of the stage, and the dominant component of such rhetoric would be Roman.

97. Trumbull, *An Elegy on the Times,* 11.

98. The author was aware of the "bright Millennial prospect" that his poem described: *Boston Gazette,* February 13, 1775.

99. "To the Inhabitants of the Colony of Massachusetts Bay," *Boston Gazette,* February 27, 1775. See also "Independens," *Freeman's Journal,* June 7, 1777.

100. For a South American context, see Lupher, *Romans in the New World.*

101. See chapter 3 in this volume.

102. *Two Dialogues on Different Subjects,* 130, 141.

103. Ibid., 130.

104. Ibid., 143.

105. Sewall, *Epilogue to Cato.*

106. Ramsay, *Oration on the Advantages of American Independence,* 20.

107. Ibid., 7.

108. "Anticipation of the Literary Fame of America," quoted in Eadie, *Classical Traditions in Early America,* 115–16.

109. Cooper, *Sermon Preached before His Excellency John Hancock, Esq.* Samuel Adams, too, envisioned America as a classical, if Christian polity, as a "Christian Sparta": Adams to John Scollay, December 30, 1780, in Cushing, *The Writings of Samuel Adams,* 4:238.

110. Zakai, *Exile and Kingdom,* 81–82.

111. "Officer of Rank in the Continental Army," in *America Invincible,* 20.

112. Ibid.

113. Wheatly, *Liberty and Peace,* 3.

114. Zakai, *Jonathan Edwards's Philosophy of History,* 145.

115. Freneau, *A Poem,* 21.

116. Richard, *The Founders and the Classics,* 57.

117. John Adams, quoted in ibid., 83.

118. Charles Lee, quoted in ibid., 84.

119. "Vox Populi," *Virginia Gazette* (Pinkney), December 15, 1774.

120. Ross, "Historical Consciousness in Nineteenth-Century America."

121. Drayton, *Memoirs of the American Revolution,* 2:386.

122. The similarities between the archaic attitudes toward time that Mircea Eliade

reveals and those that American patriots held are remarkable: Eliade, *The Myth of the Eternal Return*, 1971.

123. Quoted in Gummere, *The American Colonial Mind and the Classical Tradition*, 18.

124. Alexander Hamilton, "Catullus to Aristedes," in Morris, *Alexander Hamilton and the Founding of the Nation*, 129.

125. Quoted in Richard, *The Founders and the Classics*, 84.

126. *Account of the Commencement in the College of Philadelphia*, 3.

127. John Adams to a friend in London, February 10, 1775, in Smith, *Letters of Delegates to Congress*, 1:309.

128. Bolingbroke, *Letters on the Study and Use of History*, letter 2.

129. For an important study of eighteenth-century understandings of history, see Colbourne, *The Lamp of Experience*.

2. Britannia Corrupt

1. Hamer, *The Papers of Henry Laurens*, 15:371.

2. Quoted in Bell, *The Cult of the Nation in France*, 83.

3. Charles Salas points out that throughout the seventeenth and eighteenth centuries, both the French and the English attempted to appropriate the struggle between ancient Rome and Carthage to their benefit: Salas, "Punic Wars in France and Britain."

4. This partisan narrative was established by the works of Livy, a Roman, and Polybius, nominally a Roman, and was thus heavily slanted toward the Roman point of view.

5. Salas, "Punic Wars in France and Britain," 5.

6. Cited in Becker, *The Eve of the Revolution*, 31. Some doubt could remain, however, as even after the victory in the Seven Years' War, an English historian pointed out that "of all free states whose memory is preserved to us in history, Carthage bears the nearest resemblance to Britain, both in her commerce, opulence, sovereignty of the sea, and her method of carrying on her land by foreign mercenaries": Montagu, *Reflections on the Rise and Fall of the Antient Republicks*, 176.

7. For a detailed account of the development of British nationalism, see Colley, *Britons*, esp. chap. 1.

8. John Pocock comments on descriptions of Britain as "Augustan," which apply to the second half of the eighteenth century, as well: Pocock, *Barbarism and Religion*, 3:313.

9. Rowe, "Romans and Carthaginians in the Eighteenth Century," 204.

10. Goldsmith, *A History of England*, 241, 254.

11. For example, in 1759 Edward Montagu favorably compared the British achievements with ancient powers: Montagu, *Reflections on the Rise and Fall of the Antient Republicks*, 375.

12. Quoted in Koebner, *Empire*, 193.

13. Quoted in Miller, *Defining the Common Good*, 199, 250.

14. Armitage, *The Ideological Origins of the British Empire*, 68; see also ibid., 49–51. In this context see also Fitzmaurice, *Humanism and America*.

15. Miller, *Defining the Common Good*, 200.

16. Philip Yorke, quoted in ibid., 194.

17. John Entick, *The Present State of the British Empire*, quoted in Koebner, *Empire*, 196.

18. Ibid.

19. Otis, *The Rights of the British Colonies Asserted and Proved*, 15.

20. For the breadth and depth of the classicization of American literature, see Shields, *The American Aeneas*.

21. Young, *The Unfortunate Hero*, 7.

22. Ibid.

23. Ibid., 15.

24. Maylem, *The Conquest of Louisburg*, 1.

25. Ibid., 3. For contemporary attitudes toward the British king see McConville, *The King's Three Faces*.

26. *The Recruiting Officer*.

27. Ibid.

28. Mayhew, *Two Discourses Delivered October 9th*, 64.

29. Ibid., 65.

30. Ibid.

31. Foxcroft, *Grateful Reflexions on the Signal Appearances of Divine Providence for Great Britain and Its Colonies in America*, 30.

32. Ibid.

33. *The Military Glory of Great-Britain*, 6.

34. Yosef Haim Yerushalmi instructively conflates the notions of "history" and "meaning in history": see Yerushalmi, *Zakhor*.

35. Evans, *Ode on the Late Glorious Successes of His Majesty's Arms and Present Greatness of the English Nation*, 5.

36. Ibid., 5.

37. Ibid., 7.

38. Evans, "An Exercise Containing a Dialogue and Ode on Occasion of the Peace," 77.

39. Mainly because after the Glorious Revolution, the British monarchy was usually considered by contemporaries nominally as a republic, as it was perceived as governed by a mixed constitution with the legislative branch superior to the executive.

40. Cockings, *War*, 4.

41. Ibid., 13, 16.

42. Cockings, *The Conquest of Canada*.

43. "To the Public," in ibid., iii–v.

44. In fact, Cockings might have been so successful in glorifying Britain that a

performance of his play is said to have convinced the Continental Congress in 1775 to shut all theaters in Philadelphia: Emerson, *American Literature*, 94.

45. Thatcher, *The Sentiments of a British American*, 2.

46. Butterfield, *The Englishman and His History*, 81–82.

47. Robert Shalhope's quintessential surveys of the republican synthesis are "Republicanism and Early American Historiography" and "Toward a Republican Synthesis."

48. Bailyn, *The Ideological Origins of the American Revolution*, 35–54; idem, *The Origins of American Politics*, 54–57.

49. John Dickinson, quoted in Bailyn, *The Ideological Origins of the American Revolution*, 90.

50. Americans could, however, employ such an idiom to chastise themselves, as opposed to the metropole. See, e.g., "Philo Britannicus," in Hyneman and Lutz, *American Political Writing during the Founding Era*, 1:42–44. Although Bailyn is likely the only historian to address the images of Britain as a corrupt Rome in the context of the impending American Revolution, he comments on this phenomenon in a footnote and adds, offhandedly, that "analogies to the decline and fall of Rome sprang to the lips of almost every commentator as the crisis in Anglo-American affairs deepened": Bailyn, *The Ideological Origins of the American Revolution*, 137n40.

51. For an analysis of the Revolution as a rebellion against patriarchal authority see Fliegelman, *Prodigals and Pilgrims*. See also Burrows and Wallace, "The American Revolution"; and Jordan, "Familial Politics."

52. The authoritative account of the civic-humanistic language is Pocock, *The Machiavellian Moment*. For a discussion of the notion of luxury, see Sekora, *Luxury*.

53. By "Nerofication" I do not necessarily mean the act of depicting Britons in terms of Nero Claudius Caesar Germanicus, the last of the Julio-Claudian emperors, but, rather, the process in which many of the Caesars were employed to describe crown magistrates. Nevertheless, not only was Nero's figure prominent in those depictions, but his image was arguably the most ferocious of the evil train of emperors.

54. Otis, *The Rights of the British Colonies Asserted and Proved*, 15.

55. Ibid., 64.

56. Colonists in the British West Indies, and those in the rest of the American colonies who did not rebel, "conspicuously failed to join the pamphlet campaign against Britain." Accordingly, they also apparently did not join the classical discourse describing Britain as the Roman Empire: O'Shaughnessy, *An Empire Divided*, 81.

57. Henry's language might actually have been much more subtle than this account, and he might have apologized for the language he had used before his speech was over: see Morgan, *The Stamp Act Crisis*, 121–31.

58. "Yeoman," *Providence Gazette*, May 11, 1765.

59. Morgan, *Prologue to Revolution*, 73.

60. Hopkins, *The Rights of Colonies Examined*, 15.

61. Howard, *A Letter from a Gentleman at Halifax*, 15.

62. Otis, *A Vindication of the British Colonies Asserted and Proved*, 21–22.

63. For an English opinion of the "Roman" character of their control of their colonies, see "Anti-Sejanus," *London Chronicle*, November 28–30, 1765, quoted in Morgan, *Prologue to Revolution*, 73.

64. Dummer, *A Defense of the New-England Charters*, 39–40. See also Berry, *The Idea of Luxury*; Sekora, *Luxury*.

65. Morgan, *Prologue to Revolution*, 54. Similar language can be found in the resolves of other colonies: see ibid., 57 ff.

66. Ibid., 161.

67. "An Ode Occasioned by the Repeal of the Stamp Act," *Virginia Gazette* (Rind), supp., August 15, 1766.

68. Morgan, *The Stamp Act Crisis*, 152.

69. Quincy, *Observations on the Act of Parliament Commonly called the Boston Port-Bill*, 81.

70. "Monitor I," in Lee, *The Farmer's and Monitor's Letters*, 62.

71. "Monitor III," in Lee, *The Farmer's and Monitor's Letters*, 69.

72. Ibid.

73. William Hooper to James Iredell, letter, April 26, 1774, in Saunders, *The Colonial Records of North Carolina*, 9:985. Similarly, a year later John Adams asked, "Is not the British constitution arrived nearly to that point, where the Roman republic was when Jugurtha left it, and pronounc'd it a venal city ripe for destruction, if it can only find a purchaser?" "Novanglus 4," February 13, 1775, in Taylor, *The Papers of John Adams*, 2:265–67.

74. William Hooper to James Iredell, letter, April 26, 1774, in Saunders, *The Colonial Records of North Carolina*, 9:985–86. 75. Ibid., 9:986.

76. Quincy, *Observations on the Act of Parliament Commonly called the Boston Port-Bill*, 45.

77. Ibid., 46.

78. Such understandings were common as other Americans were comparing the British Parliament to the corrupt Roman Senate under Caesar, retaining merely its formalities but nothing of its early perfection: see, e.g., Langdon, *Government Corrupted by Vice*, 17.

79. Quincy, *Observations on the Act of Parliament Commonly called the Boston Port-Bill*, 57.

80. Samuel Chase to James Duane, February 5, 1775, in Smith, *Letters of Delegates to Congress*, 1:305. See also Shippen, "To the King," *Virginia Gazette* (Rind), August 25, 1774.

81. "To the Worthy Inhabitants of the Town of Boston," *Boston Gazette*, August 8, 1774.

82. "Westerly, 19th May, 1774," *Newport Mercury*, May 30, 1774.

83. *South Carolina Gazette*, September 26, 1775.

84. "Judge Drayton's Address to the Grand Jury at Charleston, South Carolina," speech, *American Archives*, series 4, vol. 5, April 23, 1776, 1025.

85. Drayton, *A Charge on the Rise of the American Empire*, 3. The speech was also printed in the *South Carolina Gazette,* November 14, 1776.

86. Ibid., 3.

87. François Furet accused Marxist historians for being fooled by the revolution-aries' rhetoric and thus not understanding what the French Revolution was really about. Here, however, I am excavating a contemporary trajectory and logic, not stating my own views on the causes of the French Revolution: see Furet, *Interpreting the French Revolution.*

88. Leacock, *The Fall of British Tyranny,* 51.

89. Ibid.

90. Quoted in Richard, *The Founders and the Classics,* 77.

91. Cushing, *The Writings of Samuel Adams,* 1:96.

92. Ibid., 1:109.

93. "General Parson's Reply to Governor Tyron's Letter," *Royal Gazette,* April 18, 1778.

94. "Humphrey Ploughjogger to Philanthrop," in Taylor, *The Papers of John Adams,* 1:179.

95. Ford, *Political Writings of John Dickinson,* 346, 356.

96. Lee, *The Farmer's and Monitor's Letters,* 66.

97. *Boston Gazette,* October 14, 1771.

98. Ibid.

99. Tacitus, *The Annals,* books 13–16; Suetonius, *The Lives of the Caesars,* 210–45.

100. Allan, *The American Alarm,* 3.

101. Warren, *The Adulateur,* 25.

102. Ibid., 25, 27, 30.

103. "To the Memory of Thomas Hutchinson," *Virginia Gazette* (Rind), June 2, 1774.

104. Silverman, *A Cultural History of the American Revolution,* 82.

105. Carretta, *George III and the Satirists from Hogarth to Byron,* 171.

106. Allan, *An Oration upon the Beauties of Liberty or the Essential Rights of the Americans,* ix (dedication).

107. "Virginius," *Virginia Gazette* (Pinkney), February 9, 1775.

108. John Adams to a friend in London, February 10, 1775, in Smith, *Letters of Delegates to Congress,* 1:309.

109. "Philoleutheros Americanus," *A Poem.*

110. "Cosmopolitan IX," *Massachusetts Spy,* April 26, 1776.

111. "Orthodoxus," *New Hampshire Gazette,* August 10, 1776. Orthodoxus alluded in the same essay to Nero's burning of Rome, asking, "Was not Rome burnt in sport?"

112. "Extract of a Letter from a Gentleman of Observation in London to His Friend in New-York," *Royal Gazette,* October 24, 1778.

113. Seabury, *A Discourse,* 12. For Samuel West's patriotic reply to this loyalist reasoning, see West, *On the Right to Rebel.*

114. "A Native of Pennsylvania [Hugh Williamson]," *The Plea of the Colonies on the Charges Brought against Them by Lord Mansfield*, 34.

115. Shaw, *American Patriots and the Rituals of Revolution*, 14.

116. Downes, *Democracy, Revolution, and Monarchism in Early American Literature*, 34.

117. Waldstreicher, *In the Midst of Perpetual Fetes*, 30. See also McConville, *The King's Three Faces*.

118. Downes, *Democracy, Revolution, and Monarchism in Early American Literature*, 34.

119. Waldstreicher, *In the Midst of Perpetual Fetes*, 31.

120. Sewall's remarkable *Epilogue to Cato* is examined thoroughly in chapter 3. See Litto, "Addison's Cato in the Colonies."

121. Sewall, *Epilogue to Cato*.

122. "America Independent," in Clark, *Poems of Freneau*, 1:26.

123. "A Few Reflections," in Marsh, *Prose*, 81.

124. Shields, *The American Aeneas*.

125. *A Dialogue, between the Devil and George III*, 2.

126. Ibid., 6.

127. Ibid.

128. Hatch, *The Sacred Cause of Liberty*, 86. Sacvan Bercovitch sees British Israel as a "commanding metaphor" of the eighteenth century: Bercovitch, *The American Jeremiad*.

129. Bercovitch points out that it took a century for a fully developed typology of mission, based on sacred rhetoric for secular use, to develop: ibid., 131.

3. "Judge the Future by the Past"

1. From here on, "the north" will refer to the colonies-states north of, and including, Pennsylvania, while "the south" will refer to the colonies south of, and including, New York.

2. Boas, "Cycles." See also Trompf, *The Idea of Historical Recurrence in Western Thought*. Cyclical theories were notably developed in the twentieth century by Oswald Spengler in his prophetic *The Decline of the West* and Arnold Toynbee's monumental *A Study of History*. For an application of cyclical theory to American history see Schlesinger, *The Cycles of American History*.

3. Bornstein, "Time-Schemes, Order, and Chaos"; Eliade, *The Myth of the Eternal Return*; Boas, "Cycles"; Macey, *Encyclopedia of Time*.

4. Guibbory, *The Map of Time*, 1–33, argues for the prevalence of cyclical ideas in England throughout early modernity.

5. Ruth Bloch points out that southern planters were among the few social groups in revolutionary America "notably disinclined towards millennial thought" and hence receptive to cyclical notions: Bloch, *Visionary Republic*, xv. See also Persons, "The Cyclical Theory of History in Eighteenth Century America."

6. Pocock, *Barbarism and Religion*.

7. Persons, "The Cyclical Theory of History in Eighteenth Century America," 155.

8. "The Reading of History Pleasing and Advantageous," *Virginia Gazette* (Purdie and Dixon), March 17, 1774. For earlier contemplations of decline in terms of Rome, see "A Comparison between the Present Age and Former Ages," *Virginia Gazette* (Purdie and Dixon), December 3, 1767; "The Effects of Simplicity and Luxury on a State, Exemplified from the Roman History," *Virginia Gazette* (Purdie and Dixon), September 5, 1771.

9. Sallust, *The Jugurthine War and the Conspiracy of Catiline.*

10. Gibbon, *The History of the Decline and Fall of the Roman Empire*, 81.

11. For extensive comparisons of Britain to declining Rome, see chapter 2.

12. *Virginia Gazette* (Pinkney), June 15, 1775. The oration was originally published in the *Pennsylvania Gazette*, May 31, 1775.

13. McCoy, *The Elusive Republic*, 33.

14. "The Speech of the Honorable Henry Temple Luttrell," *Carolina Gazette and Country Journal*, July 11, 1775.

15. *Virginia Gazette* (Pinkney), June 15, 1775.

16. "Remarks on Annual Elections for the Fairfax Independent Company," in Rutland, *The Papers of George Mason*, 1:230–31.

17. Pocock, *Barbarism and Religion*, 3:271.

18. Rutland, *The Papers of George Mason*, 1:230–31.

19. "Non Quis Sed Quid," *South Carolina Gazette and Country Journal*, July 4, 1774.

20. "One of the People," *South Carolina Gazette and Country Journal*, July 25, 1775.

21. "View of the Measures now pursuing by the Principle States of Europe," *South Carolina Gazette*, November 14, 1775.

22. McCoy, *The Elusive Republic*, 21.

23. For the ideological tensions between commercial and agrarian interests in America, see McCoy, *The Elusive Republic*, 5–12.

24. *South Carolina Gazette*, November 14, 1775.

25. "E.F.," *Virginia Gazette* (Purdie), May 17, 1776.

26. Drayton, *A Charge on the Rise of the American Empire*, 2.

27. Ibid., 9. In this context, see also Shippen, "To the King," *Virginia Gazette* (Rind), August 25, 1774.

28. Drayton, *A Charge on the Rise of the American Empire*, 9.

29. Idem, *The Speech of the Hon. William Henry Drayton, Esquire*, 4.

30. "Cato of Utica," *Boston Gazette*, May 30, 1774.

31. Pre-revolutionary discussions (see chapter 2) in which Rome's decline was seriously discussed were not perpetuated thereafter in the north.

32. "Americanus," *Boston Post-Boy*, February 13, 1775.

33. John Adams, letter to Nathan Webb, October 12, 1755, in Taylor, *The Papers of John Adams*, 1:5.

34. *Orations Delivered at the Request of the Inhabitants of the Town of Boston*, 101.

35. For millennialism in eighteenth-century America, see Bloch, *Visionary Republic*; Tuveson, *Redeemer Nation*. See also Juster, *Doomsayers*.

36. The literary historian John Shields analyzes classical "types" in revolutionary

America. However, Shields's revealing discussion is restricted to types that correlate to Virgil's writings: Shields, *The American Aeneas,* xli.

37. For typology in the American context, see Bercovitch, *Typology and Early American Literature,* 15–46.

38. Howe, *Language and Political Meaning in Revolutionary America,* 98. For more on metaphors, see Lakoff and Johnson, *Metaphors We Live By.*

39. Auerbach, *Mimesis,* 195–96. Hereafter, I will use "figura" and "type" interchangeably, as both indicate a biblical prefiguration, albeit in diverging Latin and Greek genealogies.

40. "Figura," in idem, *Scenes from the Drama of European Literature,* 54.

41. Korshin, *Typologies in England,* 5. A similar transformation can be identified outside the Anglophone world much earlier. Eric Auerbach, for example, sees Dante and the *Divine Comedy* as a pivotal figure in such transformation: Auerbach, *Scenes from the Drama of European Literature,* 60–76.

42. Korshin, *Typologies in England,* 74.

43. Dawson, *Christian Figural Reading and the Fashioning of Identity,* 84.

44. Korshin, *Typologies in England,* 25.

45. Miller, "Introduction," 7.

46. Munk, "Edward Taylor."

47. Bercovitch, "The Typology of the American Mission," 136.

48. Miller, "Introduction," 27.

49. For a bold statement regarding the role of Protestantism in the Revolution, see Shain, *The Myth of American Individualism.* Suggestions that revolutionary America was a place where "everything had a Protestant beginning" are found as early as the mid-nineteenth century: Schaff, *America,* 72–73. Modern scholars believe that, in America, "Puritanism provided the moral and background of fully 75 percent of the people who declared their independence in 1776": Ahlstrom, *Religious History of the American People,* 124. Indeed, Patricia Bonomi argues that "the idiom of religion penetrated all discourse, underlay all thought, marked all observances, gave meaning to every public and private crisis": Bonomi, *Under the Cope of Heaven,* 3.

50. Bonomi, *Under the Cope of Heaven,* 8–9.

51. Hammer, *The Puritan Tradition in Revolutionary, Federalist, and Whig Political Theory,* 94.

52. Hatch, *The Sacred Cause of Liberty,* 92.

53. Wood, *The Creation of the American Republic,* 118.

54. Samuel Adams to John Scollay, December 30, 1780, in Cushing, *The Writings of Samuel Adams,* 4:238.

55. In this context, see Nathan Hatch's notion of "republican millennialism": Hatch, *The Sacred Cause of Liberty,* 16.

56. Ross, "Historical Consciousness in Nineteenth-Century America," 918.

57. Korshin, *Typologies in England,* 134–35.

58. Ibid., 133–85.

59. Ibid., 370.

60. William Hooper to James Iredell, letter, April 26, 1774, in Saunders, *The Colonial Records of North Carolina*, 9:986.

61. Quincy, *Observations on the Act of Parliament Commonly called the Boston Port-Bill*, 82; Philip Freneau, "The Rising Glory of America," in Clark, *Poems of Freneau*, 1:13; *Two Dialogues on Different Subjects*, 130.

62. For metaphors in revolutionary discourse, see Howe, *Language and Political Meaning in Revolutionary America*, 98–127.

63. Burke, *The Renaissance Sense of the Past*, 4.

64. Meigs, *An Oration*, 12.

65. Dawson, *Christian Figural Reading and the Fashioning of Identity*, 85.

66. Smith, *An Oration in the Memory of General Montgomery*, 5.

67. Ibid., 19.

68. Dawson, *Christian Figural Reading and the Fashioning of Identity*, 89.

69. "Canada Invasion," quoted in Silverman, *A Cultural History of the American Revolution*, 314.

70. "Rusticus," *Remarks on a Late Pamphlet entitled Plain Truth*, 11.

71. *Two Dialogues on Different Subjects*, 134.

72. Ibid., 135.

73. "Officer of Rank in the Continental Army," in *America Invincible*, 32–33.

74. "Dialogue on the Success of Our Arms and the Rising Glory of America," in ibid., 137. After his defection, Arnold was not compared to Hannibal anymore. Instead, he was compared to the villains of antiquity. For example, in *The Fall of Lucifer*, Arnold is described in terms of a "Roman Catiline," the famous conspirator against the republic.

75. *Two Dialogues on Different Subjects*, 137.

76. The ease with which Americans compared their Canadian campaign to Carthage's (usually perceived as commercial and corrupt) invasion of Italy demonstrates that, while Roman models served Americans well, the typological logic allowed the use of other opportunities where non-Roman narratives and figures made themselves exegetically useful.

77. Brackenridge, *The Death of General Montgomery*, 12.

78. For Washington's and classical symbolism, see Cunliffe, *George Washington*; Schwartz, *George Washington*; Wills, *Cincinnatus*. Modern historians occasionally still use such language. See, e.g., Leibiger, *Founding Friendship*, 68, who calls Washington "the Cincinnatus who had accepted the sword reluctantly and surrendered it eagerly."

79. The Cincinnatian trope was arguably the most common of all, especially after the war. See the epilogue.

80. *Virginia Gazette* (Dixon and Hunter), January 24, 1777.

81. Clark, *Poems of Freneau*, 2:83.

82. Wharton, *A Poetical Epistle to His Excellency George Washington, Esq.*, 8.

83. Meyer Reinhold points out that "for most Americans of the eighteenth century it was through translation of the classics that they gained access to the classical

heritage": Reinhold, *Classica Americana*, 30. See also Winterer, *The Mirror of Antiquity*, 26.

84. For the history of Addison's Cato in America, see Furtwangler, "Cato in Valley Forge"; Litto, "Addison's Cato in the Colonies."

85. Litto, "Addison's Cato in the Colonies," 443.

86. Garry Wills believes that the play was "omnipresent in the revolutionary rhetoric in America": Wills, *Cincinnatus*, 127; see also Richard, *The Founders and the Classics*, 57–60.

87. Litto, "Addison's Cato in the Colonies," 449.

88. Ibid., 444–46.

89. Furtwangler, "Cato in Valley Forge."

90. Shields, *The American Aeneas*, 192.

91. Ibid., 174–93. Since Shields's illuminating study focuses on the myth of Aneas in America, he treats the epilogue on those terms. Litto ignores all but six lines of the text: Litto, "Addison's Cato in the Colonies," 447.

92. Sewall, *Epilogue to Cato.*

93. The *Epilogue to Cato* was not the only case in which Americans produced glossaries matching classical figures with contemporaries. A list of secret names of members of the Cliosophic Society of the College of New Jersey, 1770–76, attributed Greek or Roman classical names to about half of its sixty-seven members between the years 1770 and 1776: see McLachlan, "Classical Names, American Identities," 96–98. Another instance of such a glossary was a cipher composed by Alexander Hamilton in 1792, in which out of twenty-four politicians to whom he attributed a code name (including the president and several ministers and senators), twenty-two were classical. Washington was Scavola; Adams was Brutus; Jefferson was Scipio; and Madison was Tarquin: see Alexander Hamilton, "Letter to Gouverneur Morris," June 22, 1792, in Cooke and Syfert, *The Papers of Alexander Hamilton*, 11:546.

94. Warren, *The Adulateur.* See also pp. 100–103.

95. Jefferson, *Notes on the State of Virginia*; see McCoy, *The Elusive Republic*, 185–208. A hint of such reasoning can be found in embryonic form in the *Epilogue to Cato*, as Sewall promised Americans the whole continent. However, the idea of space for virtue was left undeveloped until after the war.

96. Wharton, *A Poetical Epistle to His Excellency George Washington, Esq.*, 24.

97. Pocock, *Barbarism and Religion*, 3:10.

98. For the aberrant nature of New England in the British Atlantic context, see Greene, *Pursuits of Happiness*, 28–54.

99. For a non-typological context of the use of the Romans in the New World, see Lupher, *Romans in the New World.*

100. Freneau, *A Poem*, 21.

101. *Boston Gazette*, February 13, 1775.

102. For illuminating overviews of the role of exceptionalism in American history, see Chaplin, "Expansion and Exceptionalism in Early American History"; Ross, *The Origins of American Social Science*, 22–52.

103. Trumbull, *An Elegy on the Times,* 12–13.
104. *Two Dialogues on Different Subjects,* 27.
105. Ibid., 27, 29–30.
106. Warren, *An Oration,* 6.
107. Ibid., 18, 10.
108. Ibid., 17, 25, 32.
109. The most influential and thorough corrective to this phenomenon is Greene, *Pursuits of Happiness.*
110. Bloch, *Visionary Republic,* 93.
111. Butler, "Enthusiasm Described and Decried."
112. Woodward, *The Burden of Southern History,* 19–20.
113. Britton, "The Decline and Fall of Nations in Antebellum Southern Thought"; Ross, *The Origins of American Social Science,* 30–31. See also Kaufman, *Capitalism, Slavery, and Republican Values.*
114. Pocock, *The Machiavellian Moment,* 505.
115. Ibid.; Rahe, *Republics Ancient and Modern,* esp. vols. 2–3.
116. Hall, *The Organization of American Culture.*
117. Ross, "Historical Consciousness in Nineteenth-Century America," 911.
118. "Figura," in Auerbach, *Scenes from the Drama of European Literature,* 59.
119. Madsen, *Allegory in America,* 3.

4. Taking the Toga

1. Alexander Hamilton to John Laurens, August 15, 1782, in Cooke and Syfert, *The Papers of Alexander Hamilton,* 3:145.
2. For a French perspective of classical revolutionary performances, see Ozouf, *Festivals of the French Revolution.*
3. For an insightful context of Americans "playing Indian," see Deloria, *Playing Indian.* Sandra Gustafson, too, points out that "the oratorical public culture of the revolution can be seen as a form of 'playing indian', as well as playing Greek or Roman": Gustafson, *Eloquence Is Power,* xix. For political acting as role playing see, Greene, "Character, Persona, and Authority."
4. Hopkinson, *An Exercise,* 6.
5. Charles Wilson Peale, "William Pitt, Mezzotint Engraving," 1768, in *The Classical Spirit in American Portraiture,* 28–29. For references of Pitt as Brutus, see Frank H. Sommer, "Thomas Hollis and the Arts of Dissent," in Morse, *Prints in and of America to 1850,* 143.
6. Engraving and broadside in *The Classical Spirit in American Portraiture,* 28–29.
7. Quoted in Mullett, "Classical Influences on the American Revolution," 103.
8. Zobel, *The Boston Massacre,* chap. 16.
9. Ramsay, *The History of the American Revolution* (1789), 1: 85.
10. Albanese, *Sons of the Fathers,* 73.
11. John Adams, quoted in Baskerville, *The People's Voice,* 13.

12. Gustafson, *Eloquence Is Power,* xxiv.

13. Ibid., 16.

14. Wood, *The Great Republic,* 236.

15. Gustafson, *Eloquence Is Power,* 186–7.

16. Fliegelman, *Declaring Independence,* 29–30.

17. Halloran and Clark, "Transformations of Public Discourse in Nineteenth Century America," 2.

18. Fliegelman, *Declaring Independence,* 29.

19. Gustafson, *Eloquence Is Power,* 46.

20. Cary, *Joseph Warren,* 10–11, 33, 201.

21. Ibid., 107.

22. *Orations Delivered at the Request of the Inhabitants of the Town of Boston,* 18–19.

23. Hutchinson, quoted in Forthingham, *Life and Times of Joseph Warren,* 178.

24. *Boston Gazette,* March 9, 1772.

25. Cary, *Joseph Warren,* viii.

26. *Boston Evening Post,* March 6, 1775. March 5, 1775, was a Sunday, so the annual oration was scheduled for Monday, March 6.

27. Cushing, *The Writings of Samuel Adams,* 3:205.

28. Magoon, *Orators of the American Revolution,* 157. See also Cary, *Joseph Warren,* 174. Cary may have relied on Magoon in this matter.

29. In his diary, Thomas Hutchinson recalled an alleged plot to assassinate Warren during his oration, as told by an English officer. The *Virginia Gazette,* reprinting a report from a London newspaper, elaborated on the egg episode but insisted that the design against the patriots was limited to seizure, not murder: Hutchinson and *Virginia Gazette,* quoted in Allan, *John Hancock,* 167.

30. Forthingham, *Life and Times of Joseph Warren,* 427.

31. MacKenzie, *Diary of Fredrick Mackenzie,* 13.

32. "A Spectator," a pseudonymous writer in the Tory newspaper *Rivington's Gazette* of New York, mentioned "some officers" who were present on the occasion: "A Spectator," *Rivington's Gazette,* March 13, 1775. In his diary, Hutchinson gave a (seemingly exaggerated) number of three hundred Redcoats at the oration: quoted in Allan, *John Hancock,* 167. British Lieutenant John Baker recalled "a great number of officers" who were assembled at the oration: John Baker, quoted in Allan, *John Hancock,* 167. Samuel Adams remarked that he had treated "many of the officers present" with civility and showed them to their seats so "that they might have no pretence to behave ill": Cushing, *The Writings of Samuel Adams,* 3:205.

33. Loring, *The Hundred Boston Orators Appointed by the Municipal Authorities and Other Public Bodies,* 59.

34. Quoted in Gustafson, *Eloquence Is Power,* 195.

35. Both "A Spectator" and MacKenzie mentioned the black cloth hung on the pulpit.

36. "A Spectator," *Rivington's Gazette,* March 16, 1775. See also MacKenzie, *Diary of Fredrick Mackenzie,* 13.

37. "A Spectator," *Rivington's Gazette,* March 16, 1775; emphasis added.

38. MacKenzie, *Diary of Fredrick Mackenzie,* 13; Loring, *The Hundred Boston Orators Appointed by the Municipal Authorities and Other Public Bodies,* 59; Magoon, *Orators of the American Revolution,* 158.

39. "A Spectator," *Rivington's Gazette,* March 16, 1775.

40. Cushing, *The Writings of Samuel Adams,* 3:205; MacKenzie, *Diary of Fredrick Mackenzie,* 13. A completely different account of the speech's progress appears in Loring's citation of the Reverend Dr. Homer: Loring, *The Hundred Boston Orators Appointed by the Municipal Authorities and Other Public Bodies,* 60.

41. *Orations Delivered at the Request of the Inhabitants of the Town of Boston,* 61.

42. Ibid., 67.

43. Samuel Adams reported that, as he advanced the motion to propose the appointment of an orator for next year's commemoration, the soldiers "began to hiss, which irritated the Assembly to the greatest degree, and confusion ensued": Cushing, *The Writings of Samuel Adams,* 3:206. MacKenzie reported that, once the oration was over, Adams stood up and asked for a volunteer to deliver the next year's oration to commemorate "the bloody massacre of the 5th of March 1770." The use of this charged phrase, which Warren refrained from using during his speech, instigated what came next. "On this several officers began to hiss; other cried out 'Oh! Fie! Fie!' and a great hustle ensued," which he describes in detail: MacKenzie, *Diary of Fredrick Mackenzie,* 13. Spectator agreed with his fellow Tory's narrative of the commotion at the end of the oration: "A Spectator," *Rivington's Gazette,* March 16, 1775. Lieutenant John Barker described a slightly different the scene: Barker, quoted in Allan, *John Hancock,* 168.

44. There are doubtful elements in the account by "A Spectator." He wanted his readers to believe the following sequence regarding Warren's arrival and entry: Warren reached the Old South Church, went to the store opposite the building with his servant, put on a "Ciceronian toga etc.," crossed the street—dressed in a toga, entered Old South, and mounted the pulpit. His detailed description of Warren's entrance into the building is omniscient: How could he have seen Warren donning the toga at the apothecary's, across the street from the Old South, if he and his friends were "gaping at each other" inside? The account of the Commemoration Oration by "A Spectator" left a trail of uncertainties regarding his identity, motives, and trustworthiness.

45. Which could explain the description by "A Spectator" of Warren's "Demosthenian posture, with a white handkerchief in his right hand, and his left in his breeches" during the speech.

46. Forthingham, *Life and Times of Joseph Warren,* 429.

47. Further support for the "deceptive narrative" comes from "An Oration Delivered March Fifteenth, 1775," by Thomas Bolton, a loyalist burlesque of Warren's second oration. In this piece, Bolton derides Warren's "enthusiasm," "sedition" and "profit in oration making," which were delivered with "uplifted voice and hand." However, Bolton suspiciously does not mention the toga, a silence that suggests the

toga may have never been worn: see Thomas Bolton, "An Oration," in Potter and Thomas, *The Colonial Idiom*, 303–304.

48. We should note that the account by "A Spectator" was not reprinted in Boston and was less available to Whig readership.

49. McLachlan, "Classical Names, American Identities," 83–84.

50. Quoted in Brown, *Knowledge Is Power*, 101.

51. Ibid., 102.

52. *Orations Delivered at the Request of the Inhabitants of the Town of Boston?*, 34.

53. Brown, *Knowledge Is Power*, 12. for an account of the "ideology of print," in which print and republicanism were integrated see Warner, "Franklin and the Republic of Letters."

54. Gustafson, *Eloquence Is Power*, 233.

55. Portelli, *The Text and the Voice*, 28.

56. Gustafson, *Eloquence Is Power*, 194.

57. Baskerville, *The People's Voice*, 13.

58. Fliegelman, *Declaring Independence*, 2.

59. Kann, *A Republic of Men*, 25.

60. Fliegelman, *Declaring Independence*, 2.

61. Ibid., 30; Diamond, *Performance and Cultural Politics*, 1.

62. See chapter 5.

63. At least one of Warren's pen names, "Paskalos," had a Greek resonance, although its referent is not clear.

64. Wahrman, "The English Problem of Identity in the American Revolution," 1260.

65. Deloria, *Playing Indian*, 12.

66. Cary, suggesting that Warren was indeed a leader in the party, admits that the evidence is only circumstantial: Cary, *Joseph Warren*, 134.

67. For an Indian context, see Deloria, *Playing Indian*, 26.

68. Samuel Adams to John Scollay, 30 December 1780, in Cushing, *The Writings of Samuel Adams*, 4:238.

69. *The Classical Spirit in American Portraiture*, 32.

70. See, e.g., Revere's engraving of John Hancock, in which the artist situated the model as a medieval soldier: *The Classical Spirit in American Portraiture*, 33.

71. From *Pennsylvania Packet*, July 3, 1775, quoted in Forthingham, *Life and Times of Joseph Warren*, 536.

72. Silverman, *A Cultural History of the American Revolution*, 279.

73. Forthingham, *Life and Times of Joseph Warren*, 538, 541.

74. If the author was referring to Leonidas, he was wrong, because Thermopylae, although a valiant last stand, was actually a defeat.

75. For a sample, see the many eulogies cited in Forthingham, *Life and Times of Joseph Warren*, 536–41.

76. Burk, *Bunker Hill*. For further detail, see chapter 6 in this volume.

77. The foremost specimen and model of the neo-Roman plays was Joseph

Addison's tragedy *Cato:* Addison, *Cato.* For a discussion of *Cato,* see chapter 3 in this volume. *The Defeat* was published in May 24 and July 19, 1773, issues of the *Boston Gazette.*

78. Winterer, *The Mirror of Antiquity,* 51. See also Ellison, *Cato's Tears and the Making of Anglo American Emotion.*

79. Otway, *The History and Fall of Caius Marius (1680),* manipulated historical time in similar, if not identical, fashion by transplanting Romeo and Juliet to republican Rome and inserting real historical characters such as Marius and Sulla in place of the Montagues and Capulets: see Kewes, "History and Its Uses," 64.

80. On March 26, 1772, *The Adulateur* appeared in Isaiah Thomas's *Massachusetts Spy,* and the April 23, 1772, issue published more pieces of the play. In 1773, the play was published anonymously in pamphlet form. On May 24 and July 19, 1773, a few excerpts from a second play that made use of a similar set of characters appeared in the *Boston Gazette.* This play, entitled *The Defeat,* was never published in its entirety.

81. Rosemarie Zagarri correlates the Roman *dramatis personae* in Warren's play with eminent Bostonian Whigs: Zagarri, *A Woman's Dilemma,* 56.

82. Ibid., 56.

83. Warren, *The Adulateur,* 8, 18.

84. This language is similar to the vision Warren produced at the concluding paragraph of her history of the Revolution some twenty years later: see Warren, *History of the Rise, Progress, and Termination of the American Revolution, II: 698.*

85. Zagarri, *A Woman's Dilemma,* 58. Edmund M. Hays, however, sees Rapatio's character develop from a semi-comic villain in *The Adulateur* into a "devilish master of policy grasping to power" in *The Defeat:* Hays, "Mercy Otis Warren," 440.

86. Warren, *Poems,* 10.

87. For Warren's philosophical view of history, see Hicks, "Portia and Marcia," 264–94.

88. Warren, *The Adulateur,* 20, 19.

89. Idem, *The Group,* 20.

90. See, among others, Miller, *Sam Adams,* 330; McLachlan "Classical Names, American Identities," 83.

91. During the French Revolution, which took place some fifteen years later, rites in which the participants wore Roman costumes were carefully planned and executed. (Before that climactic upheaval took place, Jean-Jacques Rousseau, who praised the salubriousness and aesthetics of the Roman garb, never dared exchange his breeches for a toga.). See Ozouf, *Festivals of the French Revolution;* Parker, *The Cult of Antiquity and the French Revolutionaries,* 52.

92. See Cohen, "The 'Liberty or Death' Speech"; McCants, *Patrick Henry.*

93. The quotes are in Gustafson, *Eloquence Is Power,* 161–63.

94. For the classics in Virginia, see Wright, "The Classical Tradition in Colonial Virginia."

95. McCants, *Patrick Henry,* 121.

96. Mullett, "Classical Influences on the American Revolution," 103n34. The two

were "stiled in Virginia & to the southward . . . the Demosthenes and Cicero of America": Ellis, *Founding Brothers,* 165.

97. Charles Thompson, quoted in Gummere, *The American Colonial Mind and the Classical Tradition,* 18.

98. Mason, *The Papers of George Mason,* 1:179.

99. McCants, *Patrick Henry,* 58–59; Cohen, "The 'Liberty or Death' Speech"; Gustafson, *Eloquence Is Power,* 164.

100. Randolph, quoted in Richard, *The Founders and the Classics,* 68.

101. Quoted in McCants, *Patrick Henry,* 57.

102. Gustafson, *Eloquence Is Power,* 142, 174.

103. Litto, "Addison's Cato in the Colonies," 444–45.

104. Furtwangler, "Cato in Valley Forge," 64–84. See also Litto, "Addison's Cato in the Colonies."

105. Litto, "Addison's Cato in the Colonies," 449. Wills believes that the play affected Americans both by its republican example and by the teaching of the dangers in caesarism: Wills, *Cincinnatus,* 136. For more on Addison's *Cato* and its reception, see chapter three in this volume.

106. Randolph, *The History of Virginia,* 212.

107. Tucker, quoted in Henry, *Patrick Henry,* 1:264–65.

108. Roane, quoted in ibid., 1:270.

109. A marble group of Laocoon and his sons being attacked by a monstrous sea serpent was excavated in Rome in 1506 and stirred a celebrated philosophical debate in the eighteenth century, which may have brought Laocoon to Roane's attention: see Lessing, *Laocoon;* Winckelmann, *Reflections on the Painting and Sculpture of the Greeks.*

110. It was, of course, the second time that Henry was implicated as a staunch Roman defying "Caesar," the first time having taken place a decade earlier when Henry admonished George III that he was on course to meet his Brutus: see chapter 2 in this volume.

111. Gustafson, *Eloquence Is Power,* 165. Henry's Catonic feat might be even more impressive considering the fact that some scholars, such as Gustafson, believe that his rhetoric was subversive to the elitist tradition of classical rhetoric: ibid., 161–65.

112. Randolph, *The History of Virginia,* 212.

113. Eighteenth-century toasts, parades, festivals, and theater performances are emblematic activities that we come to know mainly through written accounts, which have received extensive scholarly treatment: see, e.g., Newman, *Parades and the Politics of the Street;* Purcell, *Sealed with Blood;* Waldstreicher, *In the Midst of Perpetual Fetes.*

114. Hobsbawm, *The Invented Tradition,* 1–14.

115. Geertz, *The Interpretation of Cultures,* 7.

116. Bailyn, *The Ideological Origins of the American Revolution,* 26.

117. Alexander Hamilton to John Laurens, August 15, 1782, in Cooke and Syfert, *The Papers of Alexander Hamilton,* 3:145.

5. Cato Americanus

1. "Cato," *New York Journal,* September 27, 1787.

2. "Caesar," *Daily Advertiser,* October 1, 1787.

3. "Cato," *New York Journal,* October 11, 1787.

4. "Brutus," *New York Journal,* October 18, 1787.

5. Only a handful of scholars have noticed the symbolism of classical pseudonyms: see Adair, "A Note on Certain of Hamilton's Pseudonyms"; Hicks, "Portia and Marcia"; Richard, *The Founders and the Classics,* 39–43; Winterer, *The Mirror of Antiquity,* 45–47, 52–53.

6. For typical references that treat classical pseudonyms as texts without referring to the classical identity of their authors, see Ahern, "The Spirit of American Constitutionalism"; Cooke, "Alexander Hamilton's Authorship of 'Caesar' Letters."

7. Gillespie and Lienesch, *Ratifying the Constitution,* 2.

8. Meade, *Pseudonymity and Canon,* 1. "Normal" signatures are not completely stabilized social institutions, as well: see Kamuf, *Signature Pieces.*

9. For recent publications on anonymity and pseudonymity in the Anglophone world, see Easley, *First Person Anonymous;* Griffin, *The Faces of Anonymity;* North, *The Anonymous Renaissance.*

10. See, e.g., Groden and Kreiswirth, *The John Hopkins Guide to Literary Theory and Criticism.*

11. *Encyclopaedia Britannica* (1960), s.v. "Pseudonym."

12. Literary scholars point out that even recent scholarship about anonymity overlooks the symbolic creativity of pseudonyms: see Griffin, *The Faces of Anonymity,* 1–2.

13. Richard, *The Founders and the Classics,* 43. There were, nevertheless, borrowed pseudonyms that merely ornamented the text they signed, without correlating with its meaning.

14. Meade, *Pseudonymity and Canon,* 13.

15. Griffin, *The Faces of Anonymity,* 5.

16. Sensabaugh, *Milton in Early America,* 4.

17. No comprehensive count of those names has been conducted anywhere in the early modern Anglophone world. However, we do have some quantifying indicators of the prevalence of anonymity and pseudonymity. More than 80 percent of all novels published in Britain between 1750 and 1790 were published anonymously: Griffin, *The Faces of Anonymity,* 1.

18. Leonard, *Power of the Press,* 76.

19. Brown, *Knowledge Is Power,* 12. Warner, "Franklin and the Republic of Letters," 112.

20. Warner, *The Letters of the Republic,* 38–43.

21. Gustafson, *Eloquence Is Power,* 233.

22. Wahrman, "The English Problem of Identity in the American Revolution," 1260.

23. Shield, *Civil Tongues and Polite Letters in British America,* 263–65.

24. "Philo Publicus," in Hyneman and Lutz, *American Political Writing during the Founding Era*, 1:43.

25. "Britanus Americanus," in ibid., 1:91.

26. "The Tribune," in ibid., 1:92.

27. Gummere, *The American Colonial Mind and the Classical Tradition*, 13.

28. "Spartanus," quoted in Rakove, *The Beginnings of National Politics*, 148.

29. Although the count of the classical pseudonyms in the *Boston Gazette* that I have conducted is only rudimentary, it points to a trend. Other issues, such as the outflow of pseudonymous writings at different times, the ratio between non-classical and classical pseudonyms, and the diffusion of classical pseudonyms on a geographical basis, may be illuminated by the accumulation of further statistical data from additional contemporary newspapers.

30. Griffin, *The Faces of Anonymity*, 6–7.

31. Demonstrated throughout the eighteenth century by cases such as the Zenger trial of 1735 and the Act of Sedition of 1798.

32. Pasley, *The Tyranny of the Printers*, 35.

33. Benjamin Franklin, quoted in Warner, *The Letters of the Republic*, 68.

34. Freeman, *Affairs of Honor*, 129.

35. Bailyn, *The Ideological Origins of the American Revolution*, 23.

36. "The Censor," in Hyneman and Lutz, *American Political Writing during the Founding Era*, 1:659.

37. Bourdieu, *Language and Symbolic Power*, 46, 66.

38. Gustafson, *Eloquence Is Power*, 24.

39. Augurative names were connected to the texts they signed, yet, as we shall see, with less dramatic effect.

40. See pp. 174–176.

41. James McLachlan points out that about half of the surviving sixty-seven "secret names" of the Cliosophic Society of the College of New Jersey in the years 1770–77 were drawn from the classics; of these, 75 percent were Roman names, and 25 percent were Greek: McLachlan, "Classical Names, American Identities."

42. Alexander Hamilton, "Letter to Gouverneur Morris," 22 June, 1792, in Cooke and Syfert, *The Papers of Alexander Hamilton*, 11:546.

43. Warner, *The Letters of the Republic*, 78.

44. Davidson, *Propaganda and the American Revolution*, 225.

45. Smith, *Printers and the Press*, 38.

46. Howe, *Language and Political Meaning in Revolutionary America*, 191–92.

47. Ibid., 193.

48. For a discussion of the permeability and influence of newspapers, see pp. 11–12.

49. Kielbowicz, "The Press, Post Office, and the Flow of News in the Early Republic," 279.

50. Jensen, *A Documentary History of the Ratification of the Constitution*, 1:xvii.

51. Ibid., 1:xix.

52. Howe considers 75 percent a decline in the use of pseudonyms from a peak during 1774–76, when 90 percent of the pamphlets did not identify their true author: see Howe, *Language and Political Meaning in Revolutionary America,* 170, 174, 181. No similar attempt has been made to count pseudonyms in newspapers. However, it seems that newspapers, which Howe admits had become more important than pamphlets by the late 1780s, tell a different story—namely, one of a vast majority of anonymous and pseudonymous writing.

53. Occasionally authors would add "By" before their chosen name, such as in the case of "P. Valerius Agricola," *Albany Gazette,* November 8, 1787.

54. "Portius," *American Herald,* November 12, 1787.

55. "P. Valerius Agricola," *Albany Gazette,* November 8, 1787.

56. "Timon," *Daily Advertiser,* March 22, 1788.

57. "Anti-Cincinnatus," *Hampshire Gazette,* December 19, 1787.

58. "Valerius," *Virginia Independent Chronicle,* January 23, 1788.

59. "Brutus," *New York Journal,* October 18, 1787.

60. "Valerius," *Massachusetts Centinel,* November 28, 1787.

61. "Cassius," *Massachusetts Gazette,* November 30, 1787; "Cato," *New York Journal,* September 27, 1787.

62. At least one literary historian notes that "anonymity proves a lively game between author and audience." I would add that the potential of such a game expands exponentially with pseudonyms: see North, *The Anonymous Renaissance,* 5.

63. George Washington, "A Letter from Washington to Hamilton," 28 August 1788, in Cooke and Syfert, *The Papers of Alexander Hamilton,* 5:207.

64. Metaphors that extend other metaphors seem to be more effective than "regular" metaphors: see Mio, "Metaphor, Politics, and Persuasion," 136. For more on *Publius,* see pp. 176–77 in the present text.

65. "American Solon," quoted in Rakove, *The Beginnings of National Politics,* 17.

66. Hicks, "Portia and Marcia"; Winterer, *The Mirror of Antiquity,* 46–47.

67. Cima, "Black and Unmarked," 486.

68. "A Columbian Patriot [Mercy Warren Otis]," in Bailyn, *The Debate on the Constitution,* 2:284–303.

69. Kann, *A Republic of Men,* 16–18.

70. Although men (such as Benjamin Franklin) wrote occasionally under feminine pseudonyms, they did not take cover under feminine classical masks because of the intensely masculine classical sphere.

71. Philip Hicks demonstrates how Abigail Adams and Mercy Warren used classical pseudonyms in their correspondence. However, those names were not used in the public debates: Hicks, "Portia and Marcia."

72. See chapter 1. The quote is from Silverman, *A Cultural History of the American Revolution,* 9.

73. Robertson, "Look on This Picture," 1267.

74. Freeman, *Affairs of Honor,* 10.

75. Bailyn, *The Ideological Origins of the American Revolution,* 4.

76. For the adoption of the language of the duel between print combatants, see Freeman, *Affairs of Honor,* 132.

77. *The Institution of the Society of the Cincinnati,* 5.

78. For the construction of Washington as "the Cincinnatus of the West," see the epilogue.

79. Royster, *A Revolutionary People at War,* 353.

80. "Cassius," *Considerations on the Society or Order of Cincinnati,* 15.

81. See Richard, *The Founders and the Classics,* 89–90; Sellers, *American Republicanism,* 57.

82. Jensen, *A Documentary History of the Ratification of the Constitution,* 4:4–5.

83. *Massachusetts Chronicle,* January 4, 1788, in ibid., 13:614.

84. Gummere, *The American Colonial Mind and the Classical Tradition,* 13.

85. "Lycurgus," *Massachusetts Gazette,* October 23, 1787.

86. "Cato," *Essex Journal,* November 28, 1787.

87. "Helvidius Priscus," *Independent Chronicle,* December 27, 1787.

88. "Portius," *Massachusetts Gazette,* February 8, 1788.

89. "Brutus," *Independent Chronicle,* January 24, 1788.

90. "Junius," *Massachusetts Gazette,* January 29, 1788.

91. "A Question," *Massachusetts Centinel,* February 2, 1788.

92. "Cato," *Massachusetts Centinel,* January 26, 1788.

93. Jensen, *A Documentary History of the Ratification of the Constitution,* 20:540–49 (app. IV).

94. For some suggestive numbers, see ibid., 1:588–96 (app. II), 2:531–34 (app. IV), 3:575–81 (app. II), 4:597–607 (app. III).

95. Cooke identifies "Cato" as George Clinton and argues convincingly that Alexander Hamilton was most likely not "Caesar": Cooke, "Alexander Hamilton's Authorship of 'Caesar' Letters," 78–85.

96. "Caesar," *Daily Advertiser,* October 1, 1787. Interestingly, "Democritus," another anti-federalist under a classical pseudonym, mocked "Caesar" on December 14, 1787: "I will not (like the boyish Caesar) promise to follow you," perhaps alluding to Hamilton, the suspected "boyish" Caesar: "Democritus," *New York Journal,* December 14, 1787.

97. Rakove, *Original Meanings,* 156.

98. "Cato," *New York Journal,* October 11, 1787.

99. "Curtius," *Daily Advertiser,* October 18, 1787.

100. "Brutus," *New York Journal,* October 18, 1787.

101. Ibid., January 10, 1788.

102. "Cato," *New York Journal,* November 22, 1787.

103. "Brutus," *New York Journal,* January 24, 1788.

104. "Mark Anthony," *Independent Chronicle,* January 10, 1788.

105. "Americanus," *Daily Advertiser,* November 2, 1787.

106. Ibid., November 30, 1787.

107. Ibid., December 5, 1787.

108. Hamilton et al., *The Federalist Papers,* no. 18, 84, 88.

109. Jensen, *A Documentary History of the Ratification of the Constitution,* 8:4.

110. Greenberg, *Honor and Slavery,* 9.

111. The Publius essays reprinted in Virginian newspapers were: no. 1 in *Virginia Independent Chronicle,* 12 December 1787; no. 2 in *Richmond Pamphlet Anthology,* 15 December 1787, and *Virginia Independent Chronicle,* 19 December 1787; no. 3 in *Norfolk and Portsmouth Journal,* 12 December 1787, *Virginia Independent Chronicle,* 26 December 1787, *Richmond Pamphlet Anthology,* 15 December 1787, and *Virginia Independent Chronicle,* 26 December; no. 4 in *Virginia Gazette,* 22 December 1787; no. 5 in *Virginia Gazette,* 14 December 1787; no. 6 in *Norfolk and Portsmouth Journal,* 9 January 1788; no. 16 in *Virginia Gazette,* 9 April 1788.

112. The numbers are compiled from Jensen, *A Documentary History of the Ratification of the Constitution,* 8:588–96 (app. II).

113. Richard, *The Founders and the Classics,* 12–38; Mullett, "Classical Influences on the American Revolution"; Wright, "The Classical Tradition in Colonial Virginia," 36–50.

114. This "middle ground" may have collapsed in following years as pseudonyms adopted during the emergence of the First Party System, a mere few years after ratification, in which Federalist writers did not, as Republicans did, take pen names such as "Liberty," "Equality," or "Fraternity," or names of French revolutionaries such as "Mirabeau" or "Marat": see Ferling, *A Leap in the Dark,* 248.

115. A later exception to that may have been Gracchus, a Republican essayist, claiming in 1795 that "the funding system, the assumption and the bank are a triumvirate more dangerous to liberty than Caesar, Crassus and Pompey": "Gracchus," *Boston Gazette,* September 21, 1795. No Federalist would assume Gracchus, the social reformer of the late Roman Republic, to embody his arguments. Interestingly, a year later, the French proto-communist Gracchus Babeuf assumed the same name for his egalitarian conspiracy in Paris.

116. "Americanus," *Daily Advertiser,* December 5, 1787. The Latin motto for the Great Seal, "Novus Ordo Seclorum," has been traced to the Augustan poet Virgil's fourth *Eclogue,* the pastoral poem that expresses the longing of the world for a new era of peace and happiness.

117. Kenyon, *Men of Little Faith.*

118. "Brutus," *New York Journal,* January 24, 1788.

119. "Philadelphiensis," *Independent Gazetteer,* December 19, 1787.

120. See, e.g., "Cato," *New York Journal,* November 22, 1787; "Brutus," *Virginia Independent Chronicle,* May 14, 1788.

121. See chapter 2 in this volume.

122. "Americanus," *Daily Advertiser,* December 5, 1787.

123. "Agrippa," *Massachusetts Gazette,* January 15, 1788.

124. For an extensive and comprehensive essay on anti-Federalism, see Storing, *The Complete Anti-Federalist,* vol. 1.

125. See, e.g., Hamilton et al., *The Federalist Papers,* no. 18, 84–89.

126. Richard, *The Founders and the Classics*, 75–7.

127. Carl Richard expresses a similar notion of "the classicists' rout of the anti-classicist" in the Constitutional debates: Richard, *The Founders and the Classics*, 233.

128. "Mark Anthony," *Independent Chronicle*, January 10, 1788.

129. Bloch, *Visionary Republic*, 187. Bloch points out that "most of the millennialism that surfaced in the debate over the constitution came from the federalist side. They welcomed the prospect of change."

130. McCoy, *The Elusive Republic*, 201.

131. Darnton, *The Great Cat Massacre*, 78.

132. Beeman, *Beyond Confederation*.

133. Pocock, *The Machiavellian Moment*.

6. "The Pen of the Historian"

1. For the context of the Federal Decade, see Freeman, *Affairs of Honor*, 262–88.

2. John Adams, quoted in Ferguson, *Reading the Early Republic*, 1.

3. William C. Dowling, foreword to Humphreys, *An Essay on the Life of the Honourable Major-General Israel Putnam*, xvi.

4. See Leder, *The Colonial Legacy*; Messer, *Stories of Independence*.

5. Miles, "The Young American Nation and the Classical World," 270.

6. Ziff, *Writing in the New Nation*, 47.

7. Dowling, foreword to Humphreys, *An Essay on the Life of the Honourable Major-General Israel Putnam*, xiii. The current chapter, like this study as a whole, does not examine the loyalist outlook. For an account of loyalist revolutionary histories, see Leder, *The Colonial Legacy*, vol. 1.

8. Humphreys, *An Essay on the Life of the Honourable Major-General Israel Putnam*, 5.

9. Ramsay, *The History of the American Revolution* (1793), 1:iv.

10. Morse, *History of America in Two Books*, 2:116; Warren, *History of the Rise, Progress, and Termination of the American Revolution*, 1:81.

11. Burk, *The History of Virginia from Its First Settlement to the Present Day*, 1:6.

12. Warren, *History of the Rise, Progress, and Termination of the American Revolution*, 1:288.

13. Burk, *The History of Virginia from Its First Settlement to the Present Day*, 1:6

14. Ibid., 3:279.

15. M'Cullough, *Concise History of the United States*, 164–65.

16. Warren, *History of the Rise, Progress, and Termination of the American Revolution*, 1:97.

17. Burk, *The History of Virginia from Its First Settlement to the Present Day*, 1:6.

18. For the magisterial synthetic work on the period, see Elkins and McKitrick, *The Age of Federalism*.

19. M'Cullough, *Concise History of the United States*, 167.

20. For Ramsay's intellectual biography, see Shaffer, *To Be an American*.

21. Cohen, *The Revolutionary Histories*, 173.

22. Ramsay, *The History of the Revolution of South Carolina*, 1:11.

23. Ibid., 1:11, 1:161; Quentin Skinner, *Liberty before Liberalism*.

24. Ramsay, *The History of the Revolution of South Carolina*, 1:161.

25. David Ramsay, quoted in Hofstadter, *The Progressive Historians*, 233.

26. Ramsay, *The History of the American Revolution* (1789), 1:316.

27. Humphreys, *An Essay on the Life of the Honourable Major-General Israel Putnam*, 59.

28. Ibid., 67.

29. Dowling, foreword to Humphreys, xiv.

30. Burk, *The History of Virginia from Its First Settlement to the Present Day*, 3:279, 3:389–91.

31. To the influence of Warren's history attest not only the number of copies sold but also the fact that President Jefferson ordered copies of *History of the Rise, Progress, and Termination of the American Revolution* for all heads of federal department: Friedman and Shaffer, "Mercy Otis Warren and the Politics of Historical Nationalism," 195.

32. The other female historian writing at that time was Hannah Adams. She, however, wrote mostly religious, not political, histories: quoted in Shaffer, *The Politics of History*, 149–50. Reading the parts of Warren's history pertaining to the pre-1789 years does not, according to Friedman and Shaffer, reveal her republican stance: Friedman and Shafer, "Mercy Otis Warren and the Politics of Historical Nationalism," 206.

33. Lester Cohen underscores the theoretical similarities between Warren's earlier and later writings. Cohen points out that, while the events of the 1780s and 1790s gave focus and direction to Warren's historical theory, that theory was born much earlier and is reflected in her letters, poetry, and early plays: Cohen, "Explaining the Revolution," 203.

34. The first to coin the term during the 1930s, analyze the practice, and point at its problems was Butterfield, *The Whig Interpretation of History*.

35. Warren, *History of the Rise, Progress, and Termination of the American Revolution*, I: 126.

36. Ibid., 1:339.

37. Ibid., 1:3, 1:4, 2:3, 2:5, 2:690.

38. Ibid., 1:4–5, 1:15.

39. Ibid., 1:97–98.

40. Quoted in Cohen, "Explaining the Revolution," 209.

41. Warren, *History of the Rise, Progress, and Termination of the American Revolution*, 1:93.

42. Ibid., 1:45, 1:65, 1:212.

43. Years later, Warren expressed a similar view of historical reoccurrence when

she predicted that "America has many a worthy name / Who shall, hereafter, grace the rolls of fame. Her good Cornelias / and her Arias fair / Who, death, in its most hideous forms, can dare": idem, *Poems,* 209–10.

44. Idem, *History of the Rise, Progress, and Termination of the American Revolution,* 1:98, 1:126, 1:328.

45. Ibid., 1:49, 1:116, 1:143.

46. Ibid., 1:128, 1:160.

47. Ibid., 1:82–83, 1:264.

48. Ibid., 1:339, 2:618.

49. Richard, *The Founders and the Classics,* 84.

50. Barzoni, *The Romans in Greece,* iii.

51. For an examination of providence's role in the revolutionary historian's work, see Cohen, *The Revolutionary Histories,* 23–127.

52. Snowden, *American Revolution Written in the Style of Ancient History,* iii.

53. Ibid., 66.

54. Ibid., 93.

55. Ibid., 34, 176.

56. Ibid., 13, 17, 34, 74, 225.

57. Ibid., 64, 226.

58. Ibid., 38, 222.

59. Kewes, "History and Its Uses."

60. Burk, *Bunker Hill.* The play suffers from factual mistakes, such as its portrayal of the protagonist Warren as a high-ranking commander during the battle. In fact, Warren received his commission as a general a few days before the battle but not soon enough to actually assume his command, and he participated in his final battle as a volunteer.

61. The introduction to the play's 1798 edition says that it "played at the theatres in America for fourteen nights, with unbounded applause": Burk, *Bunker Hill,* 1.

62. Ibid., 3–4.

63. Ibid., 18, 19–21, 24.

64. Ibid., 44.

65. Litto, "Addison's Cato in the Colonies," 444–46.

66. Burk, *Bunker Hill,* 58.

67. Ibid., 22, 27, 44, 49, 52.

68. Ibid., 10, 13, 17.

69. Ibid., 43, 45.

70. Furstenberg, *In the Name of the Father,* 31.

71. For an illuminating analysis of the impact of Washington's death, see ibid., 25–46.

72. For the construction of Washington's image, see Schwartz, "The Character of Washington."

73. Gilmore, "Eulogy as Symbolic Biography," 148.

74. George Minot, "An Eulogy, Pronounced before the Inhabitants of the Town

of Boston, January 9th, 1800, at the Request of Their Committee," in *A Selection of Orations and Eulogies*, 18, 24.

75. Henry Lee, "An Oration, Pronounced at Philadelphia in the German Lutheran Church, December 26th, 1799, at the Request of the United States, in Congress Assembled," in ibid., 5–13.

76. Ames, "Eulogy on Washington," 85.

77. Thomas Paine A. M., "An Eulogy, Pronounced at Newport, January 2d, 1800," in *A Selection of Orations and Eulogies*, 111.

78. Ames, "Eulogy on Washington," 87.

79. George Minot, "An Eulogy, Pronounced before the Inhabitants of the Town of Boston, January 9th, 1800, at the Request of Their Committee," in *A Selection of Orations and Eulogies*, 23.

80. Benjamin Orr, "An Oration, Pronounced at Bedford, February 22nd, 1800," in ibid., 129–30.

81. Charles H. Atherton, "An Eulogy, Pronounced at Amherst, before the Inhabitants of the Town of Amherst, the Inhabitants of the Town of Milford and the Benevolent Lodge February 22d, 1800," in ibid., 96–97.

82. Thomas Paine A. M., "An Eulogy," in ibid., 111.

83. Ramsay, *An Oration on the Death of Lieutenant-General George Washington*, 27.

84. The eulogists unwittingly duplicated the cult of Caesar deification, a practice that had arisen in Rome only after the loss of republican freedom: Gilmore, "Eulogy as Symbolic Biography," 152.

85. Ames, "Eulogy on Washington," 71; Lee, *The Farmer's and Monitor's Letters*, 12.

86. Lee, *A Selection of Orations and Eulogies*, 4.

87. Cunliffe, *George Washington*.

88. Gilmore, "Eulogy as Symbolic Biography," 131.

89. Lee, *A Selection of Orations and Eulogies*, 13. The eulogy would be published at least twenty times in pamphlet form and in numerous newspapers across the nation: Furstenberg, *In the Name of the Father*, 32.

90. Ames, "Eulogy on Washington," 87–88.

91. Charles H. Atherton, "An Eulogy," in *A Selection of Orations and Eulogies*, 87.

92. Jeremiah Smith, "An Oration, Pronounced at Exeter, February 22nd, 1800," in ibid., 63.

93. Ames, "Eulogy on Washington," 75.

94. Thomas Paine A. M., "An Eulogy," in *A Selection of Orations and Eulogies*, 106.

95. Jeremiah Smith, "An Oration," in ibid., 82.

96. Jacob M'Gaw, "An Eulogy," in ibid., 125.

97. Furstenberg, *In the Name of the Father*, 34–39.

98. The extent and the timing of the transformation from an ethos of republicanism to that of a democracy has been much debated. For the classic account of that transformation, see Wood, *The Creation of the American Republic*, 593–615.

99. Cohen, *The Revolutionary Histories*, 186.

100. The bitter, if satiric, disappointment expressed in *The Anarchiad* attests to

such a mood: Joel Barlow, David Humphreys, John Trumbull, and Lemuel Hopkins, *The Anarchiad: A New England Poem,* published in installments in *New Haven Gazette* and *Connecticut Magazine,* October 1786–September 1787.

101. Messer, *Stories of Independence.* See also O'Brien, *Narratives of Enlightenment,* 215–16.

102. Hicks, *Neoclassical History and English Culture,* 3, *passim.*

103. Pocock, *Barbarism and Religion.*

104. Kemp, *The Estrangement of the Past.*

105. Pocock, "Review of Lester H. Cohen's *The Revolutionary Histories,*" 921.

106. Cohen, *The Revolutionary Histories,* 23–127.

107. For a brilliant account of the evolution of American historicism, see Ross, "Historical Consciousness in Nineteenth-Century America."

Epilogue

1. The comparison of present-day America to the Roman Empire is so common that some consider the metaphor already in danger of becoming "something of a cliché": Ferguson, *Colossus,* 14. For recent significant scholarly works that delve into that metaphor, see Bacevich, *American Empire;* James, *The Roman Predicament;* Maier, *Among Empires;* Murphy, *Are We Rome?*

2. The two obvious works that have recognized the significance of these two symbols in America are Miles, "The Whig Party and the Menace of Caesar," and Wills, *Cincinnatus.* This epilogue traces representations of "great men," mostly presidents or presidential candidates, portrayed either as Caesars or Cincinnati. Those Romans were repeatedly referred to in order to describe powerful citizens of the American republic because such focus was inherent to the tradition of classical history, as well as to the historical outlook of contemporary Americans, who saw in "great men" the main motivators and movers of history.

3. This "Roman dilemma" is brilliantly analyzed and traced in Pocock, *Barbarism and Religion.*

4. See chapter 2.

5. For a survey of the classical figures to which Washington was likened by his contemporaries, see also Cunliffe, *George Washington;* Schwartz, *George Washington;* Wills, *Cincinnatus.*

6. Wharton, *A Poetical Epistle to His Excellency George Washington, Esq.,* 7.

7. Schwartz, "The Character of Washington," 208.

8. Cited in Brookhiser, *Founding Father,* 59–60.

9. Quoted in Wright, *An Empire for Liberty,* 161.

10. *Philadelphia Aurora,* October 20, 1797.

11. Philip Freneau, "Cincinnatus," cited in Kaminski and McCaughan, *A Great and Good Man,* 33; Wills, *Cincinnatus,* 13.

12. Kammen, *A Season of Youth,* 85.

13. Jones, *O Strange New World,* 246.

14. An example of a less well-known withdrawal that was understood in Cincinnatian terms was Judge Henry Sanford's retirement to his farm in New York: see Reinhold, *Classica Americana*, 161.

15. Adams, quoted in Ellis, *Founding Brothers*, 123, and Richard, *The Founders and the Classics*, 55.

16. Richard, *The Founders and the Classics*, 68.

17. Jefferson, quoted in Leuchtenburg, *American Places*, 272.

18. Reinhold, *Classica Americana*, 161.

19. Warren, *History of the Rise, Progress, and Termination of the American Revolution*, 1:212.

20. David Ramsay, quoted in Hofstadter, *The Progressive Historians*, 233.

21. The story is recounted and its validity is assessed in Chernow, *Alexander Hamilton*, 398.

22. John Adams, quoted in Richard, *The Founders and the Classics*, 92.

23. William Keteltas, quoted in Chernow, *Alexander Hamilton*, 571.

24. John Adams, quoted in Richard, *The Founders and the Classics*, 92.

25. Quoted in ibid., 93.

26. *Putnam's Monthly*, vol. 3, no. 18, 1854, 611.

27. Quoted in Chernow, *Alexander Hamilton*, 407.

28. Alexander Hamilton, "Phocion No. IX," *Gazette of the United States*, October 25, 1796.

29. Harrington, "Henry Clay and the Classics," 241–42.

30. *Eastern Argus*, May 27, 1828.

31. Miles, "The Whig Party and the Menace of Caesar," 369n45.

32. Quoted in Watson, *Liberty and Power*, 156.

33. *Connecticut Courant*, vol. 73, no. 3762, February 25, 1837.

34. *New-Bedford Mercury*, February 21, 1834.

35. Quoted in Miles, "The Whig Party and the Menace of Caesar," 371.

36. Quoted in ibid., 374–75.

37. Quoted in Ward, *Andrew Jackson*, 44.

38. Quoted in ibid., 43–44.

39. Quoted in ibid., 42.

40. "Executive Usurpation," *United States Democratic Review*, vol. 3, no. 1, 1838, 279–93.

41. See, e.g., "The Policy of the Democratic Party at Home and Abroad," *United States Democratic Review*, vol. 40, no. 6, 1857, 482.

42. *New-Bedford Mercury*, March 6, 1840.

43. *New Hampshire Sentinel*, May 13, 1840. For a description of another procession using the Cincinnatian image, see *Portsmouth Journal of Literature and Politics*, May 30, 1840.

44. Broadside, Portsmouth, Ohio, 1840, in Richard P. Morgan, comp., *Morgan Bibliography of Ohio Imprints, 1796–1850*.

45. "Another Letter from Gen. Taylor," *Hudson River Chronicle*, August 24, 1847.

In "The Life of Gen. Zachary Taylor," a long biographical exposition that appeared in the *Semi-Weekly Eagle* in July 1848 to promote Taylor's candidacy, Taylor's Cincinnatian image was elaborated in detail.

46. Quoted in Kauffman, *American Brutus*, 121.

47. Ibid., 200.

48. Ibid., 200, 212.

49. Guelzo, *Abraham Lincoln.*

50. "Recollections of the Civil War," *North American Review*, vol. 166, no. 499, 1898, 740–51.

51. *Farmer's Cabinet*, October 26, 1865.

52. Twenty-two presidents did not serve a second term. The only presidents other than Rutherford B. Hayes who did not seek re-nomination were James K. Polk and James Buchanan. Polk's decision to retire may have been influenced by his weakened health by the end of his first term. Polk died a few months into retirement. James Buchanan's troubled presidency left him without his party's nomination, and he did not run again.

53. 22nd Amendment, Constitution of the United States.

54. See "Dwight Eisenhower: The Return of Cincinnatus," in Crockett, *The Opposition Presidency*. The quote is from Dwight D. Eisenhower, "Farewell Address to the Nation," speech, January 17, 1961, available online at www.ourdocuments.gov/doc.php?flash=true&doc=90.

55. Ferguson, *Colossus*, 88–89.

56. Quoted in McCullough, *Truman*, 836–37.

57. Manchester, *American Caesar*, 21.

58. The website at www.draftwesleyclark.com is still operating, and the "historic" website as it was aired in 2004 can still be viewed at www.draftwesleyclark.com/defaultold_red.htm (accessed September 12, 2006).

59. David Greenberg, "Cincinnatus for President: Listen Up Wesley Clark! Here's How Generals Get Elected President," available online at www.slate.com/id/2088306 (accessed September 2, 2006).

60. David Greenberg, "Is General Clark Presidential Material?" Available online at http://hnn.us/articles/1688.html (accessed October 4, 2006).

61. Michael McCord, "Tales from the Primary Trail: Gen. Wesley Clark to the Rescue? " available online at www.democraticunderground.com/articles/03/11/18_clark.html (accessed September 6, 2006).

62. The Republican Party, however, was quick to gain a Cincinnatus in the form of the Texan Congressman Ron Paul: see "Ron Paul—The Modern Cincinnatus," available online at www.dailypaul.com/node/124, posted May 10, 2007 (accessed May 13, 2008).

63. Frank Williams has recently pointed out the "eerie similarities [that] haunt the Bush administration's interpretation of constitutionality, civil liberties, executive privilege, and nationhood" with Lincoln's: Williams, "Lincoln and the Constitution," 5.

64. Ralph Nader, "American Caesar," available online at www.commondreams. org/views06/0408-21.htm (acessed October 3, 2006). See also Richard Heinberg, "Behold Caesar: George W. Bush and the American Empire," available online at www.newdawnmagazine.com/Article/George_W_Bush_&_the_American _Empire.html (accessed September, 21, 2006).

65. Wyke, *Julius Caesar in Western Culture,* 315.

66. Ibid., 318.

67. *Charleston Gazette,* May 12, 2003, quoted in ibid., 319

68. Ibid., 317.

69. For illuminating overviews of the role of exceptionalism in American history, see Chaplin, "Expansion and Exceptionalism in Early American History"; Ross, *The Origins of American Social Science,* 22–52.

70. Ross, "Historical Consciousness in Nineteenth-Century America," 912. On millennialism in American historical consciousness, see Bloch, *Visionary Republic;* Hatch, *The Sacred Cause of Liberty;* Lienesch, *New Order of the Ages;* Pocock, *The Machiavellian Moment,* 493; Tuveson, *Redeemer Nation.*

71. Ross, "Historical Consciousness in Nineteenth-Century America," 928; idem, *The Origins of American Social Science,* 29.

72. For revolutionary cyclical thought, see chapter 3 in this volume.

73. Miller, "Thomas Cole and Jacksonian America."

74. Ferguson, *Colossus,* 14; emphasis added.

75. Ibid., 34.

76. Drayton, *A Charge on the Rise of the American Empire,* 3.

BIBLIOGRAPHY

Primary Sources

A Dialogue, between the Devil and George III. Tyrant of Britain, &c. &c. &c. &c. Boston, 1782.

A Selection of Orations and Eulogies Pronounced in Different Parts of the United States in Commemoration of the Life, Virtues and Pre-eminent Services of Gen. George Washington Who Died at Mount Vernon, December 14, 1799, in the 68th Year of His Age. Amherst, N.H., 1800.

Account of the Commencement in the College of Philadelphia. Philadelphia, May 17, 1775.

An Impartial History of the War in America, between Great Britain and the United States. Boston, 1781.

"An Ode on the Occasion of George Washington's Birthday." *Independent Chronicle* (Boston), February 11, 1790.

Adams, John. *A Defense of the Constitutions of the Government of the United States of America,* 3 vols., repr. ed. New York: Da Capo Press, 1971.

Addison, Joseph. *Cato: A Tragedy and Selected Essays,* ed. Christine Dunn Henderson and Mark E. Yellin. Indianapolis, 2004.

Allan, John. *The American Alarm, or the Bostonian Plea, for the Rights, and Liberties, of the People.* Boston, 1773.

———. *An Oration upon the Beauties of Liberty or the Essential Rights of the Americans.* Boston, 1773.

America Invincible. An Heroic Poem. In Two Books. Danvers, Mass., 1779.

Ames, Fisher. "Eulogy on Washington." In *Works of Fisher Ames, with a Selection from His Speeches and Correspondence,* 2 vols., ed. Seth Ames. New York, 1969.

Bailyn, Bernard, ed. *The Debate on the Constitution,* 2 vols. New York: Library of America, 1993.

Barzoni, Vittorio. *The Romans in Greece, an Ancient Tale, Descriptive of Modern Events* (translated from the Italian). Boston, 1799.

"A Black Whig." *A Sermon, on the Present Situation of the Affairs of America and Great-Britain. Written by a Black, and Printed at the Request of Several Persons of Distinguished Characters.* Philadelphia, 1782.

Bolingbroke, Henry St. John. *Historical Writings.* Cambridge: Harvard University Press, 1997.

Brackenridge, Hugh Henry. *The Battle of Bunkers-Hill. A Dramatic Piece, of Five Acts in Heroic Measure.* By a Gentleman of Maryland. Philadelphia, 1776.
———. *The Death of General Montgomery, at the Siege of Quebec. A Tragedy.* Philadelphia, 1777.
Burk, John Daly. *Bunker Hill, or the Death of General Warren.* New York, 1797.
———. *The History of Virginia from Its First Settlement to the Present Day,* 4 vols. Petersburg, Va., 1804–16.
"Cassius." *Considerations on the Society or Order of Cincinnati . . . Addressed to the People of South-Carolina and Their Representatives.* Charleston, 1783.
Clark, Harry H., ed. *Poems of Freneau,* 2 vols. New York, 1929.
The Classical Spirit in American Portraiture: An Exhibition by the Department of Art. Providence, R.I.: Brown University Press, 1976.
Cockings, George. *The Conquest of Canada: Or the Siege of Quebec. An Historical Tragedy, of Five Acts.* Albany, N.Y., 1773.
———. *War: An Heroic Poem.* Portsmouth, N.H., 1762.
Cooke, Jacob E. and Harold Syfert, eds. *The Papers of Alexander Hamilton,* 26 vols. New York, 1961–79.
Cooper, Samuel. *Sermon Preached before His Excellency John Hancock, Esq.; Governour, the Honourable the Senate, and House of Representatives of the Commonwealth of Massachusetts, October 25, 1780. Being the Day of the Commencement of the Constitution, and Inauguration of the New Government.* Boston, 1780.
Cushing, Harry Alonzo, ed. *The Writings of Samuel Adams,* 4 vols. New York, 1904–1908.
Drayton, John. *Memoirs of the American Revolution, From Its Commencement to the Year 1776, Inclusive; As Relating to the State of South Carolina and Occasionally Referring to the States of North Carolina and Georgia,* 2 vols. Charleston, S.C., 1821.
Drayton, William Henry. *A Charge on the Rise of the American Empire.* Charleston, S.C., 1776.
———. *The Speech of the Hon. William Henry Drayton, Esquire, Chief Justice of South-Carolina . . . upon the Confederation of the United States of America.* Charlestown, S.C., 1778.
Dummer, Jeremiah. *A Defense of the New-England Charters.* Boston, 1765 (1721).
Evans, Nathaniel. *Ode on the Late Glorious Successes of His Majesty's Arms and Present Greatness of the English Nation.* Philadelphia, 1762.
———. "An Exercise Containing a Dialogue and Ode on Occasion of the Peace." In *Poems on Several Occasions with Some Other Compositions.* Philadelphia, 1772.
The Fall of Lucifer, an Elegiac Poem on the Infamous Defection of the Late General Arnold. Hartford, Conn., 1781.
Ford, Paul Leicester, ed. *The Political Writings of John Dickinson, 1764–1774.* New York, 1970 (1895).
Forthingham, Richard. *Life and Times of Joseph Warren.* Boston, 1865.
Foxcroft, Thomas. *Grateful Reflexions on the Signal Appearances of Divine Providence*

*for Great Britain and Its Colonies in America . . . A Sermon Preached in the Old
Church in Boston, October 9, 1760.* Boston, 1760.

Freneau, Philip. *A Poem, on the Rising Glory of America.* Philadelphia, 1772.

Gibbon, Edward. *The History of the Decline and Fall of the Roman Empire,* ed. Dero
A. Saunders. New York, 1985.

Gillespie, Michael Allen, and Michael Lienesch, eds. *Ratifying the Constitution.*
Lawrence, Kan., 1989.

Goldsmith, Oliver. *A History of England.* London, 1764.

Hamer, Philip M., ed. *The Papers of Henry Laurens,* 16 vols. Columbia, S.C., 1968–.

Hamilton, Alexander, James Madison, and John Jay. *The Federalist Papers,* ed. Garry
Wills. New York: Bantam, 1982.

Henry, William W. *Patrick Henry: Life, Correspondence and Speeches,* 3 vols. New
York, 1891.

Hopkins, Stephen. *The Rights of Colonies Examined.* Providence, R.I., 1765.

Hopkinson, Thomas. *An Exercise, Containing a Dialogue and Two Odes Performed at
the Public Commencement in the College of Philadelphia, May 20th, 1766.* Philadelphia, 1766.

Howard, Martin. *A Letter from a Gentleman at Halifax.* Newport, R.I., 1765.

Humphreys, David. *An Essay on the Life of the Honourable Major-General Israel Putnam.* Indianapolis, 2000.

Hyneman, Charles S., and Donald S. Lutz, eds. *American Political Writing during the
Founding Era, 1760–1805,* 2 vols. Indianapolis, 1983.

*The Institution of the Society of the Cincinnati. Formed by the Officers of the Army of the
United States, for the Laudable Use Therein Mentioned.* New York, 1784.

Jefferson, Thomas. *Notes on the State of Virginia.* Philadelphia, 1788.

Jensen, Merrill, ed. *A Documentary History of the Ratification of the Constitution,* 20
vols. Madison, Wis., 1981.

Kaminski, John P. *The Quotable Jefferson.* Princeton, N.J.: Princeton University Press,
2006.

Kaminski, John P., and Jill Adair McCaughan, eds. *A Great and Good Man: George
Washington in the Eyes of His Contemporaries.* Madison, Wis.: Madison House,
1989.

Langdon, Samuel. *Government Corrupted by Vice, and Recovered by Righteousness.*
Boston, 1775.

Leacock, John. *The Fall of British Tyranny, or American Liberty Triumphant: A Tragi-
Comedy of Five Acts.* Philadelphia, 1776.

Lee, Arthur. *The Farmer's and Monitor's Letters, to the Inhabitants of the British Colonies.* Williamsburg, Va., 1769.

Lessing, Gotthold Ephraim. *Laocoon* (1766), repr. ed. London, 1967.

Loring, James Spear. *The Hundred Boston Orators Appointed by the Municipal Authorities and Other Public Bodies, from 1770 to 1852; Comprising Historical Gleanings
Illustrating the Principles and Progress of Our Republican Institutions.* Boston, 1853.

MacKenzie, Frederick. *Diary of Fredrick Mackenzie: Giving a Daily Narrative of His Military Service as an Officer of the Regimen of Royal Welch Fusiliers during the Years 1775–1781 in Massachusetts, Rhode Island, and New York,* 2 vols. Cambridge, Mass., 1930.

Magoon, E. L. *Orators of the American Revolution* (1848), repr. ed. Littleton, Colo.: Fred B. Rothman, 1992.

Marsh, Philip M., ed. *Prose.* New Brunswick, N.J., 1955.

Mason, George. *The Papers of George Mason, 1725–1792,* ed. Robert Allan Rutland, 3 vols. Chapel Hill, N.C., 1970.

Mayhew, Jonathan. *Two Discourses Delivered October 9th.* Boston, 1760.

Maylem, John [Philo-Bellum]. *The Conquest of Louisburg. A Poem.* Newport, R.I., 1758.

McClosky, Robert G., ed. *Works of James Wilson,* 2 vols. Cambridge, Mass., 1967.

M'Cullough, John. *Concise History of the United States.* Philadelphia, 1795.

Meigs, Josiah. *An Oration, Pronounced before a Public Assembly in New Haven, on the 5th Day of November 1781, at the Celebration of the Glorious Victory over Lieutenant-General Earl Cornwallis.* New Haven, Conn., 1781.

The Military Glory of Great-Britain, an Entertainment, Given by the Late Candidates for Bachelor's Degree, at the Close of the Anniversary Commencement, Held in Nassau-Hall New-Jersey September 29th, 1762. Philadelphia, 1762.

Montagu, Edward W. *Reflections on the Rise and Fall of the Antient Republicks. Adapted to the Present State of Great Britain.* London, 1759.

Morgan, Edmund S., ed. *Prologue to Revolution: Sources and Documents on the Stamp Act Crisis, 1764–1766.* Chapel Hill, 1959.

Morgenthau, Hans J., "The colossus of Johnson City," *New York Review of Books,* March 31, 1966.

Morse, Jedidiah. *History of America in Two Books,* 2 vols. Philadelphia, 1790.

Morse, John D., ed. *Prints in and of America to 1850.* Charlottesville: University of Virginia Press, 1970.

"A Native of Pennsylvania [Hugh Williamson]." *The Plea of the Colonies on the Charges Brought against Them by Lord Mansfield, and Others, in a Letter to His Lordship.* Philadelphia, 1777.

"Officer of Rank in the Continental Army." *America Invincible. An Heroic Poem; in Two Books.* Boston, 1779.

Orations Delivered at the Request of the Inhabitants of the Town of Boston to Commemorate the Evening of the Fifth of March, 1770; When a Number of Citizens were Killed by a Party of British Troops, Quartered among Them in a Time of Peace. Boston, 1785.

Otis, James. *The Rights of the British Colonies Asserted and Proved.* Boston, 1764.

———. *A Vindication of the British Colonies, against the Aspersions of the Halifax Gentleman, in His Letter to a Rhode-Island Friend.* Boston, 1765.

Otis, Mercy Warren. *The Adulateur and The Defeat, in Plays and Poems of Mercy Warren Otis.* Delmar, N.Y., 1980.

Otway, Thomas. *The History and Fall of Caius Marius.* London, 1680.

"Philoleutheros Americanus." *A Poem, upon the Present Times.* New Haven, Conn., 1775.

Potter, David, and Gordon L. Thomas, eds. *The American Colonial Idiom.* Carbondale, Ill., 1970.

Quincy, Josiah. *Observations on the Act of Parliament Commonly called the Boston Port-Bill; with thoughts on civil society and standing armies.* Boston, 1774.

Ramsay, David. *Oration on the Advantages of American Independence: Spoken before a Publick Assembly of the Inhabitants of Charlestown in South-Carolina, on the Second Anniversary of that Glorious Era.* Charleston, S.C., 1778.

——. *An Oration on the Death of Lieutenant-General George Washington, Late President of the United States,* Charleston, S.C., 1800.

——. *The History of the American Revolution* (1789), 2 vols., ed. Lester Cohen. Indianapolis: Liberty Press, 1990.

——. *The History of the American Revolution* (1793), 2 vols. New York: Russell and Russell, 1968.

——. *The History of the Revolution of South Carolina, from a British Province to an Independent State,* 2 vols. Trenton, N.J., 1785.

Randolph, Edmund. *The History of Virginia,* ed. Arthur Shafer. Charlottesville, Va., 1970.

"The Recruiting Officer, Together with Yanky Doodle." Broadside, 1760.

"Rusticus." *Remarks on a Late Pamphlet entitled Plain Truth.* Philadelphia, 1776.

Rutland, Robert A., ed. *The Papers of George Mason, 1725–1792,* 3 vols. Chapel Hill, N.C., 1970.

Sallust. *The Jugurthine War and the Conspiracy of Catiline.* New York, 1982.

Saunders, William L., ed. *The Colonial Records of North Carolina.* 30 vols. New York, 1968.

Schaff, Philip. *America.* New York, 1855.

Seabury, Samuel. *A Discourse Addressed to His Majesty's Provincial Troops.* New York, 1777.

Sewall, Jonathan Mitchell. *Epilogue to Cato, Spoken at a Late Performance of That Tragedy.* Portsmouth, N.H., 1778.

Smith, Paul H., ed. *Letters of Delegates to Congress, 1774–1789,* 9 vols. Washington, D.C., 1976.

Smith, William. *An Oration in the Memory of General Montgomery.* Philadelphia, 1776.

Snowden, Richard. *American Revolution Written in the Style of Ancient History.* Philadelphia, 1793.

Suetonius. *The Lives of the Caesars,* trans. J. C. Rolfe. Cambridge, Mass.: Harvard University Press, 1964.

Tacitus. *The Annals.* New York: Penguin, 1956.

Taylor, Robert J., ed. *The Papers of John Adams,* 14 vols. Cambridge, Mass.: Belknap Press, 1977–.

Thatcher, Oxenbridge. *The Sentiments of a British American.* Boston, 1762.

Trumbull, John. *An Elegy on the Times.* New Haven, Conn., 1775.

Two Dialogues on Different Subjects, Being Exercises, Delivered on a Quarter-Day, in the Chapel of Yale-College, New-Haven, March 28, 1776. New Haven, Conn., 1776.

Walsh, Richard, ed. *The Writings of Christopher Gadsden.* Columbia, S.C., 1966.

Warren, John. *An Oration, Delivered July 4th, 1783, at the Request of the Inhabitants of the Town of Boston; in Celebration of the Anniversary of American Independence.* Boston, 1783.

Warren, Mercy Otis. *The Adulateur, a Tragedy.* Boston, 1773.

———. *The Group; as Lately Acted, and to Be Re-acted to the Wonder of All Superior Untelligences, nigh Head-quarters at Amboyne.* Boston, 1775.

———. *History of the Rise, Progress, and Termination of the American Revolution,* 2 vols, ed. Lester Cohen. Indianapolis, 1988.

———. *Poems, Dramatic and Miscellaneous.* Boston, 1790.

West, Samuel. *On the Right to Rebel against Governors.* Boston, 1776.

Wharton, Charles Henry. *A Poetical Epistle to His Excellency George Washington, Esq.; Commander in Chief of the Armies of the United States of America.* Providence, R.I., 1781.

Wheatley, Phillis. *Liberty and Peace: A Poem.* Boston, 1784.

Winckelmann, Johann Joachim. *Reflections on the Painting and Sculpture of the Greeks.* London, 1765.

Witherspoon, John. *The Humble Confession, Declaration, Recantation, and Apology of Benjamin Towne, Printer in Philadelphia.* Philadelphia, 1778.

Young, Benjamin Prime. *The Unfortunate Hero: A Pindaric Ode in Memoriam of Viscount George Augustus Howe That Fell in July of 1758.* New York, 1758.

NEWSPAPERS AND JOURNALS

Albany Gazette
American Herald
Boston Evening Post
Boston Gazette
Boston Post-Boy
Carolina Gazette and Country Journal
Charleston Gazette
Connecticut Courant
Daily Advertiser (New York)
Eastern Argus
Essex Journal
Farmer's Cabinet
Freeman's Journal
Gazette of the United States
Hampshire Gazette
Hudson River Chronicle
Independent Chronicle
Independent Gazetteer

Massachusetts Centinel
Massachusetts Chronicle
Massachusetts Gazette
Massachusetts Spy
New-Bedford Mercury
New Hampshire Gazette
New Hampshire Sentinel
New Haven Gazette
New York Journal
Newport Mercury
Norfolk and Portsmouth Journal
North American Review
Pennsylvania Gazette
Philadelphia Aurora
Portsmouth Journal of Literature and Politics
Providence Gazette
Putnam's Monthly

Richmond Dispatch

Richmond Pamphlet Anthology

Rivington's Gazette

Royal Gazette

Semi-Weekly Eagle

South Carolina Gazette

South Carolina Gazette and Country
   Journal

United States Democratic Review

Virginia Gazette

Virginia Independent Chronicle

Secondary Sources

Adair, Douglass "A Note on Certain of Hamilton's Pseudonyms." *William and Mary Quarterly* 12 (1955): 282–97.

———. *Fame and the Founding Fathers.* New York: W. W. Norton, 1974.

Adams, Willi Paul. *The First American Constitutions: Republican Ideology and the Making of the State Constitutions in the Revolutionary Era,* trans. Rita and Robert Kimber. Lanham, Md.: Rowman and Littlefield, 2001.

Ahern, Gregory S. "The Spirit of American Constitutionalism: John Dickinson's Fabius Letters." *Humanitas* 11 (1998): 57–76.

Ahlstrom, Sydney E. *Religious History of the American People.* New Haven, Conn.: Yale University Press, 1972.

Albanese, Catherine L. *Sons of the Fathers: The Civil Religion of the American Revolution.* Philadelphia: Temple University Press, 1976.

Aldridge, A. Own. "The Concept of Ancients and Moderns." In *Classical Traditions in Early America,* ed. John W. Eadie et. al., 99–118. Ann Arbor: University of Michigan Press, 1976.

Allan, Herbert S. *John Hancock: Patriot in Purple.* New York: Macmillan, 1948.

Amory, Hugh, and David D. Hall, eds. *A History of the Book in America: The Colonial Book in the Atlantic World.* New York: Cambridge University Press, 2000.

Anderson, Benedict. *Imagined Communities: Reflections of the Origin and Spread of Nationalism.* London: Verso, 1983.

Armitage, David. *The Ideological Origins of the British Empire.* Cambridge: Cambridge University Press, 2000.

Auerbach, Eric. *Mimesis: The Representation of Reality in Western Literature.* Princeton, N.J.: Princeton University Press, 1953.

———. *Scenes from the Drama of European Literature.* Gloucester, Mass.: Peter Smith, 1973.

Bacevich, Andrew J. *American Empire: The Realities and Consequences of U.S. Diplomacy.* Cambridge, Mass.: Harvard University Press, 2003.

Bailyn, Bernard. *The Ideological Origins of the American Revolution.* Cambridge, Mass.: Harvard University Press, 1967.

———. *The Origins of American Politics.* New York: Vintage, 1970.

Baskerville, Barnet. *The People's Voice: The Orator in American Society.* Lexington: University Press of Kentucky, 1979.

Becker, Carl L. *The Eve of the Revolution.* New Haven, Conn.: Yale University Press, 1918.

Beeman, Richard, ed. *Beyond Confederation: Origins of the Constitution and American National Identity.* Chapel Hill: University of North Carolina Press, 1987.

Bell, David A. *The Cult of the Nation in France.* Cambridge, Mass.: Harvard University Press, 2001.

Bercovitch, Sacvan, ed. *The American Jeremiad.* Madison: University of Wisconsin Press, 1978.

———. *Typology and Early American Literature.* Amherst: University of Massachusetts Press, 1972.

———. "The Typology of the American Mission." *American Quarterly* 30 (1978): 135–55.

Berry, Christopher J. *The Idea of Luxury: A Conceptual and Historical Investigation.* Cambridge: Cambridge University Press, 1994.

Bloch, Ruth H. *Visionary Republic: Millennial Themes in American Thought, 1756–1800.* New York: Cambridge University Press, 1985.

Boas, George. "Cycles." In *The Dictionary of the History of Ideas,* ed. Philip P. Wiener, 1:621–27. New York: Charles Scribner, 1973.

Bonomi, Patricia. *Under the Cope of Heaven: Religion, Society, and Politics in Colonial America.* New York: Oxford University Press, 1986.

Bornstein, Herbert. "Time-Schemes, Order, and Chaos: Periodization and Ideology." In *Time, Order, Chaos: The Study of Time IX,* ed. J. T. Faser, Marlene P. Soulsby, and Alexander Argyros. Madison, Conn.: International Universities Press, 1998.

Bourdieu, Pierre. *Language and Symbolic Power.* Cambridge: Polity, 1991.

Breen, Timothy H. *The Marketplace of Revolution: How Consumer Politics Shaped American Independence.* New York: Oxford University Press, 2004.

Britton, James C. "The Decline and Fall of Nations in Antebellum Southern Thought: A Study of Southern Historical Consciousness, 1846–1861." Ph.D. diss., University of North Carolina, Chapel Hill, 1989.

Brookhiser, Richard. *Founding Father.* New York: Free Press, 1996.

Brown, Richard D. *Knowledge Is Power: The Diffusion of Information in Early America.* New York: Oxford University Press, 1989.

Burke, Peter. *The Renaissance Sense of the Past.* London: Edward Arnold, 1969.

Burrows, Edwin G., and Michael Wallace. "The American Revolution: The Ideology and Psychology of National Liberation." *Perspectives in American History* 6 (1972): 167–306.

Bushman, Richard L. *The Refinement of America: Persons, Houses, Cities.* New York: Alfred A. Knopf, 1994.

Butler, Jon. "Enthusiasm Described and Decried: The Great Awakening as Interpretive Fiction," *Journal of American History* 69 (1982): 305–25.

Butterfield, Herbert. *The Englishman and His History.* Cambridge: Cambridge University Press, 1944.

———. *The Whig Interpretation of History.* New York: W. W. Norton, 1965.

Calhoun, Craig. *Nationalism.* Minneapolis: University of Minnesota Press, 1998.

Carretta, Vincent. *George III and the Satirists from Hogarth to Byron.* Athens: University of Georgia Press, 1990.

Cary, John. *Joseph Warren: Physician, Politician, Patriot.* Urbana: University of Illinois Press, 1961.

Chaplin, Joyce. "Expansion and Exceptionalism in Early American History." *Journal of American History* 89 (2003): 1431–55.

Chernow, Ron. *Alexander Hamilton.* New York: Penguin, 2004.

Cima, Gay Gibson. "Black and Unmarked: Phillis Wheatley, Mercy Otis Warren, and the Limit of Strategic Anonymity." *Theatre Journal* 52, no. 4 (2000): 469–95.

Clark, Charles E. *The Public Prints: The Newspaper in Anglo American Culture, 1665–1740.* New York: Oxford University Press, 1994.

Cohen, Charles L. "The 'Liberty or Death' Speech: A Note on Religion and Revolutionary Rhetoric." *William and Mary Quarterly* 38 (1981): 707–17.

Cohen, Lester H. "Explaining the Revolution: Ideology and Ethics in Mercy Otis Warren's Historical Theory." *William and Mary Quarterly* 37, no. 2 (1980): 200–18.

———. *The Revolutionary Histories: Contemporary Narratives of the American Revolution.* Ithaca, N.Y.: Cornell University Press, 1980.

Cohn-Haft, Louis. "The Founding Fathers and Antiquity." *Smith College Studies in History* 66 (1980): 137–53.

Colbourne, Trevor H. *The Lamp of Experience: Whig History and the Intellectual Origins of the American Revolution.* Indianapolis: Liberty Fund, 1998.

Colley, Linda. *Britons: Forging of the Nation, 1707–1837.* New Haven, Conn.: Yale University Press, 1994.

Commager, Henry Steele. "The American Enlightenment and the Ancient World: A Study in Paradox." *Proceedings of the Massachusetts Historical Society* 83 (1971): 3–15.

Cooke, Jacob E. "Alexander Hamilton's Authorship of 'Caesar' Letters." *William and Mary Quarterly* 17 (1960): 78–85.

Cremin, Lawrence A. *American Education: The Colonial Experience, 1607–1783.* New York: Harper and Row, 1970.

Crockett, David A. *The Opposition Presidency: Leadership and the Constraints of History.* College Station: Texas A&M University Press, 2002.

Cunliffe, Marcus. *George Washington: Man and Monument.* Boston: Little, Brown, 1958.

D'Andrade, Roy. "A Folk Model of the Mind." In *Cultural Models in Language and Thought,* ed. Dorothy Holland and Naomi Quinn, 112–48. New York: Cambridge University Press, 1987.

Darnton, Robert. *The Great Cat Massacre.* New York: Basic Books, 1999.

Davidson, Philip Grant. *Propaganda and the American Revolution.* New York: W. W. Norton, 1973.

Dawson, David. *Christian Figural Reading and the Fashioning of Identity.* Berkeley: University of California Press, 2002.

Deloria, Philip J. *Playing Indian.* New Haven, Conn.: Yale University Press, 1998.

Diamond, Elin. *Performance and Cultural Politics.* London: Routledge, 1996.

Downes, Paul. *Democracy, Revolution, and Monarchism in Early American Literature.* Cambridge: Cambridge University Press, 2002.

Eadie, John W., ed. *Classical Traditions in Early America.* Ann Arbor: University of Michigan Press, 1976.

Easley, Alexis. *First Person Anonymous: Women Writers and Victorian Print Media, 1830–70.* Burlington, Vt.: Ashgate, 2004.

Eliade, Mircea. *The Myth of the Eternal Return: Or, Cosmos and History.* Princeton, N.J.: Princeton University Press, 1971.

Elkins, Stanley, and Eric McKitrick, *The Age of Federalism: The Early American Republic, 1788–1800.* New York: Oxford University Press, 1995.

Ellis, Joseph J. *Founding Brothers: The Revolutionary Generation.* New York: Alfred A. Knopf, 2000.

Ellison, Julie. *Cato's Tears and the Making of Anglo American Emotion.* Chicago: University of Chicago Press, 1999.

Emerson, Everett, ed. *American Literature.* Madison: University of Wisconsin Press, 1977.

Ferguson, Niall. *Colossus: The Rise and Fall of the American Empire.* New York: Penguin, 2005.

Ferguson, Robert A. *Reading the Early Republic.* Cambridge, Mass.: Harvard University Press, 2006.

Ferling, John. *A Leap in the Dark: The Struggle to Create the American Republic.* New York: Oxford University Press, 2003.

Fink, Zera. *The Classical Republicans: An Essay in the Recovery of a Pattern of Thought in Seventeenth-Century England.* Evanston, Ill.: Northwestern University Press, 1962.

Fitzmaurice, Andrew. *Humanism and America: An Intellectual History of English Colonization, 1500–1625.* Cambridge: Cambridge University Press, 2003.

Fliegelman, Jay. *Declaring Independence: Jefferson, Natural Language and the Culture of Performance.* Stanford, Calif.: Stanford University Press, 1993.

———. *Prodigals and Pilgrims: The American Revolution against Patriarchal Authority, 1750–1800.* Cambridge: Cambridge University Press, 1984.

Forthingham, Richard. *Life and Times of Joseph Warren.* Boston: Little, Brown, 1865.

Freeman, Joanne B. *Affairs of Honor: National Politics in the New Republic.* New Haven, Conn.: Yale University Press, 2001.

Friedman, Lawrence J., and Arthur H. Shaffer. "Mercy Otis Warren and the Politics of Historical Nationalism." *New England Quarterly* 48, no. 2 (1975): 194–215.

Furet, Francois. *Interpreting the French Revolution.* New York: Cambridge University Press, 1978.

Furstenberg, Francois. *In the Name of the Father: Washington's Legacy, Slavery, and the Making of a Nation.* New York: Penguin, 2006.

Furtwangler, Albert. "Cato in Valley Forge." In *American Silhouettes: Rhetorical Identities of the Founders,* 64–84. New Haven, Conn.: Yale University Press, 1987.

Geertz, Clifford. *The Interpretation of Cultures* (1973). New York: Basic Books, 2000.

Gilmore, Michael T. "Eulogy as Symbolic Biography: The Iconography of Revolutionary Leadership, 1776–1826." In *Studies in Biography,* ed. Daniel Aaron, 131–57. Cambridge, Mass.: Harvard University Press, 1978.

Greenberg, Kenneth S. *Honor and Slavery.* Princeton, N.J.: Princeton University Press, 1996.

Greene, Jack P. "Character, Persona, and Authority: A Study of Alternative Styles of Political Leadership in Revolutionary Virginia." In *Understanding the American Revolution: Issues and Actors,* 209–46. Charlottesville: University of Virginia Press, 1995.

———. *Pursuits of Happiness: The Social Development of Early Modern British Colonies and the Formation of American Culture.* Chapel Hill: University of North Carolina Press, 1988.

Griffin, Robert J., ed. *The Faces of Anonymity: Anonymous and Pseudonymous Publication from the Sixteenth to the Twentieth Century.* New York: Palgrave Macmillan, 2003.

Groden, Michael, and Martin Kreiswirth, eds. *The John Hopkins Guide to Literary Theory and Criticism.* Baltimore: John Hopkins University Press, 1994.

Guelzo, Allan. *Abraham Lincoln: Redeemer President.* Grand Rapids, Mich.: Erdmans, 1999.

Guibbory, Achsah. *The Map of Time: Seventeenth-Century English Literature and Ideas of Pattern in History.* Urbana: University of Illinois Press, 1986.

Gummere, Richard M. *The American Colonial Mind and the Classical Tradition.* Cambridge, Mass.: Harvard University Press, 1963.

Gustafson, Sandra. *Eloquence Is Power: Oratory and Performance in Early America.* Chapel Hill: University of North Carolina Press, 2000.

Guyatt, Nicholas. *Providence and the Invention of the United States, 1607–1876.* New York: Cambridge University Press, 2007.

Hall, Peter Dobkin. *The Organization of American Culture: Private Institutions, Elites, and the Origins of American Nationality.* New York: New York University Press, 1984.

Halloran, Michael S., and Gregory Clark. "Transformations of Public Discourse in Nineteenth Century America." In *Oratorical Culture in Nineteenth Century America: Transformations in the Theory and Practice of Rhetoric,* 1–28. Carbondale: Southern Illinois University Press, 1993.

Hammer, Dean. *The Puritan Tradition in Revolutionary, Federalist, and Whig Political Theory: A Rhetoric of Origins.* New York: Peter Lang, 1998.

Harrington, J. Drew. "Henry Clay and the Classics." *Filson Club History Quarterly* 61 (1987): 234–46.

Hatch, Nathan O. *The Sacred Cause of Liberty: Republican Thought and the Millennium in Revolutionary New England.* New Haven, Conn.: Yale University Press, 1977.

Hays, Edmund M. "Mercy Otis Warren: The Defeat." *New England Quarterly* 49 (1976): 440–58.

Hicks, Philip S. *Neoclassical History and English Culture: From Clarendon to Hume.* New York: Macmillan, 1996.

———. "Portia and Marcia: Female Political Identity and the Historical Imagination, 1770–1800." *William and Mary Quarterly* 52 (2005): 265–94.

Hobsbawm, Eric. *The Invented Tradition.* New York: Cambridge University Press, 1992.

Hofstadter, Richard. *The Progressive Historians.* New York: Vintage, 1970.

Honour, Hugh. *Neo-classicism.* Middlesex: Penguin, 1968.

Howe, John. *Language and Political Meaning in Revolutionary America.* Amherst: University of Massachusetts Press, 2004.

James, Harold. *The Roman Predicament: How the Rules of International Order Create the Politics of Empire.* Princeton, N.J.: Princeton University Press, 2006.

Jones, Howard Mumford. *O Strange New World.* New York: Viking Press, 1964.

———. *Revolution and Romanticism.* Cambridge, Mass.: Belknap Press, 1974.

Johnson, Richard R. "Hellas in Hesperia: Ancient Greece and Early America." In *Paths from Ancient Greece,* ed. Carol G. Thomas, 140–67. Leiden: E. J. Brill, 1988.

Jordan, Winthrop D. "Familial Politics: Thomas Paine and the Killing of the King, 1776." *Journal of American History* 60, no. 2 (1973): 294–308

Juster, Susan. *Doomsayers: Anglo American Prophecy in the Age of Revolution.* Philadelphia: University of Pennsylvania Press, 2003.

Kammen, Michael. *A Season of Youth: The American Revolution and the Historical Imagination.* New York: Oxford University Press, 1978.

Kamuf, Peggy. *Signature Pieces: On the Institution of Authorship.* Ithaca, N.Y.: Cornell University Press, 1988.

Kann, Mark E. *A Republic of Men: The American Founders, Gendered Language, and Patriarchal Politics.* New York: New York University Press, 1998.

Kauffman, Michael W. *American Brutus: John Wilkes Booth and the Lincoln Conspiracies.* New York: Random House, 2005.

Kaufman, Allan. *Capitalism, Slavery, and Republican Values: Antebellum Political Economists, 1819–1849.* Austin: University of Texas Press, 1982.

Kelsey, Sean. *Inventing a Republic: The Political Culture of the English Commonwealth.* New York: Manchester University Press, 1997.

Kemp, Anthony. *The Estrangement of the Past: A Study in the Origins of Modern Historical Consciousness.* New York: Oxford University Press, 1991.

Kenyon, Cecelia. *Men of Little Faith: Selected Writings of Cecelia Kenyon,* ed. Stanley Elkins. Amherst, Mass.: University of Massachusetts Press, 2003.

Kerber, Linda K. *Women of the Republic: Intellect and Ideology in Revolutionary America.* Chapel Hill: University of North Carolina Press, 1997.

Kewes, Paulina. "History and Its Uses: Introduction." *Huntington Library Quarterly* 68 (2005): 1–33.

Kielbowicz, Richard B. "The Press, Post Office, and the Flow of News in the Early Republic." *Journal of the Early Republic* 3, no. 3 (1983): 255–80.

Koebner, Richard. *Empire.* Cambridge: Cambridge University Press, 1958.

Korshin, Paul J. *Typologies in England 1650–1820*. Princeton, N.J.: Princeton University Press, 1982.

Lakoff, George, and Mark Johnson. *Metaphors We Live By*. Chicago: University of Chicago Press, 2003.

Leder, Lawrence H., ed. *The Colonial Legacy*, 4 vols. New York: Harper and Row, 1971.

Leibiger, Stuart Eric. *Founding Friendship: George Washington, James Madison and the Creation of the American Republic*. Charlottesville: University of Virginia Press, 1999.

Leonard, Thomas C. *Power of the Press: The Birth of American Political Reporting*. New York: Oxford University Press, 2000.

Leuchtenburg, William E. *American Places: Encounters with History*. New York: Oxford University Press, 2000.

Lewis, Jan. "The Republican Wife: Virtue and Seduction in the Early Republic," *William and Mary Quarterly* 44 (1987): 689–721.

Lienesch, Michael. *New Order of the Ages: Time, the Constitution, and the Making of Modern American Political Thought*. Princeton, N.J.: Princeton University Press, 1988.

Litto, Fredric M. "Addison's Cato in the Colonies." *William and Mary Quarterly* 23, no. 3 (1966): 431–49.

Lupher, David A. *Romans in the New World: Classical Models in Sixteenth-Century Spanish America*. Ann Arbor: University of Michigan Press, 2003.

Macey, S. L., ed. *Encyclopedia of Time*. New York: Garland, 1994.

Madsen, Deborah L. *Allegory in America: From Puritanism to Postmodernism*. New York: St. Martin's Press, 1996.

Maier, Charles. *Among Empires: American Ascendancy and its Predecessors*. Cambridge, Mass.: Harvard University Press, 2005.

Manchester, William. *American Caesar: Douglas MacArthur, 1880–1964*. Boston: Little, Brown and Company, 1978.

McCants, David M. *Patrick Henry, the Orator*. New York: Greenwood Press, 1990.

McCoy, Drew. *The Elusive Republic: Political Economy in Jeffersonian America*. New York: W. W. Norton, 1982.

McConville, Brendan. *The King's Three Faces: The Rise and Fall of Royal America, 1688–1776*. Chapel Hill: University of North Carolina Press, 2006.

McCullough, David. *Truman*. New York: Simon and Schuster, 1993.

McLachlan, James. "Classical Names, American Identities: Some Notes on College Students and the Classical Traditions in the 1770s." In *Classical Traditions in Early America*, ed. John W. Eadie et al., 80–99. Ann Arbor: University of Michigan Press, 1976.

Meade, David G. *Pseudonymity and Canon*. Grand Rapids, Mich.: Erdmans, 1987.

Messer, Peter C. *Stories of Independence: Identity, Ideology and History in Eighteenth-Century America*. DeKalb: Northern Illinois University Press, 2005.

Miles, Edwin A. "The Whig Party and the Menace of Caesar." *Tennessee Historical Quarterly* 26, no. 4 (1968): 36–79.

———. "The Young American Nation and the Classical World." *Journal of the History of Ideas* 35, no. 2 (1974): 259–74.

Miller, Angela. "Thomas Cole and Jacksonian America: The Course of Empire as Political Allegory." *Prospects* 14 (1990): 65–92.

Miller, John C., *Sam Adams: Pioneer in Propaganda*. Boston: Little, Brown, 1936.

Miller, Perry. "Introduction." In Jonathan Edwards, *Images or Shadows of Divine Things*. New Haven, Conn.: Yale University Press, 1948.

Miller, Peter N. *Defining the Common Good: Empire, Religion and Philosophy in Eighteenth-Century Britain*. New York: Cambridge University Press, 1994.

Mio, Jeffery Scott. "Metaphor, Politics, and Persuasion." In *Metaphor: Implications and Applications*, ed. Jeffery S. Mio and Albert N. Katz, 127–46. Mahwah, N.J.: Lawrence Erlbaum, 1996.

Monaghan, Jennifer. *Learning to Read and Write in Colonial America*. Amherst: University of Massachusetts Press, 2005.

Morgan, Edmund S. *The Stamp Act Crisis: Prologue to Revolution*. New York: Macmillan, 1963.

Morris, Richard B. *Alexander Hamilton and the Founding of the Nation*. New York: Harper and Row, 1969.

Mullett, Charles F. "Classical Influences on the American Revolution." *Classical Journal* 35 (1939): 92–104.

Munk, Linda. "Edward Taylor: Typology and Puritanism." *History of European Ideas* 17 (1993): 85–94.

Murphy, Cullen. *Are We Rome? The Fall of an Empire and the Fate of America*. New York: Houghton Mifflin, 2007.

Nelson, Eric. *The Greek Tradition in Republican Thought*. New York: Cambridge University Press, 2004.

Newman, Simon P. *Parades and the Politics of the Street*. Philadelphia: University of Pennsylvania Press, 2002.

North, Marcy L. *The Anonymous Renaissance: Culture of Discretion in Tudor-Stuart England*. Chicago: University of Chicago Press, 2003.

O'Brien, Karen. *Narratives of Enlightenment: Cosmopolitan History from Voltaire to Gibbon*. New York: Cambridge University Press, 1997.

O'Shaughnessy, Andrew J. *An Empire Divided: The American Revolution and the British Caribbean*. Philadelphia: University of Pennsylvania Press, 2000.

Ozouf, Mona. *Festivals of the French Revolution*. Cambridge, Mass.: Harvard University Press, 1988.

Parker, Harold Talbot. *The Cult of Antiquity and the French Revolutionaries*. Chicago: University of Chicago Press, 1937.

Pasley, Jeffrey L. *The Tyranny of the Printers: Newspaper Politics in the Early American Republic*. Charlottesville: University of Virginia Press, 2001.

Persons, Stow. "The Cyclical Theory of History in Eighteenth Century America." *American Quarterly* 6 (1954): 147–63.

Pocock, J. G. A. *Barbarism and Religion: The First Decline and Fall,* 4 vols. New York: Cambridge University Press, 2005.

———. *The Machiavellian Moment: Florentine Political Thought and the Atlantic Republican Tradition,* 2d ed. Princeton, N.J.: Princeton University Press, 2003 (1975).

———. *Politics, Language and Time: Essays on Political Thought and History.* Chicago: University of Chicago Press, 1989.

———. "Review of Lester H. Cohen's *The Revolutionary Histories." Journal of American History* 68, no. 4 (1982): 920–21.

———. *Virtue, Commerce and History.* Cambridge: Cambridge University Press, 1985.

Portelli, Alessandro. *The Text and the Voice: Writing, Speaking and Democracy in America.* New York: Columbia University Press, 1994.

Purcell, Sarah. *Sealed with Blood: War, Sacrifice, and Memory in Revolutionary America.* Philadelphia: University of Pennsylvania Press, 2002.

Rahe, Paul A. *Republics Ancient and Modern.* Tulsa: University of North Oklahoma Press, 1992.

Rakove, Jack N. *The Beginnings of National Politics: An Interpretive History of the Continental Congress.* New York: Alfred A. Knopf, 1979.

———. *Original Meanings: Politics and Ideas in the Making of the Constitution.* New York: Alfred A. Knopf, 1997.

Reinhold, Meyer. *Classica Americana: The Greek and Roman Heritage in the United States.* Detroit: Wayne State University Press, 1984.

Richard, Carl J. *The Founders and the Classics: Greece, Rome and the American Enlightenment.* Cambridge, Mass.: Harvard University Press, 1994.

———. *The Battle for the American Mind.* Lanham, Md.: Rowman and Littlefield, 2004.

Robertson, Andrew W. "'Look on This Picture . . . and on This!' Nationalism, Localism, and Partisan Images of Otherness in the United States, 1787–1820." *American Historical Review* 106 (2001): 1236–80.

Ross, Dorothy. "Historical Consciousness in Nineteenth-Century America." *American Historical Review* 89, no. 4 (1984): 909–28

———. *The Origins of American Social Science.* New York: Cambridge University Press, 1991.

Rowe, Nicholas. "Romans and Carthaginians in the Eighteenth Century: Imperial Ideology and National Identity in Britain and France during the Seven Years' War." Ph.D. diss., Boston College, 1997.

Royster, Charles. *A Revolutionary People at War: The Continental Army and American Character, 1775–1783.* Chapel Hill: University of North Carolina Press, 1979.

Salas, Charles G. "Punic Wars in France and Britain." Ph.D. diss., Claremont Graduate School, Claremont, Calif., 1996.

Schlesinger Jr., Arthur. *The Cycles of American History.* Boston: Houghton Mifflin, 1986.

Schwartz, Barry. "The Character of Washington: A Study in Republican Culture." *American Quarterly* 38, no. 3 (1986): 202–22.

———. *George Washington: The Making of a Symbol.* New York: Free Press, 1987.

Sekora, John. *Luxury: The Concept in Western Thought from Eden to Smollett.* Baltimore: Johns Hopkins University Press, 1977.

Sellers, M. N. S. *American Republicanism: Roman Ideology in the United States Constitution.* New York: New York University Press, 1994.

Sensabaugh, George F. *Milton in Early America.* Princeton, N.J.: Princeton University Press, 1964.

Shaffer, Arthur H. *The Politics of History.* Chicago: Precedent, 1975.

———. *To Be an American: David Ramsay and the Making of the American Consciousness.* Columbia: University of South Carolina Press, 1992.

Shain, Barry Allan. *The Myth of American Individualism: The Protestant Origins of American Political Thought.* Princeton, N.J.: Princeton University Press, 1996.

Shalhope, Robert. "Republicanism and Early American Historiography." *William and Mary Quarterly* 39 (1982): 334–56.

———. "Toward a Republican Synthesis: The Emergence of an Understanding of Republicanism in American Historiography." *William and Mary Quarterly* 29 (1972): 49–80.

Shaw, Peter. *American Patriots and the Rituals of Revolution.* Cambridge, Mass.: Harvard University Press, 1981.

Shield, David S. *Civil Tongues and Polite Letters in British America.* Chapel Hill: University of North Carolina Press, 1997.

Shields, John C. *The American Aeneas: Classical Origins of the American Self.* Knoxville: University of Tennessee Press, 2001.

Silverman, Kenneth. *A Cultural History of the American Revolution: Painting, Music, Literature, and the Theatre in the Colonies and the United States from the Treaty of Paris to the Inauguration of George Washington, 1763–1789.* New York: Crowell, 1976.

Skinner, Quentin. *Liberty before Liberalism.* New York: Cambridge University Press, 1998.

Sloan, David W. *The Early American Press, 1690–1780.* Westport, Conn.: Greenwood Press, 1994.

Smith, Jeffery A. *Printers and the Press: The Ideology of American Journalism.* New York: Oxford University Press, 1990.

Spengler, Oswald. *The Decline of the West.* New York: Alfred A. Knopf, 1929.

Storing, Herbert J., *The Complete Anti-Federalist: Edited with Commentary and Notes,* 7 vols. Chicago: University of Chicago Press, 1981.

Toynbee, Arnold. *A Study of History,* 12 vols. London: Oxford University Press, 1935–61.

Trompf, G. W. *The Idea of Historical Recurrence in Western Thought: From Antiquity to the Reformation.* Berkeley: University of California Press, 1979.

Tuveson, Ernest Lee. *Redeemer Nation: The Idea of America's Millennial Role.* Chicago: Chicago University Press, 1968.

Wahrman, Dror. "The English Problem of Identity in the American Revolution." *American Historical Review* 106, no. 4 (2001): 1236–62.

Waldstreicher, David. *In the Midst of Perpetual Fetes: The Making of American Nationalism, 1776–1820.* Chapel Hill: University of North Carolina Press, 1997.

Ward, John William. *Andrew Jackson: Symbol for an Age.* New York: Oxford University Press, 1955.

Warner, Michael. "Franklin and the Republic of Letters." *Representations* 16, no. 3 (1986): 110–30.

———. *The Letters of the Republic: Publication and the Public Sphere in America in the Eighteenth-Century America.* Cambridge, Mass.: Harvard University Press, 2006.

Watson, Harry L. *Liberty and Power: The Politics of Jacksonian America.* New York: Hill and Wang, 1990.

Williams, Frank J. "Lincoln and the Constitution." *Magazine of History* 21 (2007): 5–8.

Wills, Garry. *Cincinnatus: George Washington and the Enlightenment.* Garden City, N.Y.: Doubleday, 1984.

Winterer, Caroline. *The Culture of Classicism: Ancient Greece and Rome in American Intellectual Life, 1780–1910.* Baltimore: Johns Hopkins University Press, 2001.

———. "From Royal to Republican: The Classical Image in Early America." *Journal of American History* 91, no. 4 (2005): 1264–90.

———. *The Mirror of Antiquity: American Women and the Classical Tradition, 1750–1900.* Ithaca, N.Y.: Cornell University Press, 2007.

Wood, Gordon S. *The Creation of the American Republic, 1776–1787.* Chapel Hill: University of North Carolina Press, 1969.

———. *The Great Republic: A History of the American People.* Boston: Little, Brown, 1977.

———. *The Radicalism of the American Revolution.* New York: Vintage, 1991.

Woodward, C. Vann. *The Burden of Southern History.* Baton Rouge: Louisiana State University Press, 1993.

Wright, Esmond. *An Empire for Liberty: From Washington to Lincoln.* New York: Blackwell, 1995.

Wright, Louis B. "The Classical Tradition in Colonial Virginia." *Papers of the Bibliographical Society in America* 33 (1939): 36–50.

Wyke, Maria, ed. *Julius Caesar in Western Culture.* Malden, Mass.: Blackwell, 2006.

Yerushalmi, Yosef Haim. *Zakhor: Jewish History and Jewish Memory.* Seattle: University of Washington Press, 1996.

Zagarri, Rosemarie. *A Woman's Dilemma: Mercy Otis Warren and the American Revolution.* Wheeling, Ill.: Harlan Davidson, 1995.

Zakai, Avihu. *Exile and Kingdom: History and Apocalypse in the Puritan Migration to America.* New York: Cambridge University Press, 1992.

———. *Jonathan Edwards's Philosophy of History: The Reenchantment of the World in the Age of Enlightenment.* Princeton, N.J.: Princeton University Press, 2003.

Ziff, Larzer. *Writing in the New Nation: Prose, Print and Politics in the Early United States.* New Haven, Conn.: Yale University Press, 1991.

Zobel, Hiller B. *The Boston Massacre.* New York: W. W. Norton, 1970.

INDEX

American Revolution: Written in the Style of Ancient History (Snowden), 202–5
"Americanus" (pseudonym), 85–86, 176
America rising to be new Rome, 28–35; ability to avoid downturn of historical cycle, 76, 86–87, 92, 106, 110, 198, 236–37, 240; Americans as reincarnated classical heroes, 92–99, 149–50; analogy between Hannibal's Italian campaign and American campaign in Canada, 94–96, 200, 255n76; British belief in, 78; in Burk's history of American Revolution, 209; continuing use of comparisons to Cincinnatus and Caesar, 217–40; decline expected as part of cycle, 76, 77, 85, 105, 106, 111, 112, 186–87, 198; nineteenth century's diminished use of analogy, 218; present-day America's use of this metaphor, 272n1; in southern discourse, 78, 85, 104, 105, 106, 111, 112; taking place of England, 125, 219; third millennium view of American decline to parallel Rome, 217–18; warring with corrupt British–Romans, 209; westward expansion to preserve America's upward cycle, 104, 256n95
Ames, Fisher, 211, 212
Ames, Nathaniel, 30
anonymity: British novels published anonymously (1750–1790), 263n17; distinguished from pseudonyms, 154, 263n12; as game between reader and writer, 265n62
"Anti-Cincinnatus" (pseudonym), 163, 179
"Anticipation of the Literary Fame of America" (poem), 34
anti-federalists: commonality of pseudonyms with federalists, 178–82, 180t; in debate over U.S. Constitution, 167–78, 184. *See also* pseudonymous writing; Republicans

arcanum imperii, 79
Areopagitica (Milton), 155
Aristedes, 16
"Aristedes" (pseudonym), 184, 185
Aristotle, 78, 81
Arnold, Benedict, 95, 96, 97, 98, 101, 102, 200, 255n74
Articles of Confederation, 85, 186
"Asiatic Luxury" and ruin of Rome, 63
assassination, presidential: Jackson, attempt on, 226; of Lincoln, 226, 229–30
assassination of Caesar. *See* Brutus, Marcus Junius
Athenian Thirty, 59
Atherton, Charles, 211
Auerbach, Erich, 87, 95, 113
"Aurelia" (pseudonym), 27
Austin, Jonathan, 86

Babeuf, Gracchus, 267n115
Bailyn, Bernard, 51, 249n50
Baker, John, 258n32
Battle of. *See names of individual battles*
Battle of Bunker Hill, The (Brackenridge), 21
Bercovitch, Sacvan, 72, 89
Berkeley, George, 29
Bernard, Francis, 65, 121
Bible, 13, 88–89. *See also* New Testament; Old Testament
biblical style, American Revolution history written in, 202–5
bipartisan American politics, origins of, 168–69, 191
"Black Whig, A" (sermon), 27–28
Bloch, Ruth, 111, 252n5, 268n129
Bolton, Thomas, 258n47
Bonomi, Patricia, 89–90, 254n49
books and bookstores, 11–12
Booth, John Wilkes, 226, 230
Boston: ban on plays in, 136; classicizing of, 119–37; compared to Carthage,

Bush, George W., 234–35, 274n63
Butterfield, Herbert, 50

"Caesar" (pseudonym), 160, 174–75,
181–82, 266n95
Caesar, Julius. *See* Julius Caesar
Calhoun, John C., 225–26
Caligula Gaius Caesar, 55–56, 64, 65
Camillus, 16, 45
Carretta, Vincent, 67
Carter, Mrs. Robert, 26
Carthage, 42, 46–47, 62, 63, 182, 247n6.
See also Punic Wars
Caspipina, Letters of, 31
Cassius (Gaius Longinus Cassius),
31–32, 72, 135, 137, 169, 200
"Cassius" (pseudonym), 164, 169, 177–78
Catholic Church, 14
Catiline (Lucius Sergius Catilina), 2, 24,
198–99, 255n74
"Catiline" (pseudonym), 160
Cato the Younger: animosity with
Caesar and death of, 25, 99, 174, 219;
Arnold (Benedict) compared to,
97–98; in eighteenth century America,
219; English Whigs favoring link
with, 155; Henry re-creating in "Give
Me Liberty or Give Me Death" oration, 115, 142–47; popularity of name
for praising patriots, 6, 23; in revolutionary America, 151, 199–200, 219;
Revolutionary period not referring to,
72; South Carolinian nullifiers comparing selves to, 226; Warren (Joseph)
compared to, 131, 132, 207
Cato (Addison's play): federalist use of,
175; Henry (Patrick) speech based on,
6, 115, 208; Sewall writing epilogue
to, 70, 99, 100–104, 256n93; Warren's
(Mercy Otis) plays compared to, 133,
206; as well-known work throughout
colonial America, 13, 99–101, 144,
260–61n77

"Cato" (pseudonym): choice of, 160;
Clinton (George) using, 266n95; com-
mon use by both federalists and anti-
federalists, 179; in debate over ratifica-
tion of U.S. Constitution, 171, 173–75;
letters by Virginian "Cato," 178;
popularity of, 155; in *South Carolina
Gazette*, 17
"Cato of Utica" (pseudonym), 16, 21, 85,
130
Cato's Letters (Trenchard & Gordon),
99, 155
"Catullus" (pseudonym), 37–38, 184, 224
"Censor, The" (pseudonym), 159
*A Charge on the Rise of the American
Empire* (Drayton), 63, 83–84
Charles I (king of England), 55, 88
Charleston Gazette on George W. Bush
as Julius Caesar, 234
Chase, Samuel, 61
Chelsea, Mass., 23
Chesterfield, Earl of, 18
Christ, analogies to, 88, 106, 110
Church, Benjamin, 102, 120, 128
Cicero: address by read to Continental
Congress, 18; American reverence
of, 2, 31; Catiline orations of, 198;
Continental Congress compared
to, 24; educational studies of, 11;
Henry (Patrick) compared to, 144;
Warren (Joseph) compared to, 125,
131; Washington (George) compared
to, 98
Cincinnatus: connection to land of, 235;
as continuing character in American
political discourse, 218–37; early patriot's view of, 2, 6, 25; in eighteenth
century America, 219–23; generals
compared to, 45, 230–31, 233–34, 235;
Hamilton (Alexander) comparing self
to, 224–25; presidents compared to,
226–32; Putnam (Israel) compared to,
193–94; Revolutionary period not re-

familiarity with, 12–13, 26–27; education of, 12; political affairs and, 26, 27; pseudonym use by, 165–66, 265n72; as writers, 139
Woodward, C. Vann, 112
Writs of Assistance, 54
Wyke, Maria, 234
Wythe, George, 36

"Yeoman" letter in *Providence Gazette,* 55
Yerushalmi, Yosef Haim, 248n34
Yorke, Philip, 44
Yorktown, battle of, 93
Young, Benjamin Prime, 45

Zagarri, Rosmarie, 135–36, 261n81

Jan Ellen Lewis and Peter
S. Onuf, editors
*Sally Hemings and Thomas Jefferson:
History, Memory, and Civic Culture*

Peter S. Onuf
*Jefferson's Empire: The Language
of American Nationhood*

Catherine Allgor
*Parlor Politics: In Which the
Ladies of Washington Help Build
a City and a Government*

Jeffrey L. Pasley
*"The Tyranny of Printers": Newspaper
Politics in the Early American Republic*

Herbert E. Sloan
*Principle and Interest: Thomas Jefferson
and the Problem of Debt (reprint)*

James Horn, Jan Ellen Lewis,
and Peter S. Onuf, editors
*The Revolution of 1800: Democracy,
Race, and the New Republic*

Phillip Hamilton
*The Making and Unmaking of
a Revolutionary Family: The
Tuckers of Virginia, 1752–1830*

Robert M. S. McDonald, editor
*Thomas Jefferson's Military
Academy: Founding West Point*

Martha Tomhave Blauvelt
*The Work of the Heart: Young
Women and Emotion, 1780–1830*

Francis D. Cogliano
Thomas Jefferson: Reputation and Legacy

Albrecht Koschnik
*"Let a Common Interest Bind Us
Together": Associations, Partisanship,
and Culture in Philadelphia, 1775–1840*

John Craig Hammond
*Slavery, Freedom, and Expansion in
the Early American West, 1787–1820*

David Andrew Nichols
*Red Gentlemen and White Savages:
Indians, Federalists, and the Search
for Order on the American Frontier*

Douglas Bradburn
*The Citizenship Revolution:
Politics and the Creation of the
American Union, 1774–1804*

Clarence E. Walker
*Mongrel Nation: The America Begotten
by Thomas Jefferson and Sally Hemings*

Timothy Mason Roberts
*Distant Revolutions: 1848 and the
Challenge to American Exceptionalism*

Peter J. Kastor and François
Weil, editors
*Empires of the Imagination: Transatlantic
Histories of the Louisiana Purchase*

Eran Shalev
*Rome Reborn on Western Shores:
Historical Imagination and the
Creation of the American Republic*